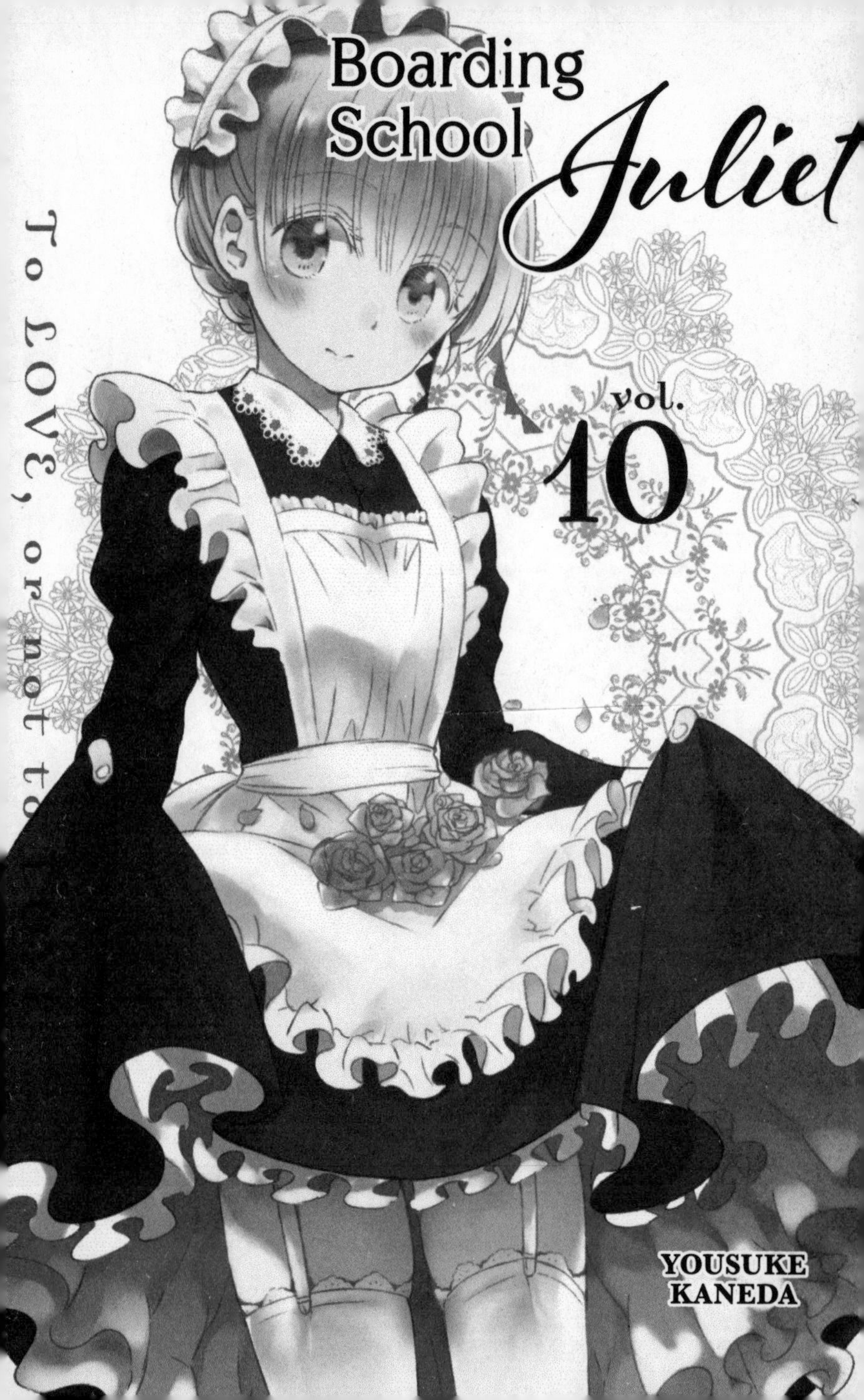
Boarding School
Juliet
To LOVE, or not to
vol.
10
YOUSUKE
KANEDA

THE PLAYERS

character

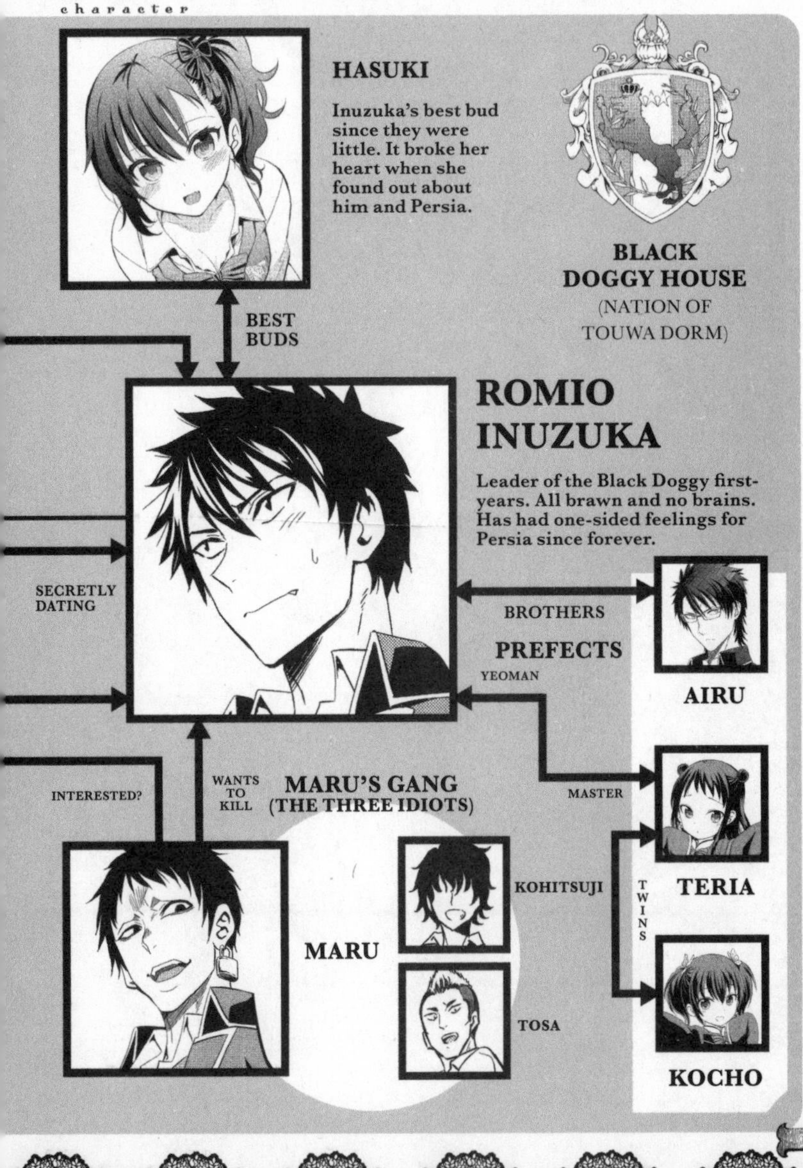
HASUKI
Inuzuka's best bud since they were little. It broke her heart when she found out about him and Persia.
BLACK DOGGY HOUSE
(NATION OF TOUWA DORM)
BEST BUDS
ROMIO INUZUKA
Leader of the Black Doggy first-years. All brawn and no brains. Has had one-sided feelings for Persia since forever.
SECRETLY DATING
BROTHERS
PREFECTS
YEOMAN
AIRU
MASTER
INTERESTED?
WANTS TO KILL
MARU'S GANG (THE THREE IDIOTS)
KOHITSUJI
TERIA
TWINS
MARU
TOSA
KOCHO

BOARDING SCHOOL JULIET

To LOVE, or not to LOVE

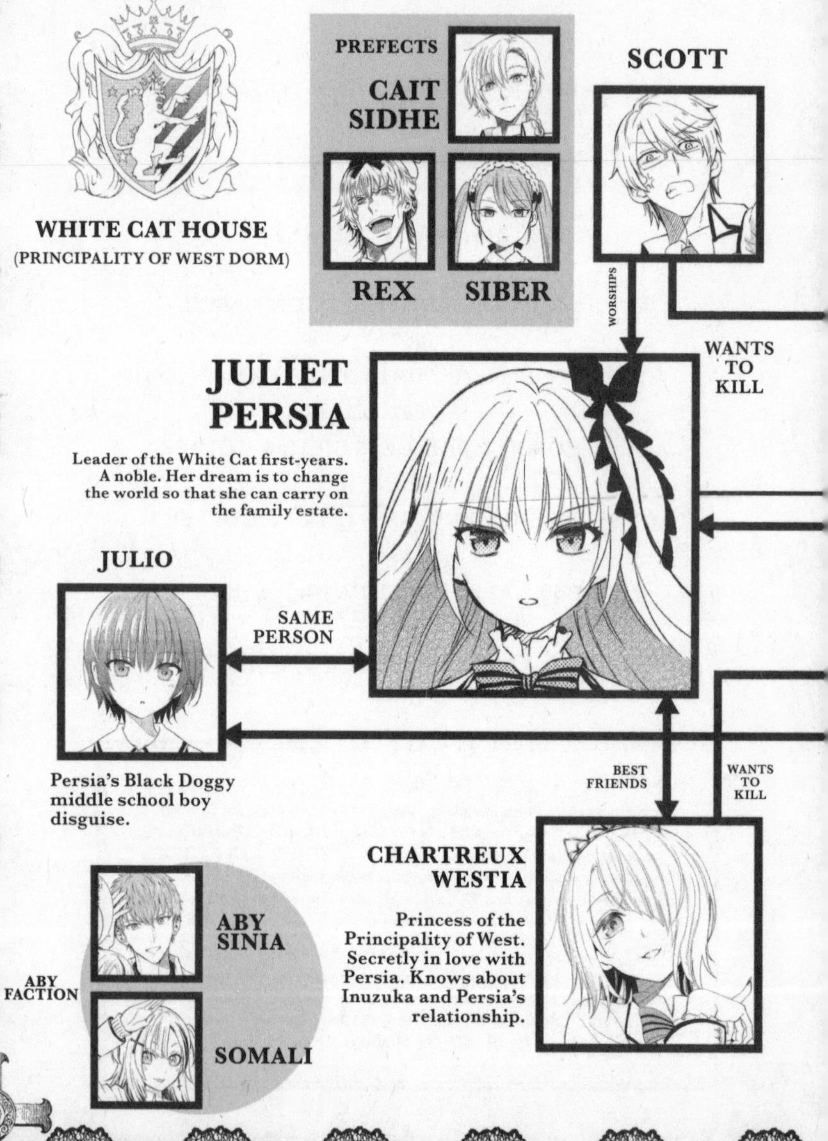
WHITE CAT HOUSE
(PRINCIPALITY OF WEST DORM)
PREFECTS
CAIT SIDHE
REX
SIBER
SCOTT
WORSHIPS
WANTS TO KILL
JULIET PERSIA
Leader of the White Cat first-years. A noble. Her dream is to change the world so that she can carry on the family estate.
JULIO
SAME PERSON
Persia's Black Doggy middle school boy disguise.
BEST FRIENDS
WANTS TO KILL
CHARTREUX WESTIA
Princess of the Principality of West. Secretly in love with Persia. Knows about Inuzuka and Persia's relationship.
ABY SINIA
ABY FACTION
SOMALI

contents

ACT 59: ROMIO & JULIET & THE TOUWA DATE

005

ACT 60: ROMIO & REON

027

ACT 61: SCOTT & JULIET

047

ACT 62: ROMIO & THE PREFECT ASSEMBLY

067

ACT 63: ROMIO & HASUKI & THE YEOMAN JOB

087

ACT 64: ROMIO & PRINCESS CHAR & COFFEE I

107

ACT 65: ROMIO & PRINCESS CHAR & COFFEE II

127

ACT 66: VALENTINE'S DAY & JULIET I

147

ACT 67: VALENTINE'S DAY & JULIET II

167

story

At boarding school Dahlia Academy, attended by students from two feuding countries, one first-year longs for a forbidden love. His name: Romio Inuzuka, leader of the Black Doggy House first-years. The apple of his eye: Juliet Persia, leader of the White Cat House first-years. It all begins when Inuzuka confesses his feelings to her. This is Inuzuka and Persia's star-crossed, secret love story...

One of the couple's worst fears has come to pass—during Persia's visit to Touwa, Airu discovered Julio's true identity! The furious Airu presented his brother with two choices: break up with Persia, or be ousted from the Inuzuka family. Naturally, Romio's response was to challenge his big bro to a do-or-die brawl. And now, it's the morning after their climactic showdown...

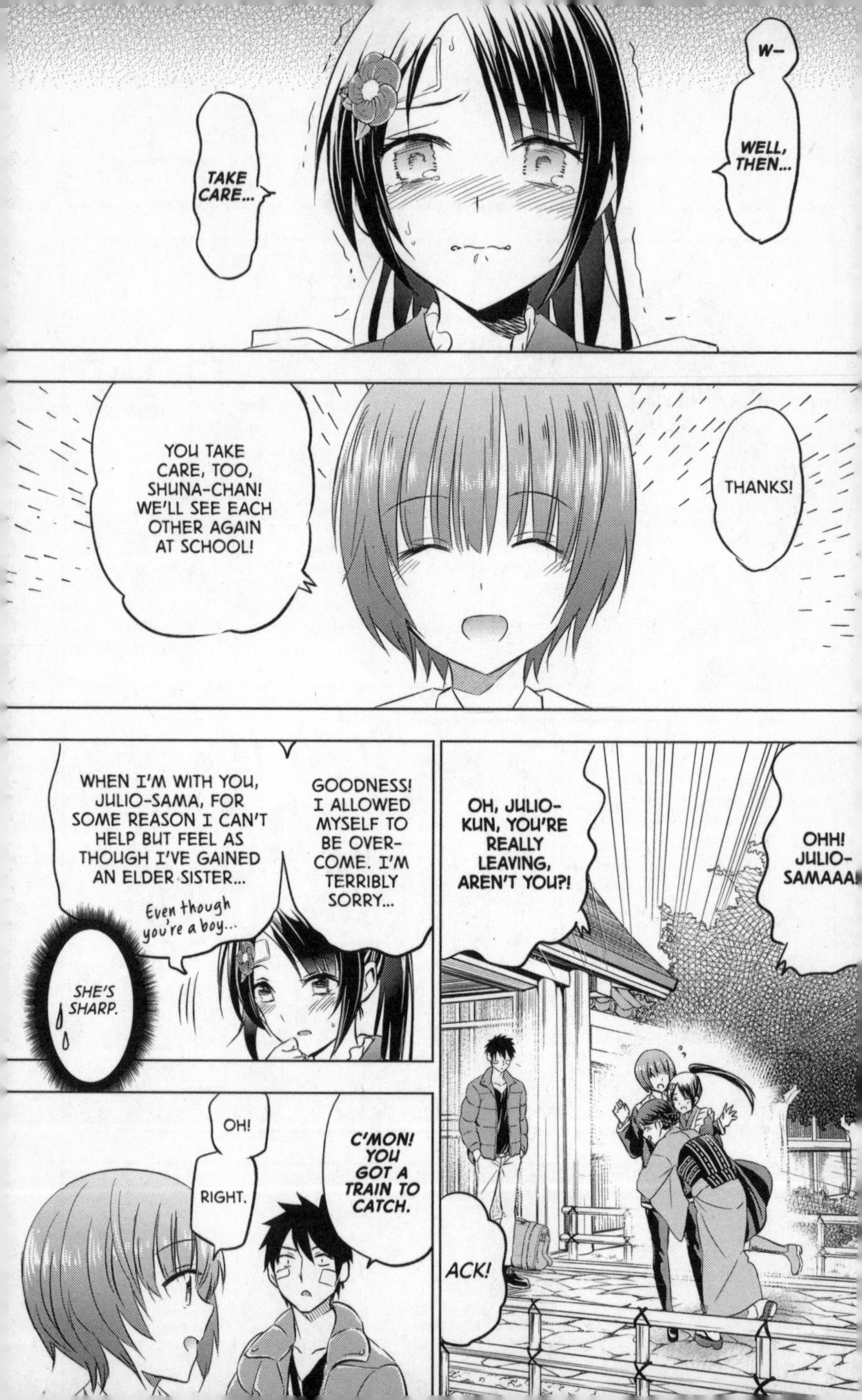

W—
WELL, THEN...
TAKE CARE...
YOU TAKE CARE, TOO, SHUNA-CHAN! WE'LL SEE EACH OTHER AGAIN AT SCHOOL!
THANKS!
OHH! JULIO-SAMAAA!
OH, JULIO-KUN, YOU'RE REALLY LEAVING, AREN'T YOU?!
ACK!
GOODNESS! I ALLOWED MYSELF TO BE OVER-COME. I'M TERRIBLY SORRY...
WHEN I'M WITH YOU, JULIO-SAMA, FOR SOME REASON I CAN'T HELP BUT FEEL AS THOUGH I'VE GAINED AN ELDER SISTER...
Even though you're a boy...
SHE'S SHARP.
C'MON! YOU GOT A TRAIN TO CATCH.
OH!
RIGHT.

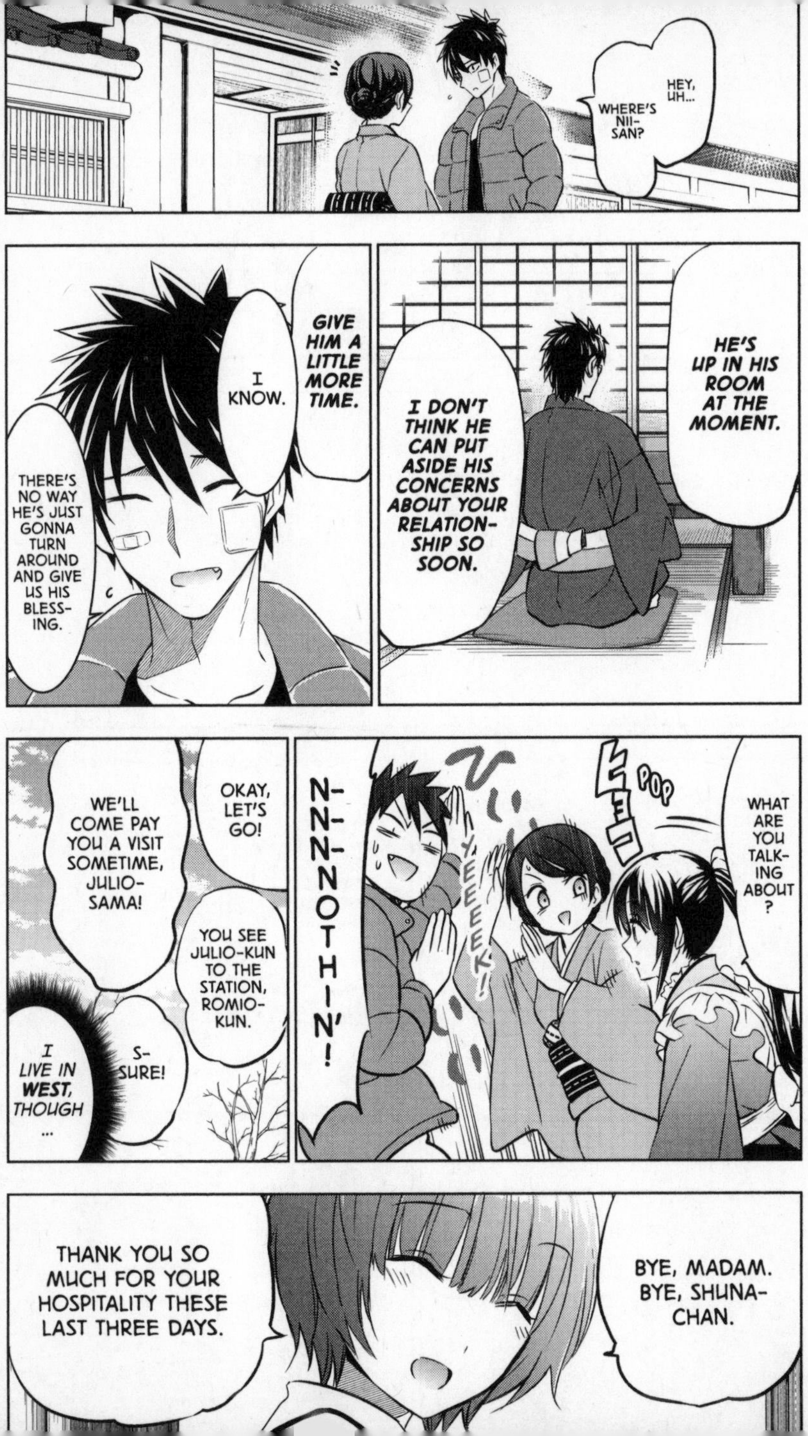
HEY, UH... WHERE'S NII-SAN?
HE'S UP IN HIS ROOM AT THE MOMENT.
I DON'T THINK HE CAN PUT ASIDE HIS CONCERNS ABOUT YOUR RELATIONSHIP SO SOON.
GIVE HIM A LITTLE MORE TIME.
I KNOW.
THERE'S NO WAY HE'S JUST GONNA TURN AROUND AND GIVE US HIS BLESSING.
WHAT ARE YOU TALKING ABOUT?
POP
YEEEEK!
N-N-N-NOTHIN'!
OKAY, LET'S GO!
WE'LL COME PAY YOU A VISIT SOMETIME, JULIO-SAMA!
YOU SEE JULIO-KUN TO THE STATION, ROMIO-KUN.
S-SURE!
I LIVE IN WEST, THOUGH...
BYE, MADAM. BYE, SHUNA-CHAN.
THANK YOU SO MUCH FOR YOUR HOSPITALITY THESE LAST THREE DAYS.

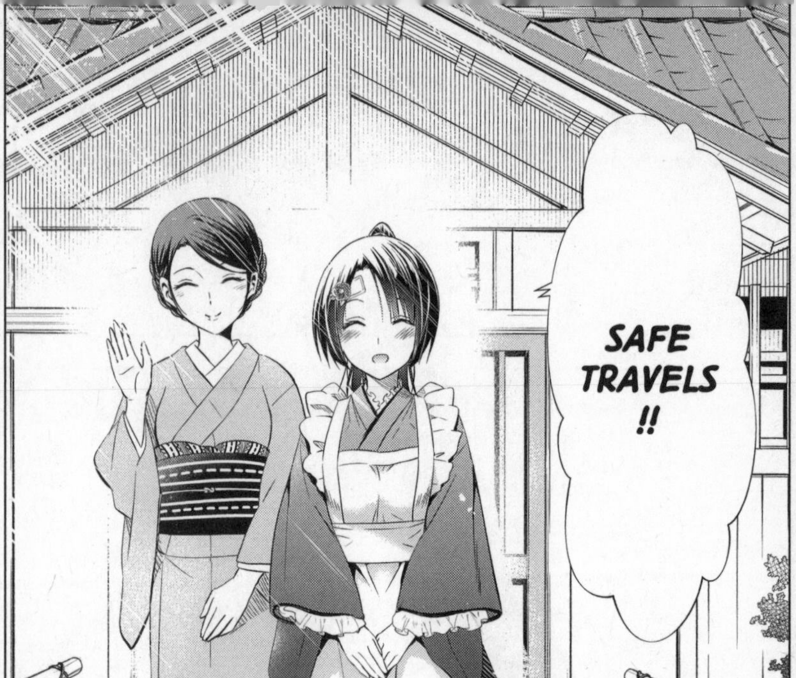
SAFE TRAVELS !!
ACT 59:
ROMIO & JULIET & THE TOUWA-DATE
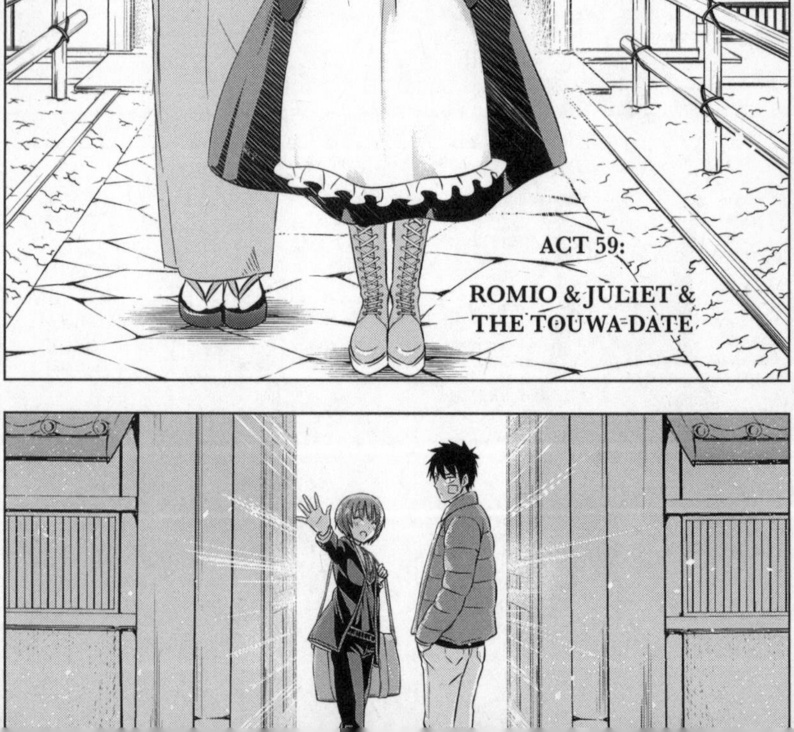

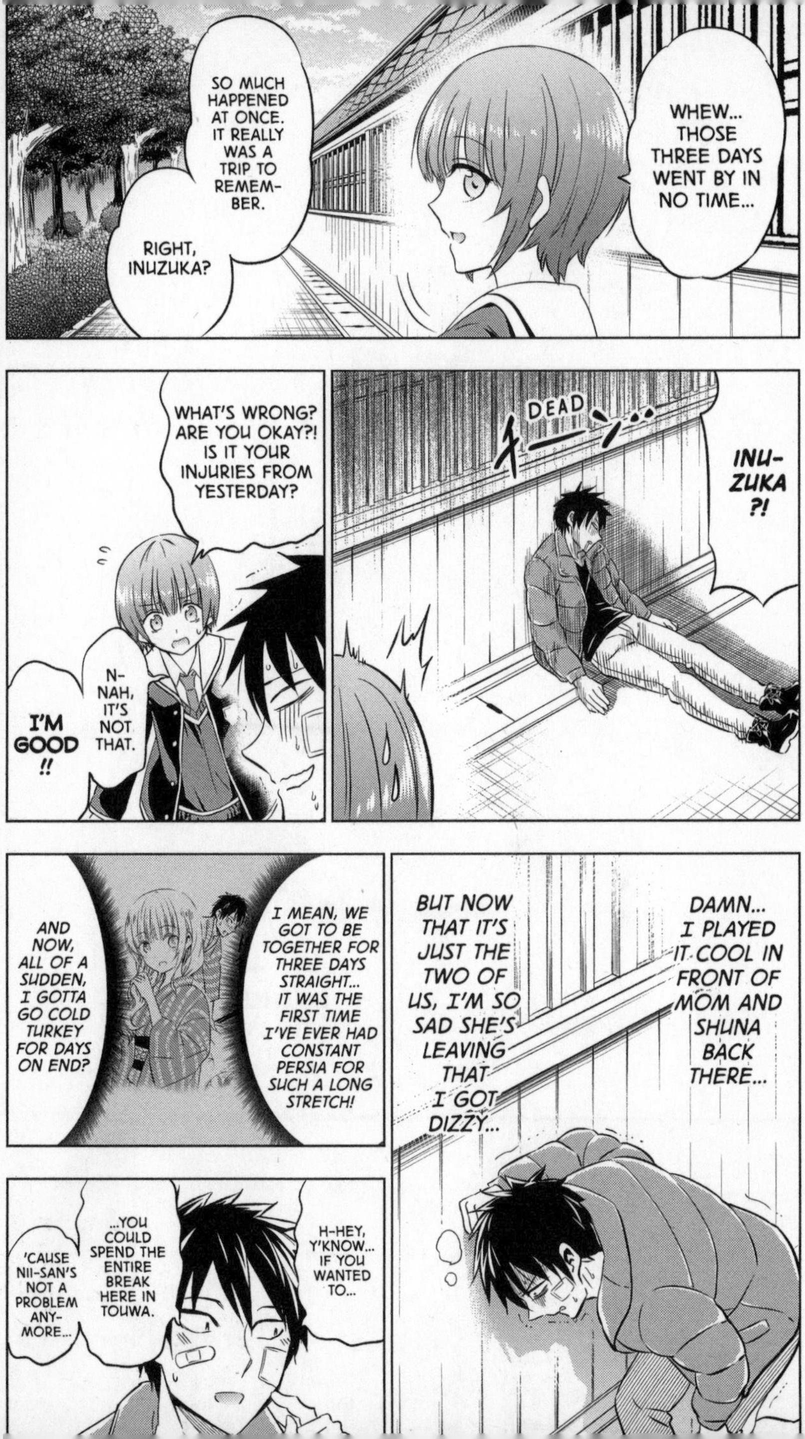
WHEW... THOSE THREE DAYS WENT BY IN NO TIME...
SO MUCH HAPPENED AT ONCE. IT REALLY WAS A TRIP TO REMEMBER.
RIGHT, INUZUKA?
INU-ZUKA?!
DEAD
WHAT'S WRONG? ARE YOU OKAY?! IS IT YOUR INJURIES FROM YESTERDAY?
N-NAH, IT'S NOT THAT.
I'M GOOD!!
DAMN... I PLAYED IT COOL IN FRONT OF MOM AND SHUNA BACK THERE...
BUT NOW THAT IT'S JUST THE TWO OF US, I'M SO SAD SHE'S LEAVING THAT I GOT DIZZY...
I MEAN, WE GOT TO BE TOGETHER FOR THREE DAYS STRAIGHT... IT WAS THE FIRST TIME I'VE EVER HAD CONSTANT PERSIA FOR SUCH A LONG STRETCH!
AND NOW, ALL OF A SUDDEN, I GOTTA GO COLD TURKEY FOR DAYS ON END?
H-HEY, Y'KNOW... IF YOU WANTED TO...
...YOU COULD SPEND THE ENTIRE BREAK HERE IN TOUWA.
'CAUSE NII-SAN'S NOT A PROBLEM ANYMORE...

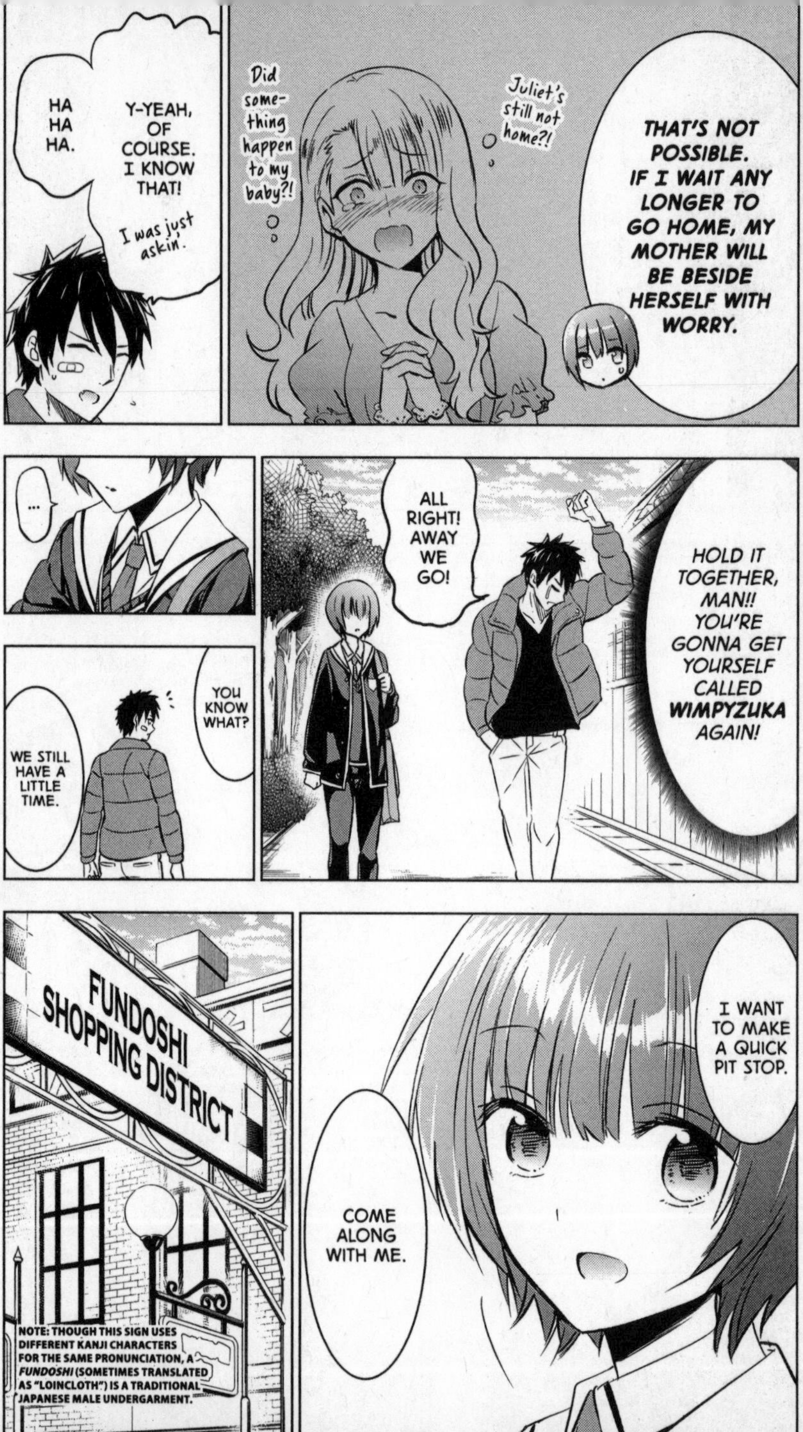
THAT'S NOT POSSIBLE. IF I WAIT ANY LONGER TO GO HOME, MY MOTHER WILL BE BESIDE HERSELF WITH WORRY.
Juliet's still not home?!
Did something happen to my baby?!
Y-YEAH, OF COURSE. I KNOW THAT!
HA HA HA.
I was just askin'.
HOLD IT TOGETHER, MAN!! YOU'RE GONNA GET YOURSELF CALLED WIMPYZUKA AGAIN!
ALL RIGHT! AWAY WE GO!
...
YOU KNOW WHAT?
WE STILL HAVE A LITTLE TIME.
I WANT TO MAKE A QUICK PIT STOP.
COME ALONG WITH ME.
FUNDOSHI SHOPPING DISTRICT
NOTE: THOUGH THIS SIGN USES DIFFERENT KANJI CHARACTERS FOR THE SAME PRONUNCIATION, A FUNDOSHI (SOMETIMES TRANSLATED AS "LOINCLOTH") IS A TRADITIONAL JAPANESE MALE UNDERGARMENT.

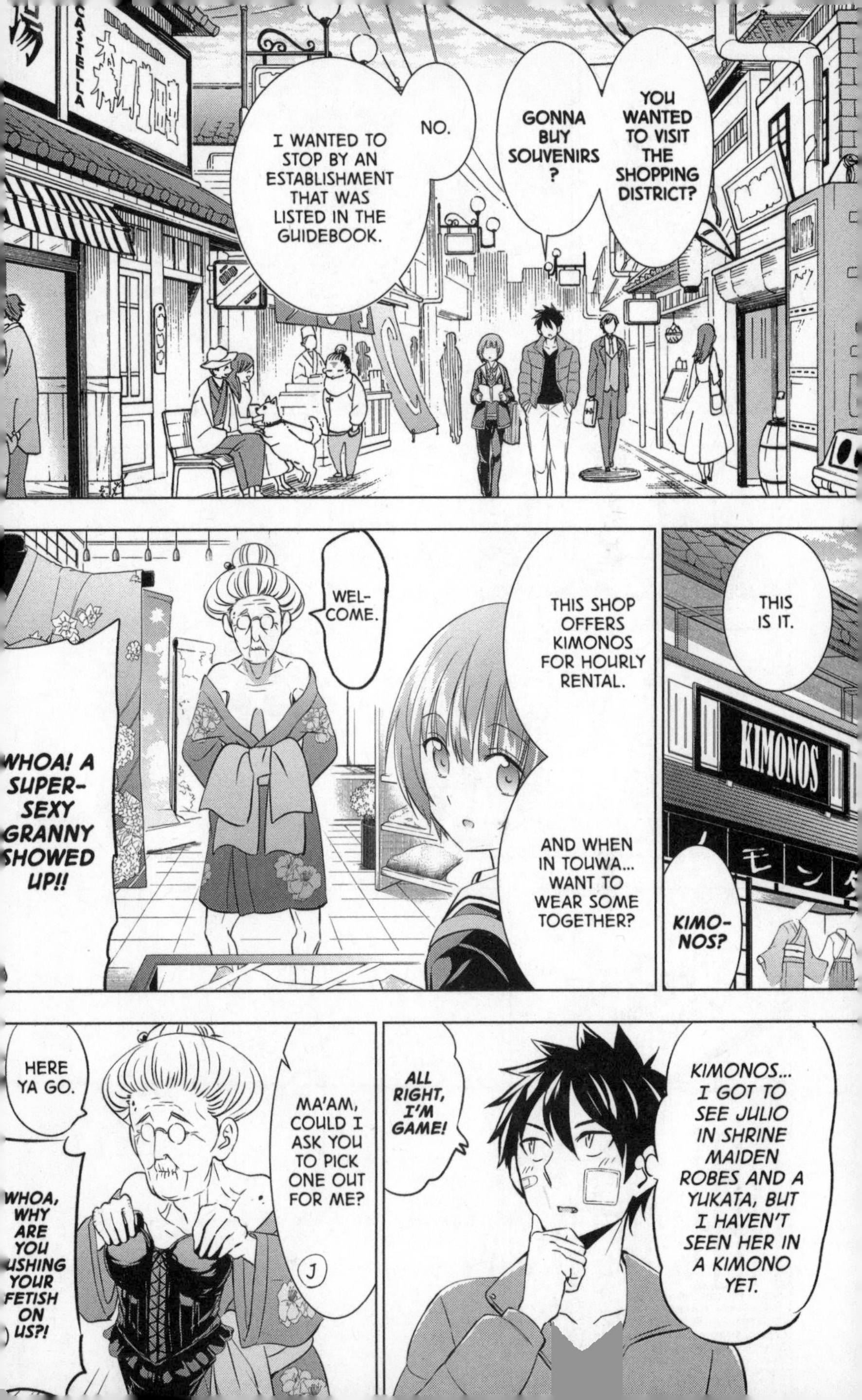
CASTELLA
YOU WANTED TO VISIT THE SHOPPING DISTRICT?
GONNA BUY SOUVENIRS?
NO.
I WANTED TO STOP BY AN ESTABLISHMENT THAT WAS LISTED IN THE GUIDEBOOK.
THIS IS IT.
KIMONOS
KIMO-NOS?
THIS SHOP OFFERS KIMONOS FOR HOURLY RENTAL.
AND WHEN IN TOUWA... WANT TO WEAR SOME TOGETHER?
WEL-COME.
WHOA! A SUPER-SEXY GRANNY HOWED UP!!
KIMONOS... I GOT TO SEE JULIO IN SHRINE MAIDEN ROBES AND A YUKATA, BUT I HAVEN'T SEEN HER IN A KIMONO YET.
ALL RIGHT, I'M GAME!
MA'AM, COULD I ASK YOU TO PICK ONE OUT FOR ME?
HERE YA GO.
WHOA, WHY ARE YOU USHING YOUR FETISH ON US?!

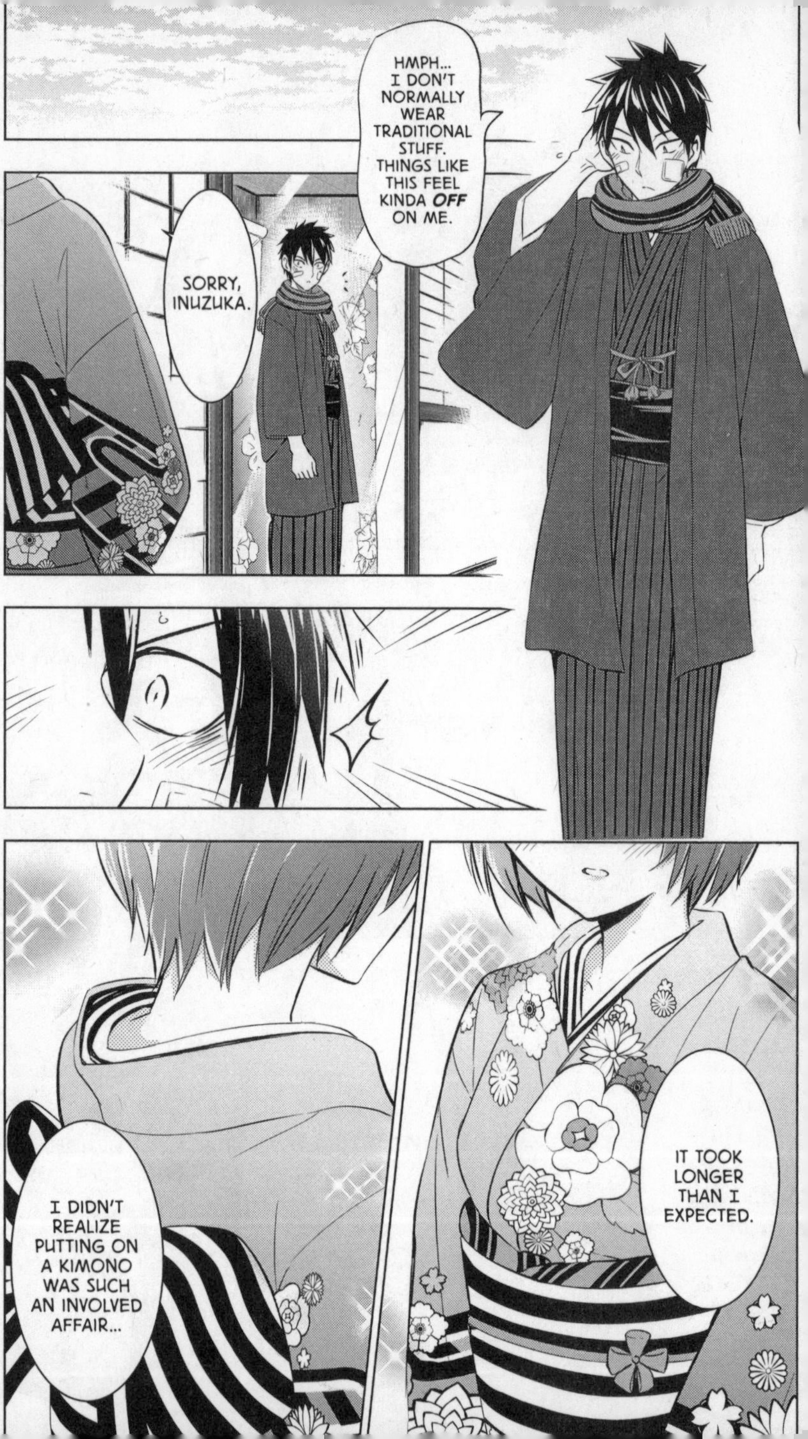
HMPH... I DON'T NORMALLY WEAR TRADITIONAL STUFF. THINGS LIKE THIS FEEL KINDA *OFF* ON ME.
SORRY, INUZUKA.
IT TOOK LONGER THAN I EXPECTED.
I DIDN'T REALIZE PUTTING ON A KIMONO WAS SUCH AN INVOLVED AFFAIR...

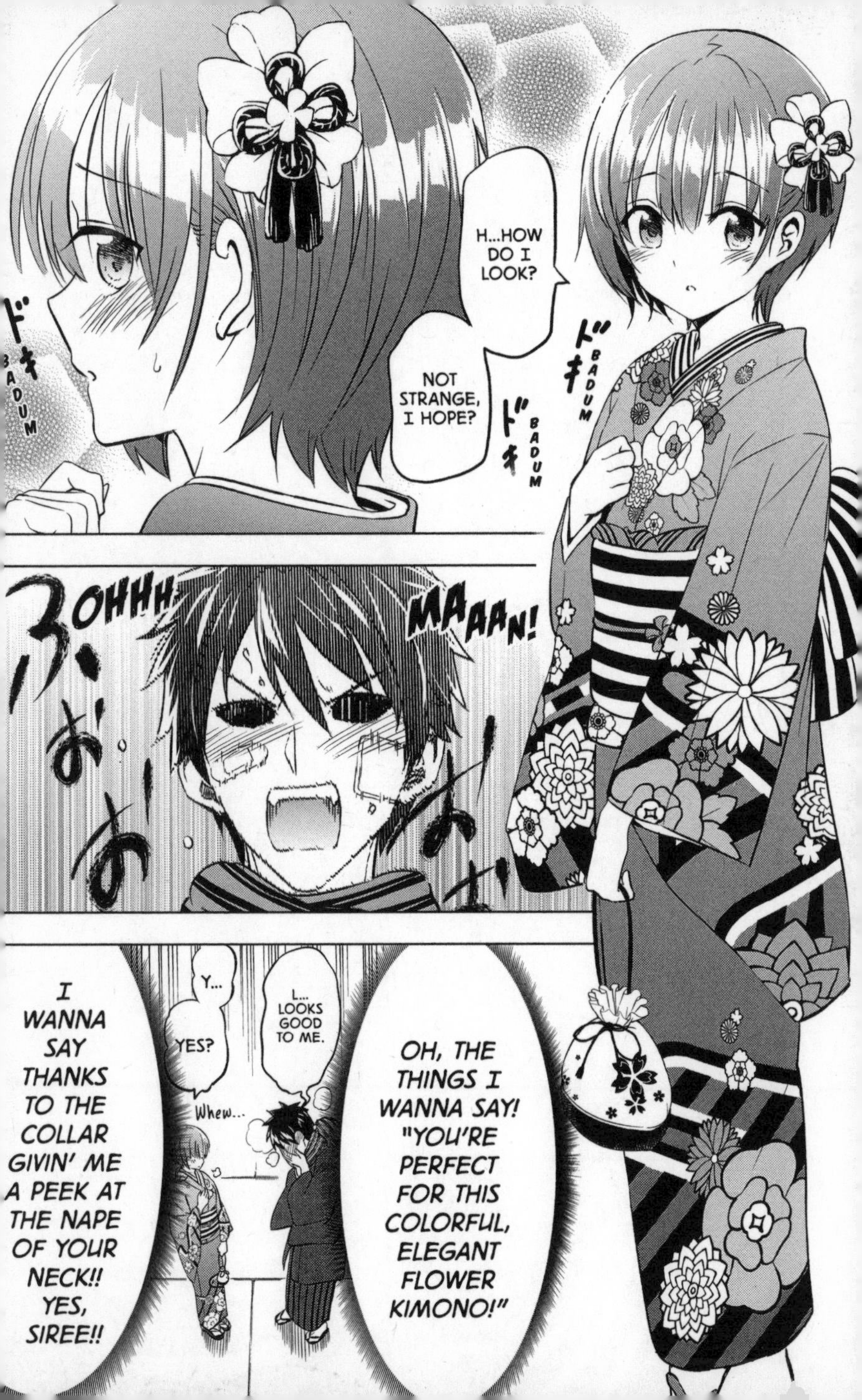
H...HOW DO I LOOK?
NOT STRANGE, I HOPE?
ドキ BADUM
ドキ BADUM
ドキ BADUM
ふぉぉぉ OHHHH-MAAAN!
OH, THE THINGS I WANNA SAY! "YOU'RE PERFECT FOR THIS COLORFUL, ELEGANT FLOWER KIMONO!"
L... LOOKS GOOD TO ME.
Y... YES?
Whew...
I WANNA SAY THANKS TO THE COLLAR GIVIN' ME A PEEK AT THE NAPE OF YOUR NECK!! YES, SIREE!!

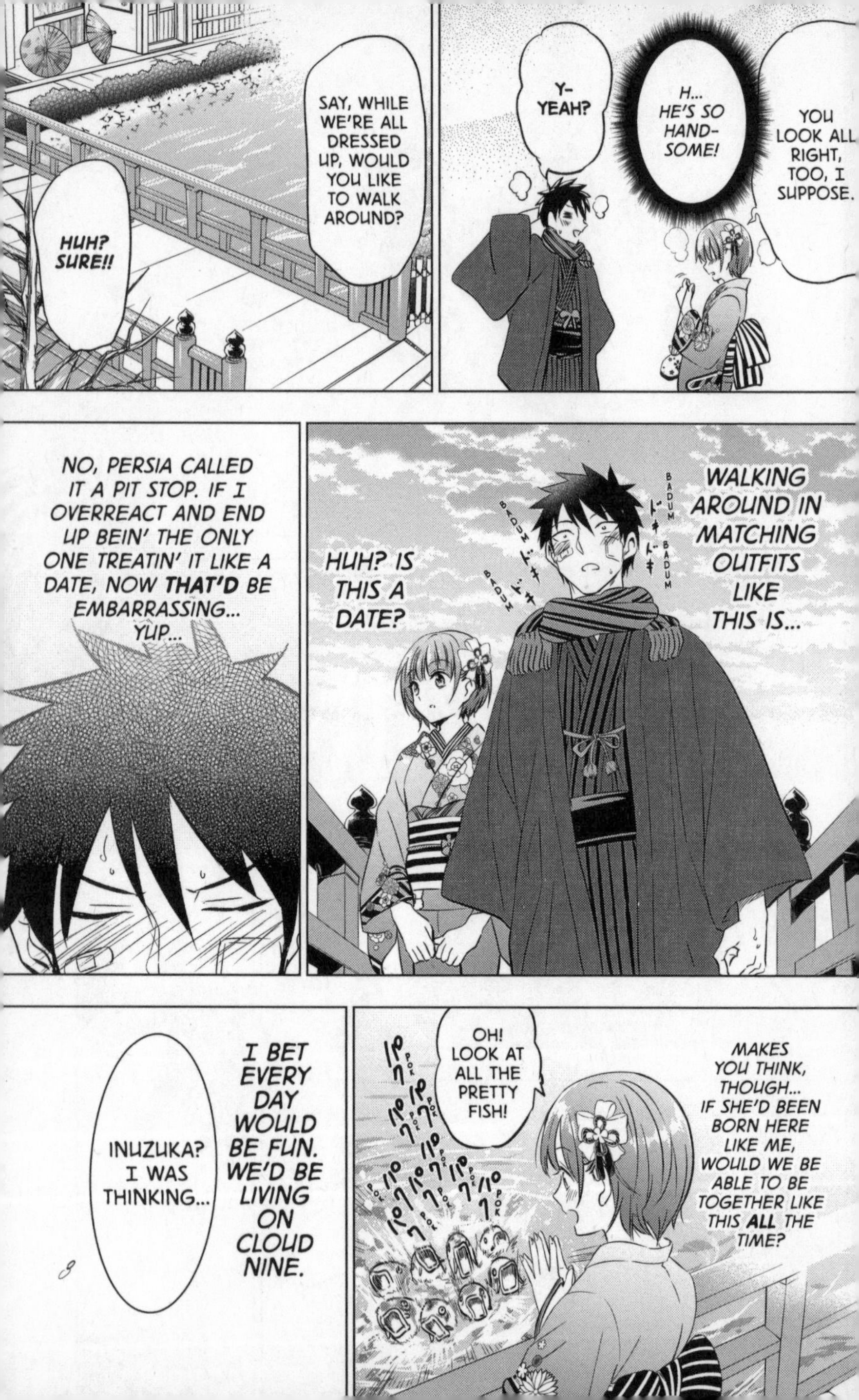
YOU LOOK ALL RIGHT, TOO, I SUPPOSE.
H... HE'S SO HAND-SOME!
Y-YEAH?
SAY, WHILE WE'RE ALL DRESSED UP, WOULD YOU LIKE TO WALK AROUND?
HUH? SURE!!
WALKING AROUND IN MATCHING OUTFITS LIKE THIS IS...
BADUM
BADUM
BADUM
BADUM
HUH? IS THIS A DATE?
NO, PERSIA CALLED IT A PIT STOP. IF I OVERREACT AND END UP BEIN' THE ONLY ONE TREATIN' IT LIKE A DATE, NOW **THAT'D** BE EMBARRASSING... YUP...
MAKES YOU THINK, THOUGH... IF SHE'D BEEN BORN HERE LIKE ME, WOULD WE BE ABLE TO BE TOGETHER LIKE THIS **ALL** THE TIME?
OH! LOOK AT ALL THE PRETTY FISH!
POK POK POK POK POK POK POK POK
I BET EVERY DAY WOULD BE FUN. WE'D BE LIVING ON CLOUD NINE.
INUZUKA? I WAS THINKING...

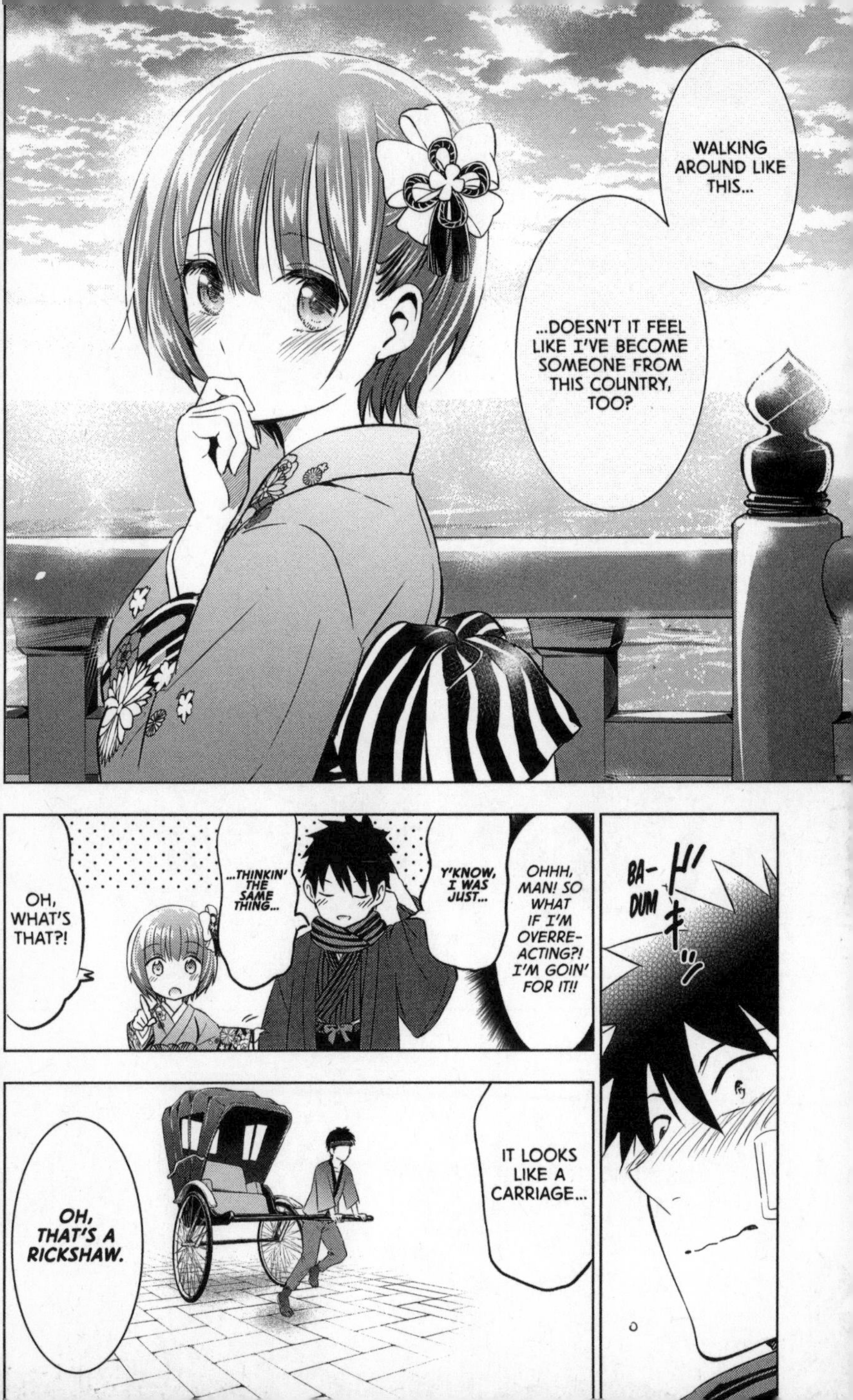
WALKING AROUND LIKE THIS...
...DOESN'T IT FEEL LIKE I'VE BECOME SOMEONE FROM THIS COUNTRY, TOO?
BA-DUM
ドキッ
OHHH, MAN! SO WHAT IF I'M OVERRE-ACTING?! I'M GOIN' FOR IT!!
Y'KNOW, I WAS JUST...
...THINKIN' THE SAME THING...
OH, WHAT'S THAT?!
IT LOOKS LIKE A CARRIAGE...
OH, THAT'S A RICKSHAW.

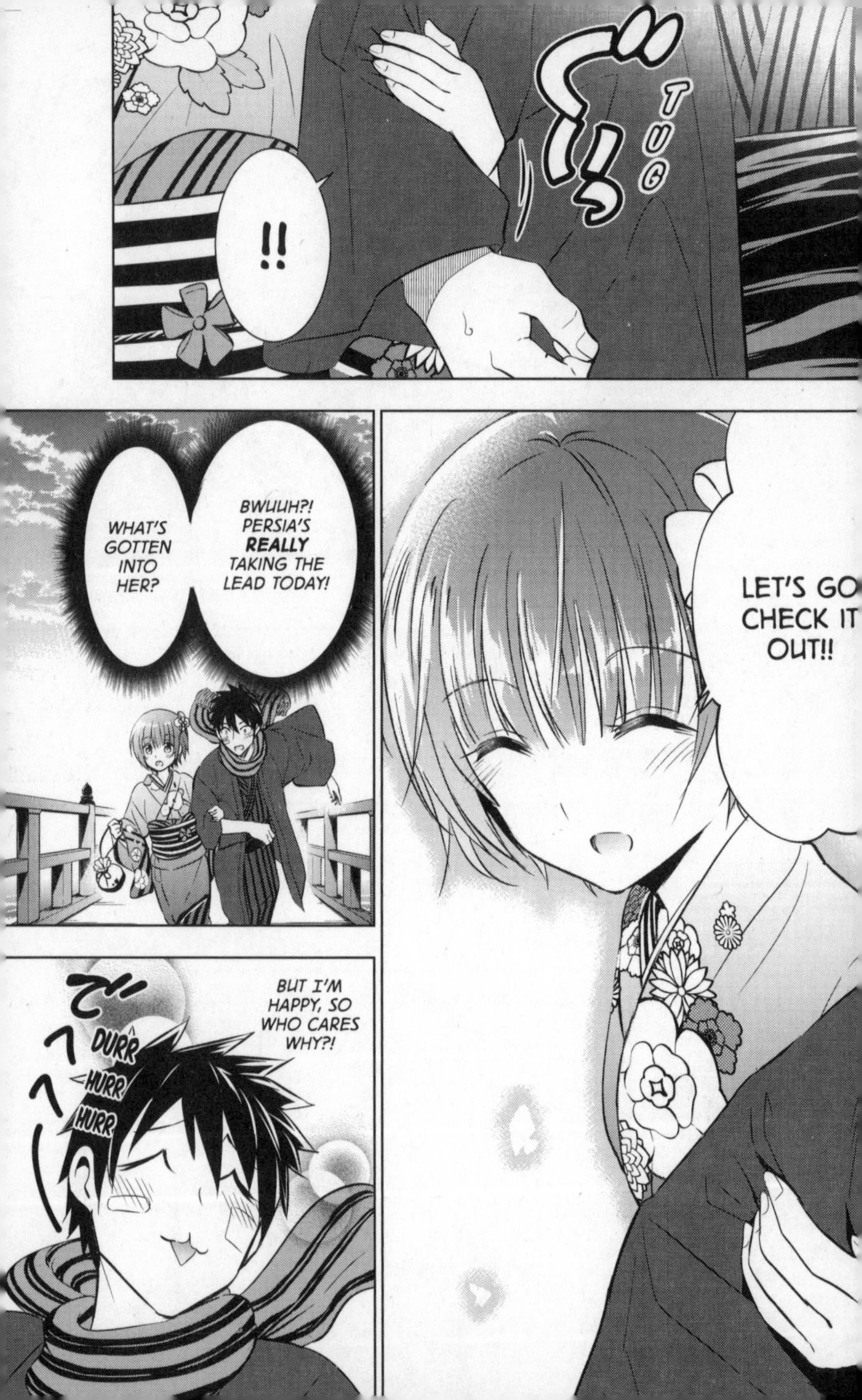
TUG
!!
LET'S GO CHECK IT OUT!!
BWUUH?! PERSIA'S **REALLY** TAKING THE LEAD TODAY!
WHAT'S GOTTEN INTO HER?
BUT I'M HAPPY, SO WHO CARES WHY?!
DURR
HURR
HURR

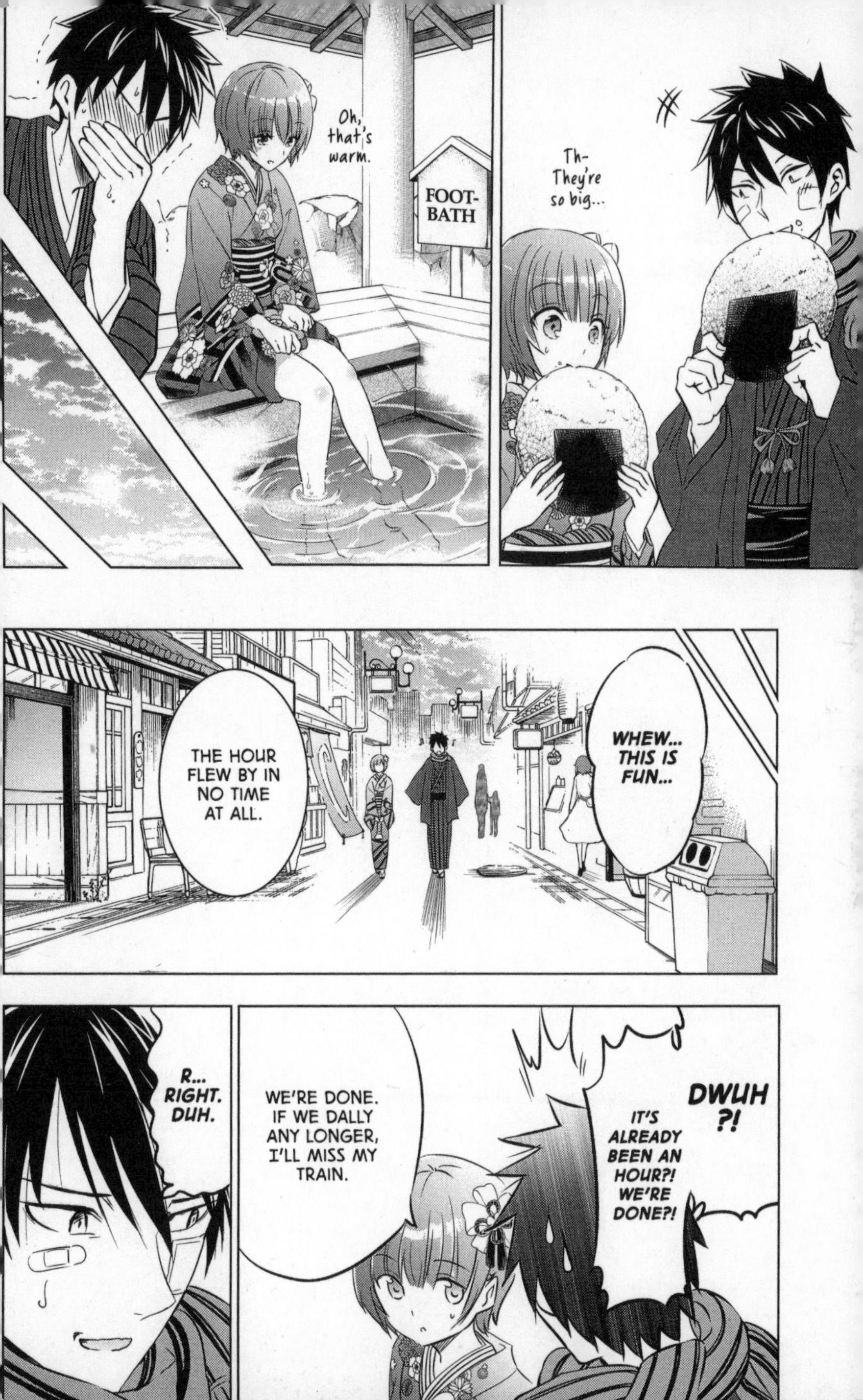
Th- They're so big...
Oh, that's warm.
FOOT-BATH
WHEW... THIS IS FUN...
THE HOUR FLEW BY IN NO TIME AT ALL.
DWUH ?!
IT'S ALREADY BEEN AN HOUR?! WE'RE DONE?!
WE'RE DONE. IF WE DALLY ANY LONGER, I'LL MISS MY TRAIN.
R... RIGHT. DUH.

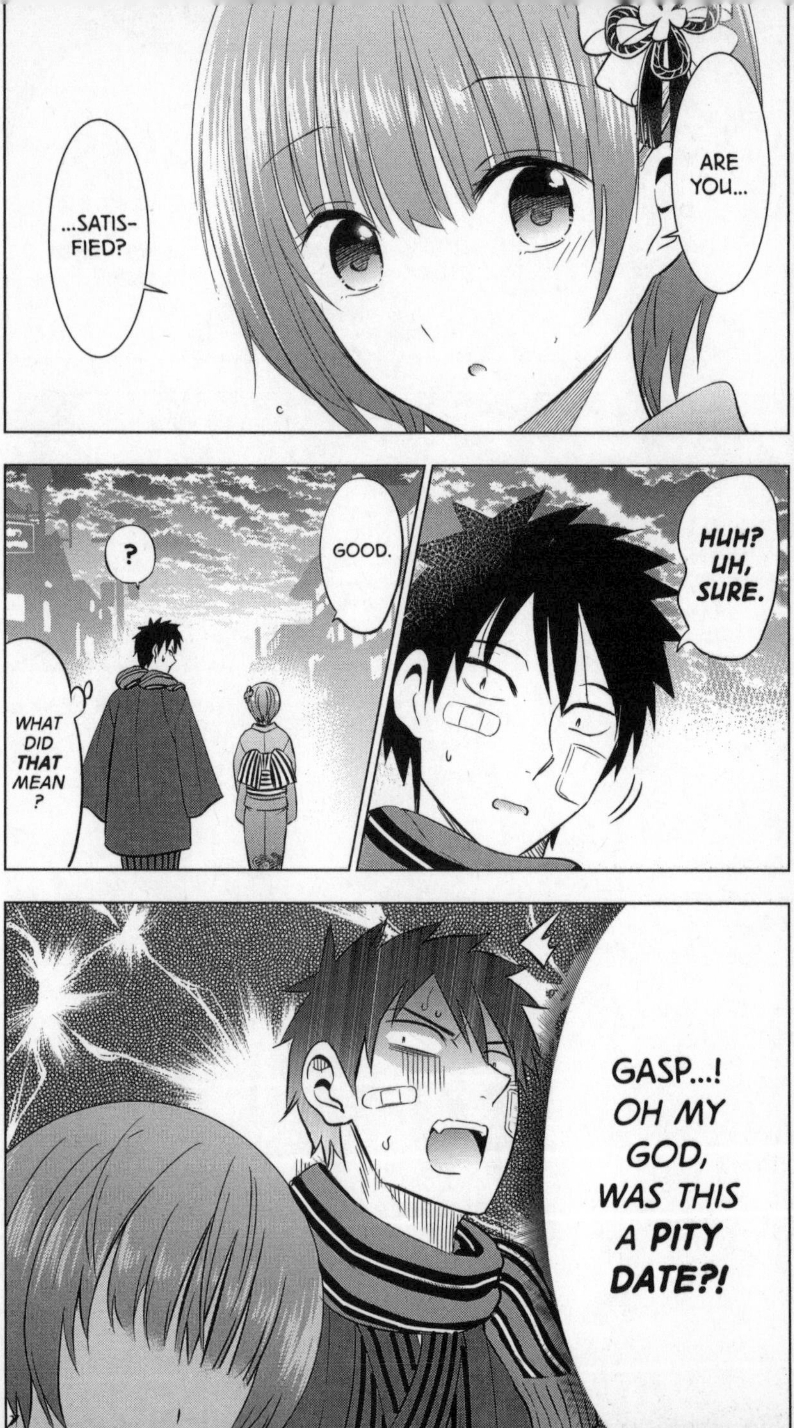
ARE YOU...
...SATIS-FIED?
HUH? UH, SURE.
GOOD.
?
WHAT DID THAT MEAN?
GASP...! OH MY GOD, WAS THIS A PITY DATE?!

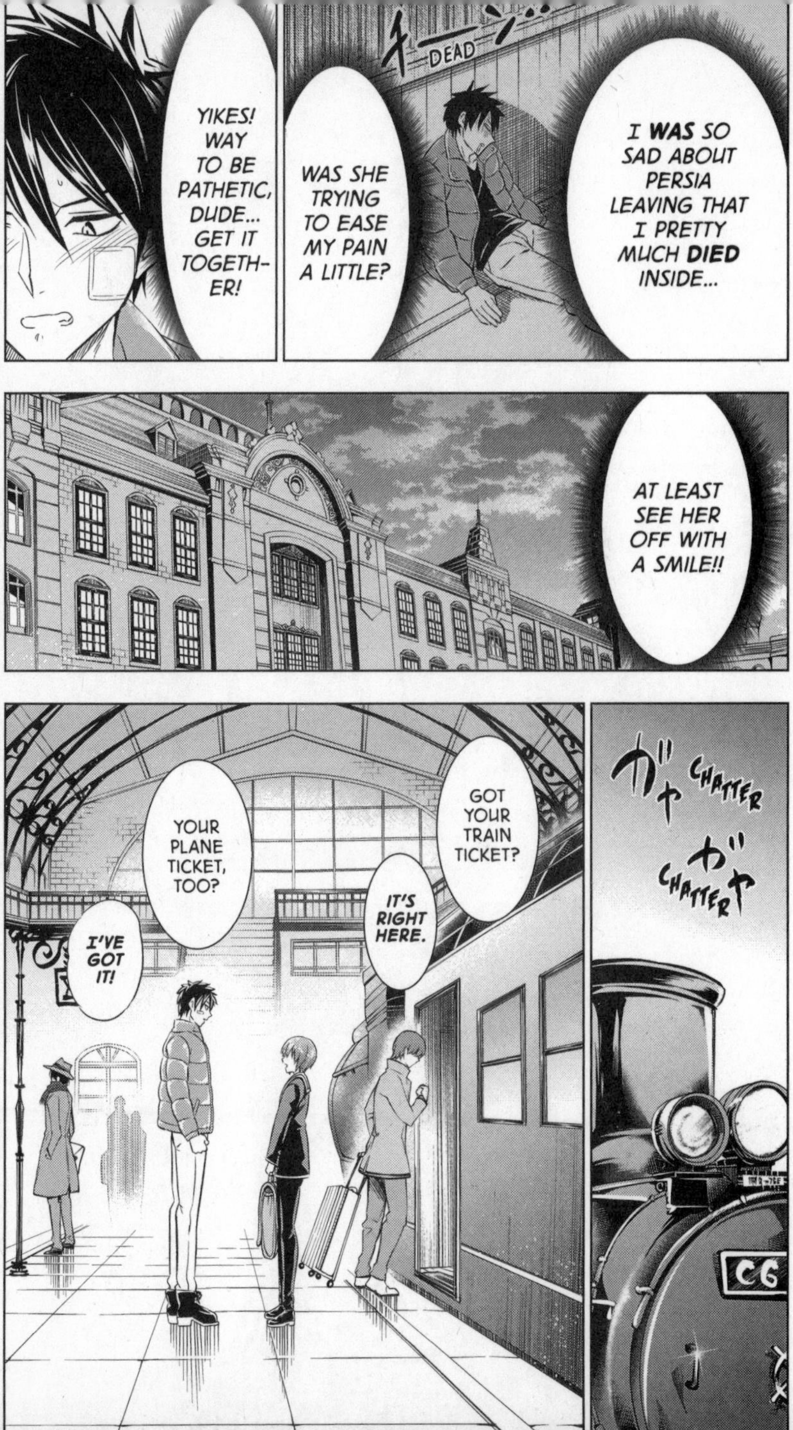
DEAD
I WAS SO SAD ABOUT PERSIA LEAVING THAT I PRETTY MUCH DIED INSIDE...
WAS SHE TRYING TO EASE MY PAIN A LITTLE?
YIKES! WAY TO BE PATHETIC, DUDE... GET IT TOGETH-ER!
AT LEAST SEE HER OFF WITH A SMILE!!
CHATTER
CHATTER
GOT YOUR TRAIN TICKET?
IT'S RIGHT HERE.
YOUR PLANE TICKET, TOO?
I'VE GOT IT!
CG

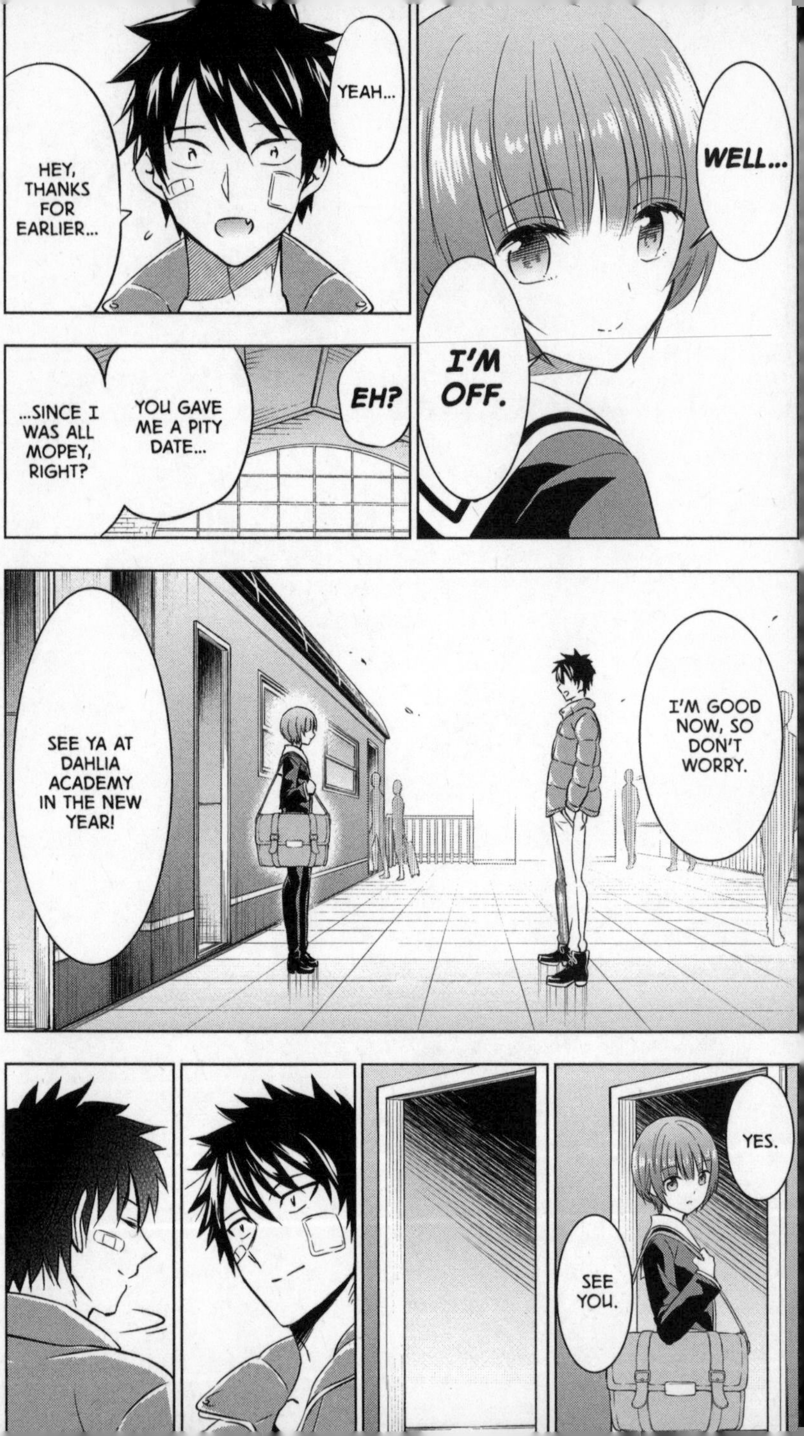
WELL...
I'M OFF.
YEAH...
HEY, THANKS FOR EARLIER...
EH?
YOU GAVE ME A PITY DATE...
...SINCE I WAS ALL MOPEY, RIGHT?
I'M GOOD NOW, SO DON'T WORRY.
SEE YA AT DAHLIA ACADEMY IN THE NEW YEAR!
YES.
SEE YOU.

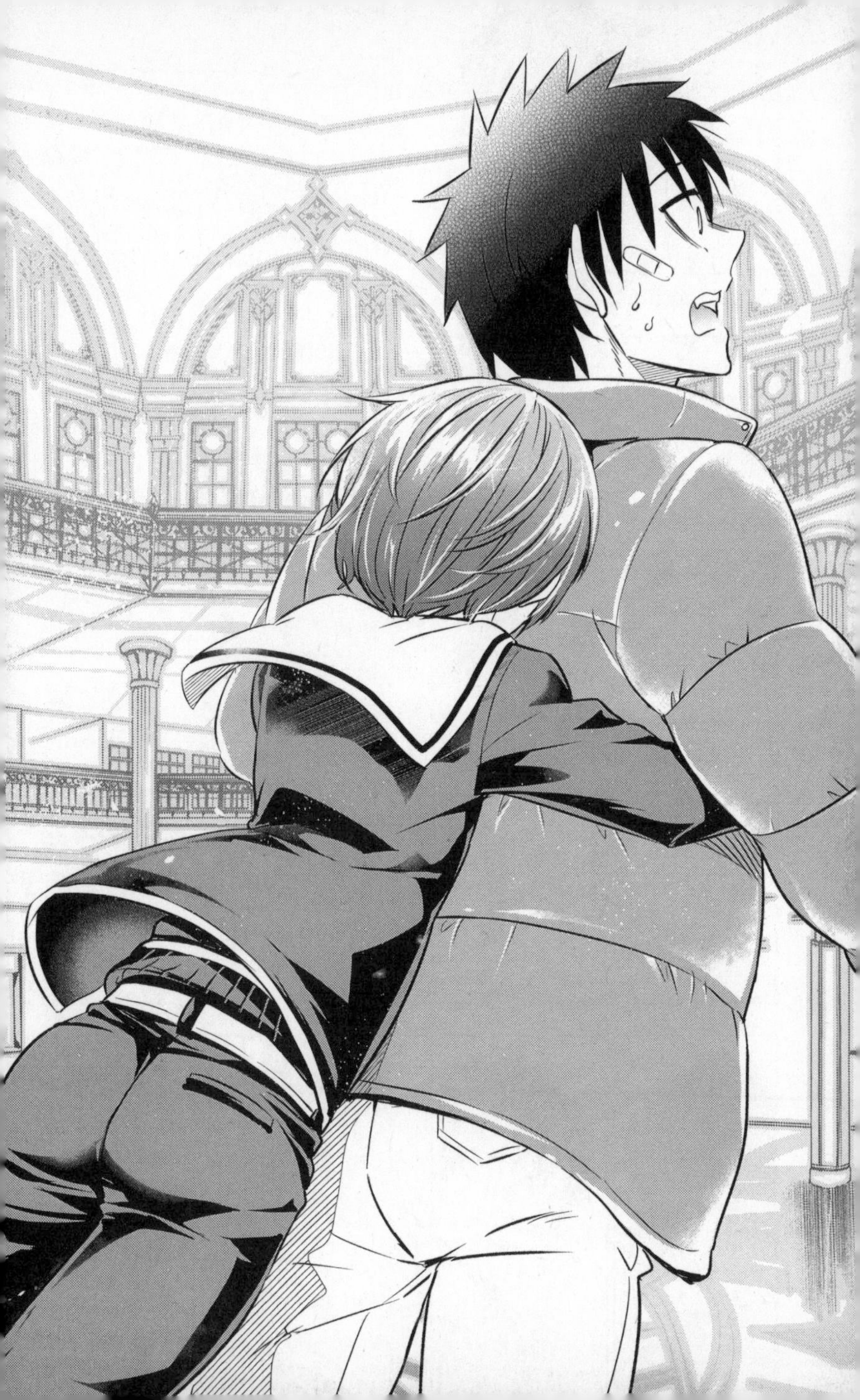

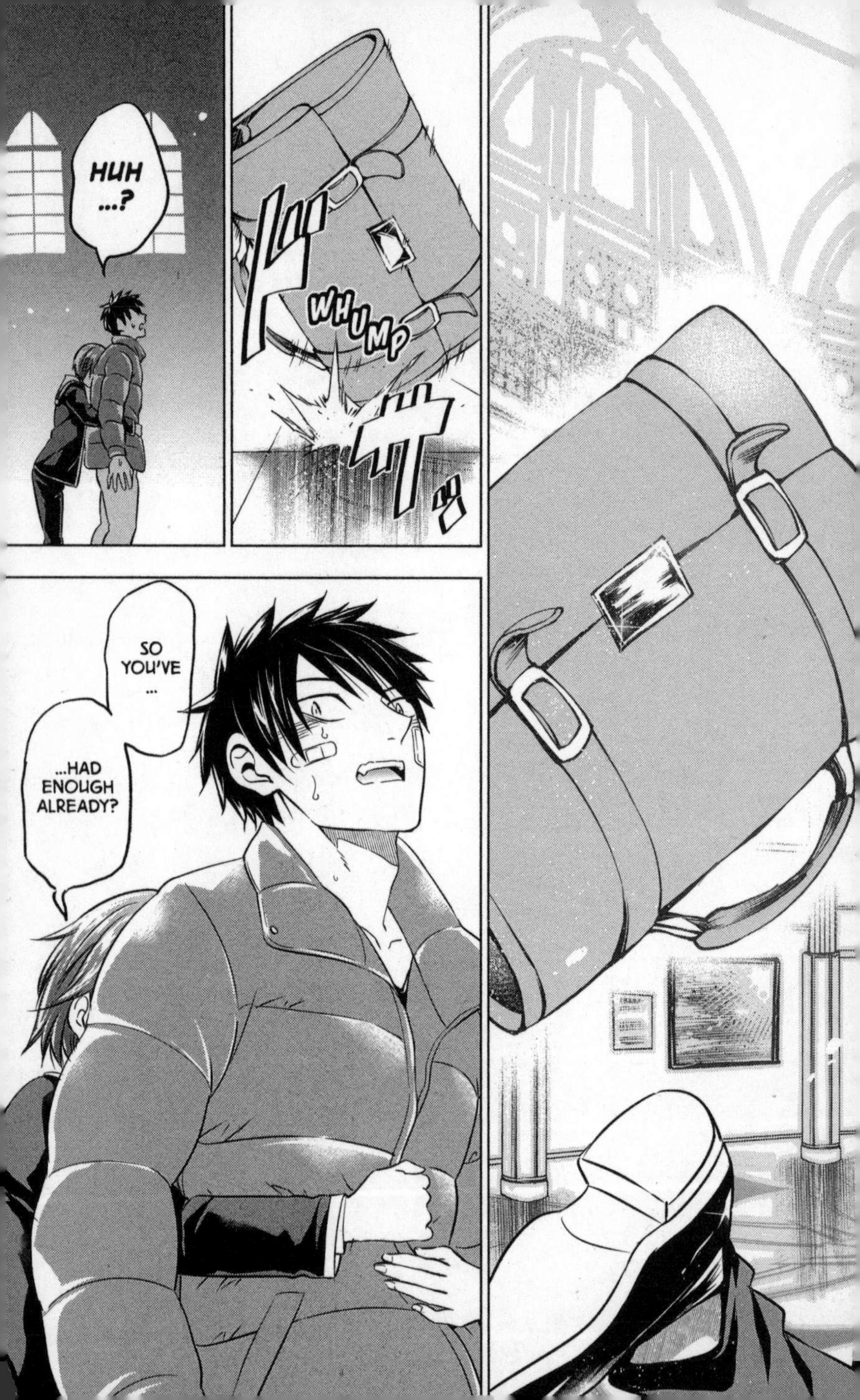
ドサッ
WHUMP
HUH ...?
SO YOU'VE ...
...HAD ENOUGH ALREADY?

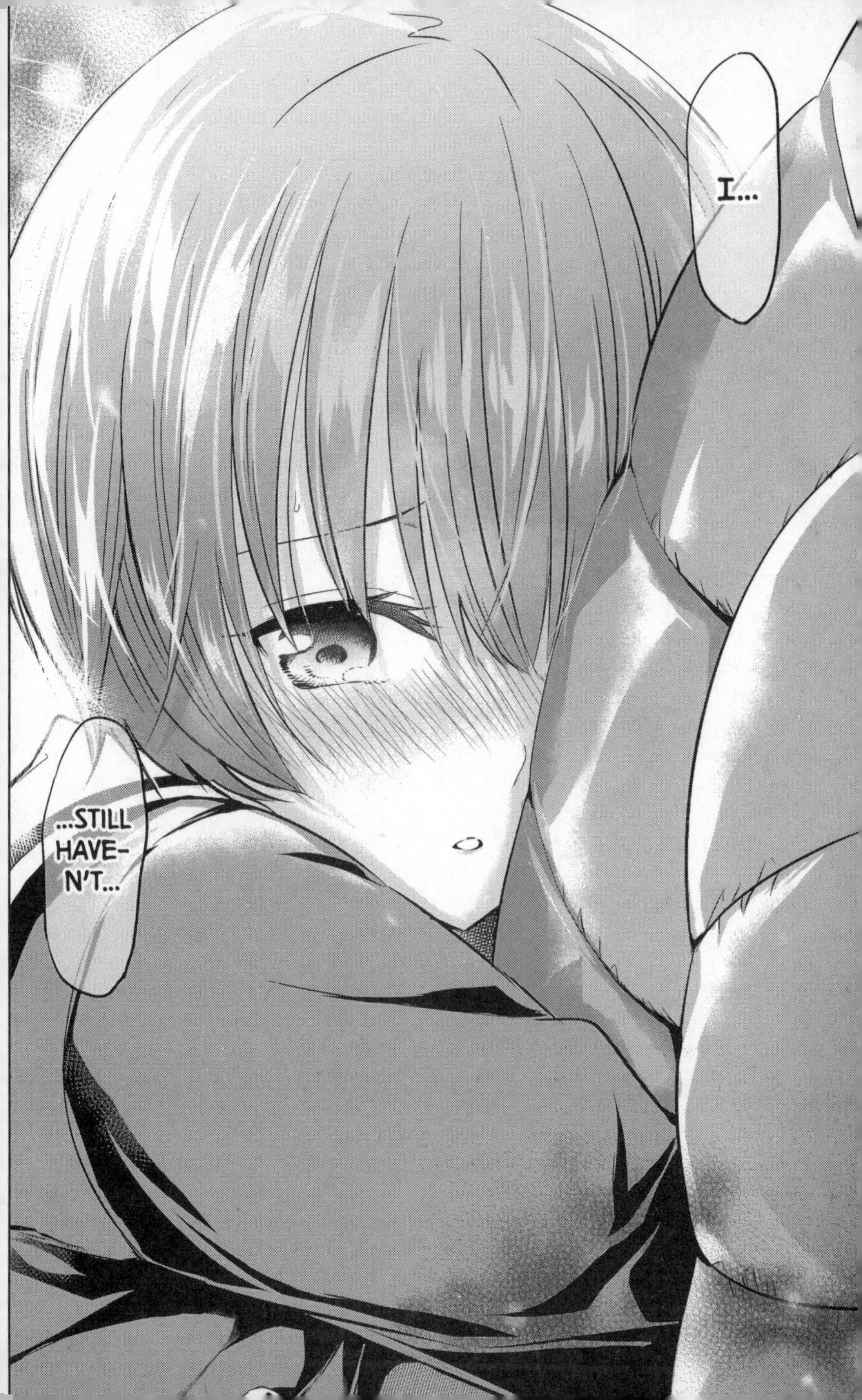
I...
...STILL HAVE-N'T...

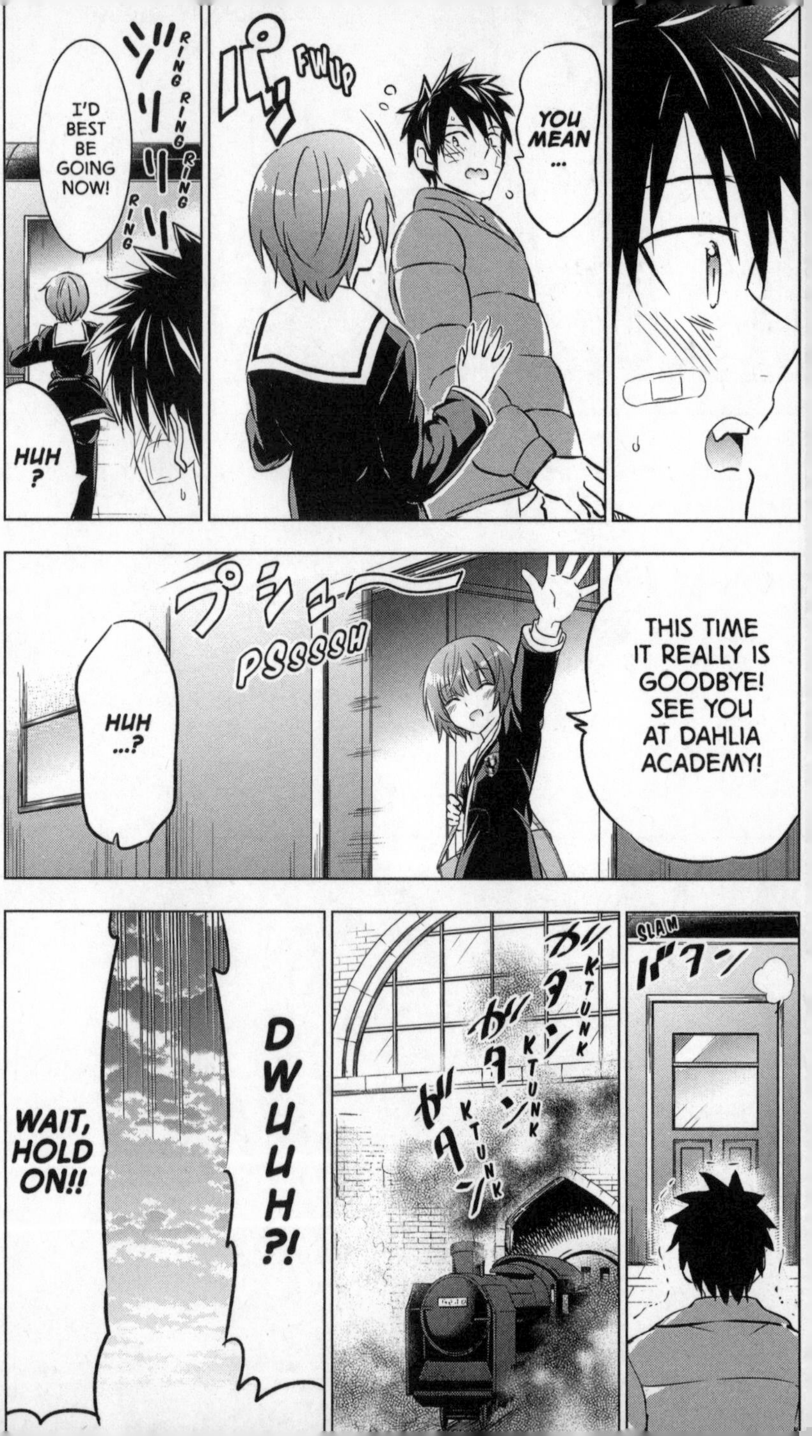
YOU MEAN ...
パッ
FWUP
ジリリリ
RING RING RING RING
I'D BEST BE GOING NOW!
HUH?
THIS TIME IT REALLY IS GOODBYE! SEE YOU AT DAHLIA ACADEMY!
プシュー
PSSSSH
HUH ...?
バタン
SLAM
ガタン ガタン ガタン
KTUNK KTUNK KTUNK
DWUUUH?!
WAIT, HOLD ON!!

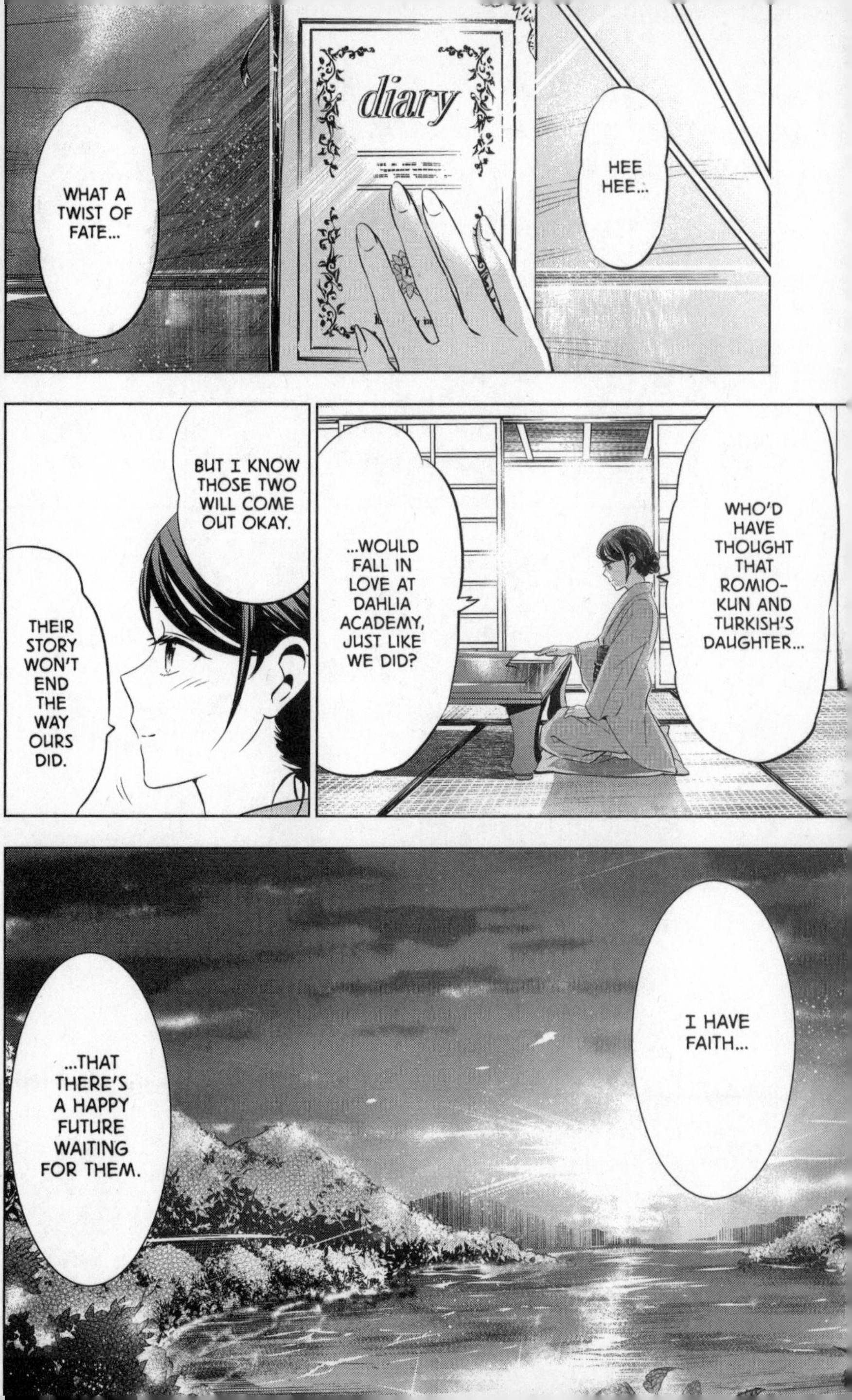
HEE HEE...
WHAT A TWIST OF FATE...
WHO'D HAVE THOUGHT THAT ROMIO-KUN AND TURKISH'S DAUGHTER...
...WOULD FALL IN LOVE AT DAHLIA ACADEMY, JUST LIKE WE DID?
BUT I KNOW THOSE TWO WILL COME OUT OKAY.
THEIR STORY WON'T END THE WAY OURS DID.
I HAVE FAITH...
...THAT THERE'S A HAPPY FUTURE WAITING FOR THEM.

Boarding
School *Juliet*

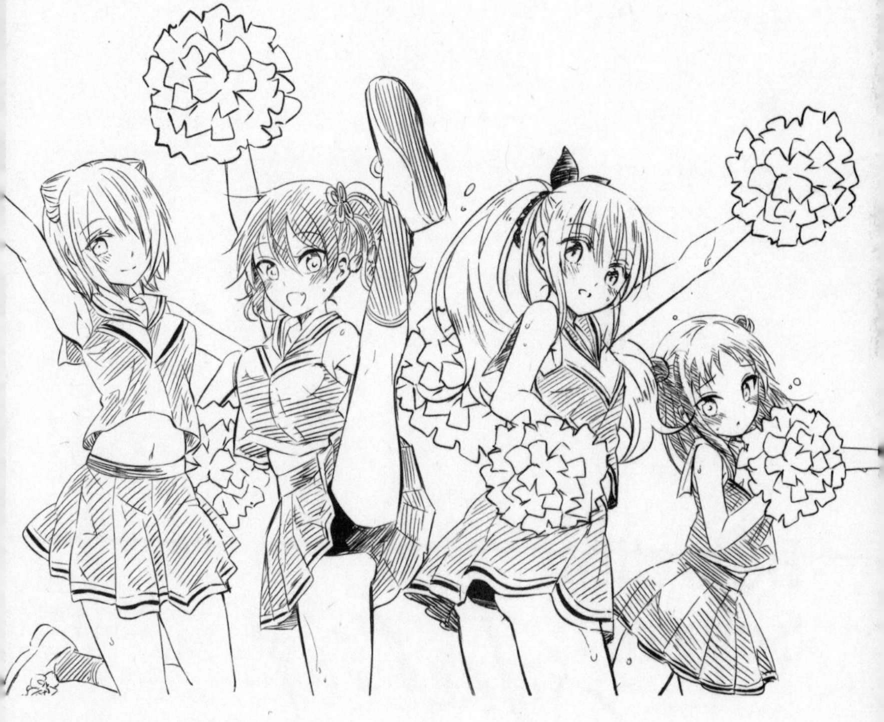

To LOVE, or not to LOVE

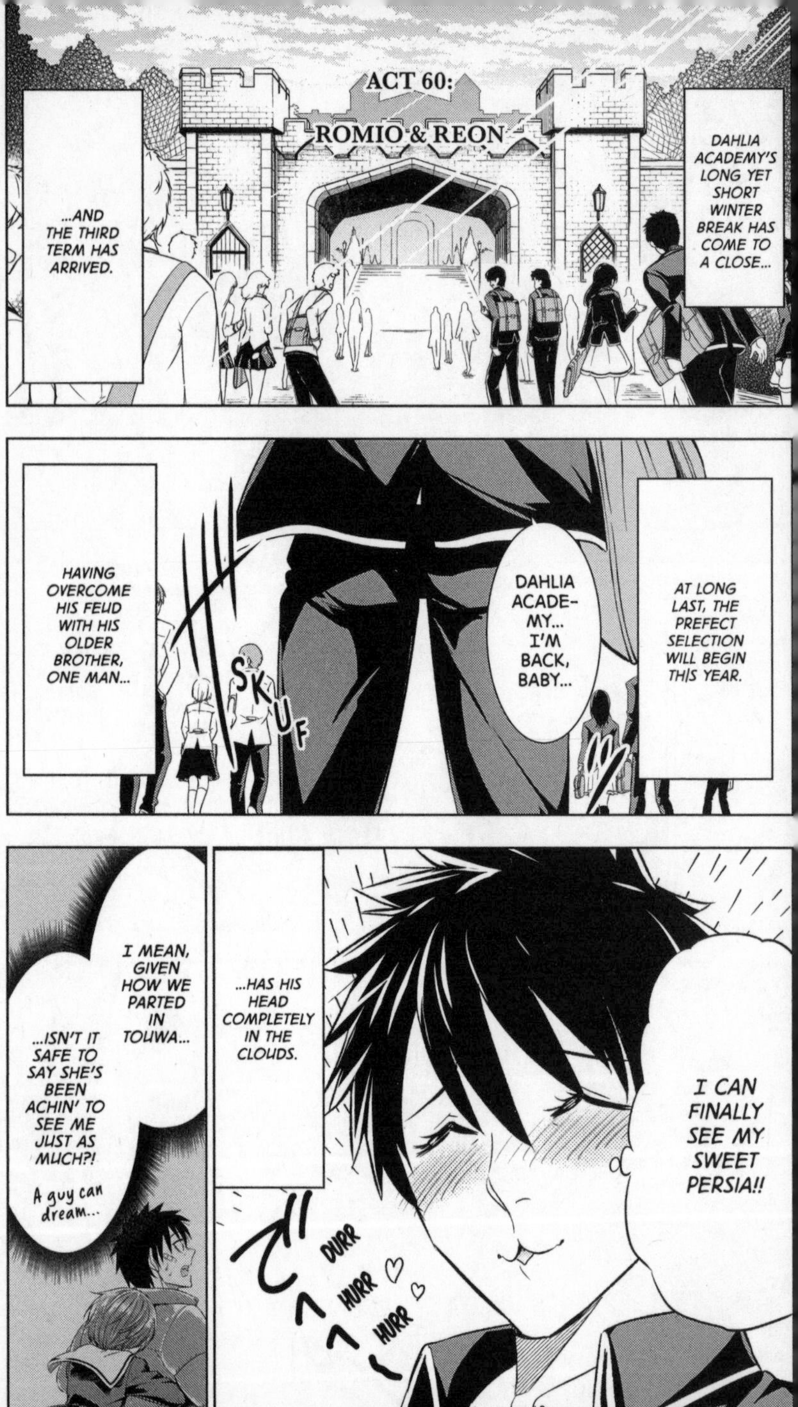
ACT 60:
ROMIO & REON
DAHLIA ACADEMY'S LONG YET SHORT WINTER BREAK HAS COME TO A CLOSE...
...AND THE THIRD TERM HAS ARRIVED.
AT LONG LAST, THE PREFECT SELECTION WILL BEGIN THIS YEAR.
DAHLIA ACADE-MY... I'M BACK, BABY...
SKUF
HAVING OVERCOME HIS FEUD WITH HIS OLDER BROTHER, ONE MAN...
I CAN FINALLY SEE MY SWEET PERSIA!!
DURR HURR HURR
...HAS HIS HEAD COMPLETELY IN THE CLOUDS.
I MEAN, GIVEN HOW WE PARTED IN TOUWA...
...ISN'T IT SAFE TO SAY SHE'S BEEN ACHIN' TO SEE ME JUST AS MUCH?!
A guy can dream...

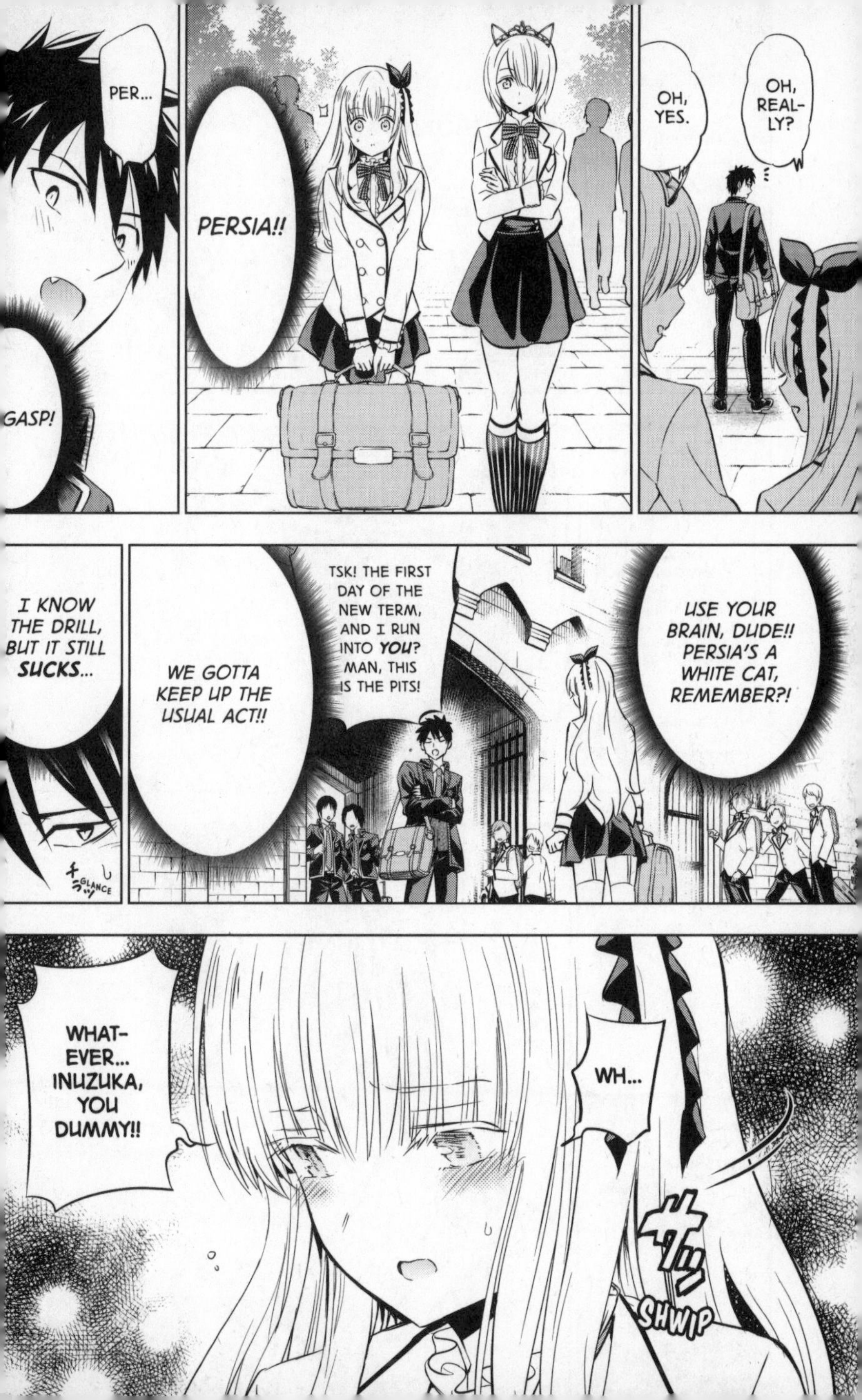
OH, REAL-LY?
OH, YES.
PERSIA!!
PER...
GASP!
USE YOUR BRAIN, DUDE!! PERSIA'S A WHITE CAT, REMEMBER?!
TSK! THE FIRST DAY OF THE NEW TERM, AND I RUN INTO YOU? MAN, THIS IS THE PITS!
WE GOTTA KEEP UP THE USUAL ACT!!
I KNOW THE DRILL, BUT IT STILL SUCKS...
GLANCE
WH...
SHWIP
WHAT-EVER... INUZUKA, YOU DUMMY!!

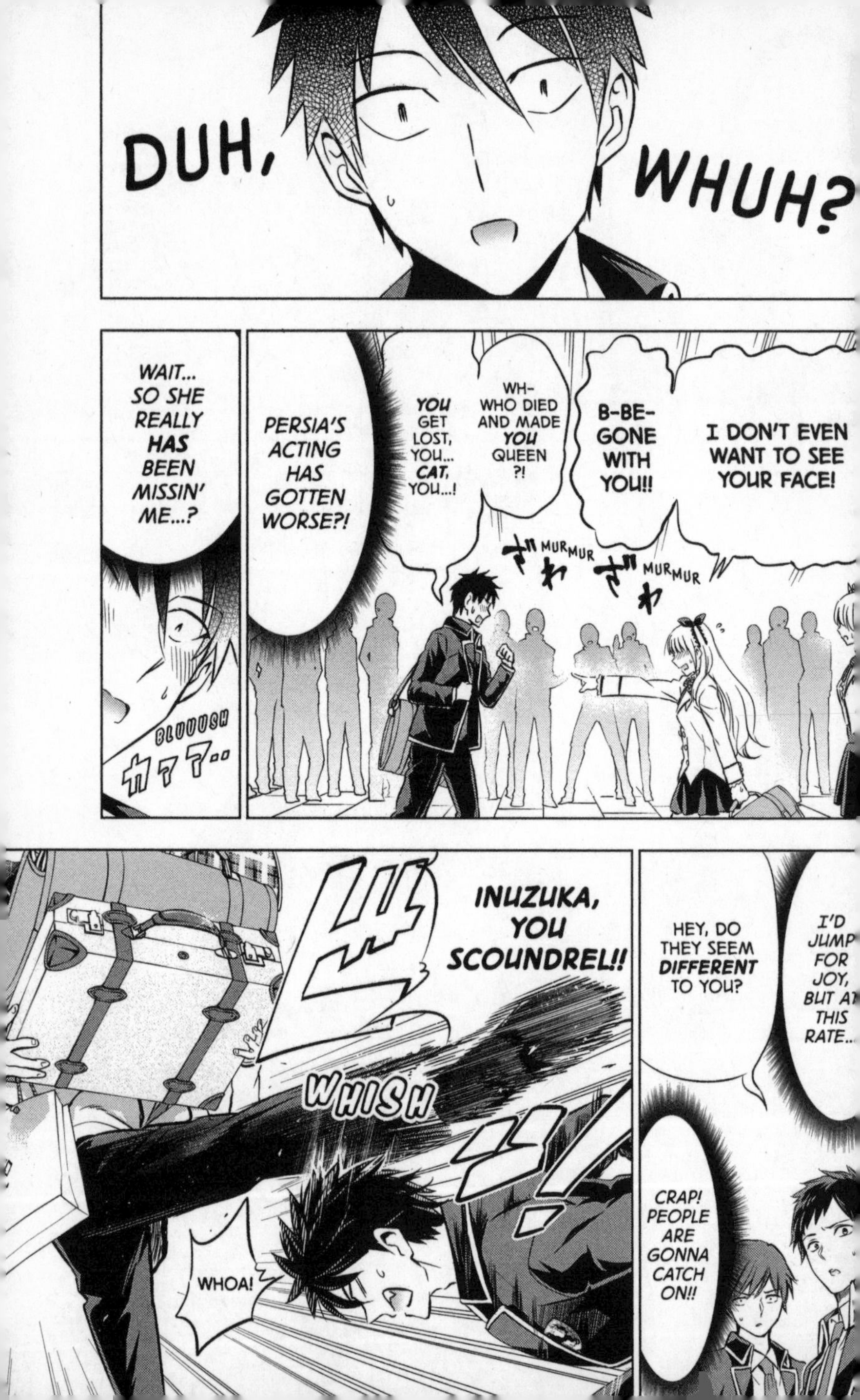
DUH, WHUH?
I DON'T EVEN WANT TO SEE YOUR FACE!
B-BE-GONE WITH YOU!!
WH- WHO DIED AND MADE YOU QUEEN?!
YOU GET LOST, YOU... CAT, YOU...!
MURMUR MURMUR
PERSIA'S ACTING HAS GOTTEN WORSE?!
WAIT... SO SHE REALLY HAS BEEN MISSIN' ME...?
BLUUUSH
I'D JUMP FOR JOY, BUT AT THIS RATE...
HEY, DO THEY SEEM DIFFERENT TO YOU?
CRAP! PEOPLE ARE GONNA CATCH ON!!
INUZUKA, YOU SCOUNDREL!!
WHISH
WHOA!

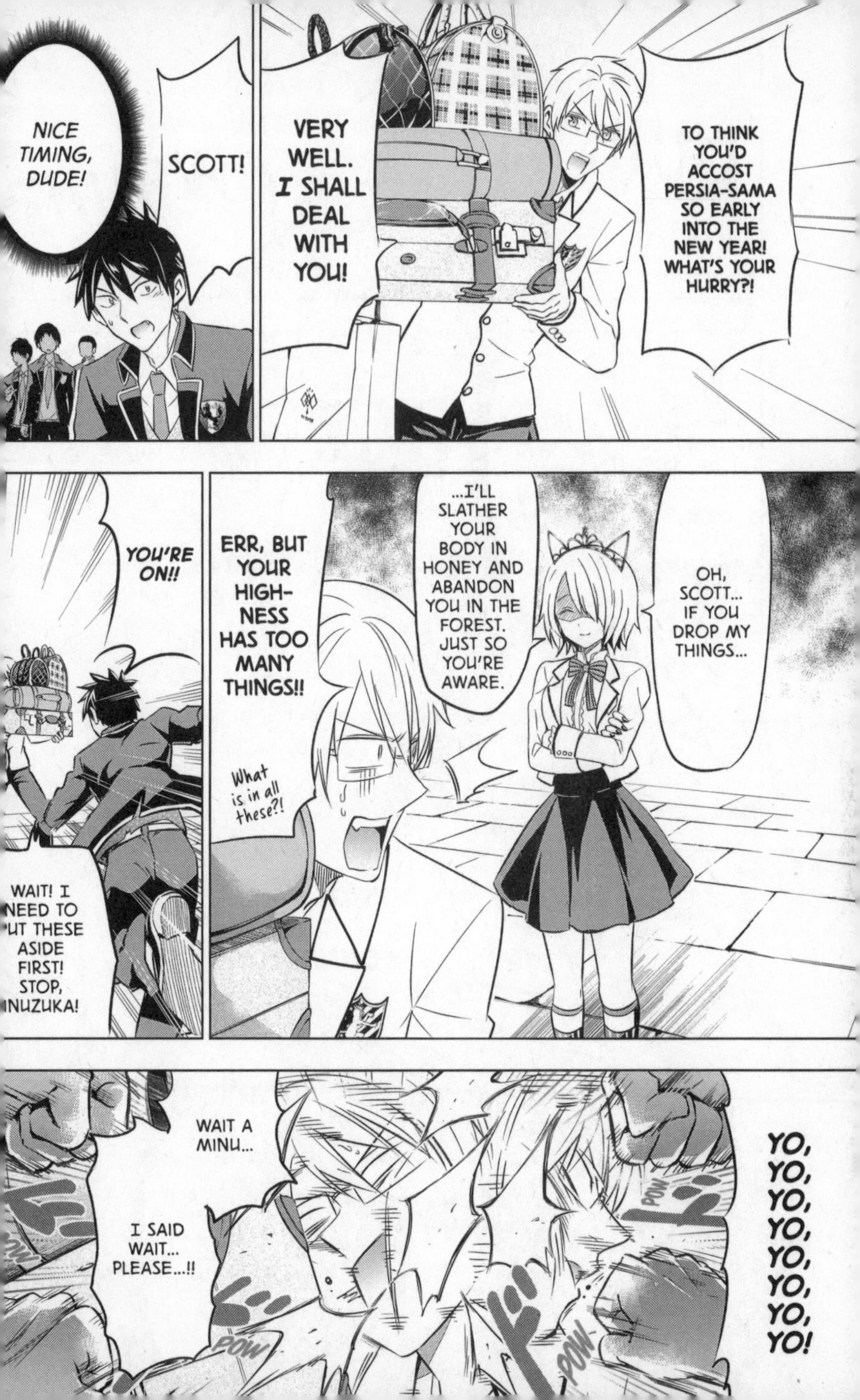
TO THINK YOU'D ACCOST PERSIA-SAMA SO EARLY INTO THE NEW YEAR! WHAT'S YOUR HURRY?!
VERY WELL. I SHALL DEAL WITH YOU!
SCOTT!
NICE TIMING, DUDE!
OH, SCOTT... IF YOU DROP MY THINGS...
...I'LL SLATHER YOUR BODY IN HONEY AND ABANDON YOU IN THE FOREST. JUST SO YOU'RE AWARE.
ERR, BUT YOUR HIGHNESS HAS TOO MANY THINGS!!
What is in all these?!
YOU'RE ON!!
WAIT! I NEED TO UT THESE ASIDE FIRST! STOP, INUZUKA!
YO, YO, YO, YO, YO, YO, YO, YO!
POW
WAIT A MINU...
I SAID WAIT... PLEASE...!!
POW
POW
POW

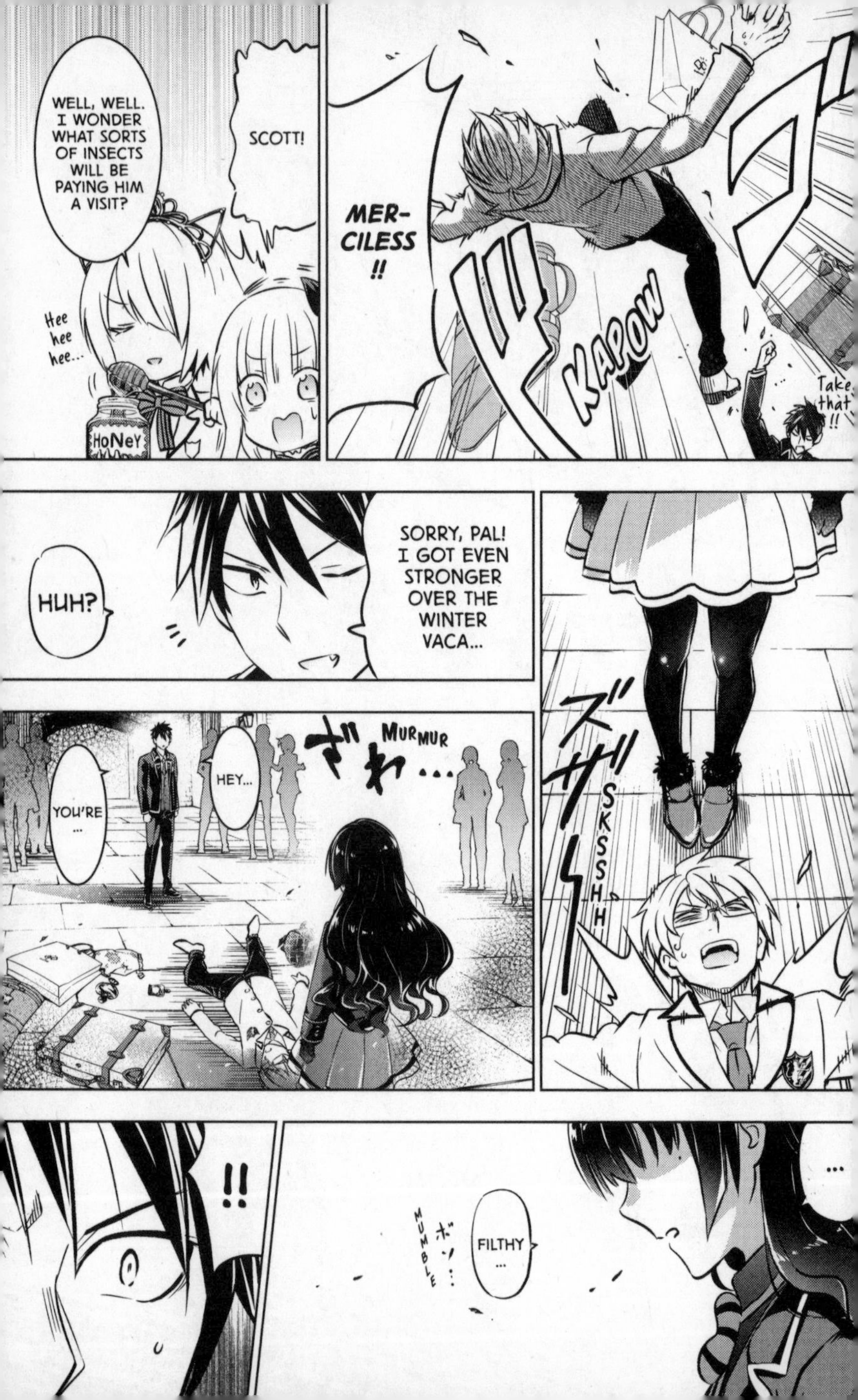
MER-CILESS!!
KAPOW
...
Take that!!
SCOTT!
WELL, WELL. I WONDER WHAT SORTS OF INSECTS WILL BE PAYING HIM A VISIT?
Hee hee hee...
HoNeY
SKSSHH
SORRY, PAL! I GOT EVEN STRONGER OVER THE WINTER VACA...
HUH?
MURMUR
HEY...
YOU'RE...
...
FILTHY...
MUMBLE
!!

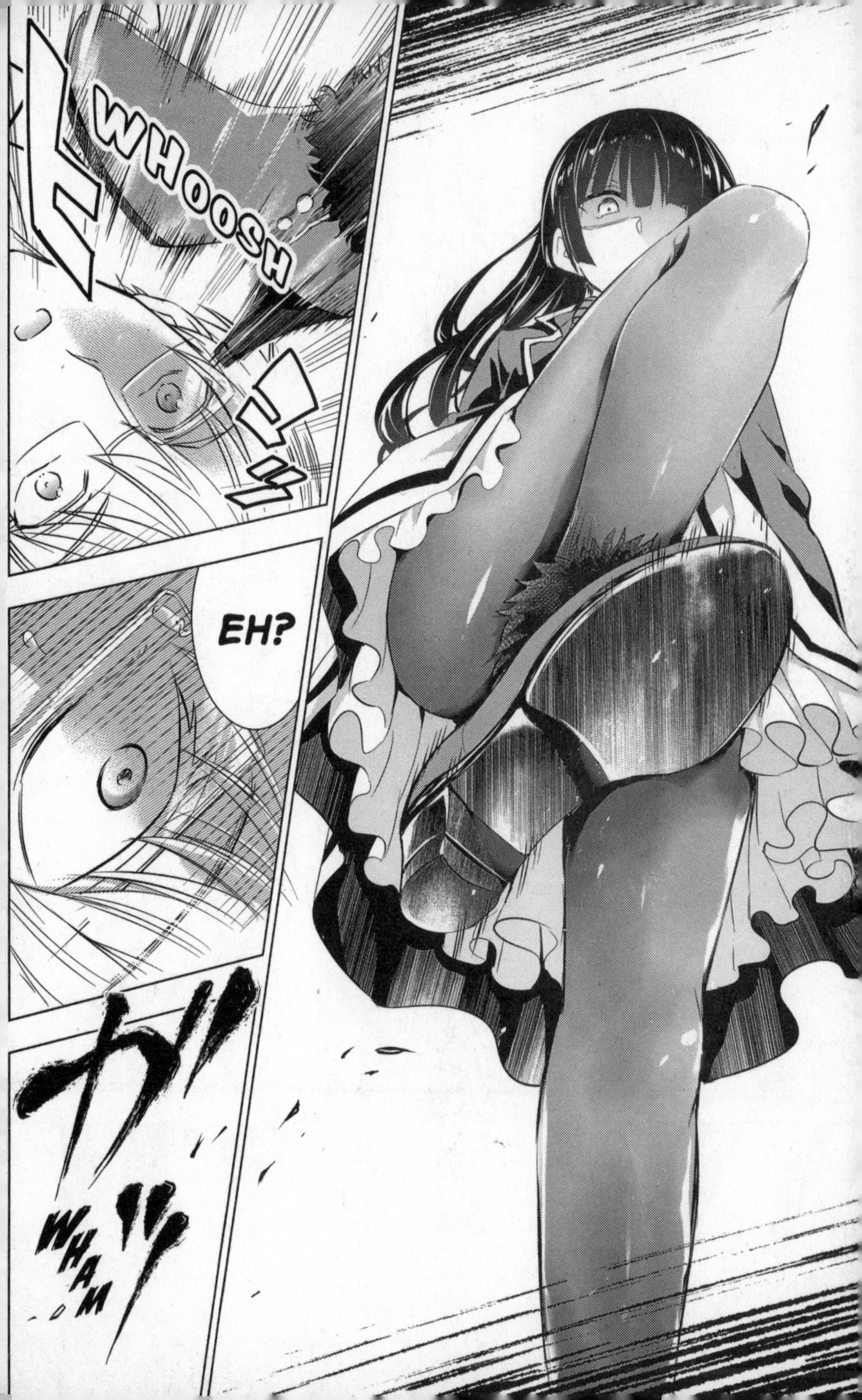
WHOOSH
!!
EH?
ガッ
WHAM

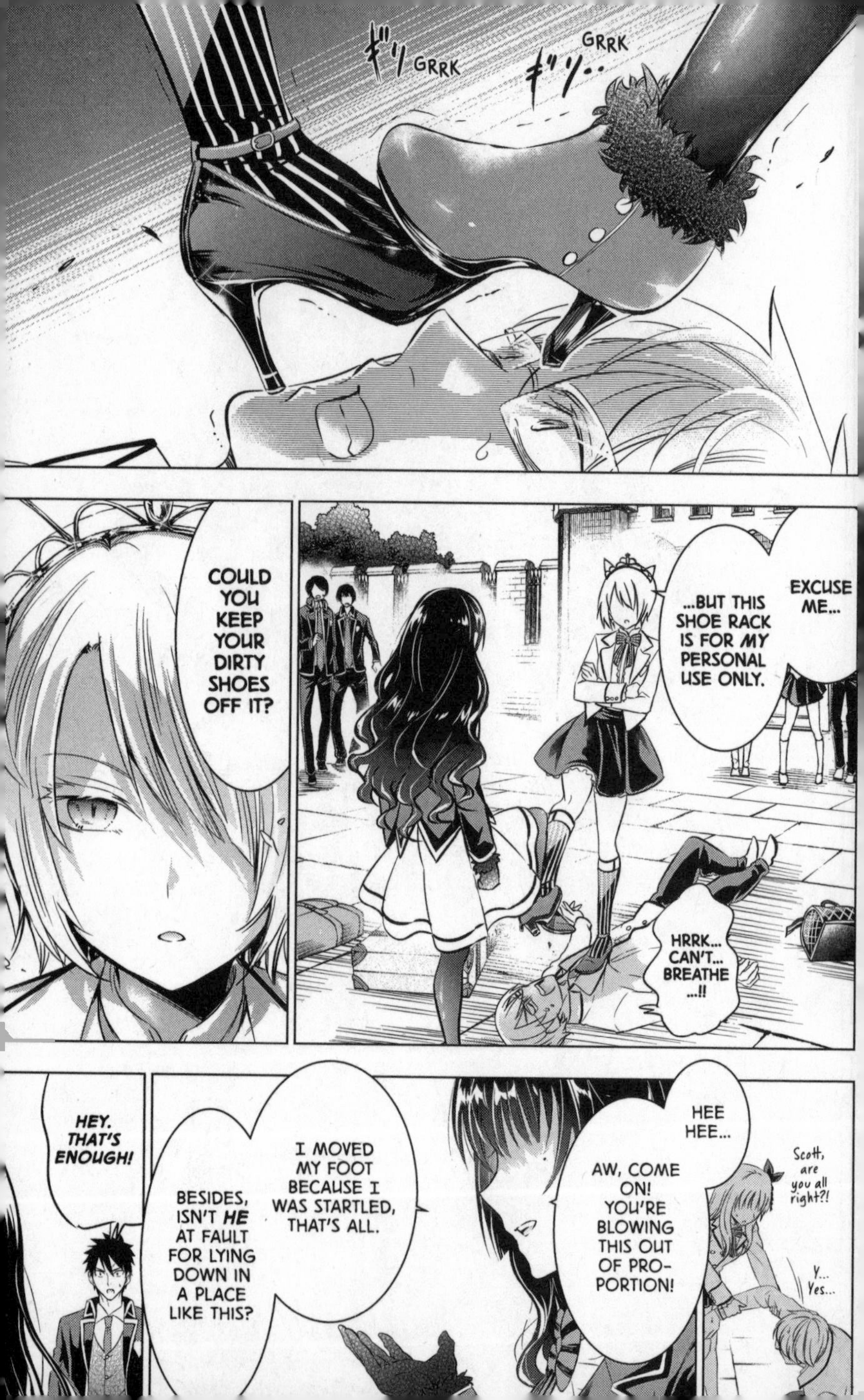
ギリッ.. GRRK
ギリ GRRK
EXCUSE ME...
...BUT THIS SHOE RACK IS FOR *MY* PERSONAL USE ONLY.
HRRK... CAN'T... BREATHE ...!!
COULD YOU KEEP YOUR DIRTY SHOES OFF IT?
HEE HEE...
AW, COME ON! YOU'RE BLOWING THIS OUT OF PRO-PORTION!
Scott, are you all right?!
Y... Yes...
I MOVED MY FOOT BECAUSE I WAS STARTLED, THAT'S ALL.
BESIDES, ISN'T *HE* AT FAULT FOR LYING DOWN IN A PLACE LIKE THIS?
HEY. THAT'S ENOUGH!

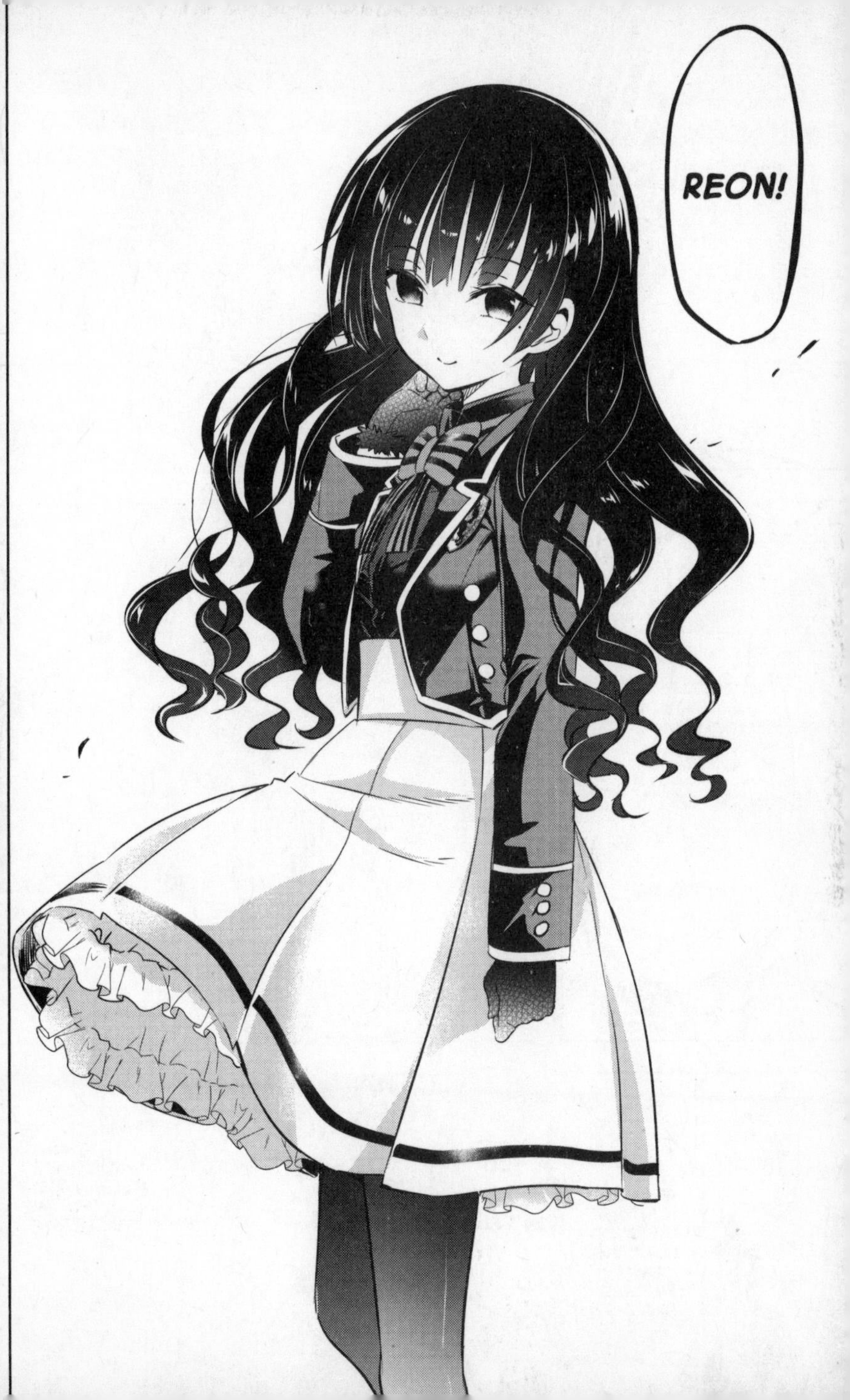
REON!

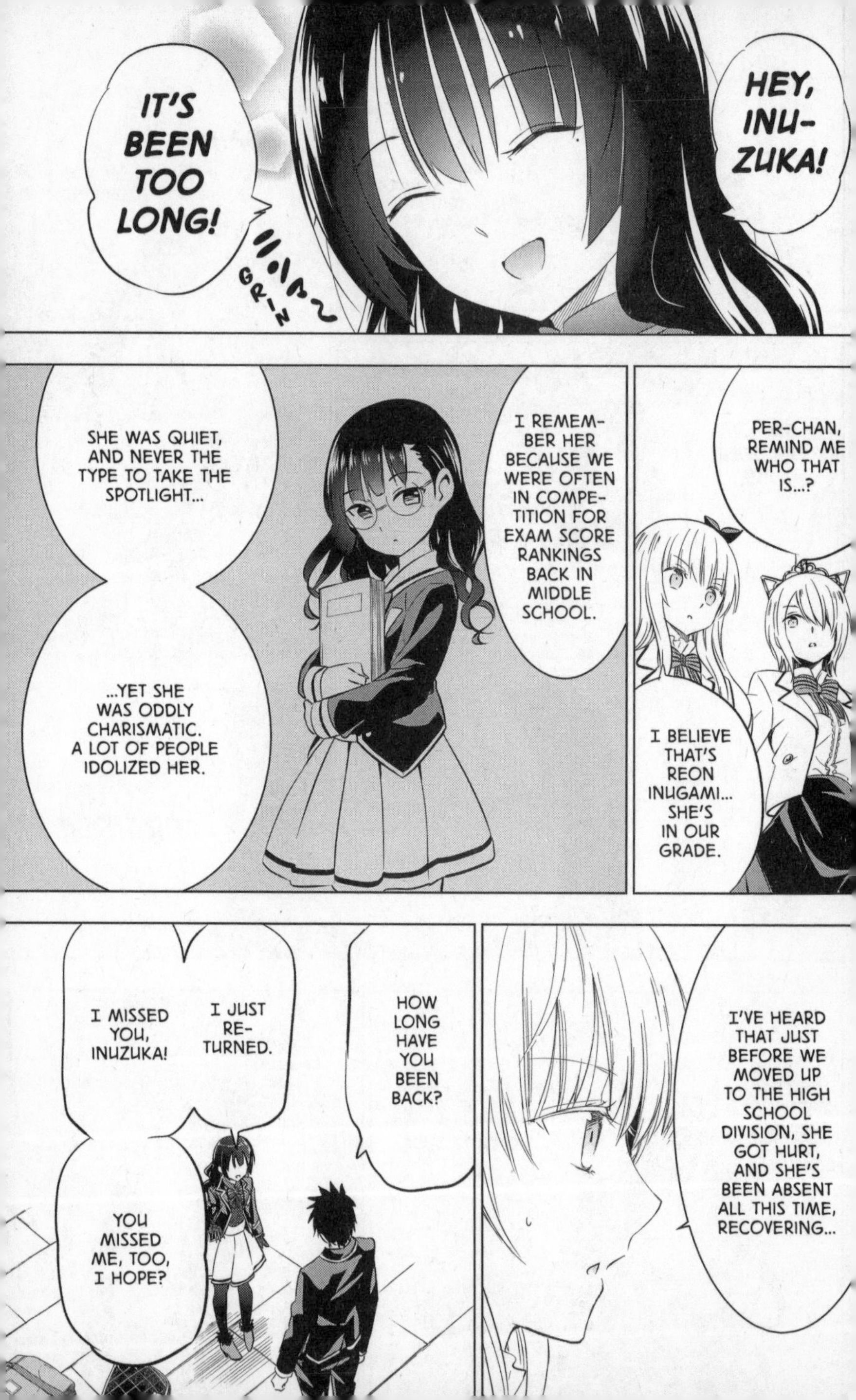
HEY, INU-ZUKA!
IT'S BEEN TOO LONG!
GRIN
PER-CHAN, REMIND ME WHO THAT IS...?
I BELIEVE THAT'S REON INUGAMI... SHE'S IN OUR GRADE.
I REMEM-BER HER BECAUSE WE WERE OFTEN IN COMPE-TITION FOR EXAM SCORE RANKINGS BACK IN MIDDLE SCHOOL.
SHE WAS QUIET, AND NEVER THE TYPE TO TAKE THE SPOTLIGHT...
...YET SHE WAS ODDLY CHARISMATIC. A LOT OF PEOPLE IDOLIZED HER.
I'VE HEARD THAT JUST BEFORE WE MOVED UP TO THE HIGH SCHOOL DIVISION, SHE GOT HURT, AND SHE'S BEEN ABSENT ALL THIS TIME, RECOVERING...
HOW LONG HAVE YOU BEEN BACK?
I JUST RE-TURNED.
I MISSED YOU, INUZUKA!
YOU MISSED ME, TOO, I HOPE?

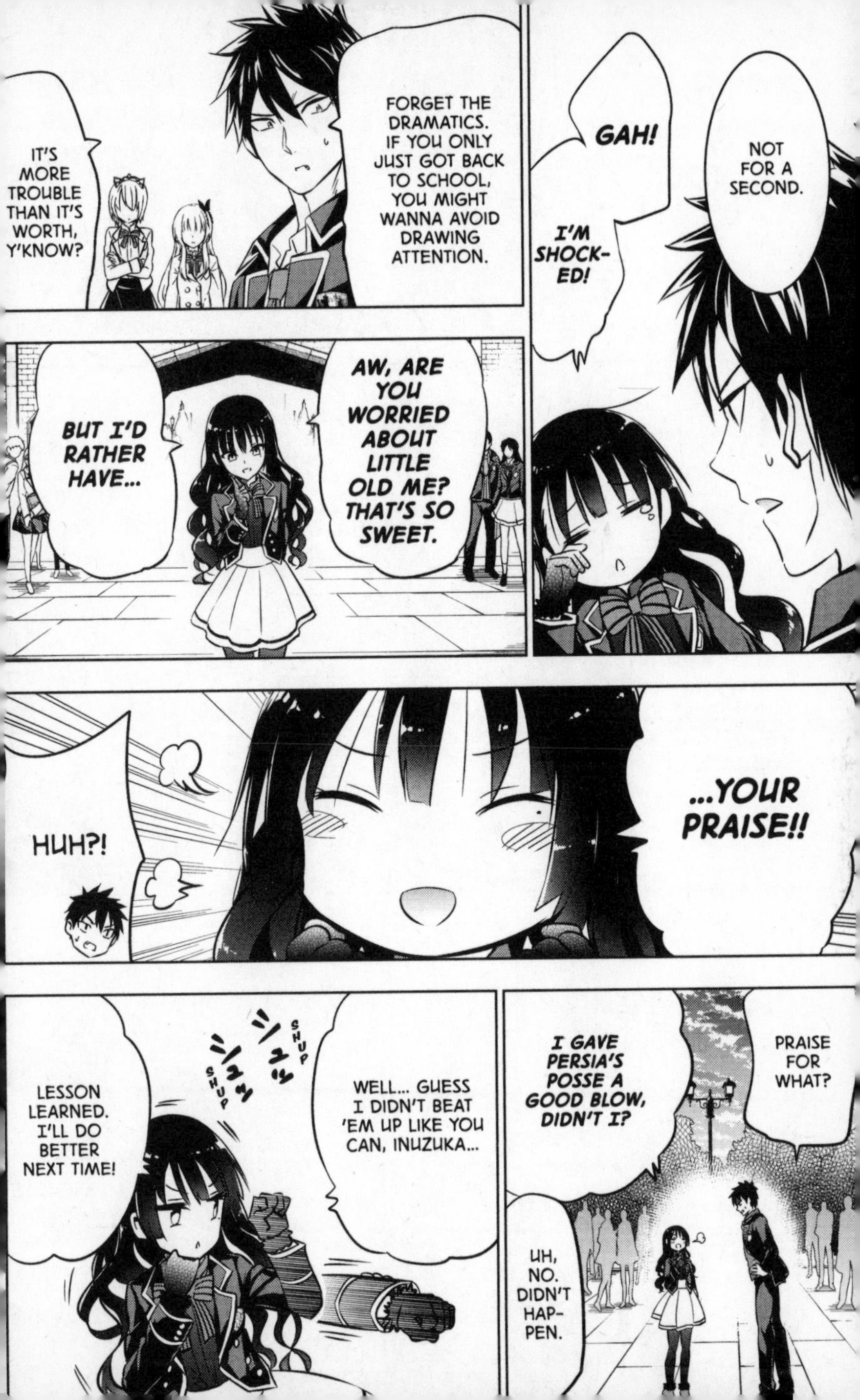
NOT FOR A SECOND.
GAH!
I'M SHOCKED!
FORGET THE DRAMATICS. IF YOU ONLY JUST GOT BACK TO SCHOOL, YOU MIGHT WANNA AVOID DRAWING ATTENTION.
IT'S MORE TROUBLE THAN IT'S WORTH, Y'KNOW?
AW, ARE YOU WORRIED ABOUT LITTLE OLD ME? THAT'S SO SWEET.
BUT I'D RATHER HAVE...
...YOUR PRAISE!!
HUH?!
PRAISE FOR WHAT?
I GAVE PERSIA'S POSSE A GOOD BLOW, DIDN'T I?
UH, NO. DIDN'T HAP-PEN.
WELL... GUESS I DIDN'T BEAT 'EM UP LIKE YOU CAN, INUZUKA...
SHUP
SHUP
LESSON LEARNED. I'LL DO BETTER NEXT TIME!

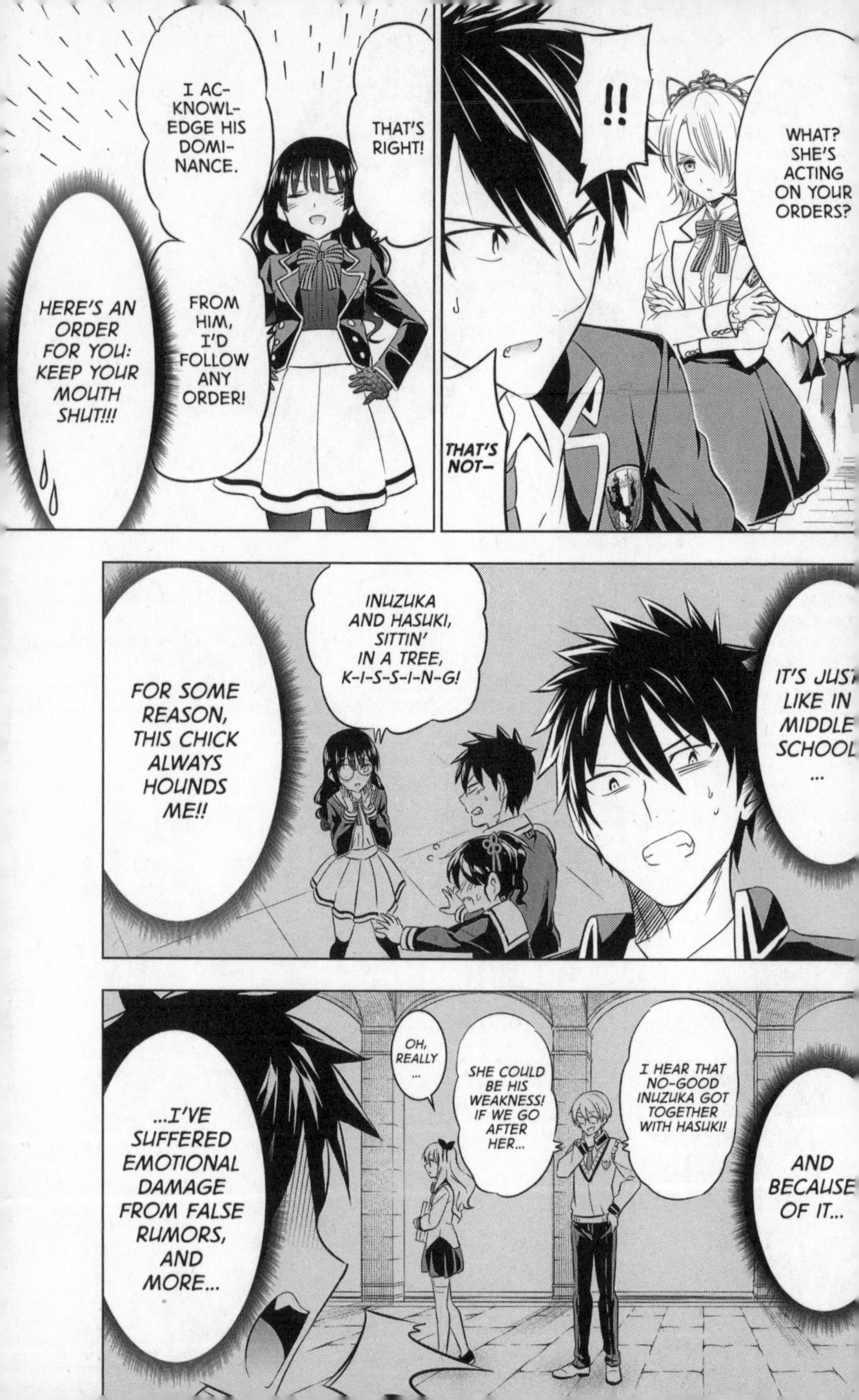
WHAT? SHE'S ACTING ON YOUR ORDERS?
!!
THAT'S NOT—
THAT'S RIGHT!
I ACKNOWLEDGE HIS DOMINANCE.
FROM HIM, I'D FOLLOW ANY ORDER!
HERE'S AN ORDER FOR YOU: KEEP YOUR MOUTH SHUT!!!
IT'S JUST LIKE IN MIDDLE SCHOOL ...
INUZUKA AND HASUKI, SITTIN' IN A TREE, K-I-S-S-I-N-G!
FOR SOME REASON, THIS CHICK ALWAYS HOUNDS ME!!
AND BECAUSE OF IT...
I HEAR THAT NO-GOOD INUZUKA GOT TOGETHER WITH HASUKI!!
SHE COULD BE HIS WEAKNESS! IF WE GO AFTER HER...
OH, REALLY ...
...I'VE SUFFERED EMOTIONAL DAMAGE FROM FALSE RUMORS, AND MORE...

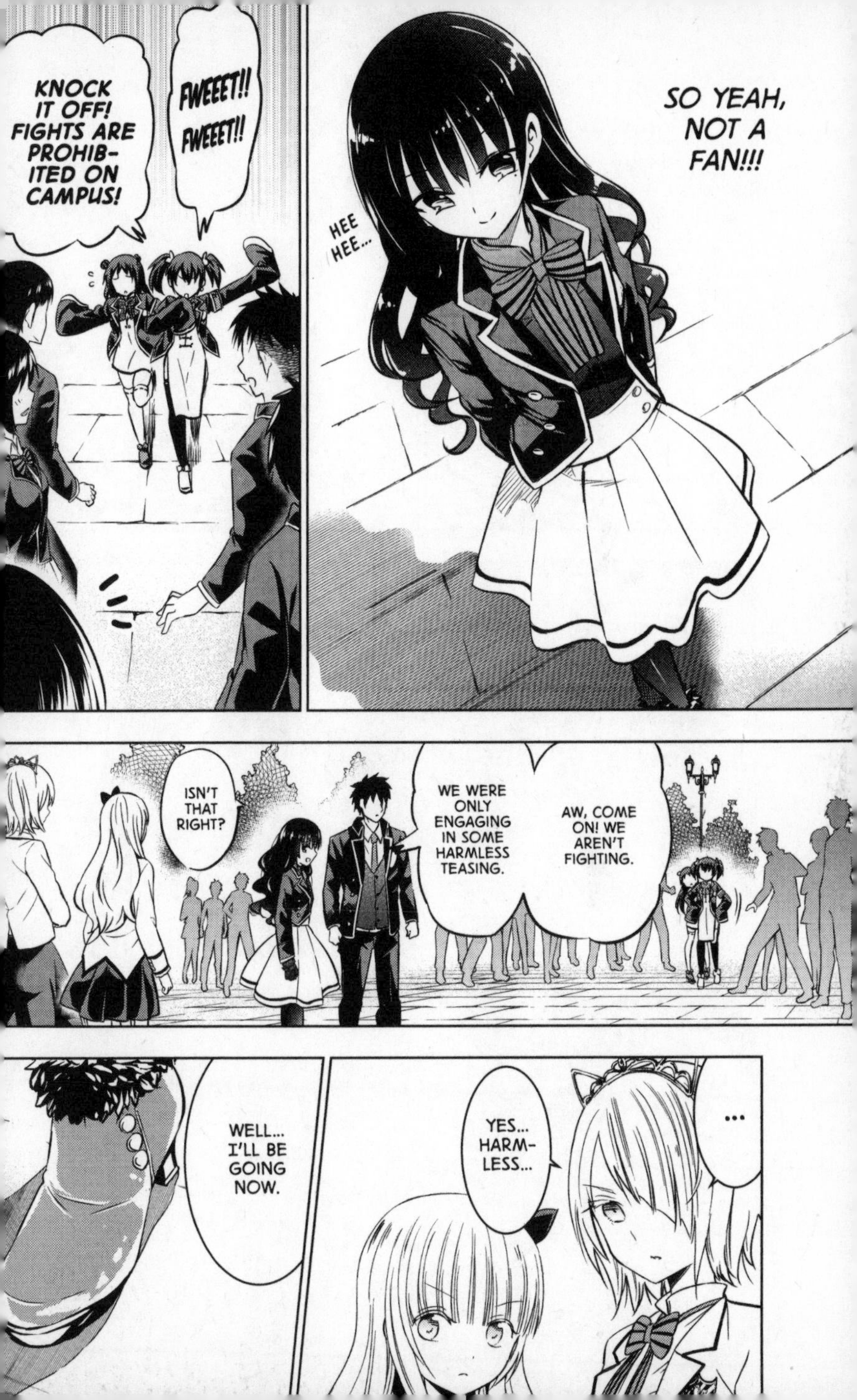
SO YEAH, NOT A FAN!!!
HEE HEE...
FWEEEET!! FWEEEET!!
KNOCK IT OFF! FIGHTS ARE PROHIB-ITED ON CAMPUS!
AW, COME ON! WE AREN'T FIGHTING.
WE WERE ONLY ENGAGING IN SOME HARMLESS TEASING.
ISN'T THAT RIGHT?
...
YES... HARM-LESS...
WELL... I'LL BE GOING NOW.

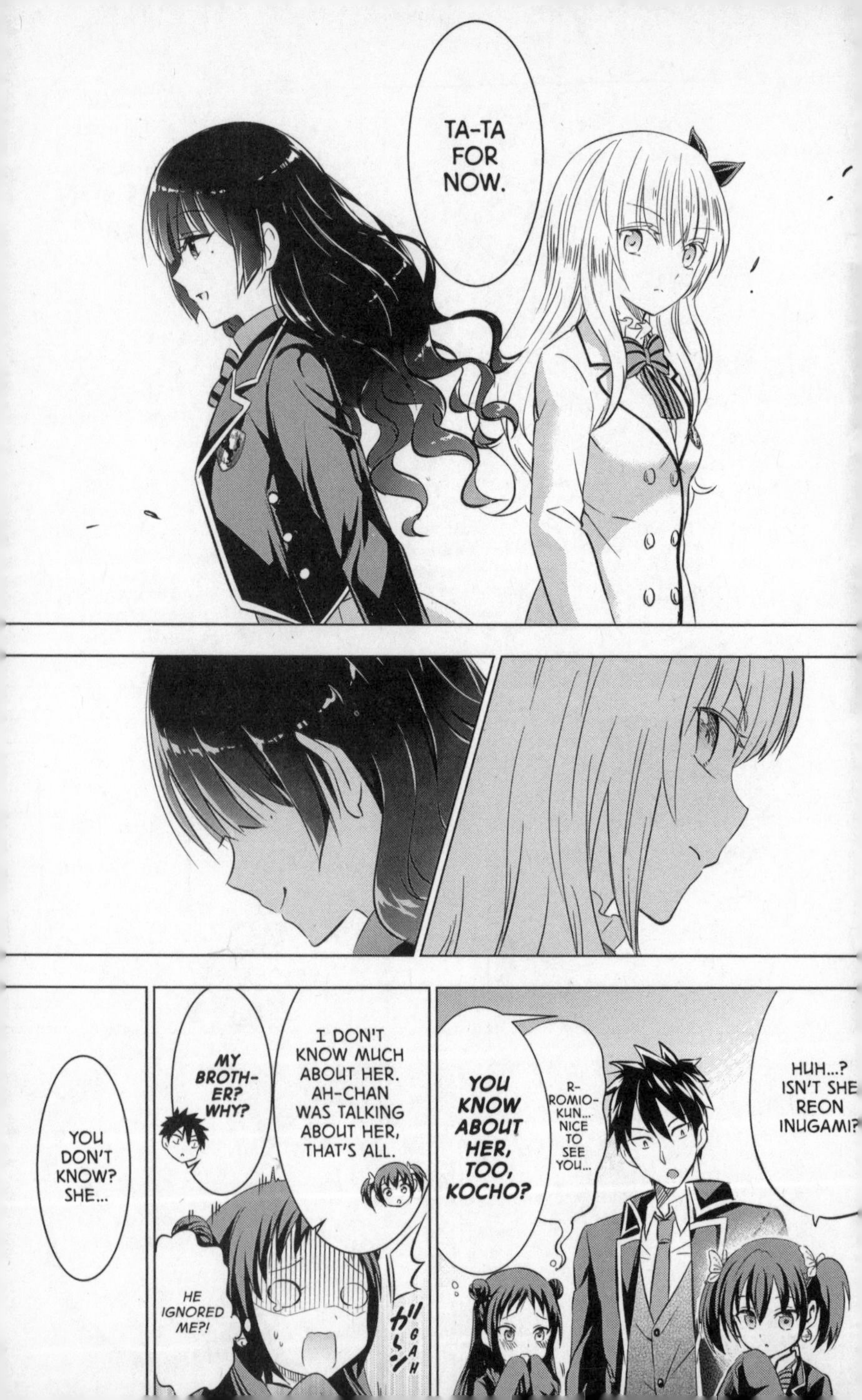

TA-TA FOR NOW.
HUH...? ISN'T SHE REON INUGAMI?
R-ROMIO-KUN... NICE TO SEE YOU...
YOU KNOW ABOUT HER, TOO, KOCHO?
I DON'T KNOW MUCH ABOUT HER. AH-CHAN WAS TALKING ABOUT HER, THAT'S ALL.
MY BROTHER? WHY?
HE IGNORED ME?!
GAH
YOU DON'T KNOW? SHE...

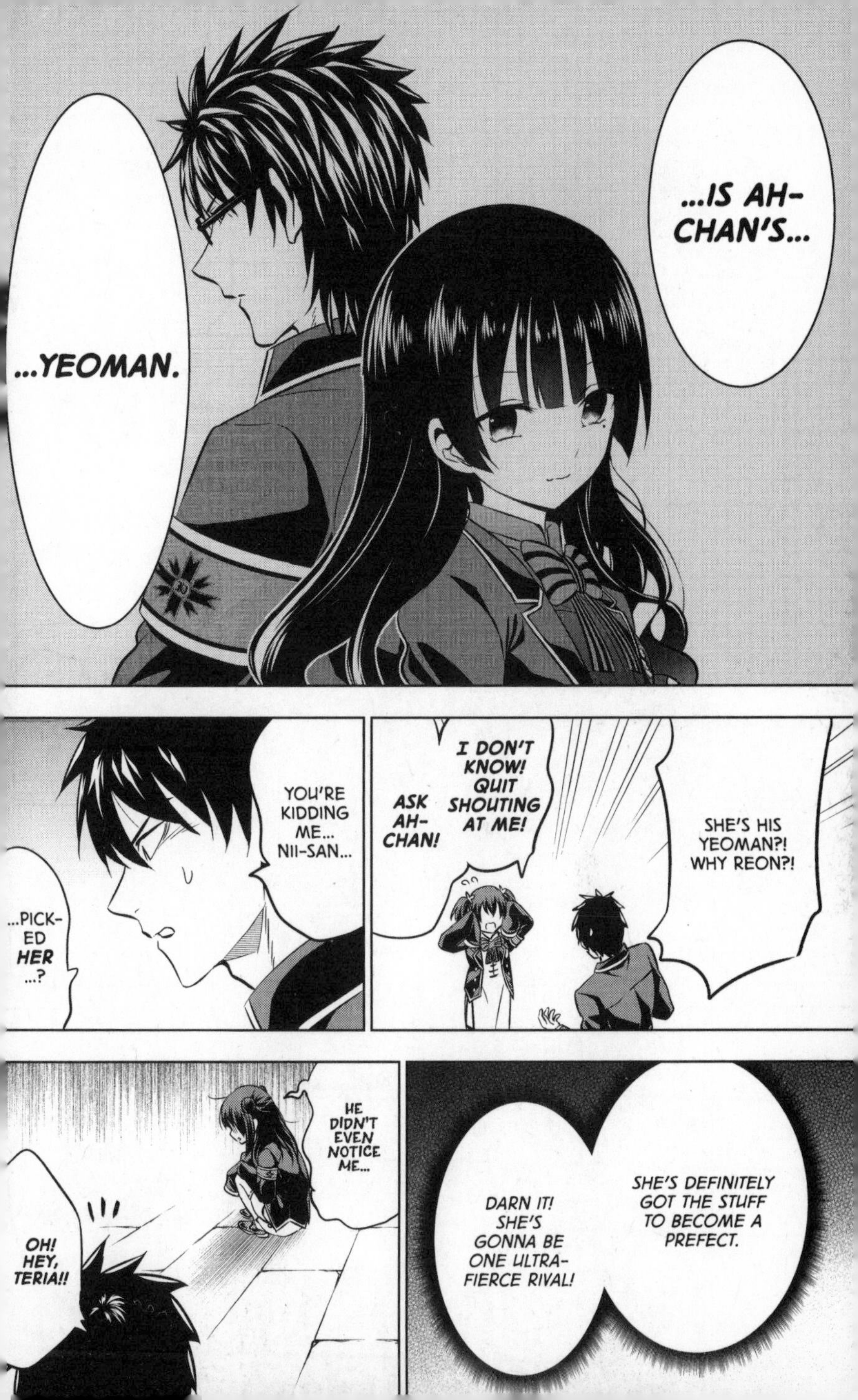
...IS AH-CHAN'S...
...YEOMAN.
SHE'S HIS YEOMAN?! WHY REON?!
I DON'T KNOW! QUIT SHOUTING AT ME!
ASK AH-CHAN!
YOU'RE KIDDING ME... NII-SAN...
...PICK-ED HER ...?
SHE'S DEFINITELY GOT THE STUFF TO BECOME A PREFECT.
DARN IT! SHE'S GONNA BE ONE ULTRA-FIERCE RIVAL!
HE DIDN'T EVEN NOTICE ME...
OH! HEY, TERIA!!

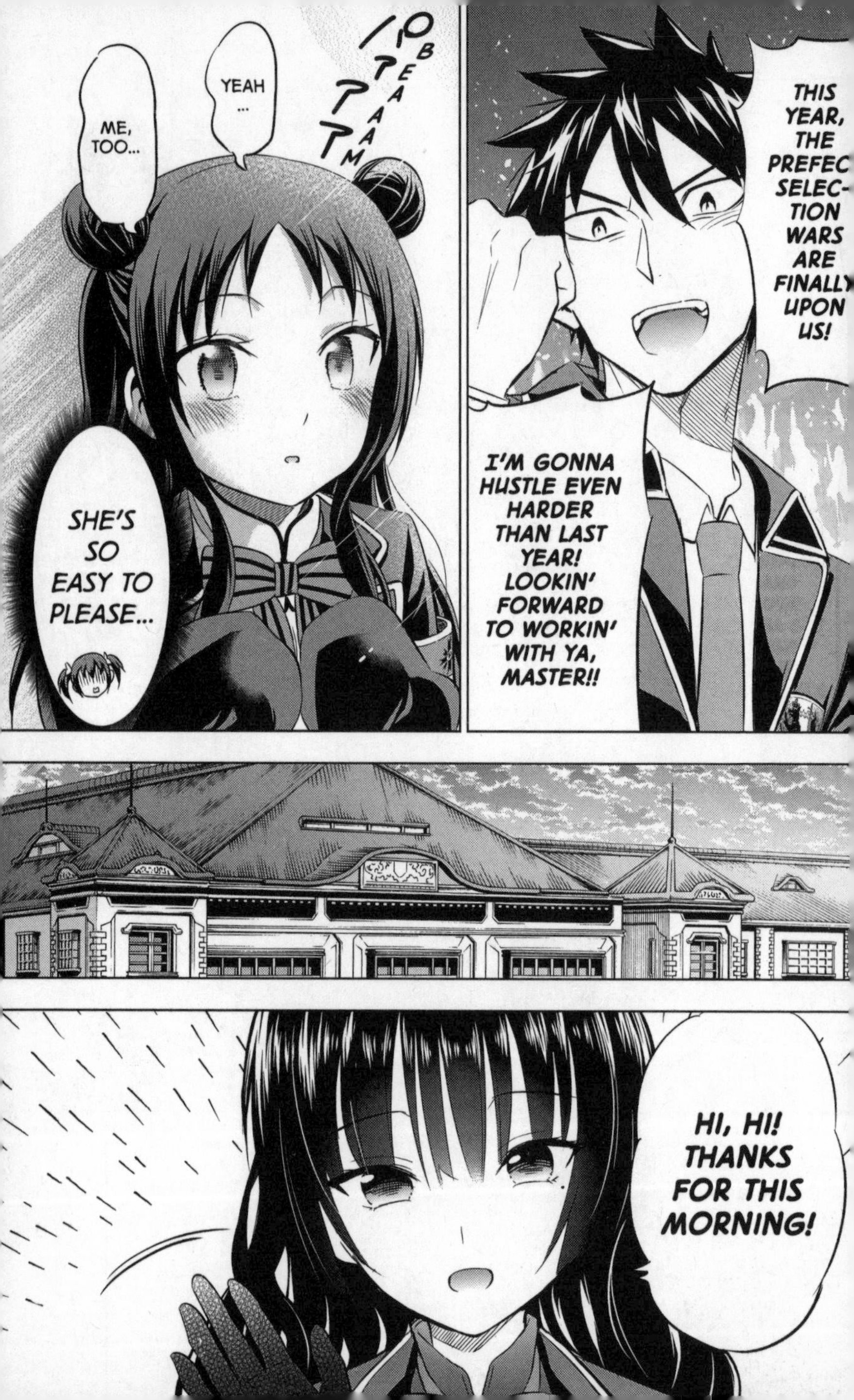
THIS YEAR, THE PREFEC SELECTION WARS ARE FINALLY UPON US!
I'M GONNA HUSTLE EVEN HARDER THAN LAST YEAR! LOOKIN' FORWARD TO WORKIN' WITH YA, MASTER!!
BEAAAM
YEAH ...
ME, TOO...
SHE'S SO EASY TO PLEASE...
HI, HI! THANKS FOR THIS MORNING!

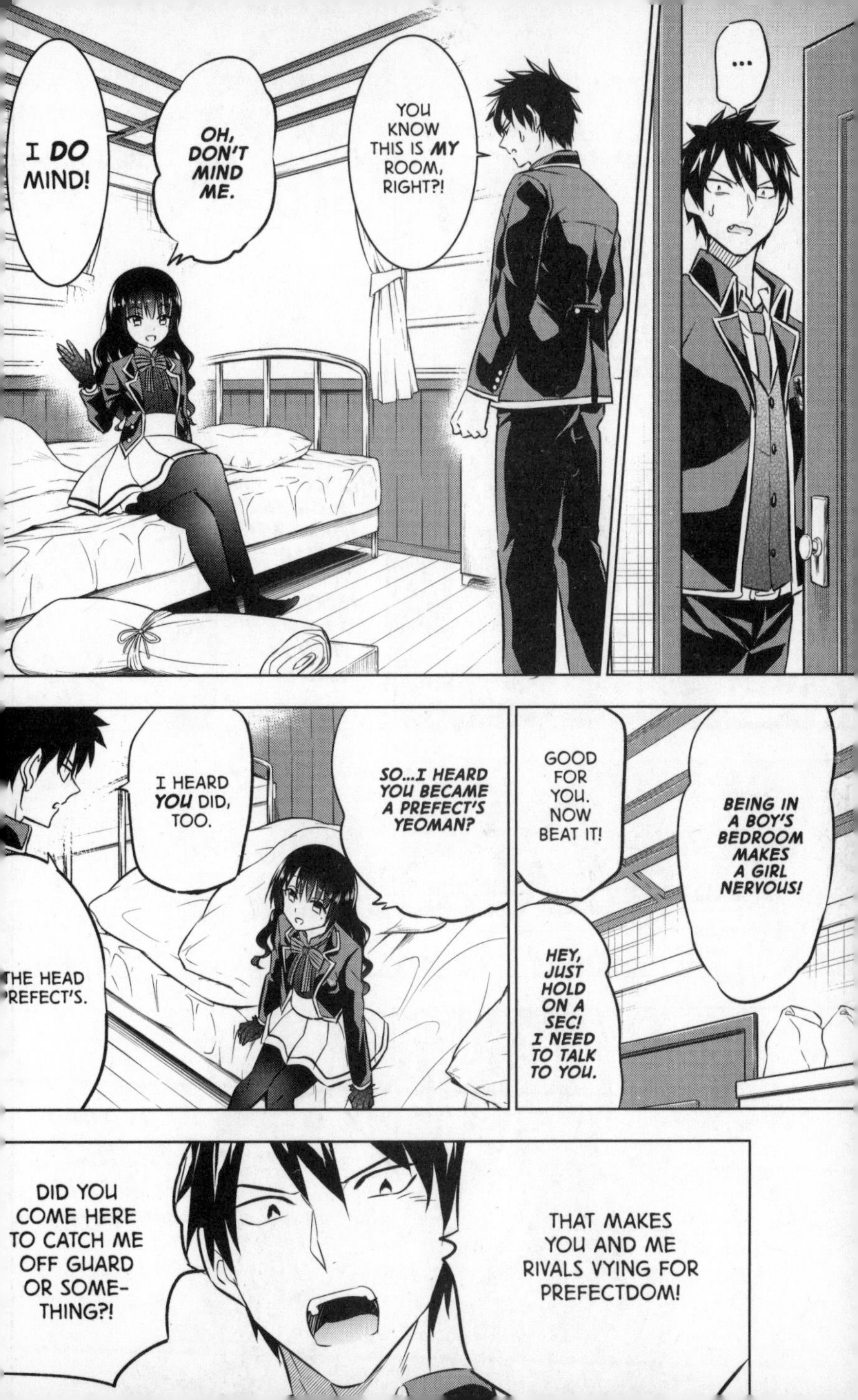
...
YOU KNOW THIS IS MY ROOM, RIGHT?!
OH, DON'T MIND ME.
I DO MIND!
BEING IN A BOY'S BEDROOM MAKES A GIRL NERVOUS!
GOOD FOR YOU. NOW BEAT IT!
HEY, JUST HOLD ON A SEC! I NEED TO TALK TO YOU.
SO...I HEARD YOU BECAME A PREFECT'S YEOMAN?
I HEARD YOU DID, TOO.
THE HEAD 'REFECT'S.
THAT MAKES YOU AND ME RIVALS VYING FOR PREFECTDOM!
DID YOU COME HERE TO CATCH ME OFF GUARD OR SOME-THING?!

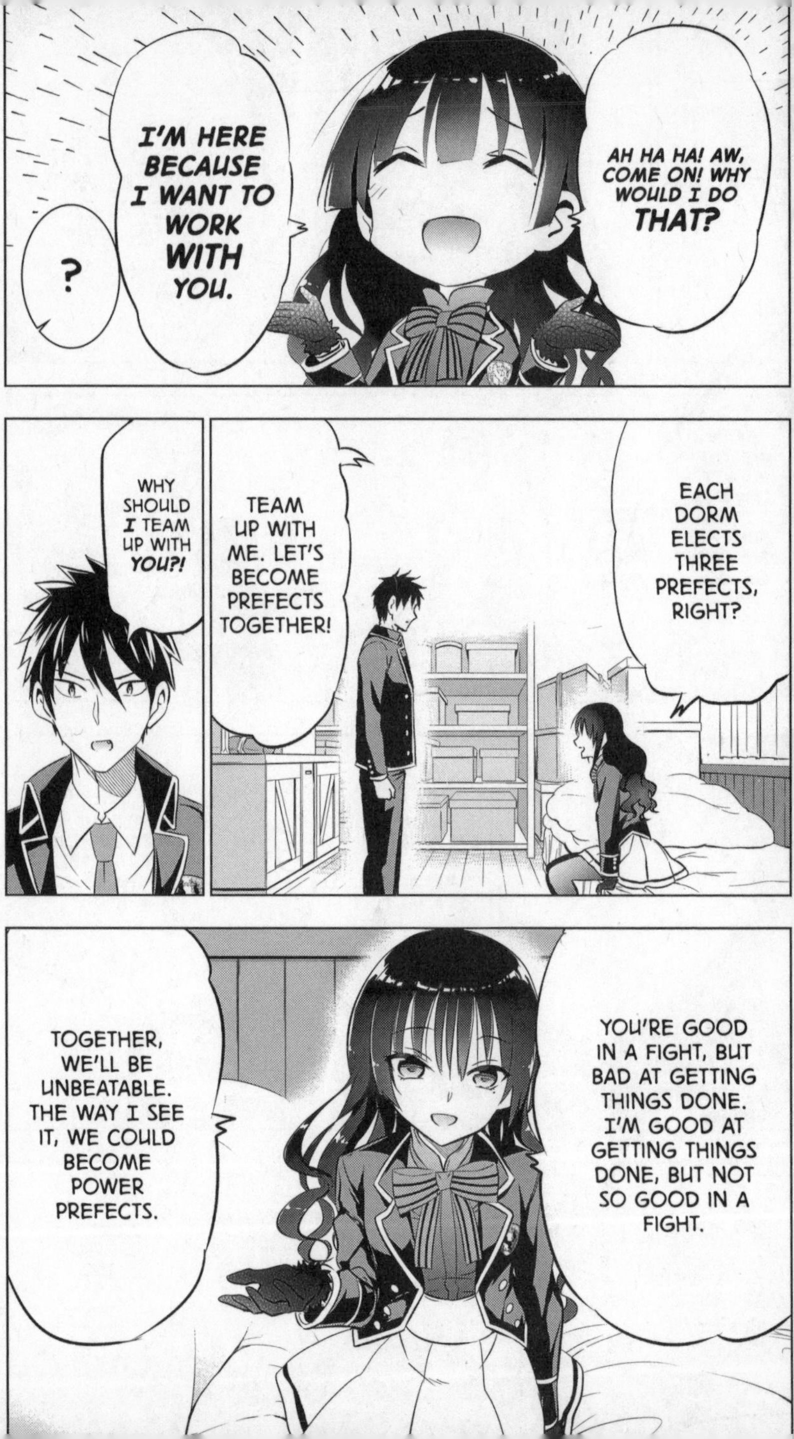
AH HA HA! AW, COME ON! WHY WOULD I DO THAT?
I'M HERE BECAUSE I WANT TO WORK WITH YOU.
?
EACH DORM ELECTS THREE PREFECTS, RIGHT?
TEAM UP WITH ME. LET'S BECOME PREFECTS TOGETHER!
WHY SHOULD I TEAM UP WITH YOU?!
YOU'RE GOOD IN A FIGHT, BUT BAD AT GETTING THINGS DONE. I'M GOOD AT GETTING THINGS DONE, BUT NOT SO GOOD IN A FIGHT.
TOGETHER, WE'LL BE UNBEATABLE. THE WAY I SEE IT, WE COULD BECOME POWER PREFECTS.

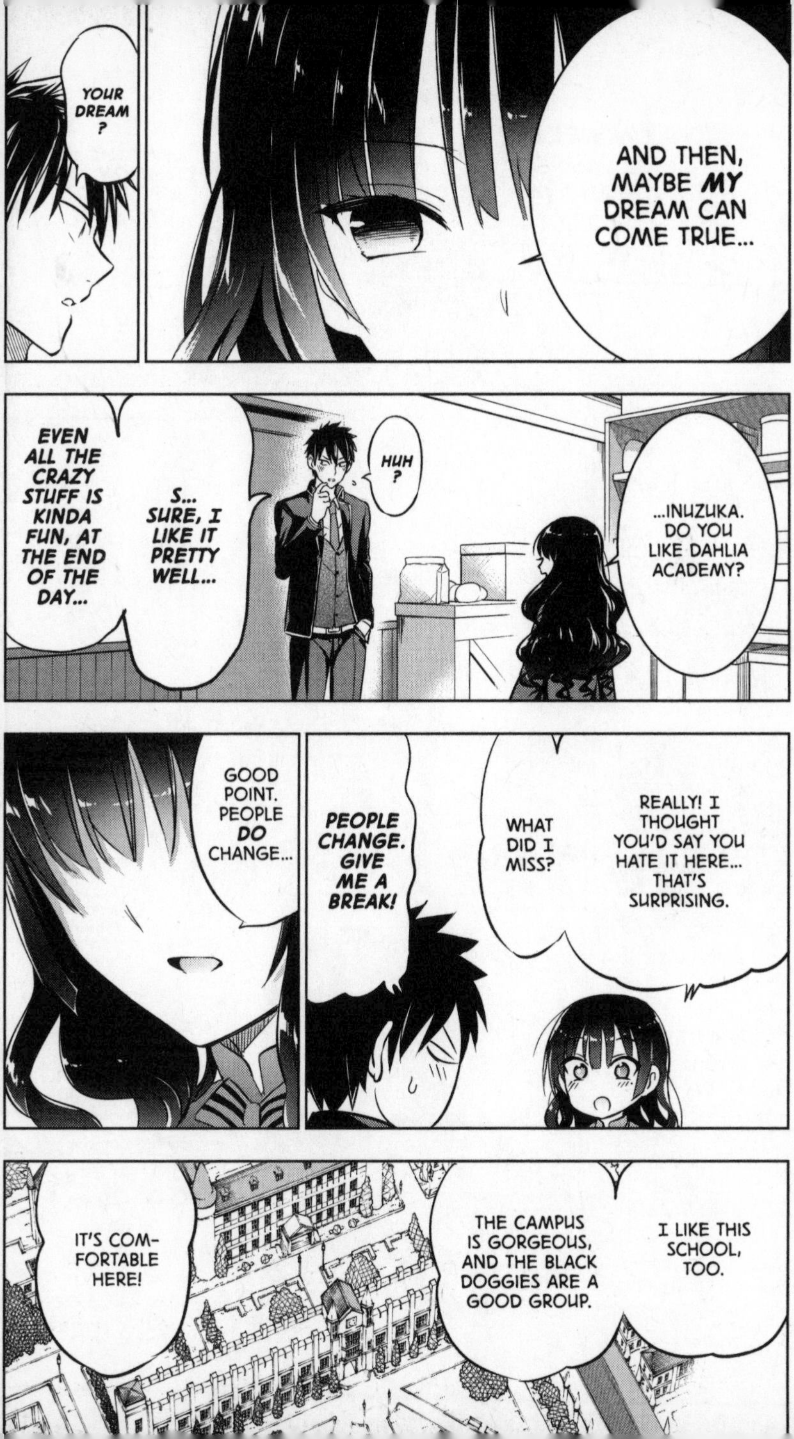
AND THEN, MAYBE MY DREAM CAN COME TRUE...
YOUR DREAM ?
...INUZUKA. DO YOU LIKE DAHLIA ACADEMY?
HUH ?
S... SURE, I LIKE IT PRETTY WELL...
EVEN ALL THE CRAZY STUFF IS KINDA FUN, AT THE END OF THE DAY...
REALLY! I THOUGHT YOU'D SAY YOU HATE IT HERE... THAT'S SURPRISING.
WHAT DID I MISS?
PEOPLE CHANGE. GIVE ME A BREAK!
GOOD POINT. PEOPLE DO CHANGE...
I LIKE THIS SCHOOL, TOO.
THE CAMPUS IS GORGEOUS, AND THE BLACK DOGGIES ARE A GOOD GROUP.
IT'S COM-FORTABLE HERE!

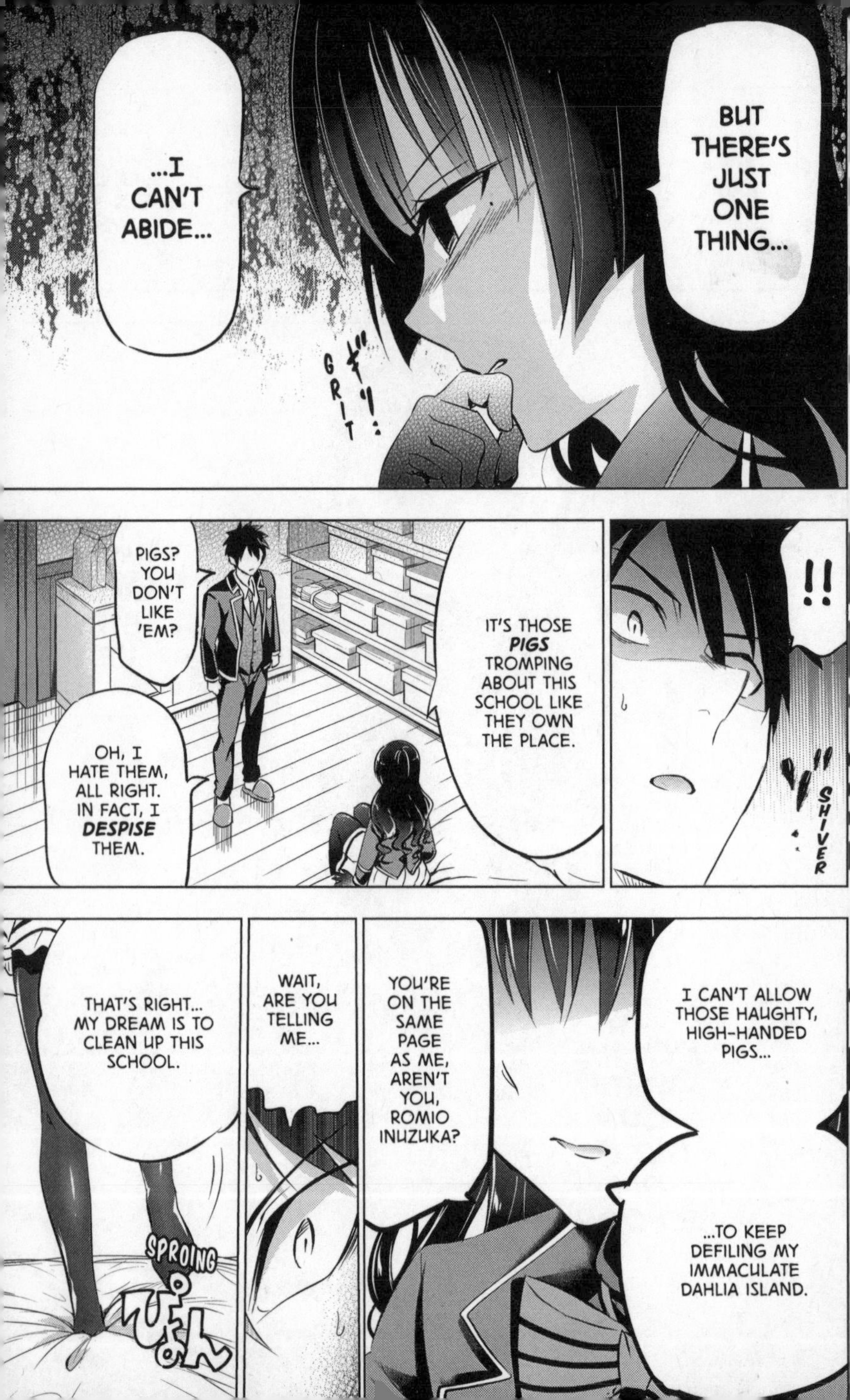
BUT THERE'S JUST ONE THING...
...I CAN'T ABIDE...
GRIT
!!
SHIVER
IT'S THOSE *PIGS* TROMPING ABOUT THIS SCHOOL LIKE THEY OWN THE PLACE.
PIGS? YOU DON'T LIKE 'EM?
OH, I HATE THEM, ALL RIGHT. IN FACT, I *DESPISE* THEM.
I CAN'T ALLOW THOSE HAUGHTY, HIGH-HANDED PIGS...
...TO KEEP DEFILING MY IMMACULATE DAHLIA ISLAND.
YOU'RE ON THE SAME PAGE AS ME, AREN'T YOU, ROMIO INUZUKA?
WAIT, ARE YOU TELLING ME...
THAT'S RIGHT... MY DREAM IS TO CLEAN UP THIS SCHOOL.
SPROING
ぴょん

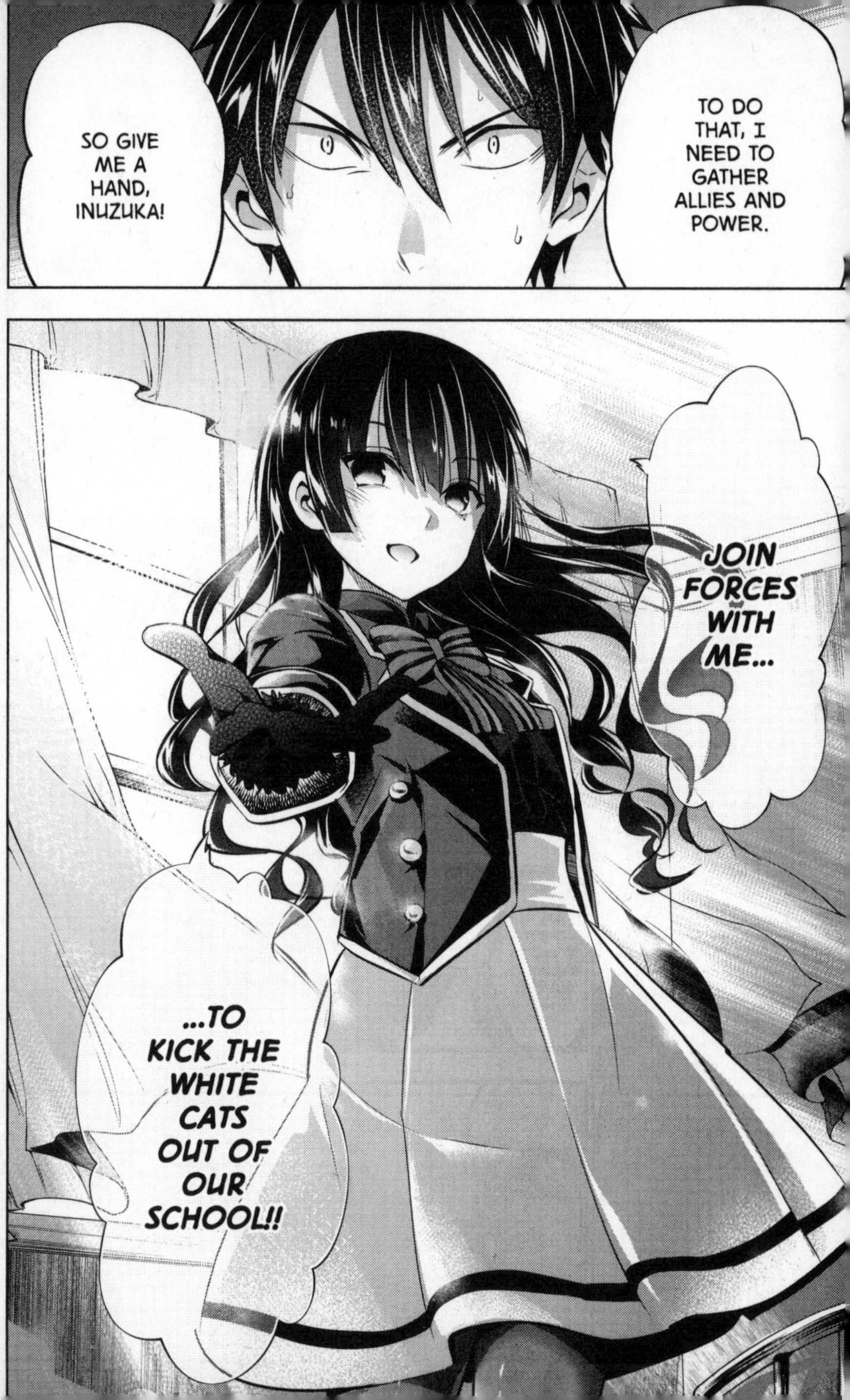
TO DO THAT, I NEED TO GATHER ALLIES AND POWER.
SO GIVE ME A HAND, INUZUKA!
JOIN FORCES WITH ME...
...TO KICK THE WHITE CATS OUT OF OUR SCHOOL!!

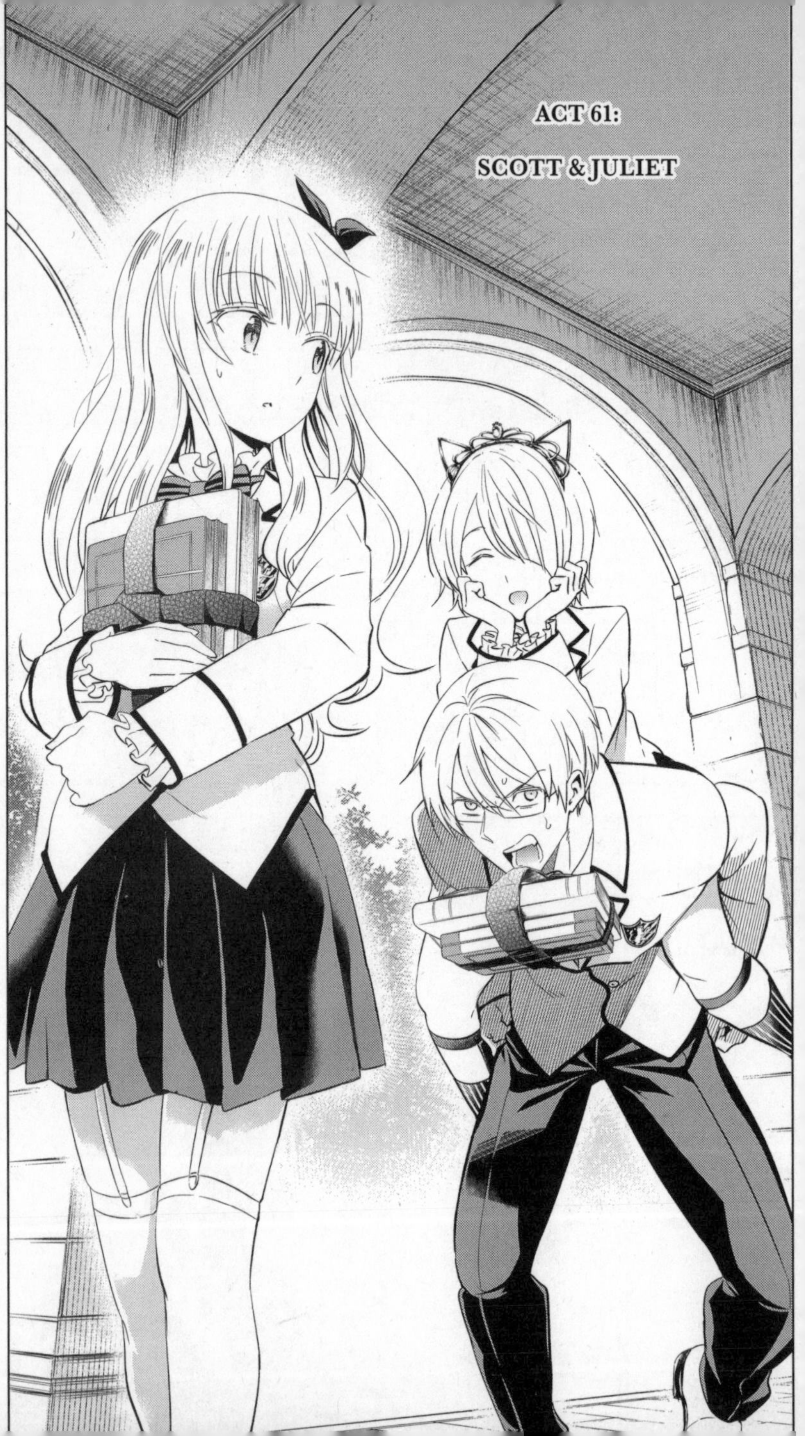
ACT 61:
SCOTT & JULIET

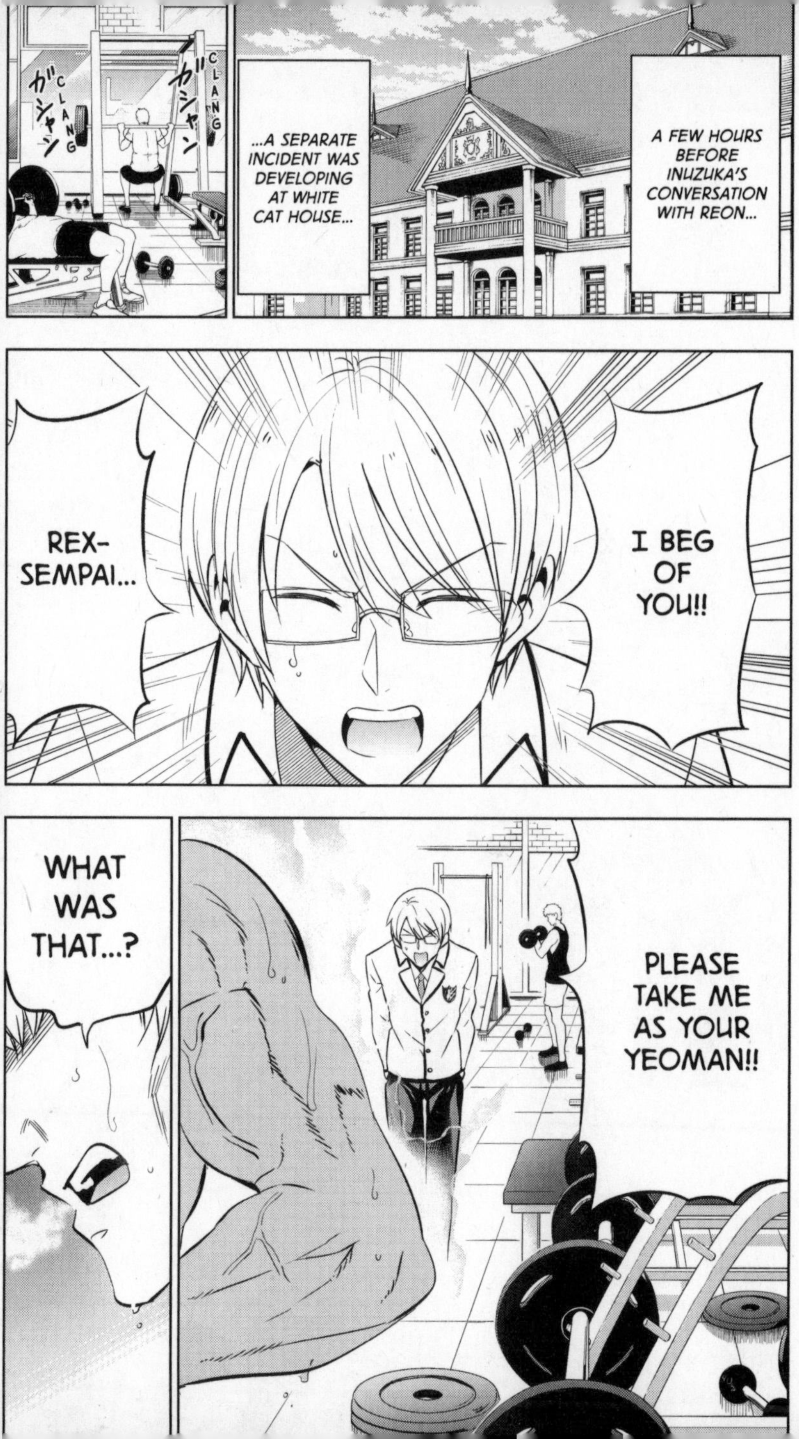
A FEW HOURS BEFORE INUZUKA'S CONVERSATION WITH REON...
...A SEPARATE INCIDENT WAS DEVELOPING AT WHITE CAT HOUSE...
ガシャン
CLANG
ガシャン
CLANG
I BEG OF YOU!!
REX-SEMPAI...
PLEASE TAKE ME AS YOUR YEOMAN!!
WHAT WAS THAT...?

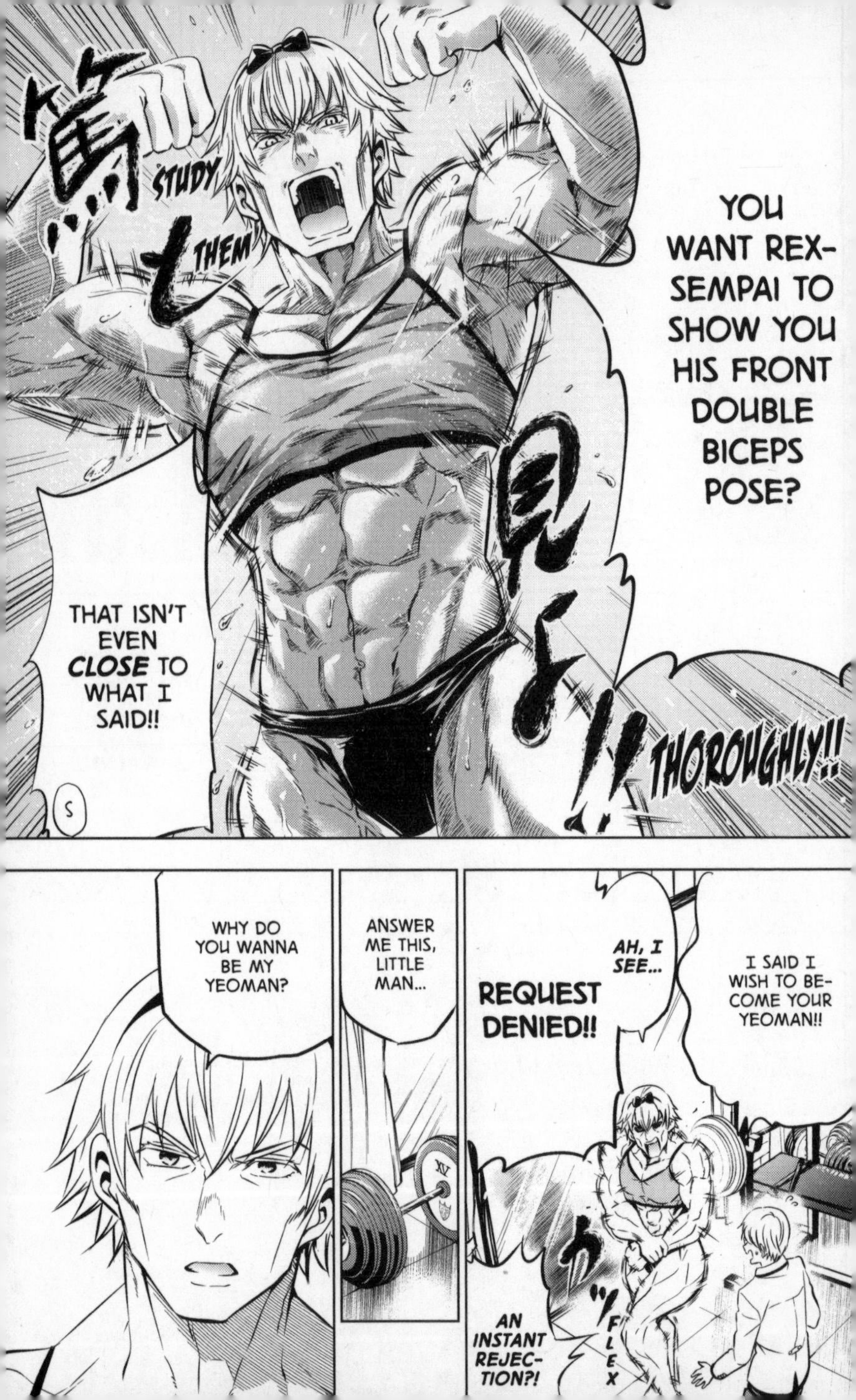
YOU WANT REX-SEMPAI TO SHOW YOU HIS FRONT DOUBLE BICEPS POSE?
STUDY THEM
THOROUGHLY!!
THAT ISN'T EVEN CLOSE TO WHAT I SAID!!
I SAID I WISH TO BE-COME YOUR YEOMAN!!
AH, I SEE...
REQUEST DENIED!!
FLEX
AN INSTANT REJEC-TION?!
ANSWER ME THIS, LITTLE MAN...
WHY DO YOU WANNA BE MY YEOMAN?

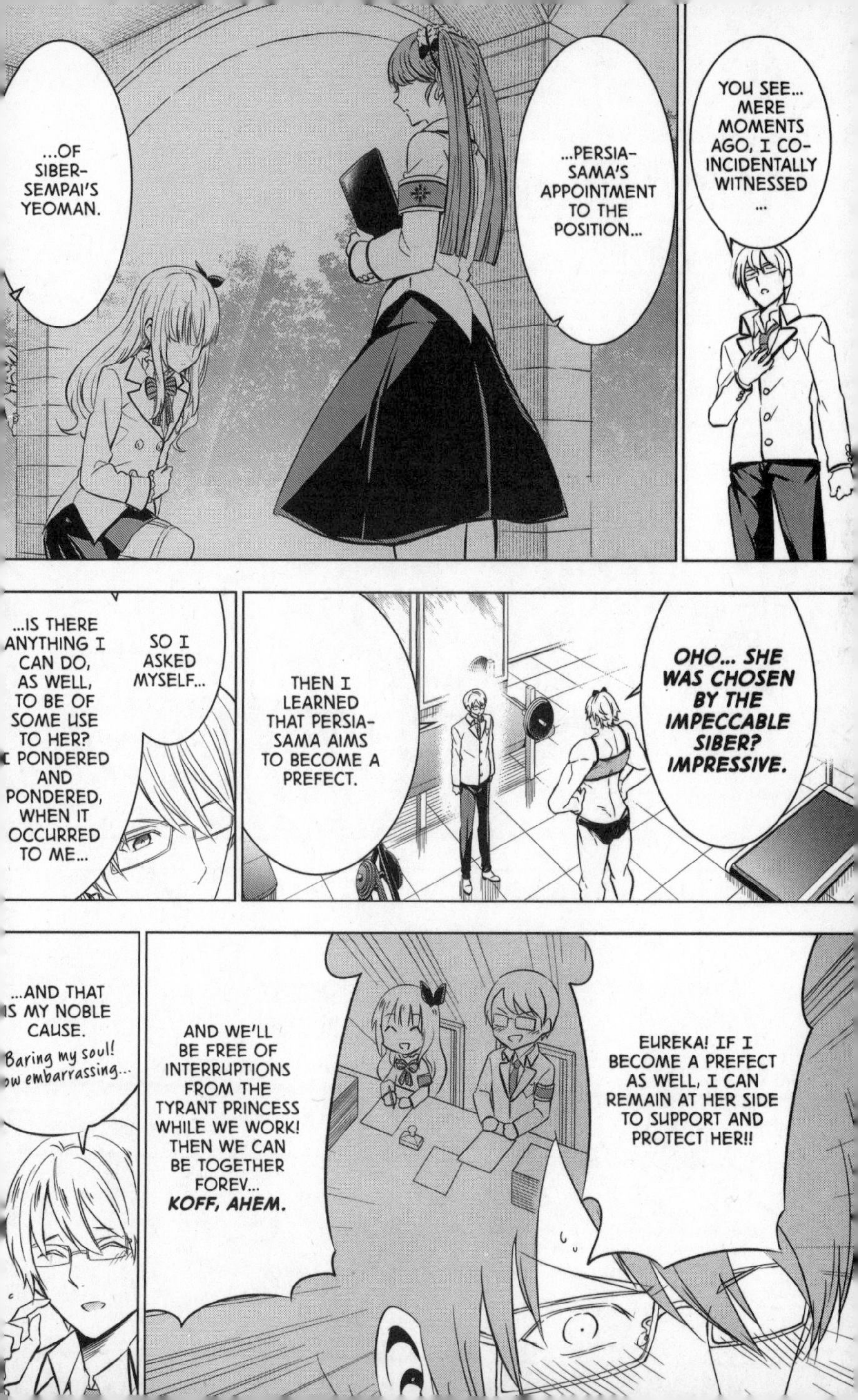
YOU SEE... MERE MOMENTS AGO, I CO-INCIDENTALLY WITNESSED ...
...PERSIA-SAMA'S APPOINTMENT TO THE POSITION...
...OF SIBER-SEMPAI'S YEOMAN.
OHO... SHE WAS CHOSEN BY THE IMPECCABLE SIBER? IMPRESSIVE.
THEN I LEARNED THAT PERSIA-SAMA AIMS TO BECOME A PREFECT.
SO I ASKED MYSELF...
...IS THERE ANYTHING I CAN DO, AS WELL, TO BE OF SOME USE TO HER? I PONDERED AND PONDERED, WHEN IT OCCURRED TO ME...
EUREKA! IF I BECOME A PREFECT AS WELL, I CAN REMAIN AT HER SIDE TO SUPPORT AND PROTECT HER!!
AND WE'LL BE FREE OF INTERRUPTIONS FROM THE TYRANT PRINCESS WHILE WE WORK! THEN WE CAN BE TOGETHER FOREV... KOFF, AHEM.
...AND THAT IS MY NOBLE CAUSE.
Baring my soul! ow embarrassing...

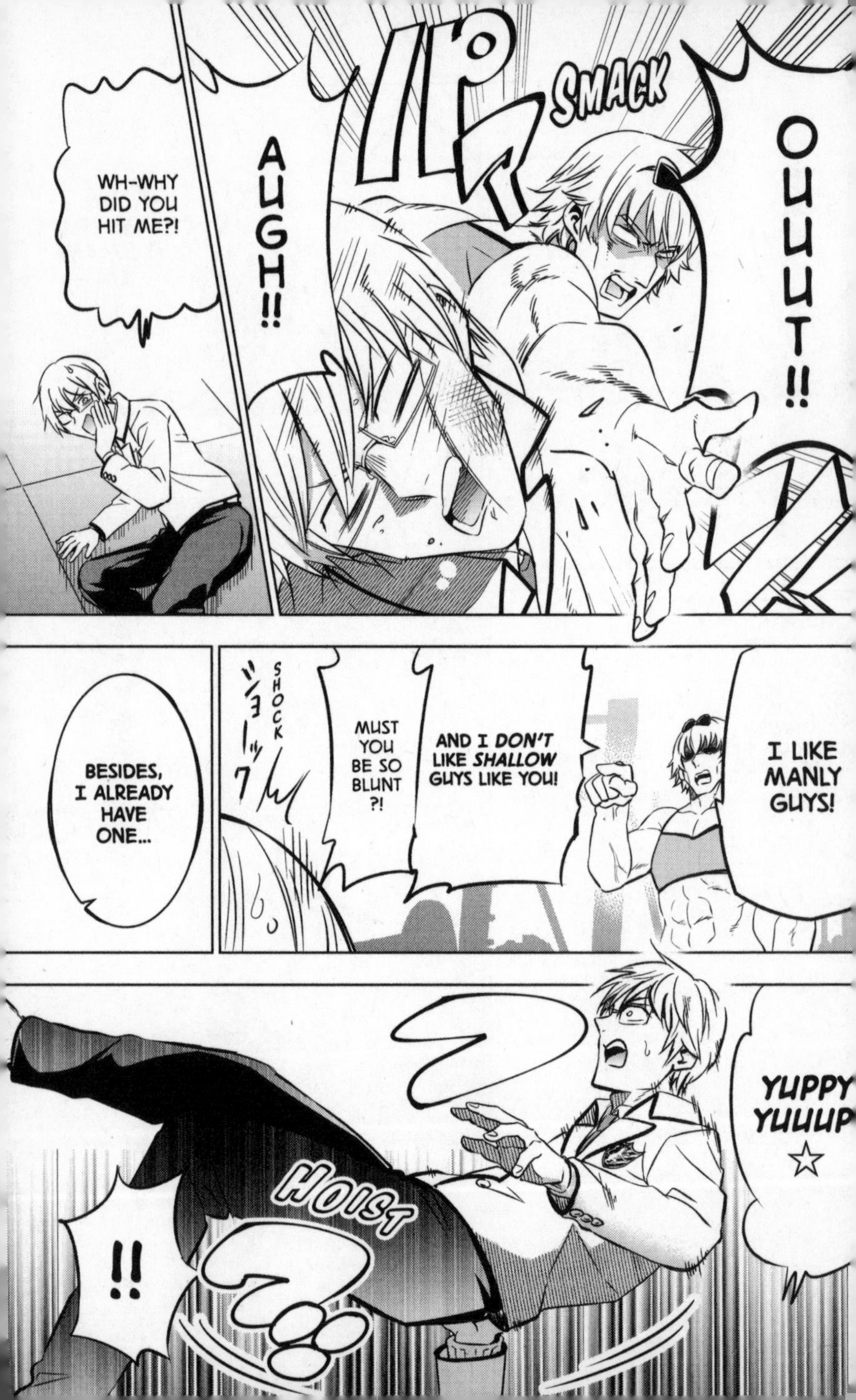
OUUUT!!
SMACK
AUGH!!
WH-WHY DID YOU HIT ME?!
I LIKE MANLY GUYS!
AND I *DON'T* LIKE *SHALLOW* GUYS LIKE YOU!
MUST YOU BE SO BLUNT ?!
SHOCK
BESIDES, I ALREADY HAVE ONE...
YUPPY YUUUP ☆
HOIST
!!

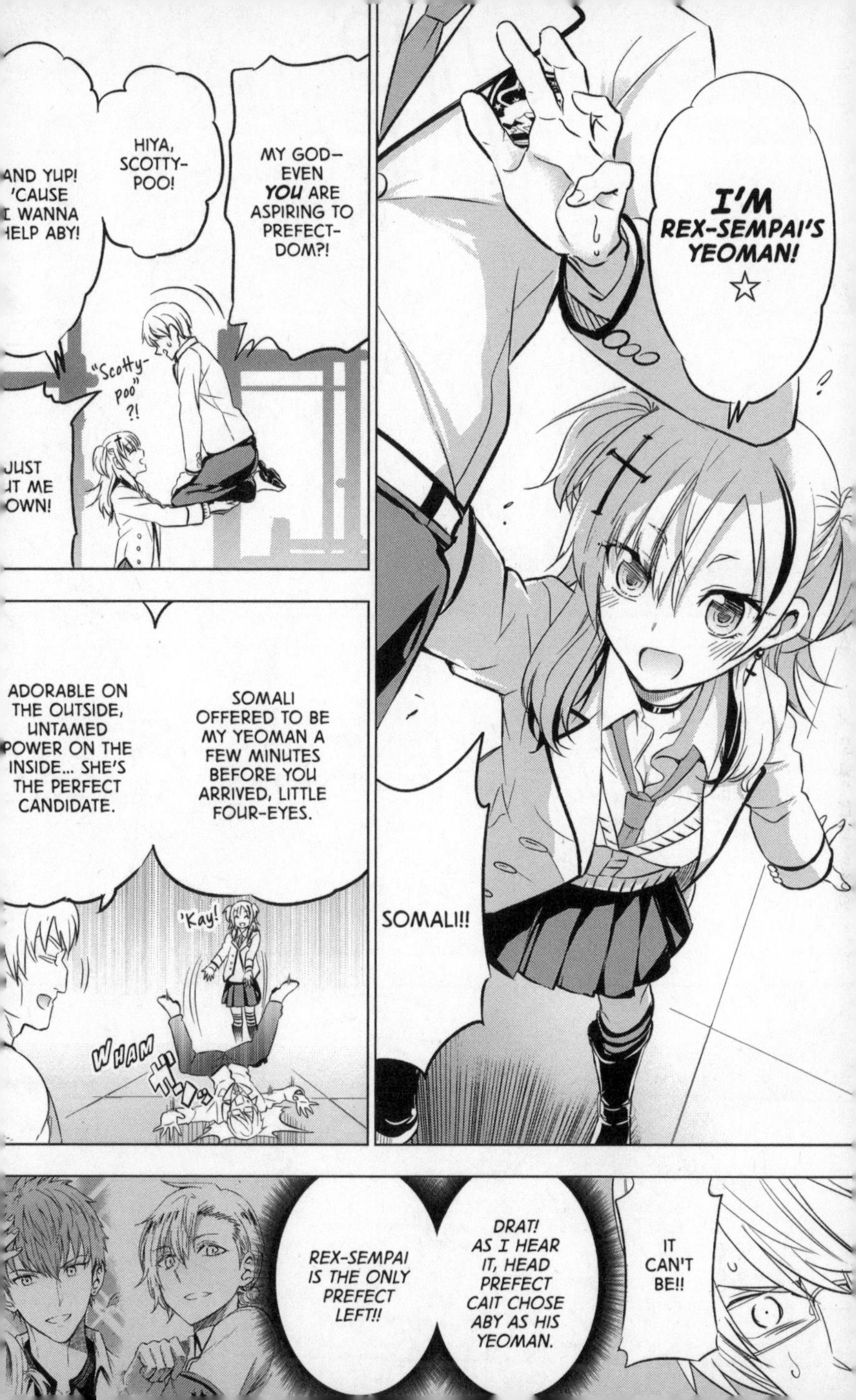

I'M REX-SEMPAI'S YEOMAN! ☆
SOMALI!!
MY GOD—EVEN YOU ARE ASPIRING TO PREFECTDOM?!
HIYA, SCOTTY-POO!
AND YUP! 'CAUSE I WANNA HELP ABY!
"Scotty-poo"?!
JUST
SOMALI OFFERED TO BE MY YEOMAN A FEW MINUTES BEFORE YOU ARRIVED, LITTLE FOUR-EYES.
ADORABLE ON THE OUTSIDE, UNTAMED POWER ON THE INSIDE... SHE'S THE PERFECT CANDIDATE.
'Kay!
WHAM
IT CAN'T BE!!
DRAT! AS I HEAR IT, HEAD PREFECT CAIT CHOSE ABY AS HIS YEOMAN.
REX-SEMPAI IS THE ONLY PREFECT LEFT!!

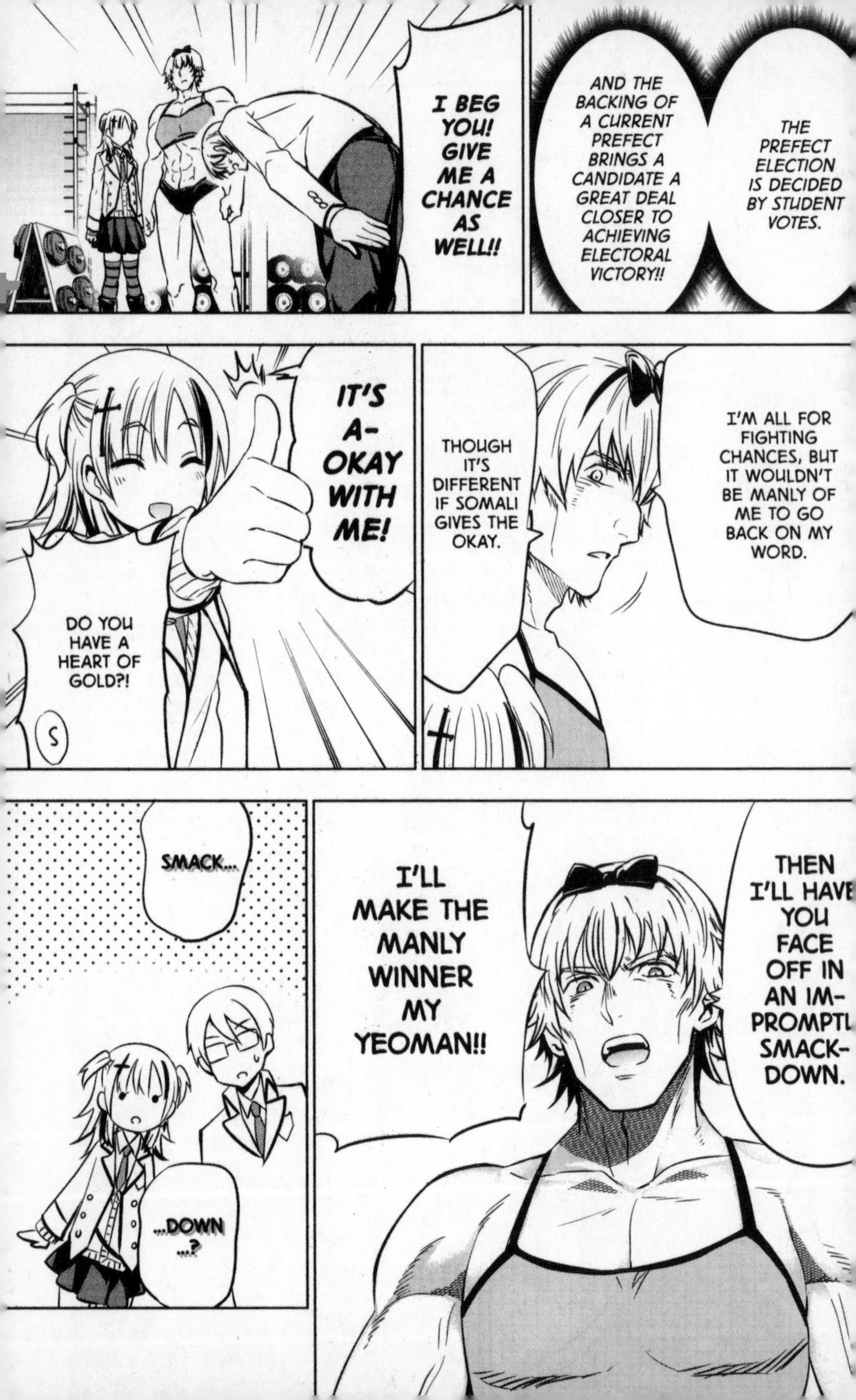
THE PREFECT ELECTION IS DECIDED BY STUDENT VOTES.
AND THE BACKING OF A CURRENT PREFECT BRINGS A CANDIDATE A GREAT DEAL CLOSER TO ACHIEVING ELECTORAL VICTORY!!
I BEG YOU! GIVE ME A CHANCE AS WELL!!
I'M ALL FOR FIGHTING CHANCES, BUT IT WOULDN'T BE MANLY OF ME TO GO BACK ON MY WORD.
THOUGH IT'S DIFFERENT IF SOMALI GIVES THE OKAY.
IT'S A-OKAY WITH ME!
DO YOU HAVE A HEART OF GOLD?!
S
THEN I'LL HAVE YOU FACE OFF IN AN IM-PROMPTU SMACK-DOWN.
I'LL MAKE THE MANLY WINNER MY YEOMAN!!
SMACK...
...DOWN ...?

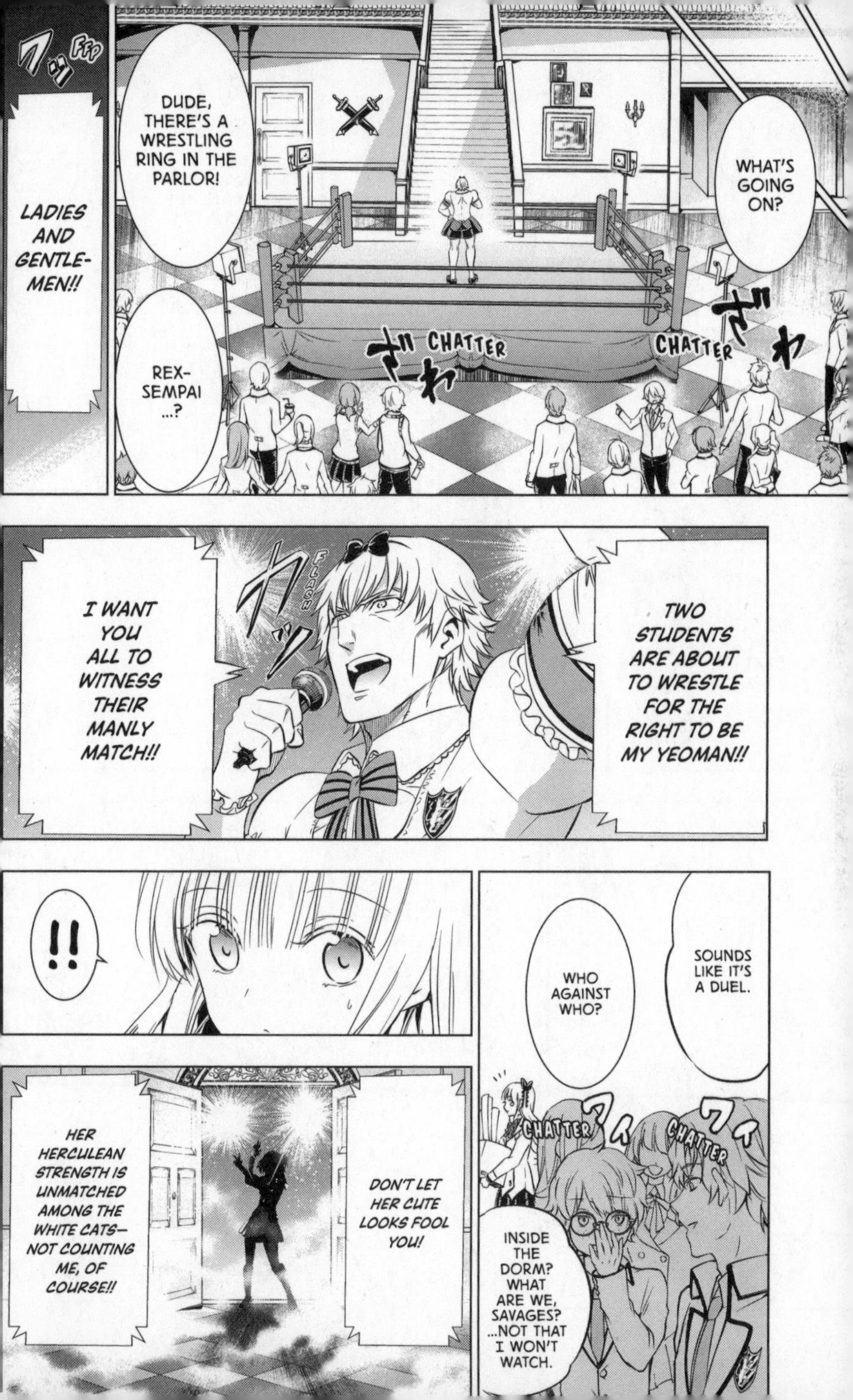
WHAT'S GOING ON?
CHATTER
DUDE, THERE'S A WRESTLING RING IN THE PARLOR!
CHATTER
REX-SEMPAI ...?
FFP
LADIES AND GENTLEMEN!!
TWO STUDENTS ARE ABOUT TO WRESTLE FOR THE RIGHT TO BE MY YEOMAN!!
FLASH
I WANT YOU ALL TO WITNESS THEIR MANLY MATCH!!
SOUNDS LIKE IT'S A DUEL.
WHO AGAINST WHO?
CHATTER
CHATTER
INSIDE THE DORM? WHAT ARE WE, SAVAGES? ...NOT THAT I WON'T WATCH.
!!
DON'T LET HER CUTE LOOKS FOOL YOU!
HER HERCULEAN STRENGTH IS UNMATCHED AMONG THE WHITE CATS—NOT COUNTING ME, OF COURSE!!

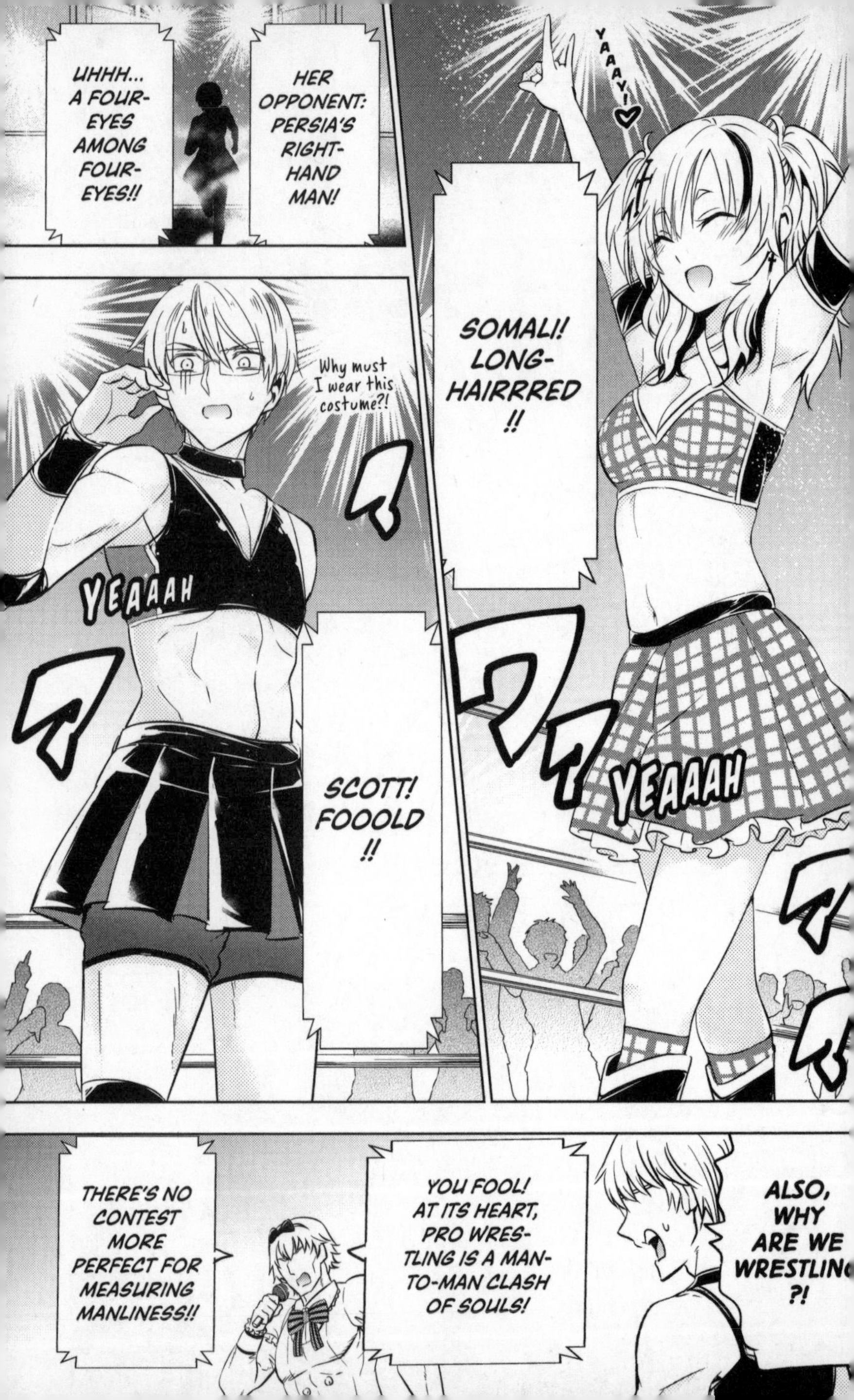
YAAAY! ♥
SOMALI! LONG-HAIRRRED!!
YEAAAH
HER OPPONENT: PERSIA'S RIGHT-HAND MAN!
UHHH... A FOUR-EYES AMONG FOUR-EYES!!
SCOTT! FOOOLD!!
Why must I wear this costume?!
YEAAAH
ALSO, WHY ARE WE WRESTLING?!
YOU FOOL! AT ITS HEART, PRO WRESTLING IS A MAN-TO-MAN CLASH OF SOULS!
THERE'S NO CONTEST MORE PERFECT FOR MEASURING MANLINESS!!

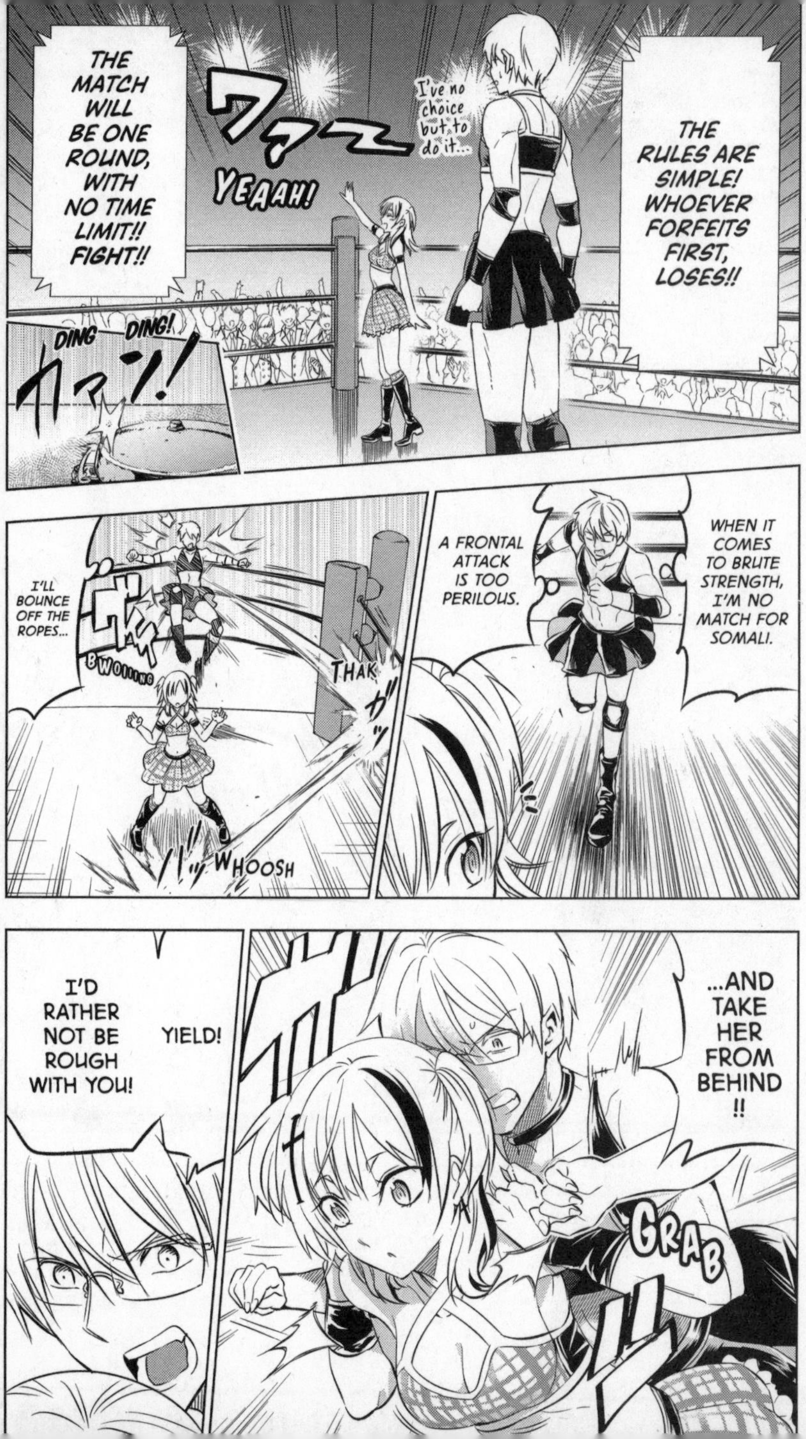

THE RULES ARE SIMPLE! WHOEVER FORFEITS FIRST, LOSES!!
I've no choice but to do it...
YEAAH!
THE MATCH WILL BE ONE ROUND, WITH NO TIME LIMIT!! FIGHT!!
DING DING!
カァン!
WHEN IT COMES TO BRUTE STRENGTH, I'M NO MATCH FOR SOMALI.
A FRONTAL ATTACK IS TOO PERILOUS.
I'LL BOUNCE OFF THE ROPES...
THAK
BWOIIING
WHOOSH
...AND TAKE HER FROM BEHIND!!
GRAB
YIELD!
I'D RATHER NOT BE ROUGH WITH YOU!

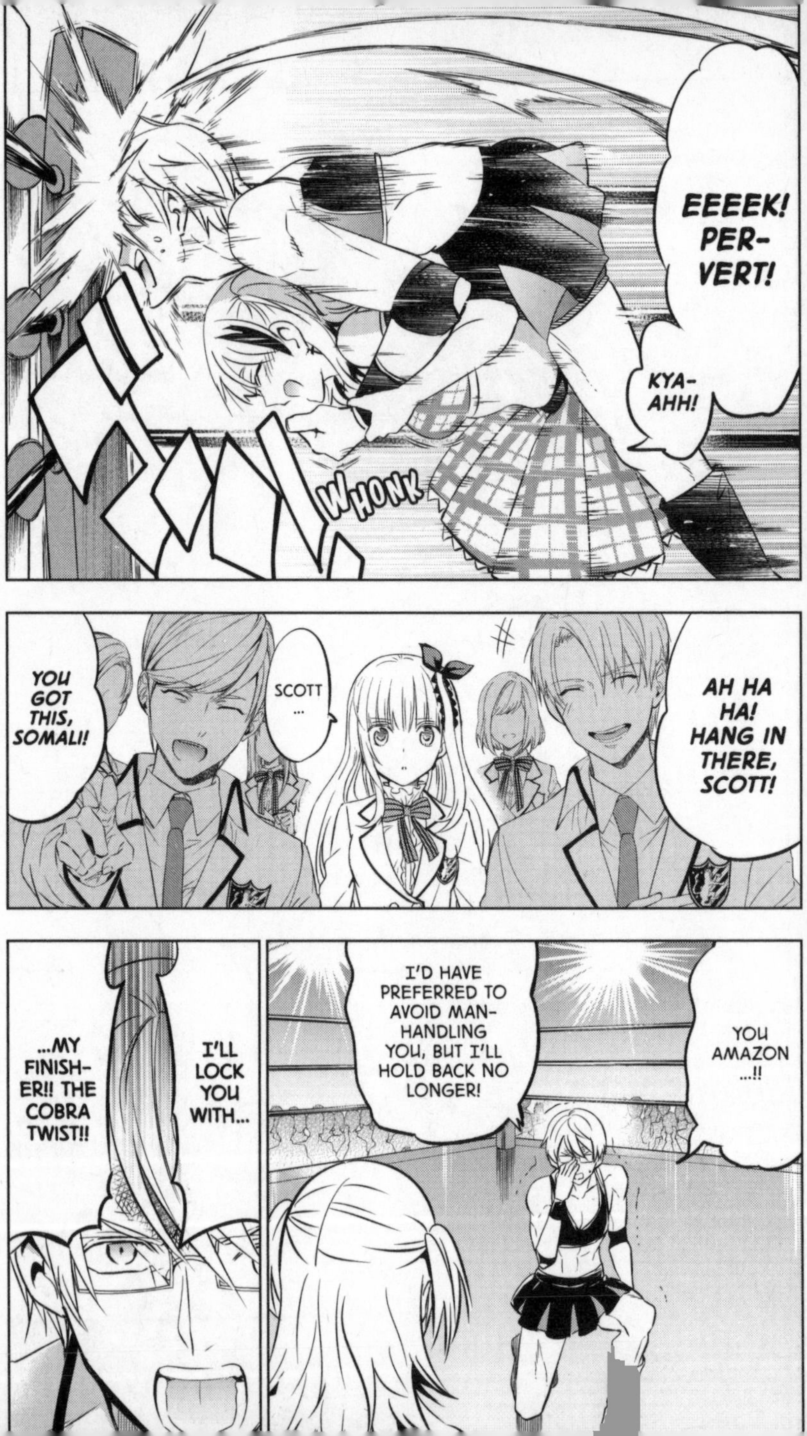
EEEEK! PER-VERT!
KYA-AHH!
WHONK
AH HA HA! HANG IN THERE, SCOTT!
SCOTT ...
YOU GOT THIS, SOMALI!
YOU AMAZON ...!!
I'D HAVE PREFERRED TO AVOID MAN-HANDLING YOU, BUT I'LL HOLD BACK NO LONGER!
I'LL LOCK YOU WITH...
...MY FINISH-ER!! THE COBRA TWIST!!

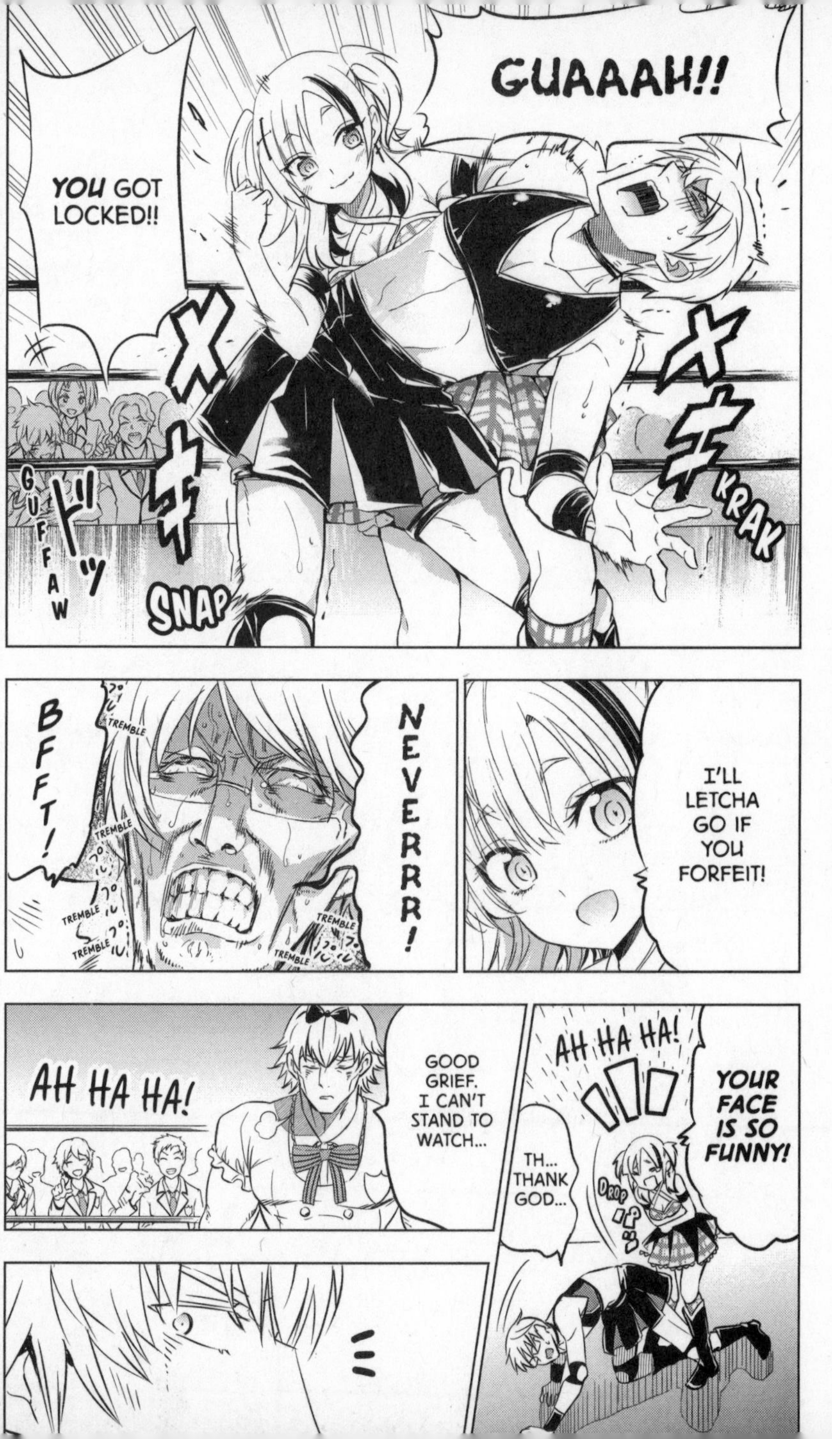
GUAAAH!!
YOU GOT LOCKED!!
KRAK
SNAP
GUFFAW
I'LL LETCHA GO IF YOU FORFEIT!
NEVERRRR!
BFFT!
TREMBLE
TREMBLE
TREMBLE
TREMBLE
TREMBLE
TREMBLE
TREMBLE
AH HA HA!
YOUR FACE IS SO FUNNY!
TH... THANK GOD...
DROP
GOOD GRIEF. I CAN'T STAND TO WATCH...
AH HA HA!

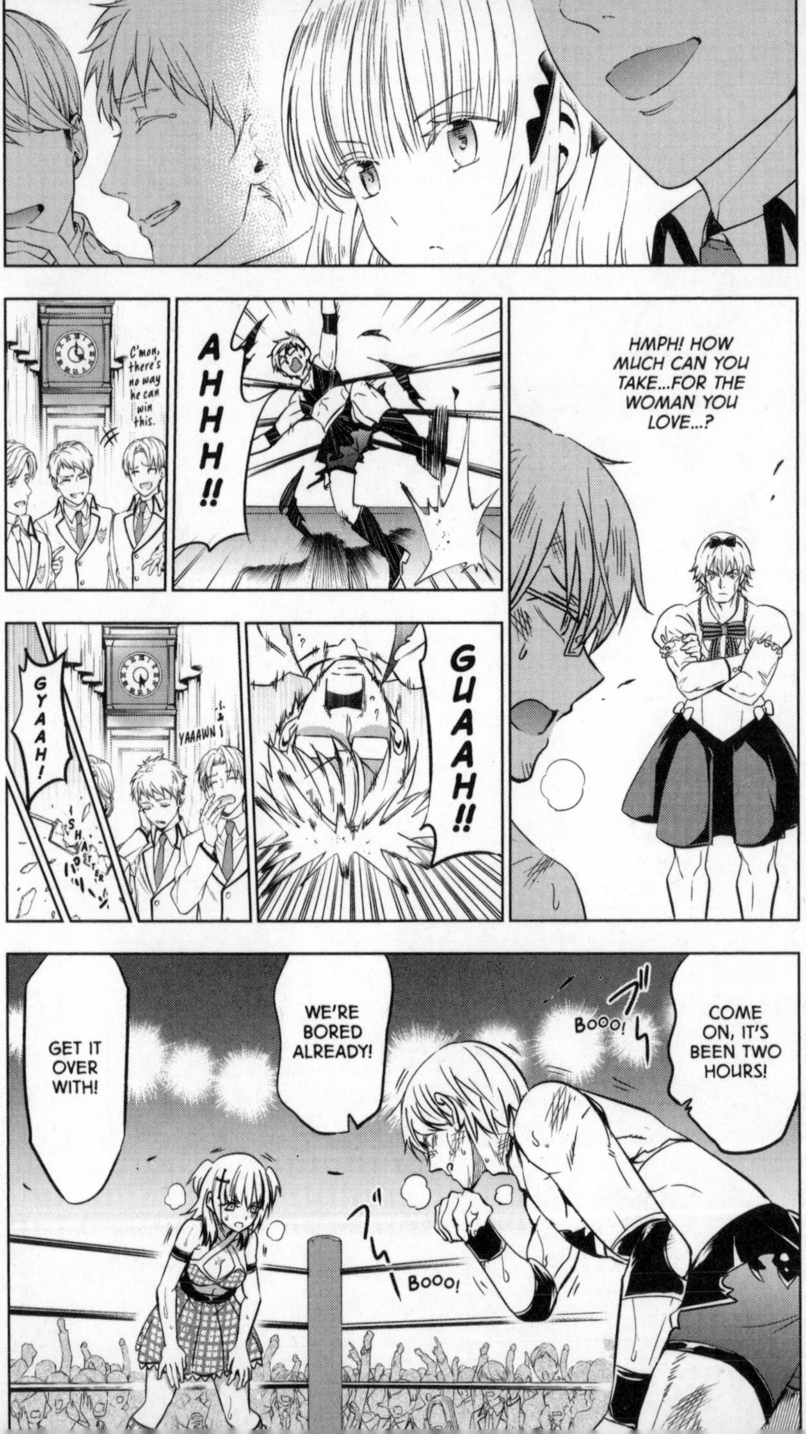

HMPH! HOW MUCH CAN YOU TAKE...FOR THE WOMAN YOU LOVE...?
AHHH!!
C'mon, there's no way he can win this.
GUAAAH!!
YAAAWN
GYAAAH!
SHATTER
COME ON, IT'S BEEN TWO HOURS!
BOOO!
WE'RE BORED ALREADY!
GET IT OVER WITH!
BOOO!

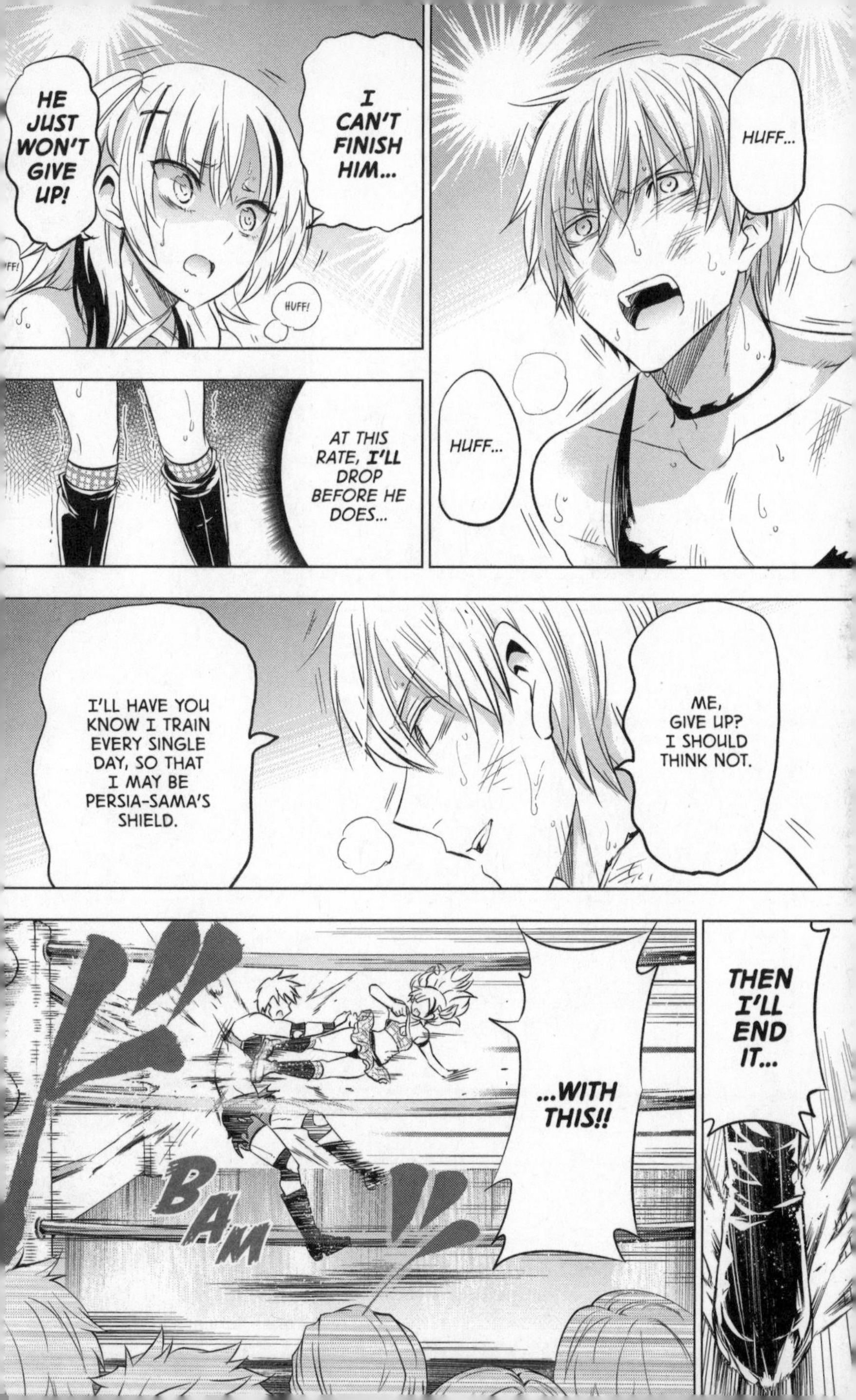
HUFF...
HUFF...
I CAN'T FINISH HIM...
HE JUST WON'T GIVE UP!
HUFF!
AT THIS RATE, I'LL DROP BEFORE HE DOES...
ME, GIVE UP? I SHOULD THINK NOT.
I'LL HAVE YOU KNOW I TRAIN EVERY SINGLE DAY, SO THAT I MAY BE PERSIA-SAMA'S SHIELD.
THEN I'LL END IT...
...WITH THIS!!
BAM!!

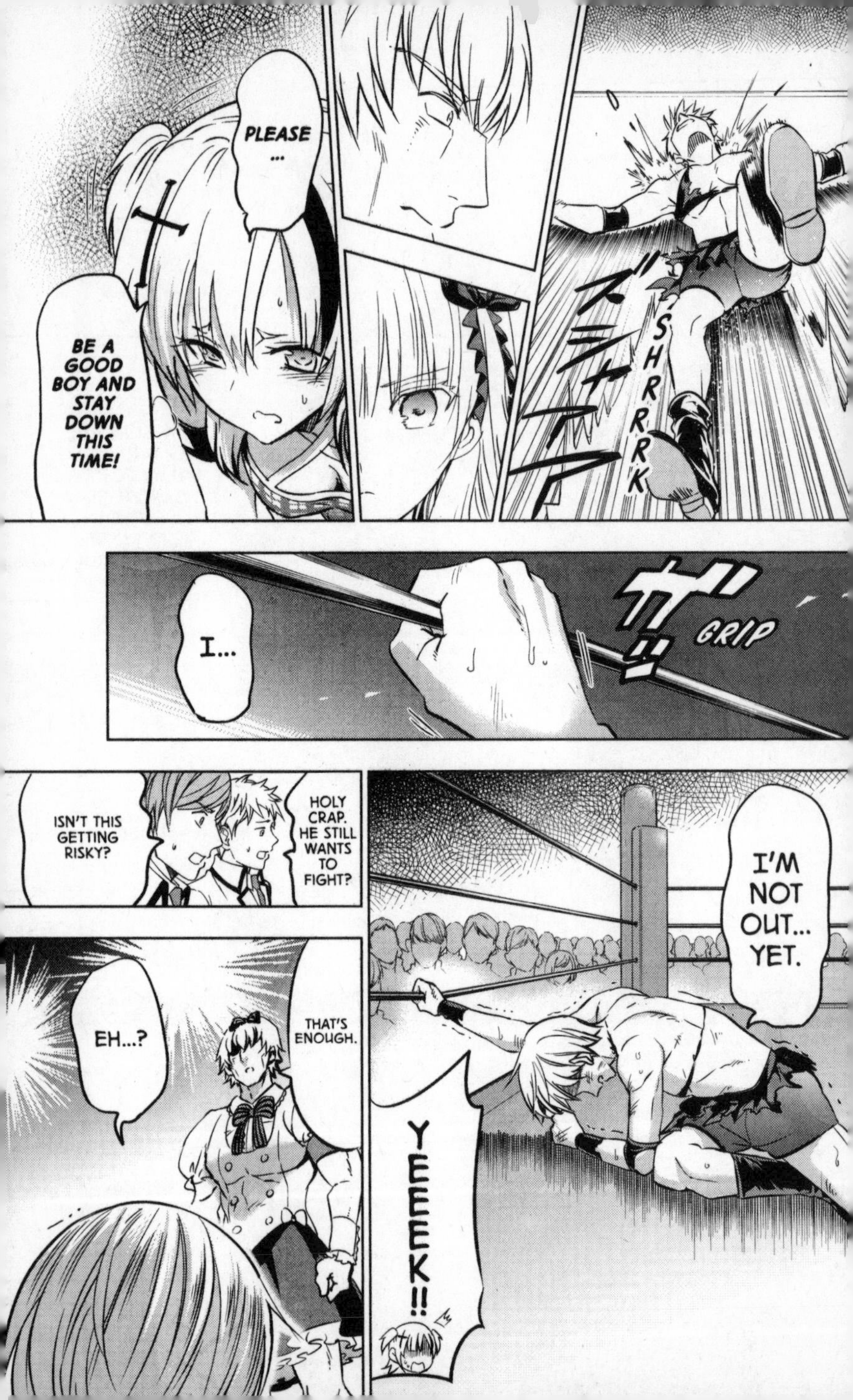
SHRRRK
PLEASE ...
BE A GOOD BOY AND STAY DOWN THIS TIME!
GRIP
I...
I'M NOT OUT... YET.
HOLY CRAP. HE STILL WANTS TO FIGHT?
ISN'T THIS GETTING RISKY?
YEEEK!!
THAT'S ENOUGH.
EH...?

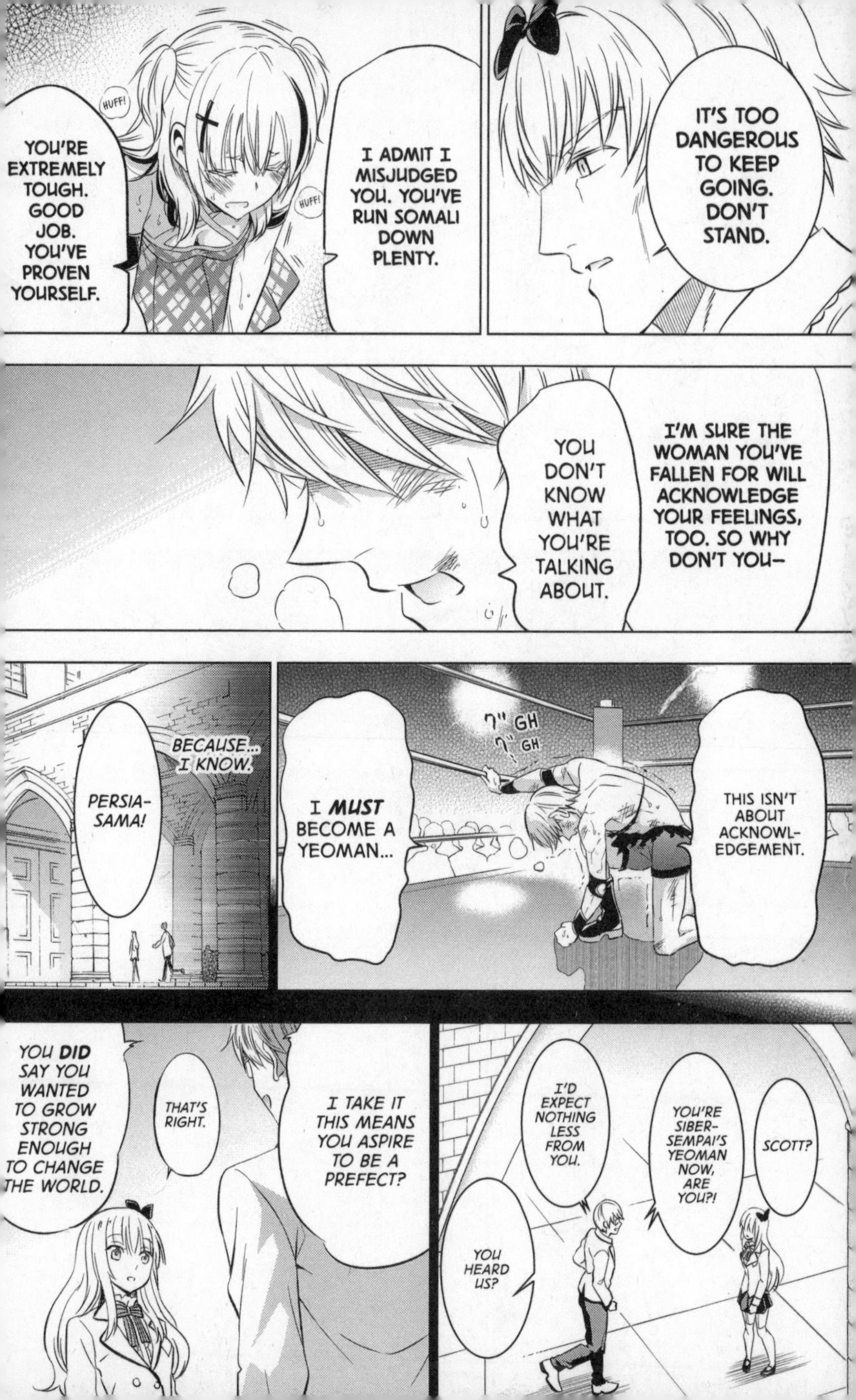
IT'S TOO DANGEROUS TO KEEP GOING. DON'T STAND.
HUFF!
I ADMIT I MISJUDGED YOU. YOU'VE RUN SOMALI DOWN PLENTY.
HUFF!
YOU'RE EXTREMELY TOUGH. GOOD JOB. YOU'VE PROVEN YOURSELF.
I'M SURE THE WOMAN YOU'VE FALLEN FOR WILL ACKNOWLEDGE YOUR FEELINGS, TOO. SO WHY DON'T YOU–
YOU DON'T KNOW WHAT YOU'RE TALKING ABOUT.
THIS ISN'T ABOUT ACKNOWL-EDGEMENT.
GH
GH
I **MUST** BECOME A YEOMAN...
BECAUSE... I KNOW.
PERSIA-SAMA!
SCOTT?
YOU'RE SIBER-SEMPAI'S YEOMAN NOW, ARE YOU?!
I'D EXPECT NOTHING LESS FROM YOU.
YOU HEARD US?
I TAKE IT THIS MEANS YOU ASPIRE TO BE A PREFECT?
THAT'S RIGHT.
YOU **DID** SAY YOU WANTED TO GROW STRONG ENOUGH TO CHANGE THE WORLD.

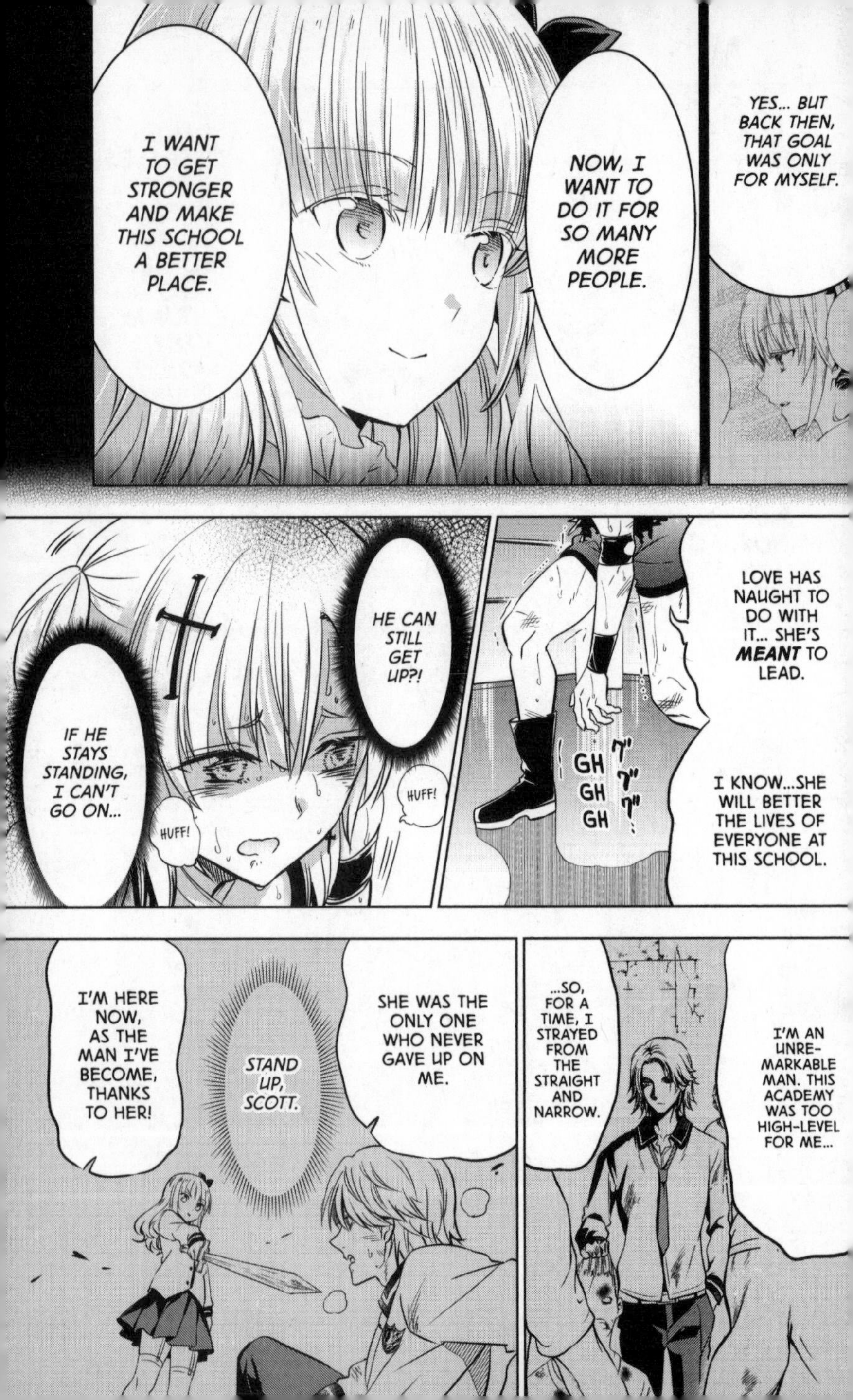
YES... BUT BACK THEN, THAT GOAL WAS ONLY FOR MYSELF.
NOW, I WANT TO DO IT FOR SO MANY MORE PEOPLE.
I WANT TO GET STRONGER AND MAKE THIS SCHOOL A BETTER PLACE.
LOVE HAS NAUGHT TO DO WITH IT... SHE'S **MEANT** TO LEAD.
I KNOW...SHE WILL BETTER THE LIVES OF EVERYONE AT THIS SCHOOL.
GH GH GH
HE CAN STILL GET UP?!
HUFF!
IF HE STAYS STANDING, I CAN'T GO ON...
HUFF!
I'M AN UNRE-MARKABLE MAN. THIS ACADEMY WAS TOO HIGH-LEVEL FOR ME...
...SO, FOR A TIME, I STRAYED FROM THE STRAIGHT AND NARROW.
SHE WAS THE ONLY ONE WHO NEVER GAVE UP ON ME.
STAND UP, SCOTT.
I'M HERE NOW, AS THE MAN I'VE BECOME, THANKS TO HER!

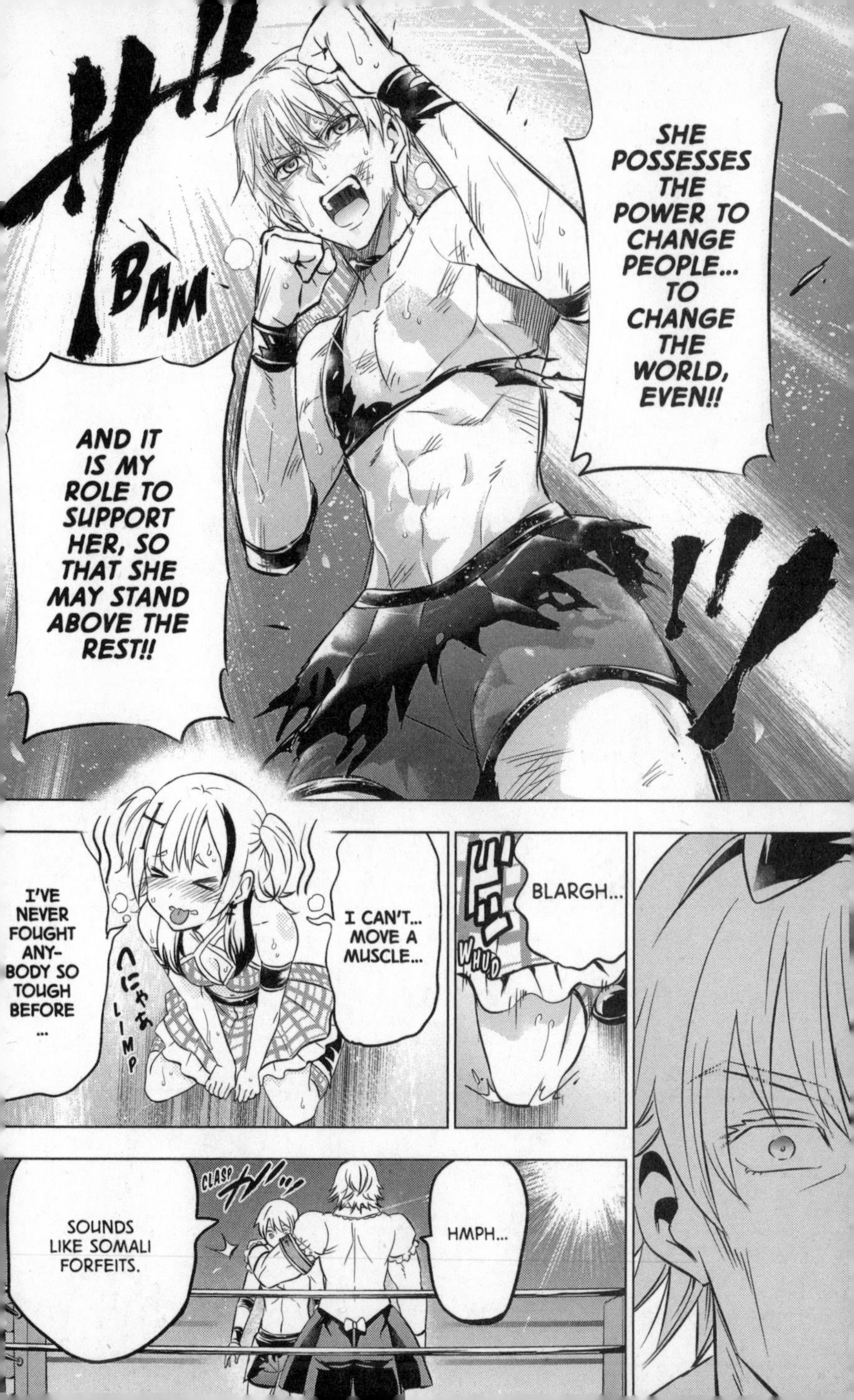
SHE POSSESSES THE POWER TO CHANGE PEOPLE... TO CHANGE THE WORLD, EVEN!!
BAM
AND IT IS MY ROLE TO SUPPORT HER, SO THAT SHE MAY STAND ABOVE THE REST!!
WHUD
BLARGH...
I CAN'T... MOVE A MUSCLE...
LIMP
I'VE NEVER FOUGHT ANY-BODY SO TOUGH BEFORE ...
HMPH...
CLASP
SOUNDS LIKE SOMALI FORFEITS.

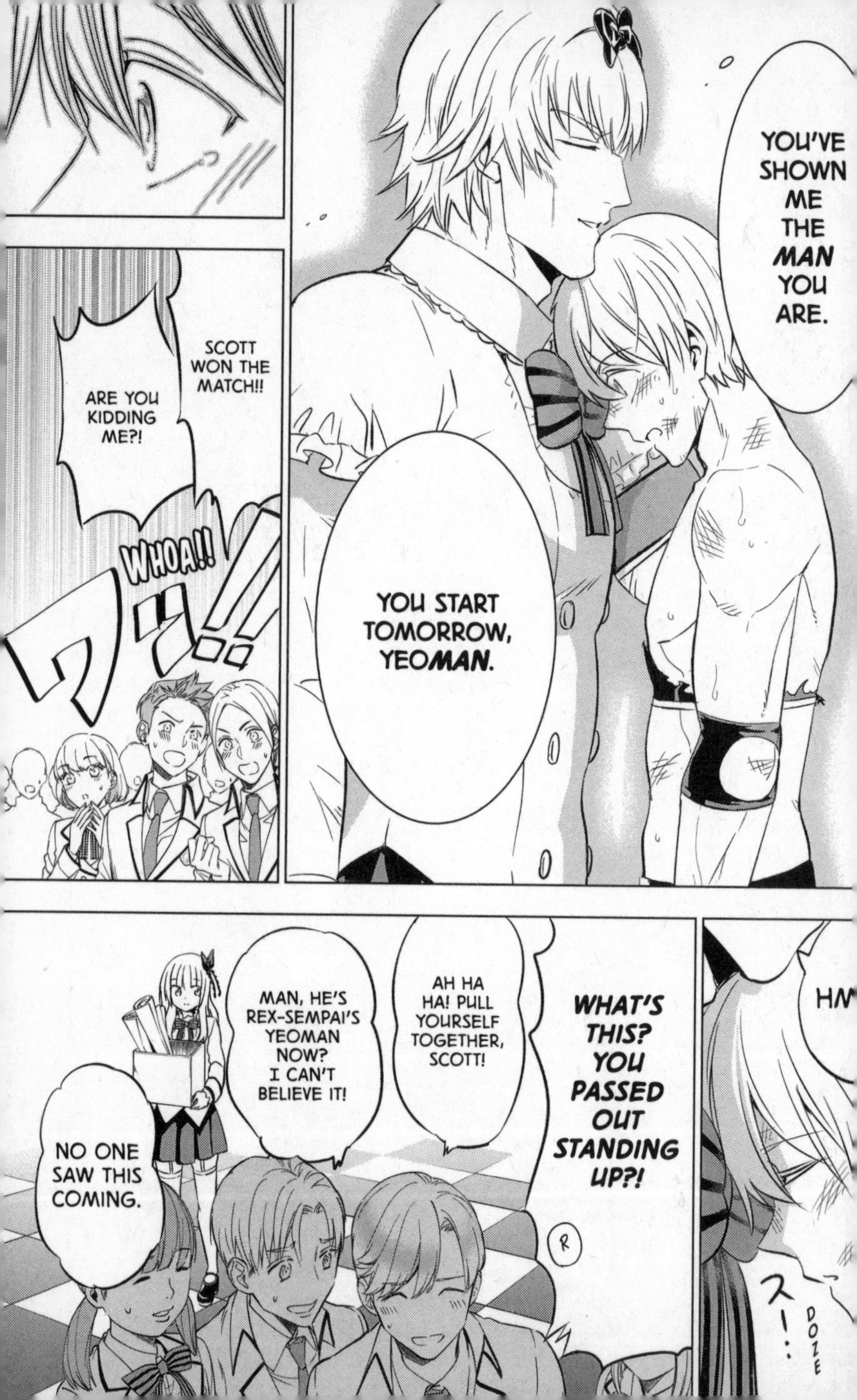

YOU'VE SHOWN ME THE MAN YOU ARE.
YOU START TOMORROW, YEOMAN.
SCOTT WON THE MATCH!!
ARE YOU KIDDING ME?!
WHOA!!
HM
DOZE
WHAT'S THIS? YOU PASSED OUT STANDING UP?!
AH HA HA! PULL YOURSELF TOGETHER, SCOTT!
MAN, HE'S REX-SEMPAI'S YEOMAN NOW? I CAN'T BELIEVE IT!
NO ONE SAW THIS COMING.

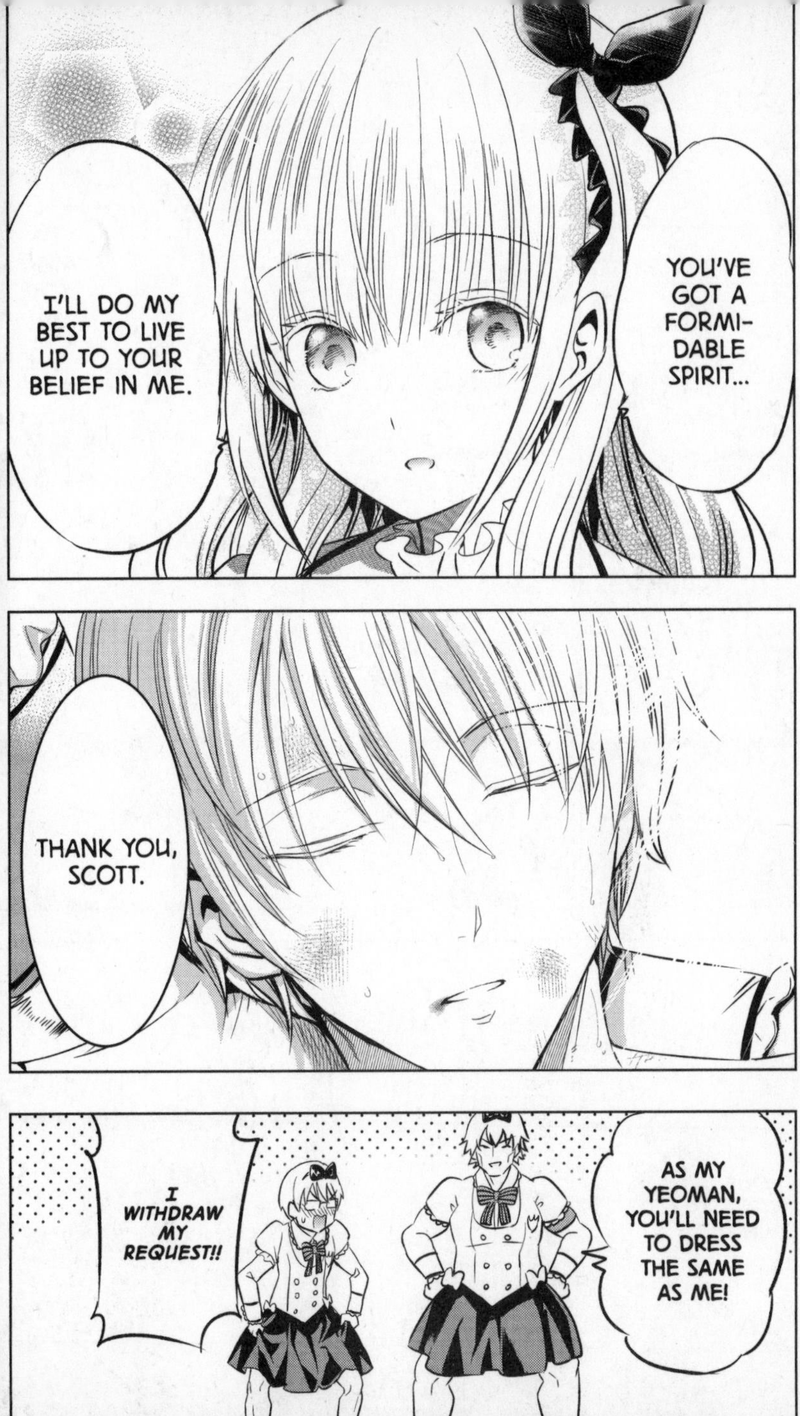
YOU'VE GOT A FORMIDABLE SPIRIT...
I'LL DO MY BEST TO LIVE UP TO YOUR BELIEF IN ME.
THANK YOU, SCOTT.
AS MY YEOMAN, YOU'LL NEED TO DRESS THE SAME AS ME!
I WITHDRAW MY REQUEST!!

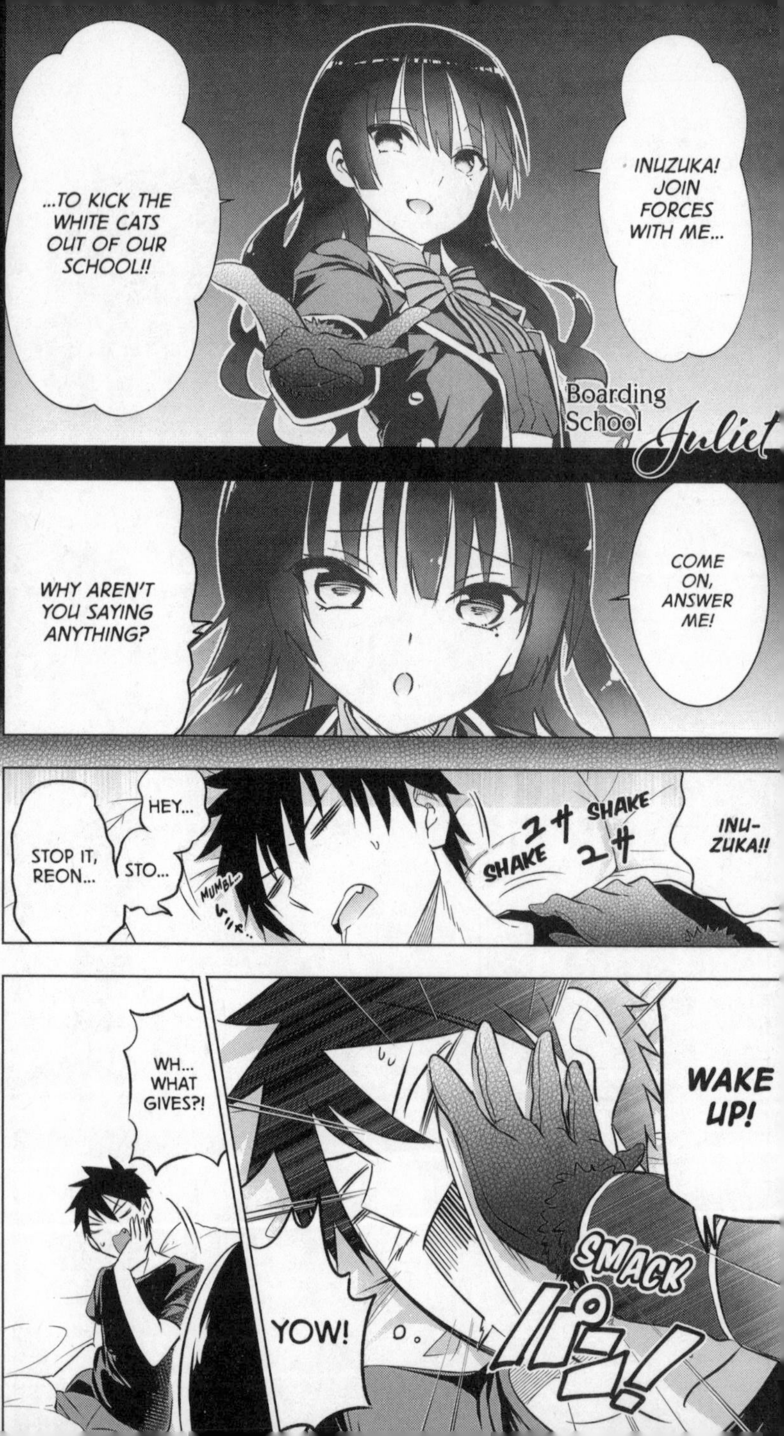
INUZUKA! JOIN FORCES WITH ME...
...TO KICK THE WHITE CATS OUT OF OUR SCHOOL!!
Boarding School Juliet
COME ON, ANSWER ME!
WHY AREN'T YOU SAYING ANYTHING?
INU-ZUKA!!
SHAKE
SHAKE
HEY...
STO...
STOP IT, REON...
MUMBL...
WAKE UP!
SMACK
YOW!
WH... WHAT GIVES?!

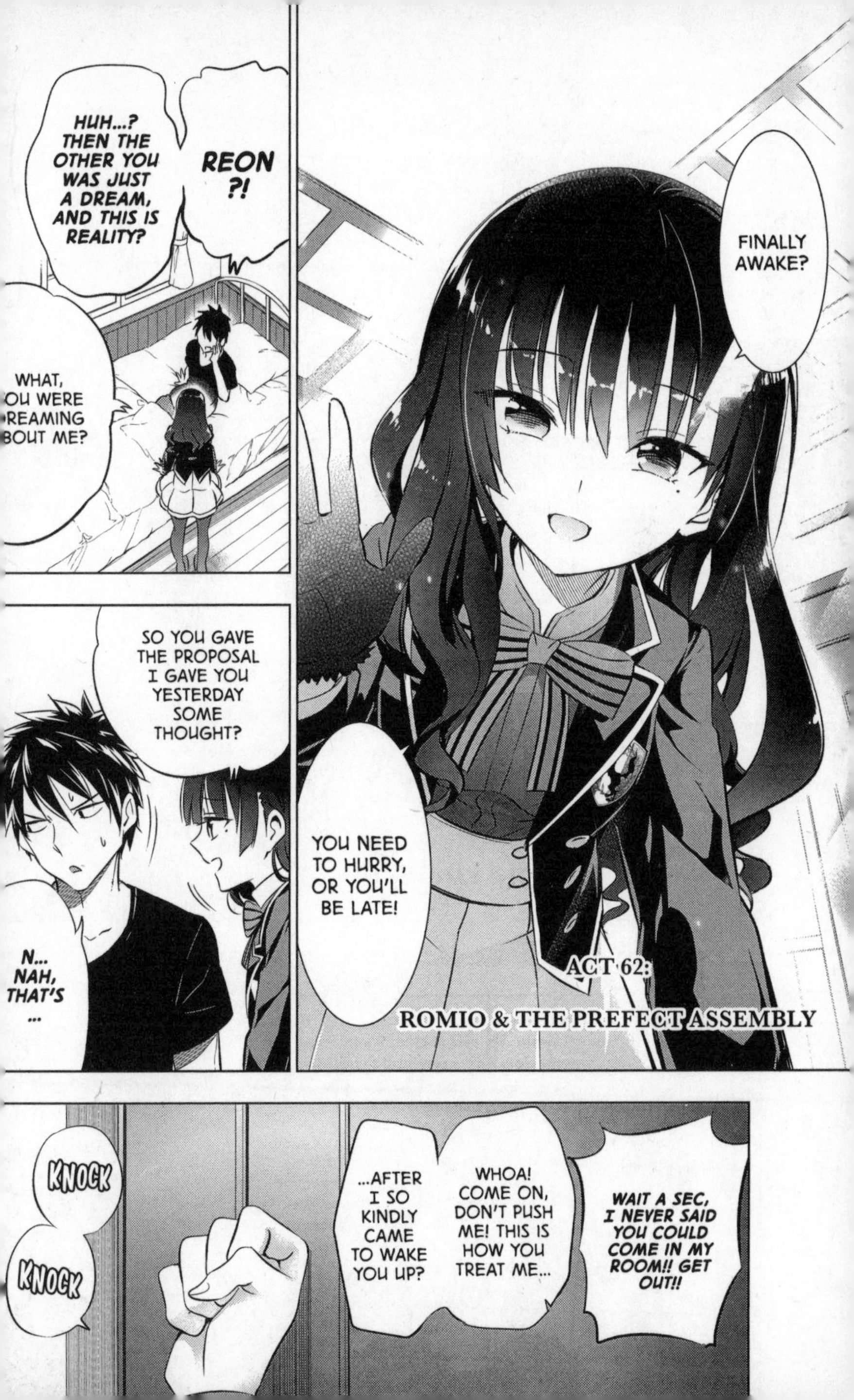

FINALLY AWAKE?
YOU NEED TO HURRY, OR YOU'LL BE LATE!
ACT 62:
ROMIO & THE PREFECT ASSEMBLY
REON ?!
HUH...? THEN THE OTHER YOU WAS JUST A DREAM, AND THIS IS REALITY?
WHAT, OU WERE REAMING BOUT ME?
SO YOU GAVE THE PROPOSAL I GAVE YOU YESTERDAY SOME THOUGHT?
N... NAH, THAT'S ...
WAIT A SEC, I NEVER SAID YOU COULD COME IN MY ROOM!! GET OUT!!
WHOA! COME ON, DON'T PUSH ME! THIS IS HOW YOU TREAT ME...
...AFTER I SO KINDLY CAME TO WAKE YOU UP?
KNOCK
KNOCK

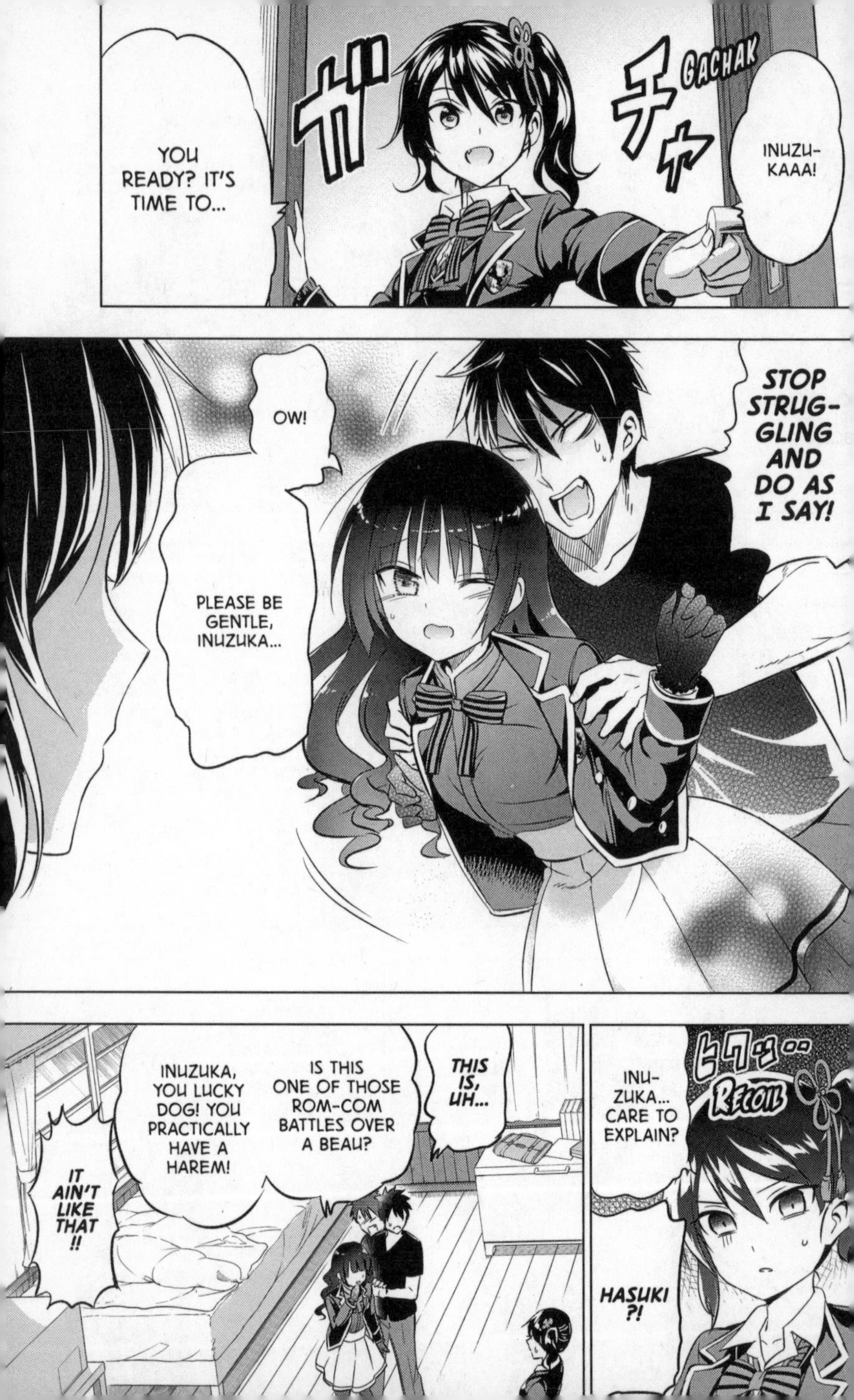
GACHAK
INUZU-KAAA!
YOU READY? IT'S TIME TO...
STOP STRUG-GLING AND DO AS I SAY!
OW!
PLEASE BE GENTLE, INUZUKA...
RECOIL
INU-ZUKA... CARE TO EXPLAIN?
HASUKI ?!
THIS IS, UH...
IS THIS ONE OF THOSE ROM-COM BATTLES OVER A BEAU?
INUZUKA, YOU LUCKY DOG! YOU PRACTICALLY HAVE A HAREM!
IT AIN'T LIKE THAT !!

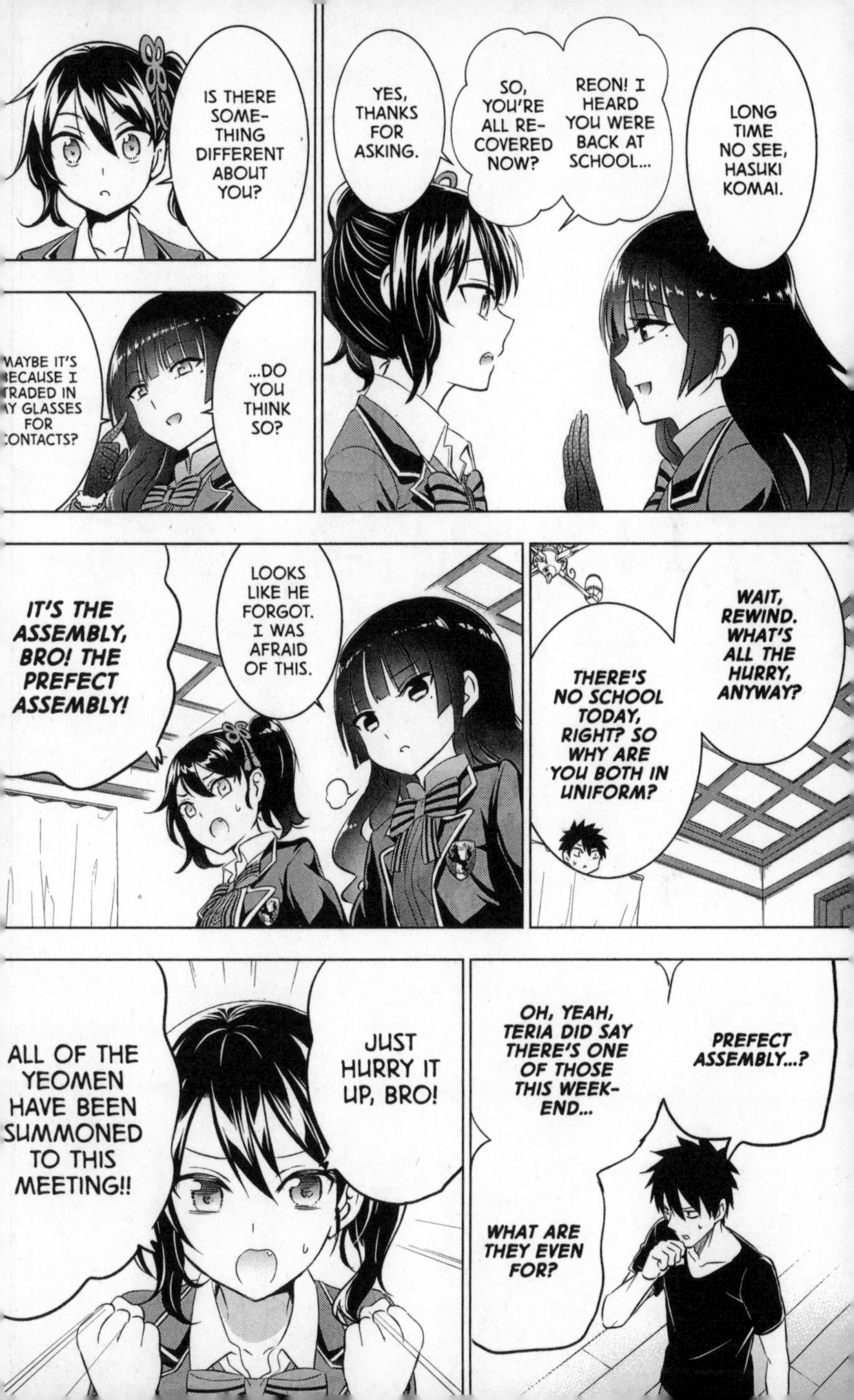
LONG TIME NO SEE, HASUKI KOMAI.
REON! I HEARD YOU WERE BACK AT SCHOOL...
SO, YOU'RE ALL RE-COVERED NOW?
YES, THANKS FOR ASKING.
IS THERE SOME-THING DIFFERENT ABOUT YOU?
...DO YOU THINK SO?
MAYBE IT'S BECAUSE I TRADED IN MY GLASSES FOR CONTACTS?
WAIT, REWIND. WHAT'S ALL THE HURRY, ANYWAY?
THERE'S NO SCHOOL TODAY, RIGHT? SO WHY ARE YOU BOTH IN UNIFORM?
LOOKS LIKE HE FORGOT. I WAS AFRAID OF THIS.
IT'S THE ASSEMBLY, BRO! THE PREFECT ASSEMBLY!
PREFECT ASSEMBLY...?
OH, YEAH, TERIA DID SAY THERE'S ONE OF THOSE THIS WEEK-END...
WHAT ARE THEY EVEN FOR?
JUST HURRY IT UP, BRO!
ALL OF THE YEOMEN HAVE BEEN SUMMONED TO THIS MEETING!!

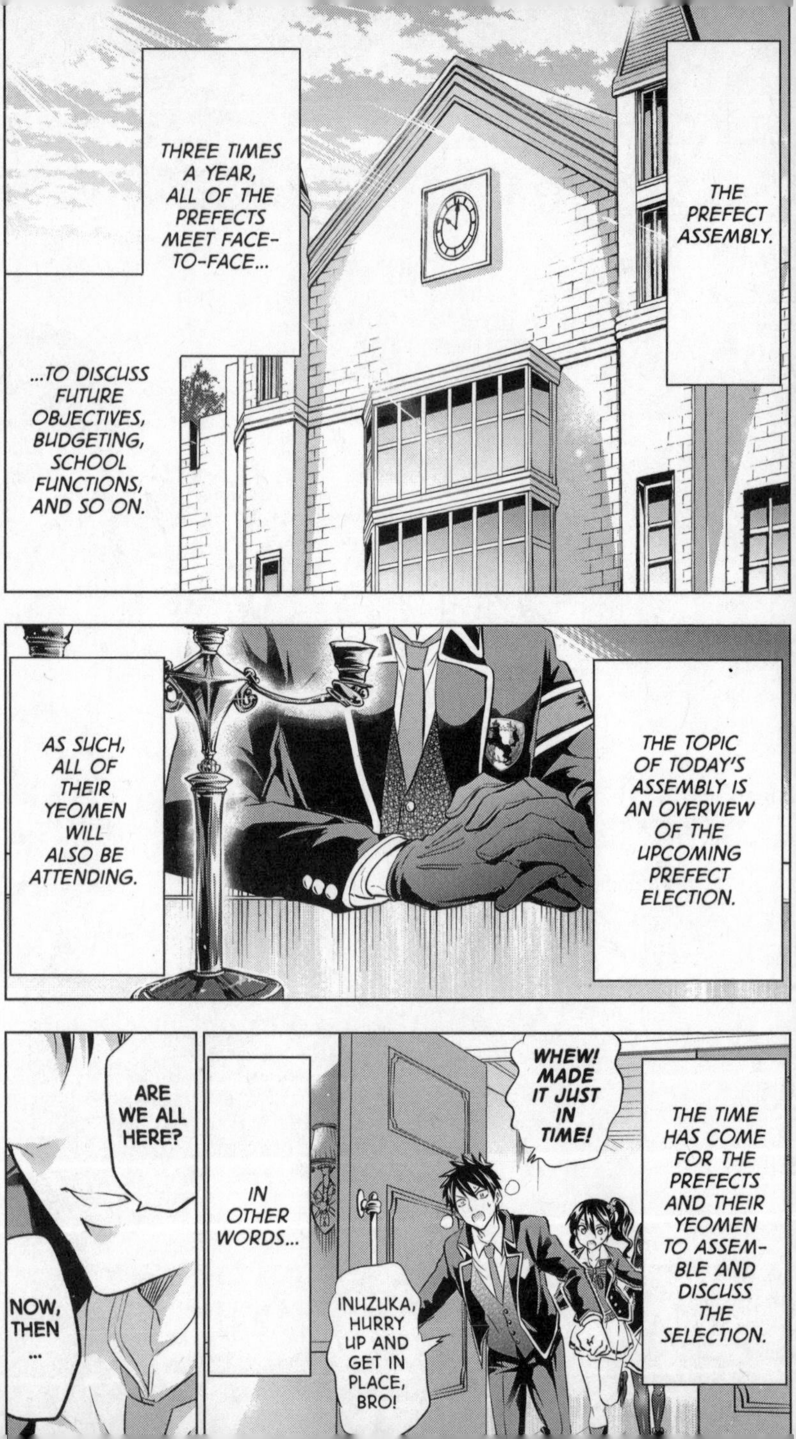
THE PREFECT ASSEMBLY.
THREE TIMES A YEAR, ALL OF THE PREFECTS MEET FACE-TO-FACE...
...TO DISCUSS FUTURE OBJECTIVES, BUDGETING, SCHOOL FUNCTIONS, AND SO ON.
THE TOPIC OF TODAY'S ASSEMBLY IS AN OVERVIEW OF THE UPCOMING PREFECT ELECTION.
AS SUCH, ALL OF THEIR YEOMEN WILL ALSO BE ATTENDING.
THE TIME HAS COME FOR THE PREFECTS AND THEIR YEOMEN TO ASSEM-BLE AND DISCUSS THE SELECTION.
WHEW! MADE IT JUST IN TIME!
IN OTHER WORDS...
INUZUKA, HURRY UP AND GET IN PLACE, BRO!
ARE WE ALL HERE?
NOW, THEN ...

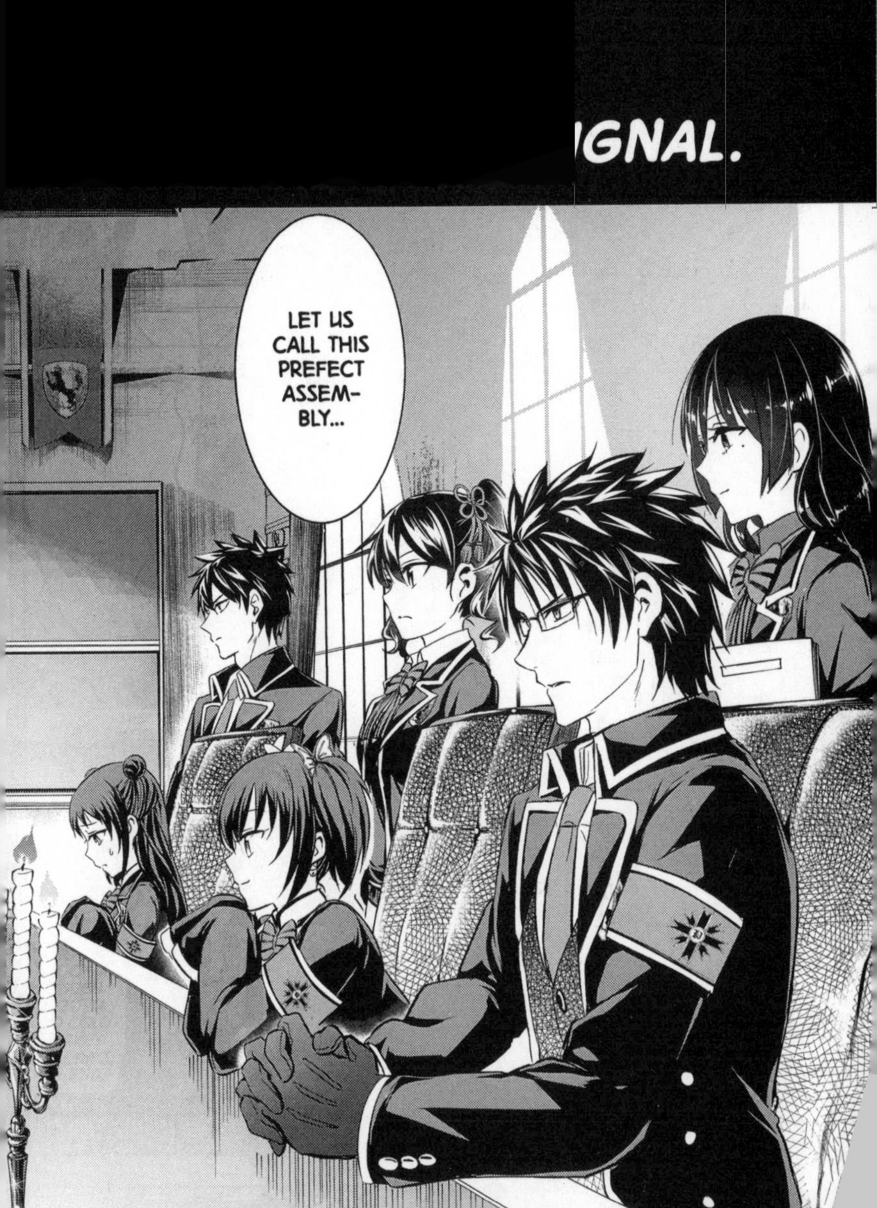
[redacted]
LET US CALL THIS PREFECT ASSEM-BLY...

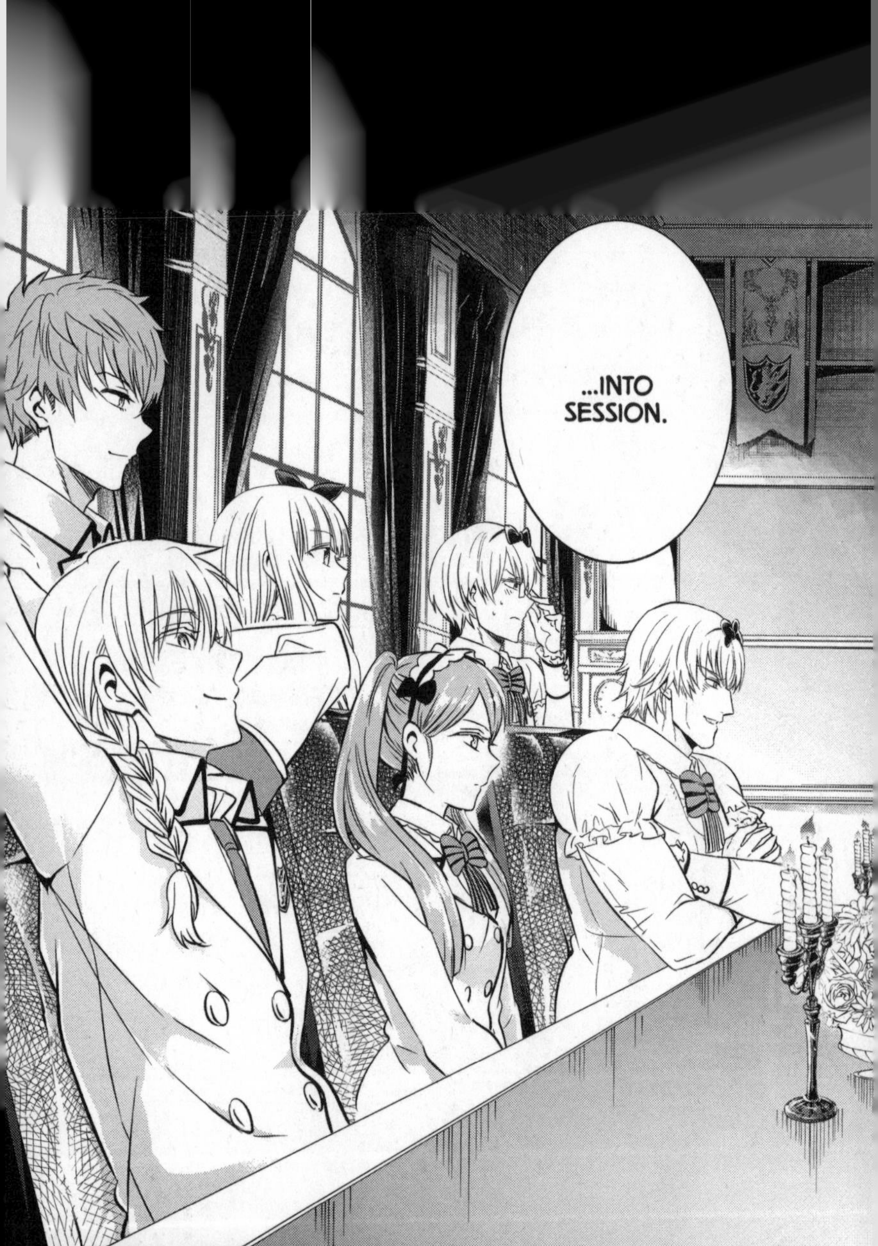
...INTO SESSION.

THE PREFECT SELECTION WAR

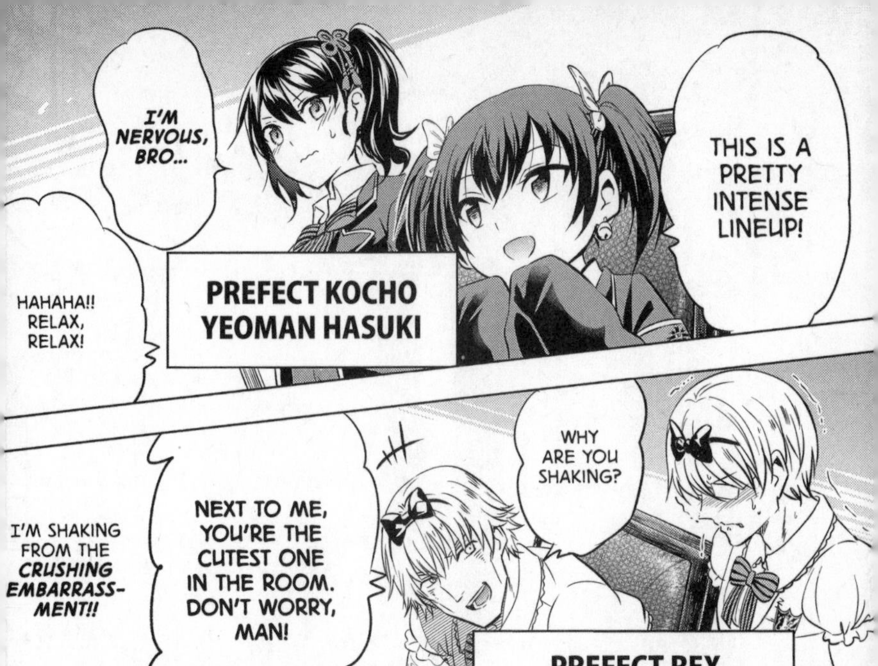
THIS IS A PRETTY INTENSE LINEUP!
I'M NERVOUS, BRO...
HAHAHA!! RELAX, RELAX!
PREFECT KOCHO YEOMAN HASUKI
WHY ARE YOU SHAKING?
NEXT TO ME, YOU'RE THE CUTEST ONE IN THE ROOM. DON'T WORRY, MAN!
I'M SHAKING FROM THE *CRUSHING EMBARRASSMENT!!*
PREFECT REX YEOMAN SCOTT
I-I'M S-S...SO NERVOUS, I FEEL QUEASY...
WRITE "PERSON" ON YOUR PALM THREE TIMES AND SWALLOW IT!
PREFECT TERIA YEOMAN ROMIO

TE: INUZUKA IS REFERRING TO THE JAPANESE IDIOM "*HITO WO NOMU*," OR "SWALLOW A PERSON." THE PRACTICE REFERS TO WRITING THE JAPANESE KANJI FOR "PERSON" ON 'S PALM, AND THEN PRETENDING TO SWALLOW IT, AS A WAY TO OVERCOME ONE'S NERVOUSNESS AND FEAR OF SPEAKING IN FRONT OF AN AUDIENCE.

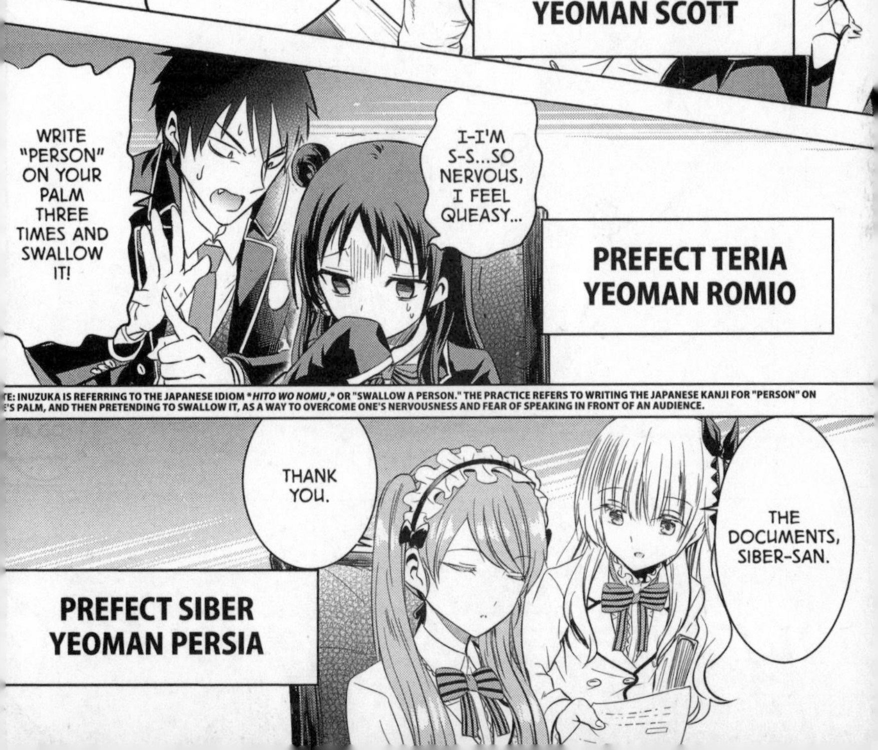
THE DOCUMENTS, SIBER-SAN.
THANK YOU.
PREFECT SIBER YEOMAN PERSIA

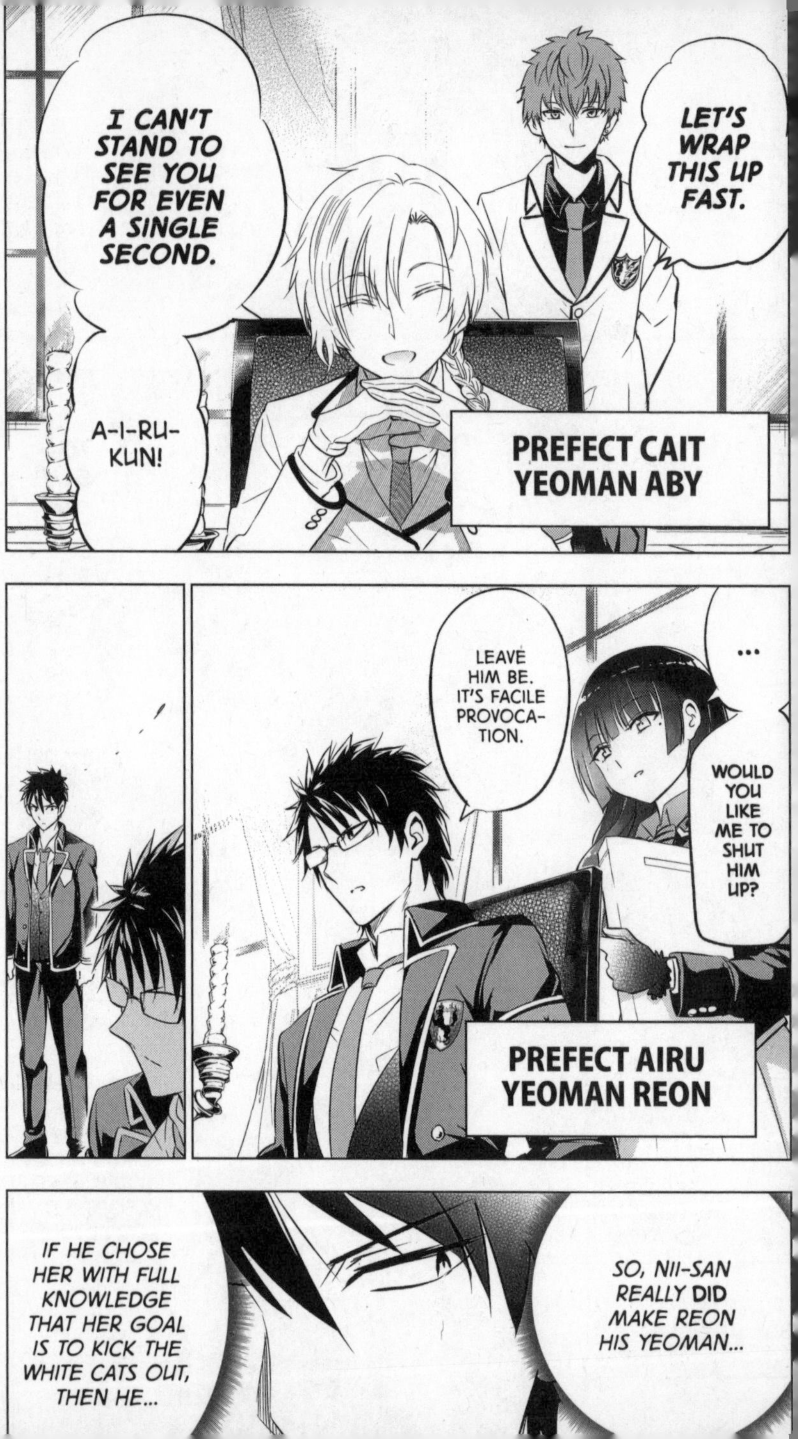
LET'S WRAP THIS UP FAST.
I CAN'T STAND TO SEE YOU FOR EVEN A SINGLE SECOND.
A-I-RU-KUN!
PREFECT CAIT YEOMAN ABY
...
WOULD YOU LIKE ME TO SHUT HIM UP?
LEAVE HIM BE. IT'S FACILE PROVOCA-TION.
PREFECT AIRU YEOMAN REON
SO, NII-SAN REALLY DID MAKE REON HIS YEOMAN...
IF HE CHOSE HER WITH FULL KNOWLEDGE THAT HER GOAL IS TO KICK THE WHITE CATS OUT, THEN HE...

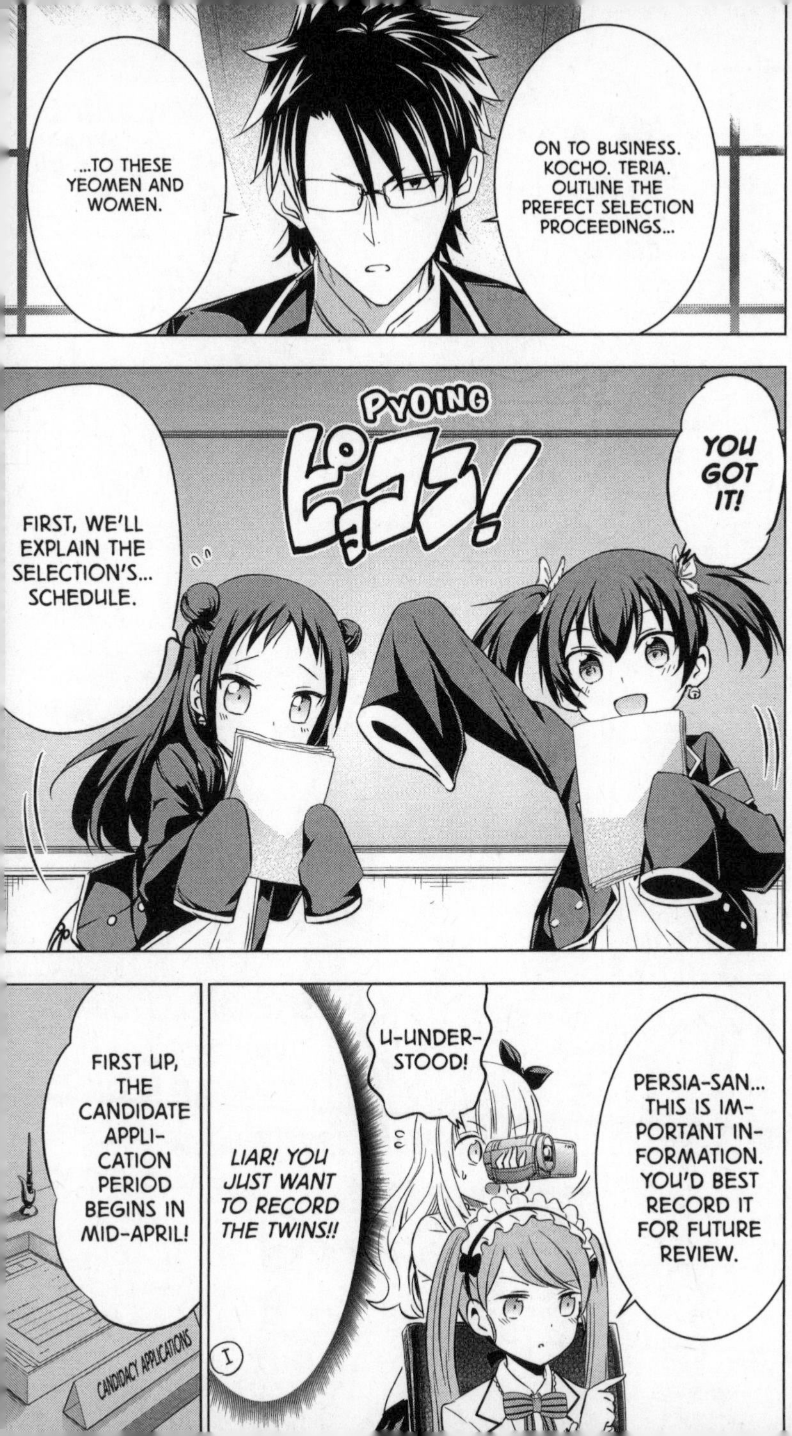
ON TO BUSINESS. KOCHO. TERIA. OUTLINE THE PREFECT SELECTION PROCEEDINGS...
...TO THESE YEOMEN AND WOMEN.
YOU GOT IT!
PYOING
ピョコン!
FIRST, WE'LL EXPLAIN THE SELECTION'S... SCHEDULE.
PERSIA-SAN... THIS IS IMPORTANT INFORMATION. YOU'D BEST RECORD IT FOR FUTURE REVIEW.
U-UNDERSTOOD!
LIAR! YOU JUST WANT TO RECORD THE TWINS!!
FIRST UP, THE CANDIDATE APPLICATION PERIOD BEGINS IN MID-APRIL!
CANDIDACY APPLICATIONS

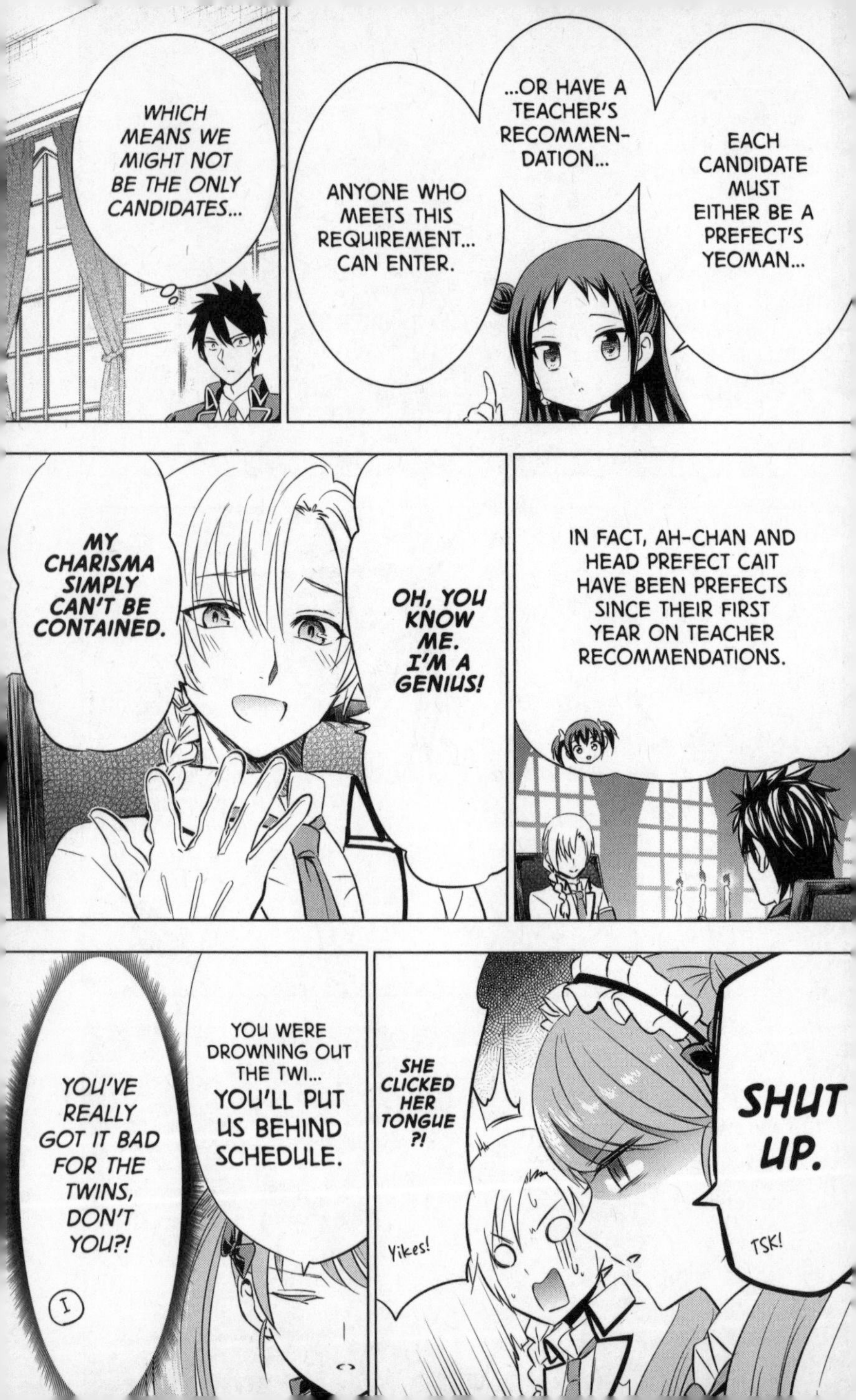
EACH CANDIDATE MUST EITHER BE A PREFECT'S YEOMAN...
...OR HAVE A TEACHER'S RECOMMEN-DATION...
ANYONE WHO MEETS THIS REQUIREMENT... CAN ENTER.
WHICH MEANS WE MIGHT NOT BE THE ONLY CANDIDATES...
IN FACT, AH-CHAN AND HEAD PREFECT CAIT HAVE BEEN PREFECTS SINCE THEIR FIRST YEAR ON TEACHER RECOMMENDATIONS.
OH, YOU KNOW ME. I'M A GENIUS!
MY CHARISMA SIMPLY CAN'T BE CONTAINED.
SHUT UP.
TSK!
SHE CLICKED HER TONGUE?!
Yikes!
YOU WERE DROWNING OUT THE TWI... YOU'LL PUT US BEHIND SCHEDULE.
YOU'VE REALLY GOT IT BAD FOR THE TWINS, DON'T YOU?!

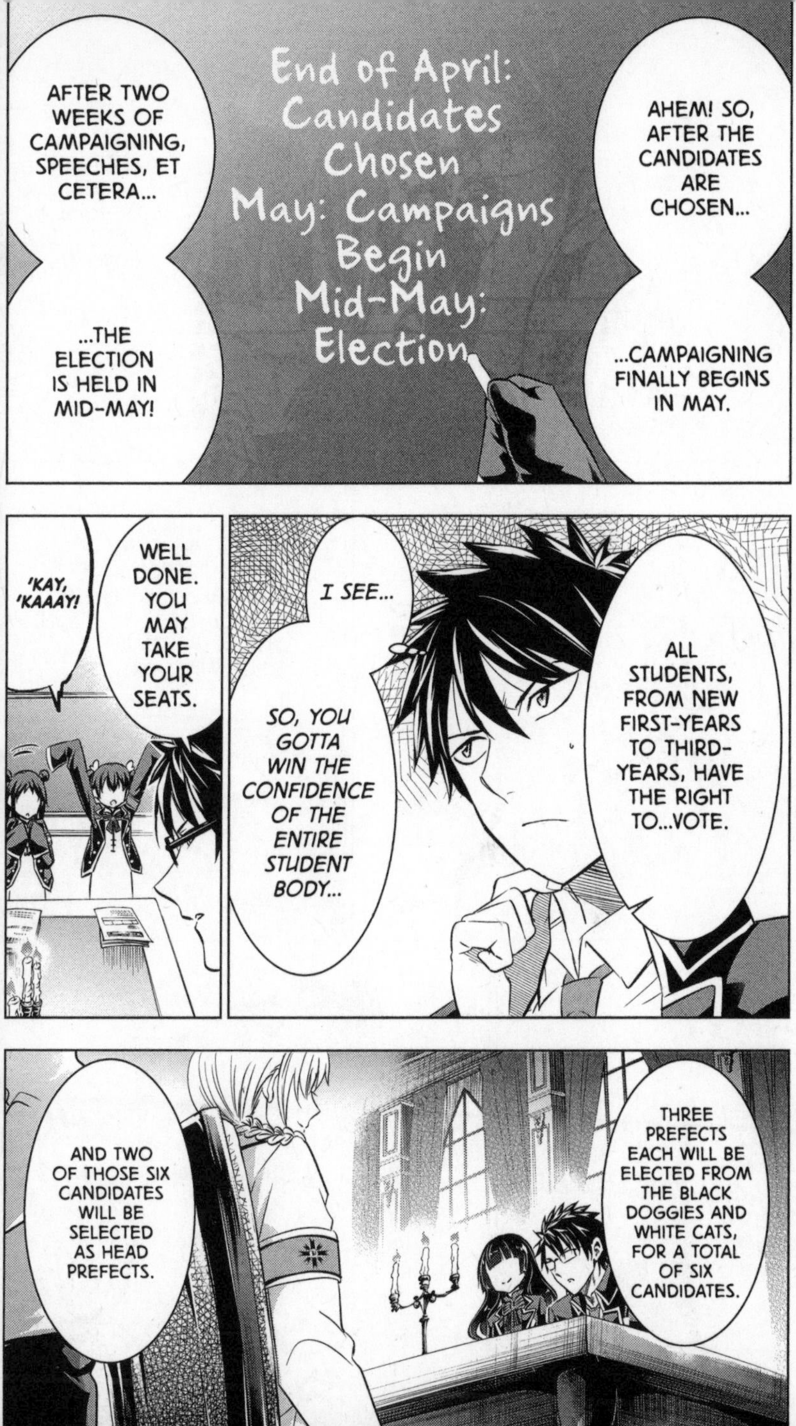
AHEM! SO, AFTER THE CANDIDATES ARE CHOSEN...
...CAMPAIGNING FINALLY BEGINS IN MAY.
End of April: Candidates Chosen
May: Campaigns Begin
Mid-May: Election
AFTER TWO WEEKS OF CAMPAIGNING, SPEECHES, ET CETERA...
...THE ELECTION IS HELD IN MID-MAY!
ALL STUDENTS, FROM NEW FIRST-YEARS TO THIRD-YEARS, HAVE THE RIGHT TO...VOTE.
I SEE...
SO, YOU GOTTA WIN THE CONFIDENCE OF THE ENTIRE STUDENT BODY...
WELL DONE. YOU MAY TAKE YOUR SEATS.
'KAY, 'KAAAY!
THREE PREFECTS EACH WILL BE ELECTED FROM THE BLACK DOGGIES AND WHITE CATS, FOR A TOTAL OF SIX CANDIDATES.
AND TWO OF THOSE SIX CANDIDATES WILL BE SELECTED AS HEAD PREFECTS.

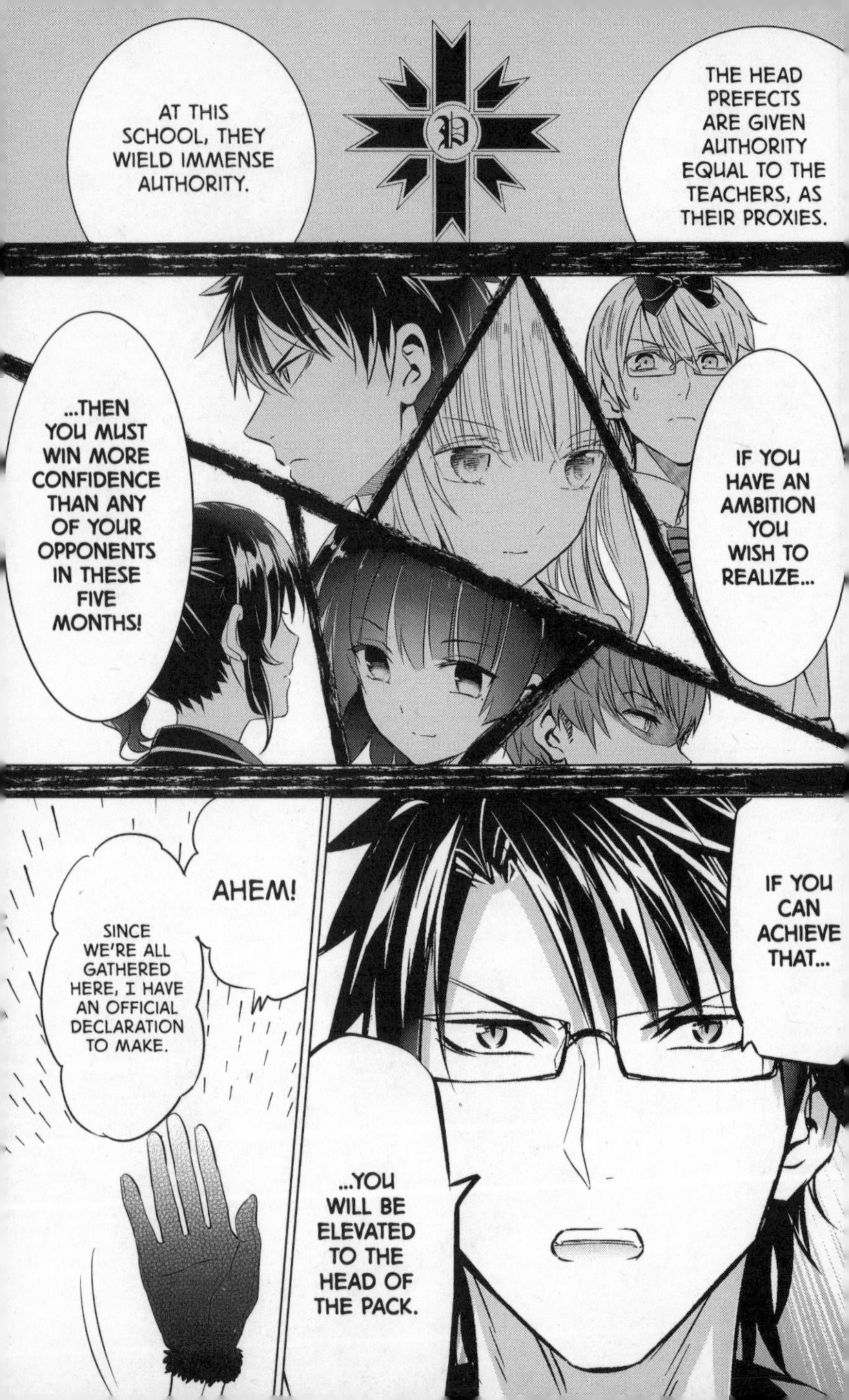
THE HEAD PREFECTS ARE GIVEN AUTHORITY EQUAL TO THE TEACHERS, AS THEIR PROXIES.
AT THIS SCHOOL, THEY WIELD IMMENSE AUTHORITY.
IF YOU HAVE AN AMBITION YOU WISH TO REALIZE...
...THEN YOU MUST WIN MORE CONFIDENCE THAN ANY OF YOUR OPPONENTS IN THESE FIVE MONTHS!
IF YOU CAN ACHIEVE THAT...
...YOU WILL BE ELEVATED TO THE HEAD OF THE PACK.
AHEM!
SINCE WE'RE ALL GATHERED HERE, I HAVE AN OFFICIAL DECLARATION TO MAKE.

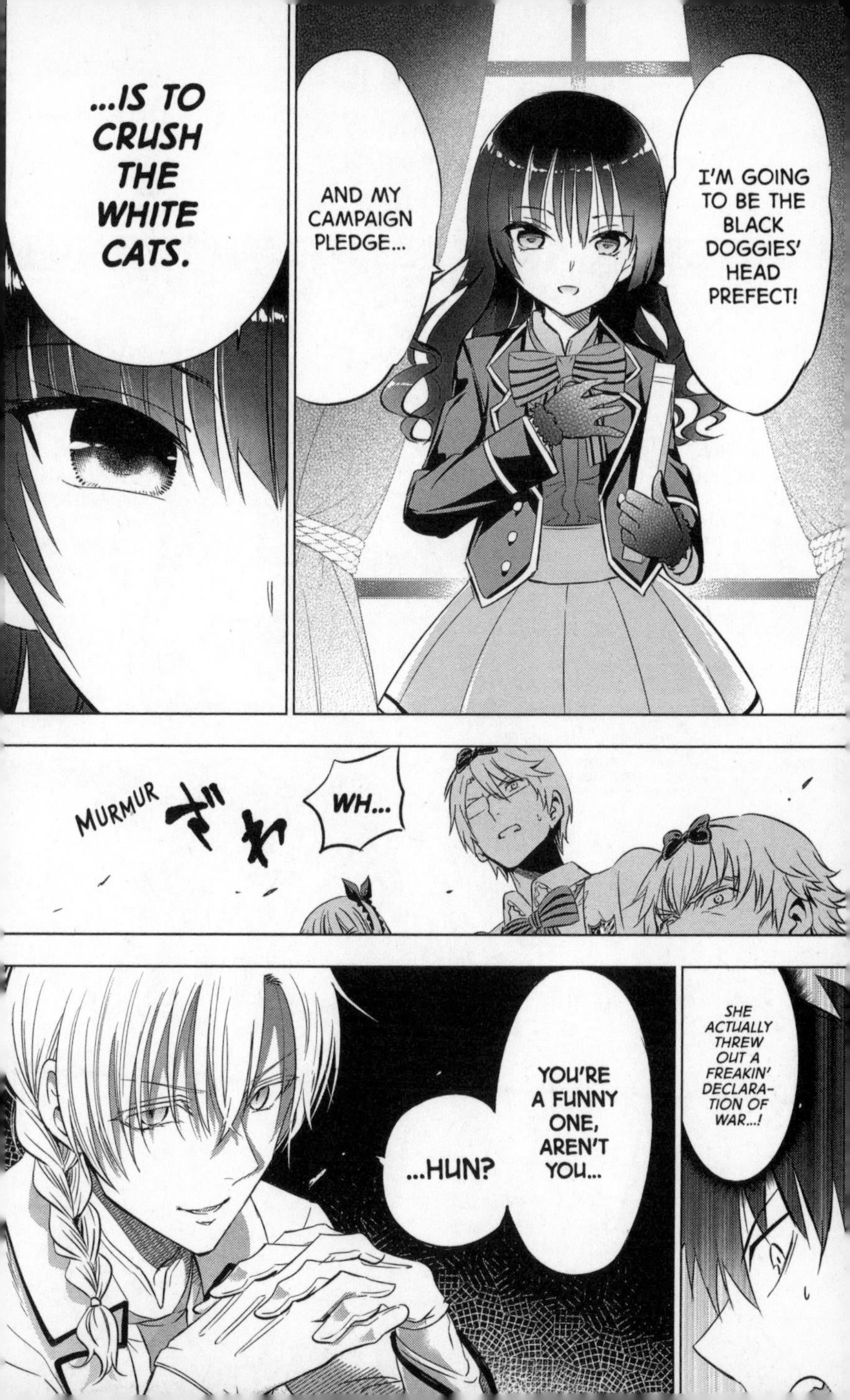
I'M GOING TO BE THE BLACK DOGGIES' HEAD PREFECT!
AND MY CAMPAIGN PLEDGE...
...IS TO CRUSH THE WHITE CATS.
WH...
ざわ
MURMUR
SHE ACTUALLY THREW OUT A FREAKIN' DECLARATION OF WAR...!
YOU'RE A FUNNY ONE, AREN'T YOU...
...HUN?

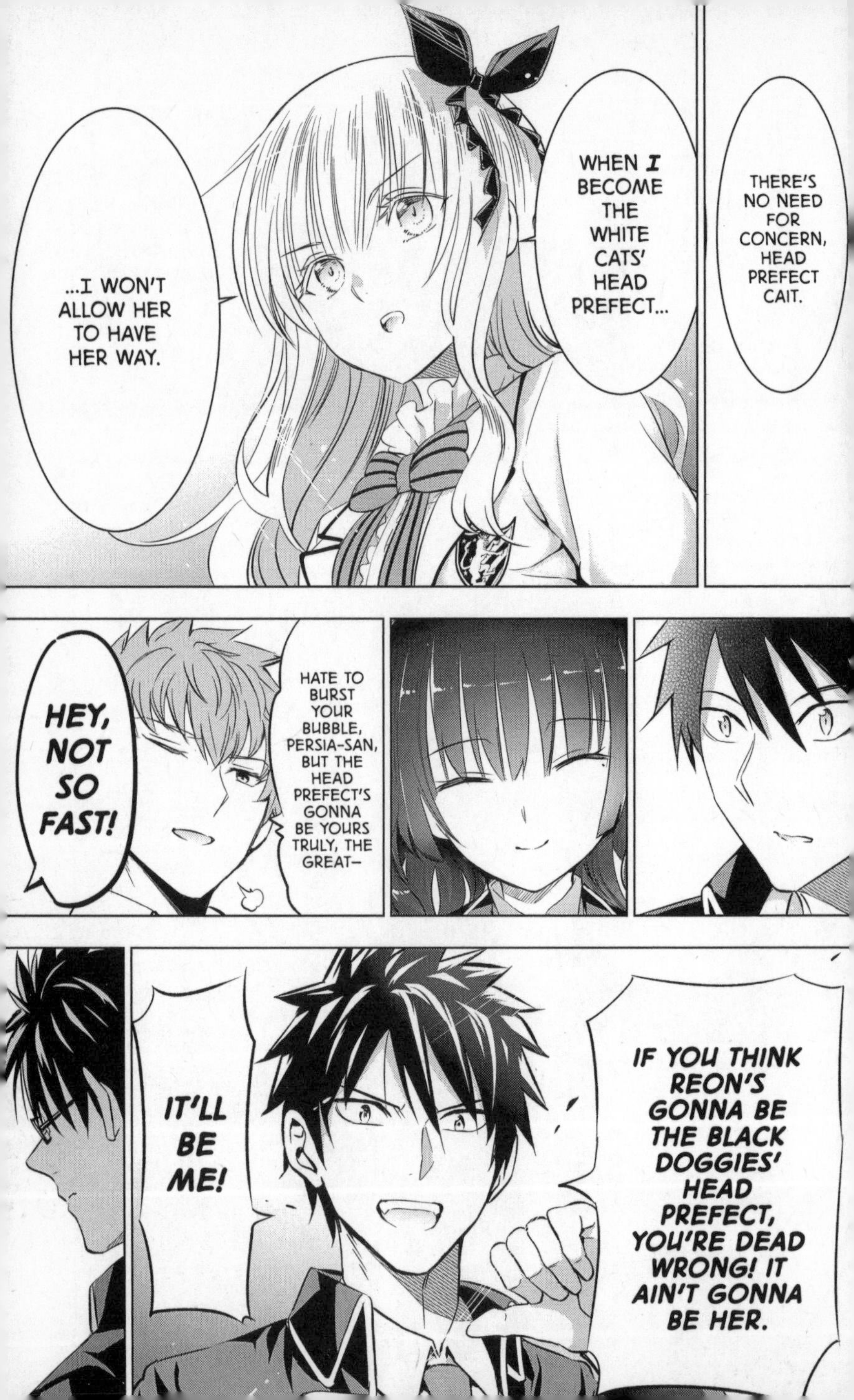
THERE'S NO NEED FOR CONCERN, HEAD PREFECT CAIT.
WHEN *I* BECOME THE WHITE CATS' HEAD PREFECT...
...I WON'T ALLOW HER TO HAVE HER WAY.
HATE TO BURST YOUR BUBBLE, PERSIA-SAN, BUT THE HEAD PREFECT'S GONNA BE YOURS TRULY, THE GREAT—
HEY, NOT SO FAST!
IF YOU THINK REON'S GONNA BE THE BLACK DOGGIES' HEAD PREFECT, YOU'RE DEAD WRONG! IT AIN'T GONNA BE HER.
IT'LL BE ME!

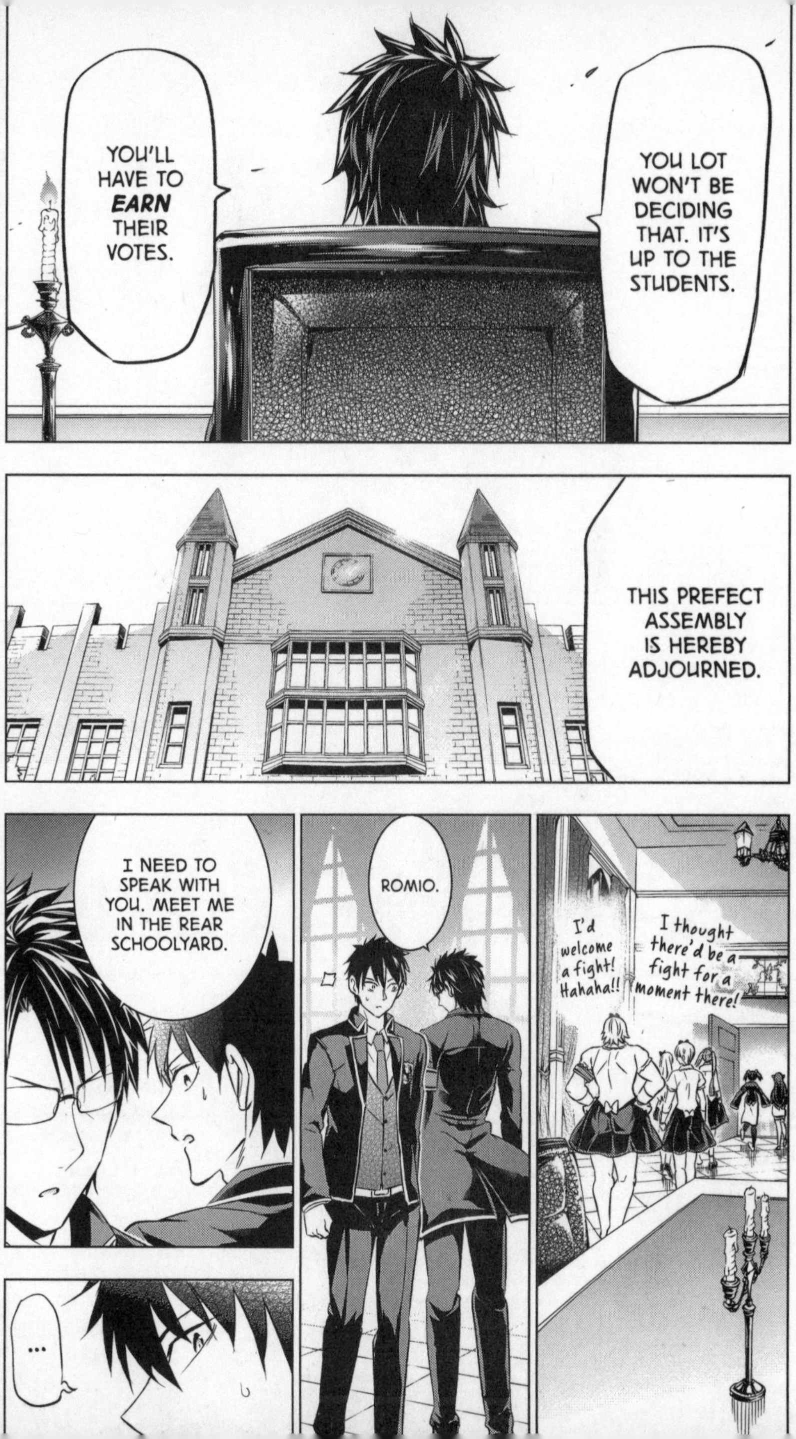
YOU LOT WON'T BE DECIDING THAT. IT'S UP TO THE STUDENTS.
YOU'LL HAVE TO **EARN** THEIR VOTES.
THIS PREFECT ASSEMBLY IS HEREBY ADJOURNED.
I thought there'd be a fight for a moment there!
I'd welcome a fight! Hahaha!!
ROMIO.
I NEED TO SPEAK WITH YOU. MEET ME IN THE REAR SCHOOLYARD.
...

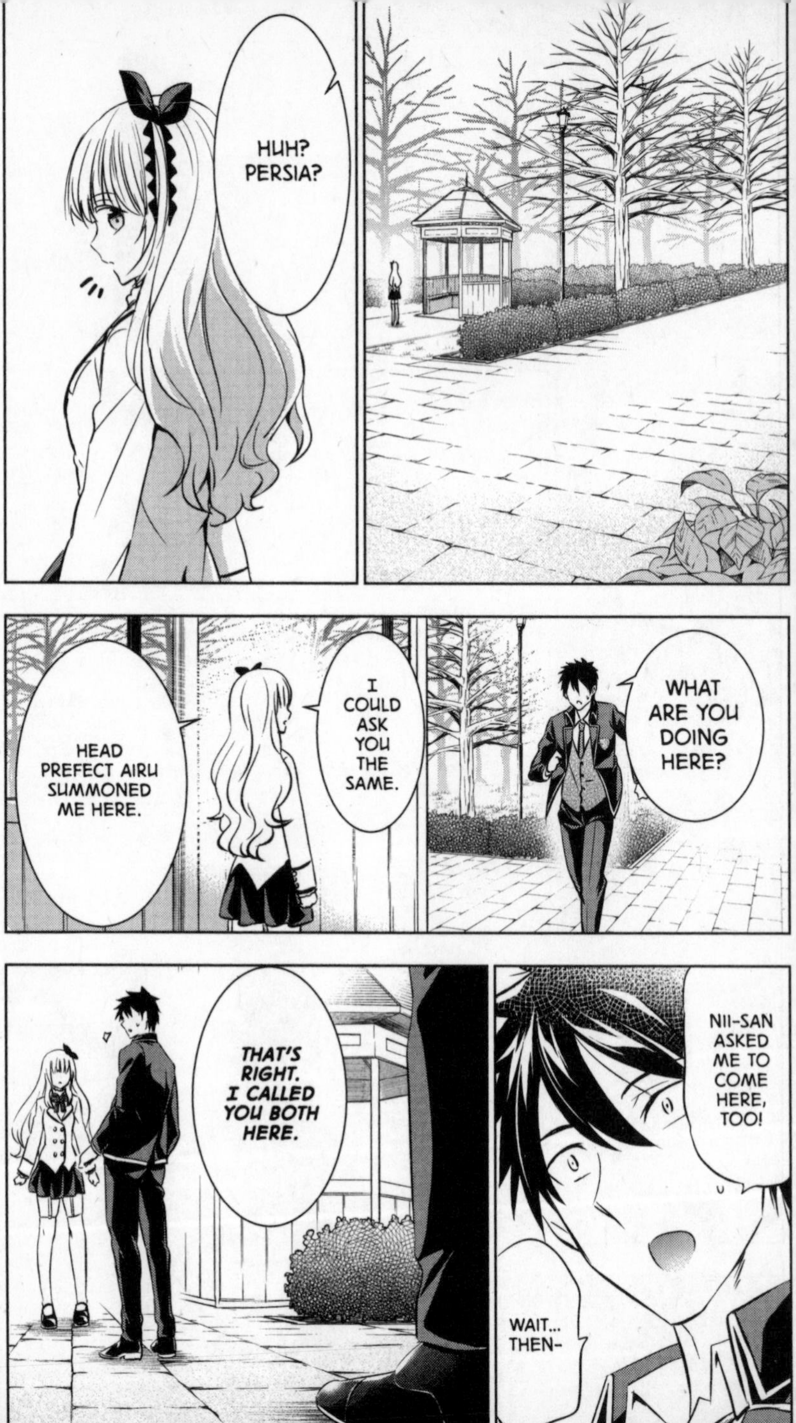
HUH? PERSIA?
WHAT ARE YOU DOING HERE?
I COULD ASK YOU THE SAME.
HEAD PREFECT AIRU SUMMONED ME HERE.
NII-SAN ASKED ME TO COME HERE, TOO!
WAIT... THEN-
THAT'S RIGHT. I CALLED YOU BOTH HERE.

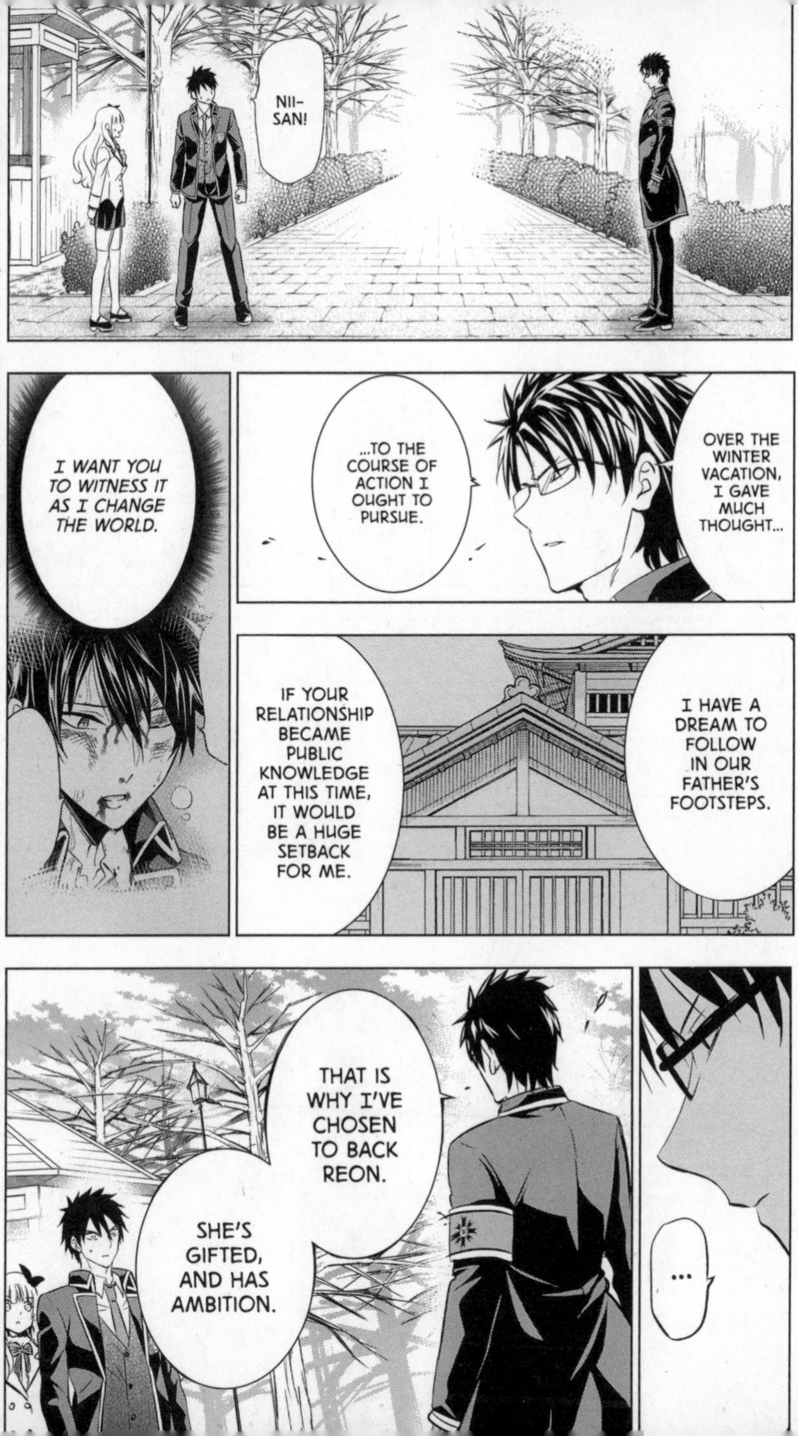
NII-SAN!
OVER THE WINTER VACATION, I GAVE MUCH THOUGHT...
...TO THE COURSE OF ACTION I OUGHT TO PURSUE.
I HAVE A DREAM TO FOLLOW IN OUR FATHER'S FOOTSTEPS.
IF YOUR RELATIONSHIP BECAME PUBLIC KNOWLEDGE AT THIS TIME, IT WOULD BE A HUGE SETBACK FOR ME.
I WANT YOU TO WITNESS IT AS I CHANGE THE WORLD.
...
THAT IS WHY I'VE CHOSEN TO BACK REON.
SHE'S GIFTED, AND HAS AMBITION.

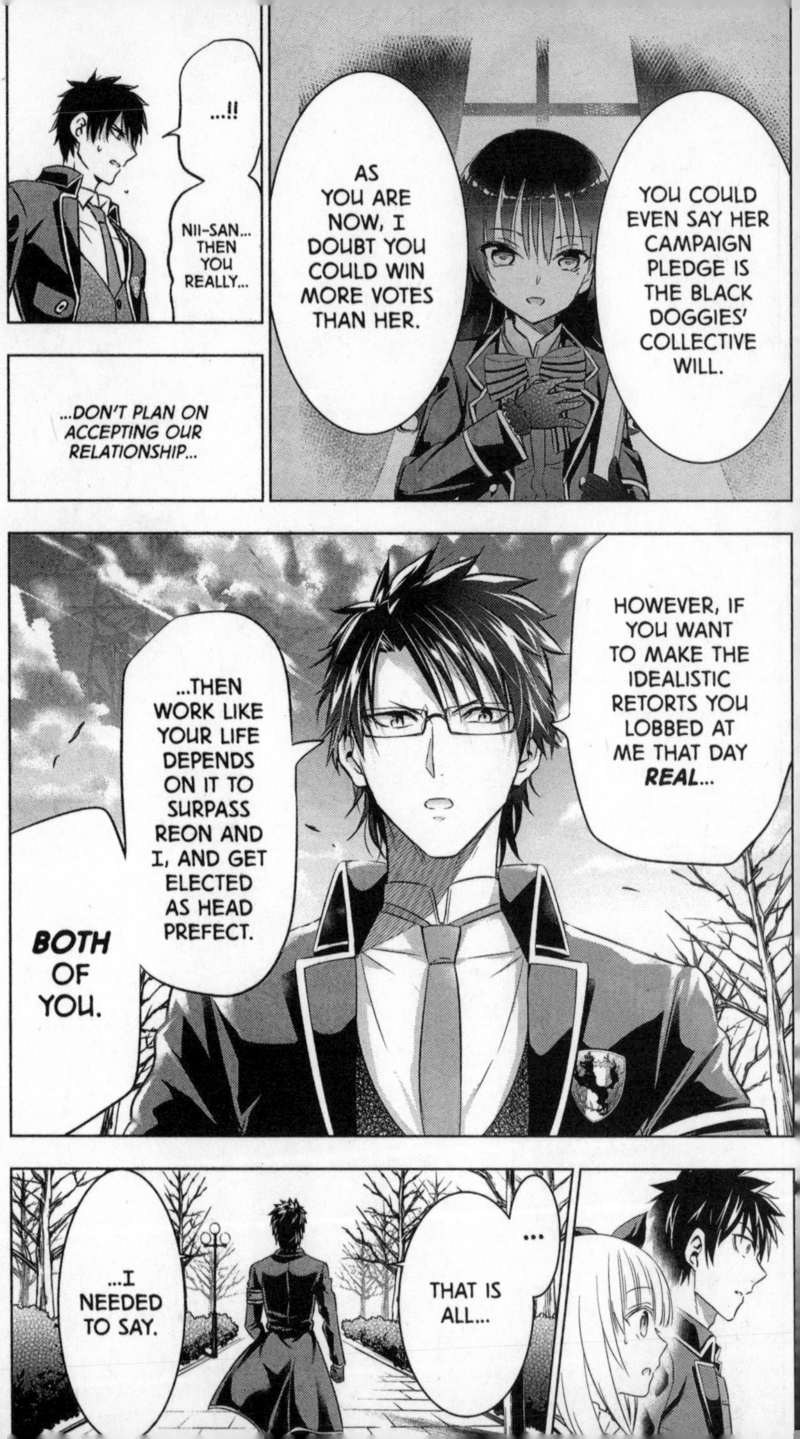
YOU COULD EVEN SAY HER CAMPAIGN PLEDGE IS THE BLACK DOGGIES' COLLECTIVE WILL.
AS YOU ARE NOW, I DOUBT YOU COULD WIN MORE VOTES THAN HER.
...!!
NII-SAN... THEN YOU REALLY...
...DON'T PLAN ON ACCEPTING OUR RELATIONSHIP...
HOWEVER, IF YOU WANT TO MAKE THE IDEALISTIC RETORTS YOU LOBBED AT ME THAT DAY ***REAL***...
...THEN WORK LIKE YOUR LIFE DEPENDS ON IT TO SURPASS REON AND I, AND GET ELECTED AS HEAD PREFECT.
BOTH OF YOU.
...
THAT IS ALL...
...I NEEDED TO SAY.

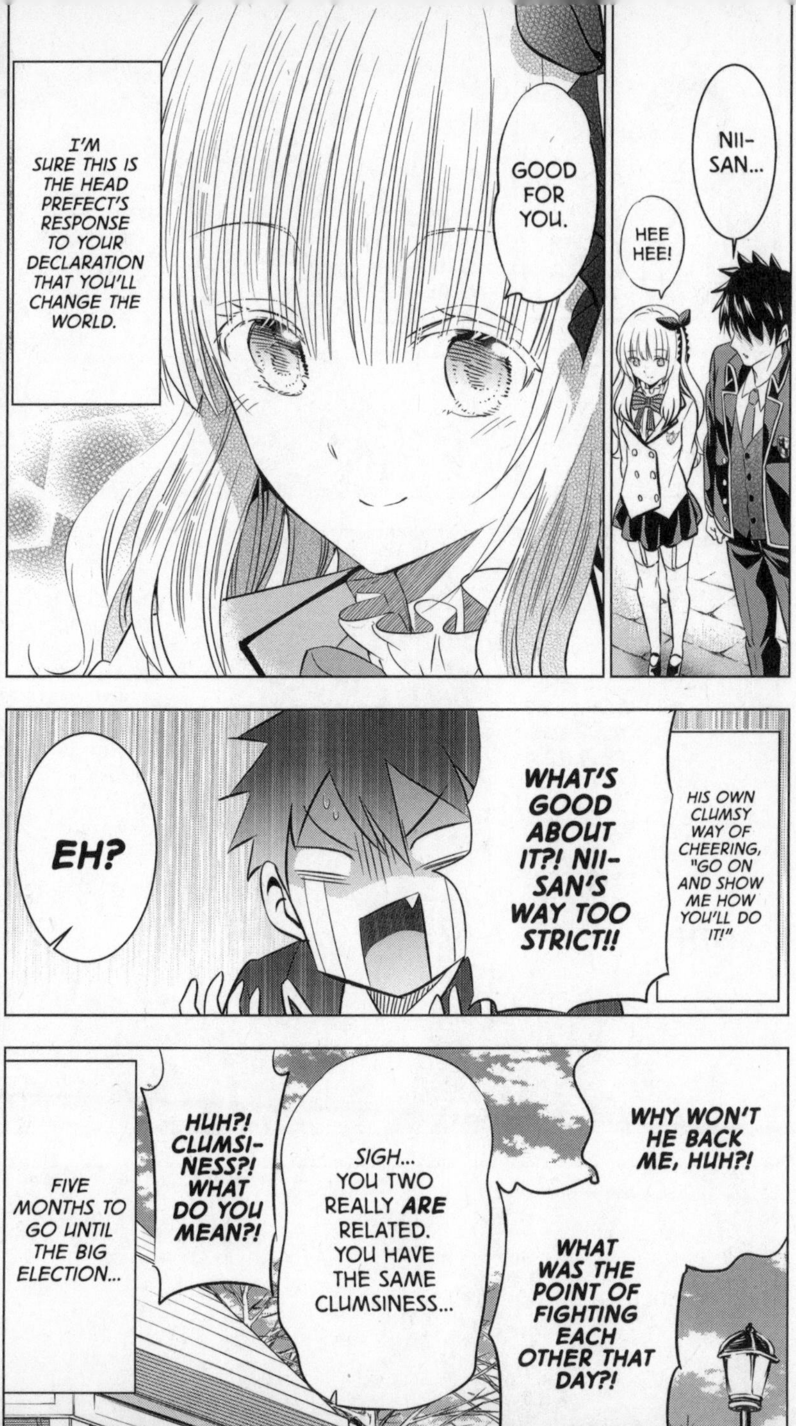
NII-SAN...
HEE HEE!
GOOD FOR YOU.
I'M SURE THIS IS THE HEAD PREFECT'S RESPONSE TO YOUR DECLARATION THAT YOU'LL CHANGE THE WORLD.
HIS OWN CLUMSY WAY OF CHEERING, "GO ON AND SHOW ME HOW YOU'LL DO IT!"
WHAT'S GOOD ABOUT IT?! NII-SAN'S WAY TOO STRICT!!
EH?
WHY WON'T HE BACK ME, HUH?!
WHAT WAS THE POINT OF FIGHTING EACH OTHER THAT DAY?!
SIGH... YOU TWO REALLY ARE RELATED. YOU HAVE THE SAME CLUMSINESS...
HUH?! CLUMSINESS?! WHAT DO YOU MEAN?!
FIVE MONTHS TO GO UNTIL THE BIG ELECTION...

ACT 63:

ROMIO & HASUKI & THE YEOMAN JOB

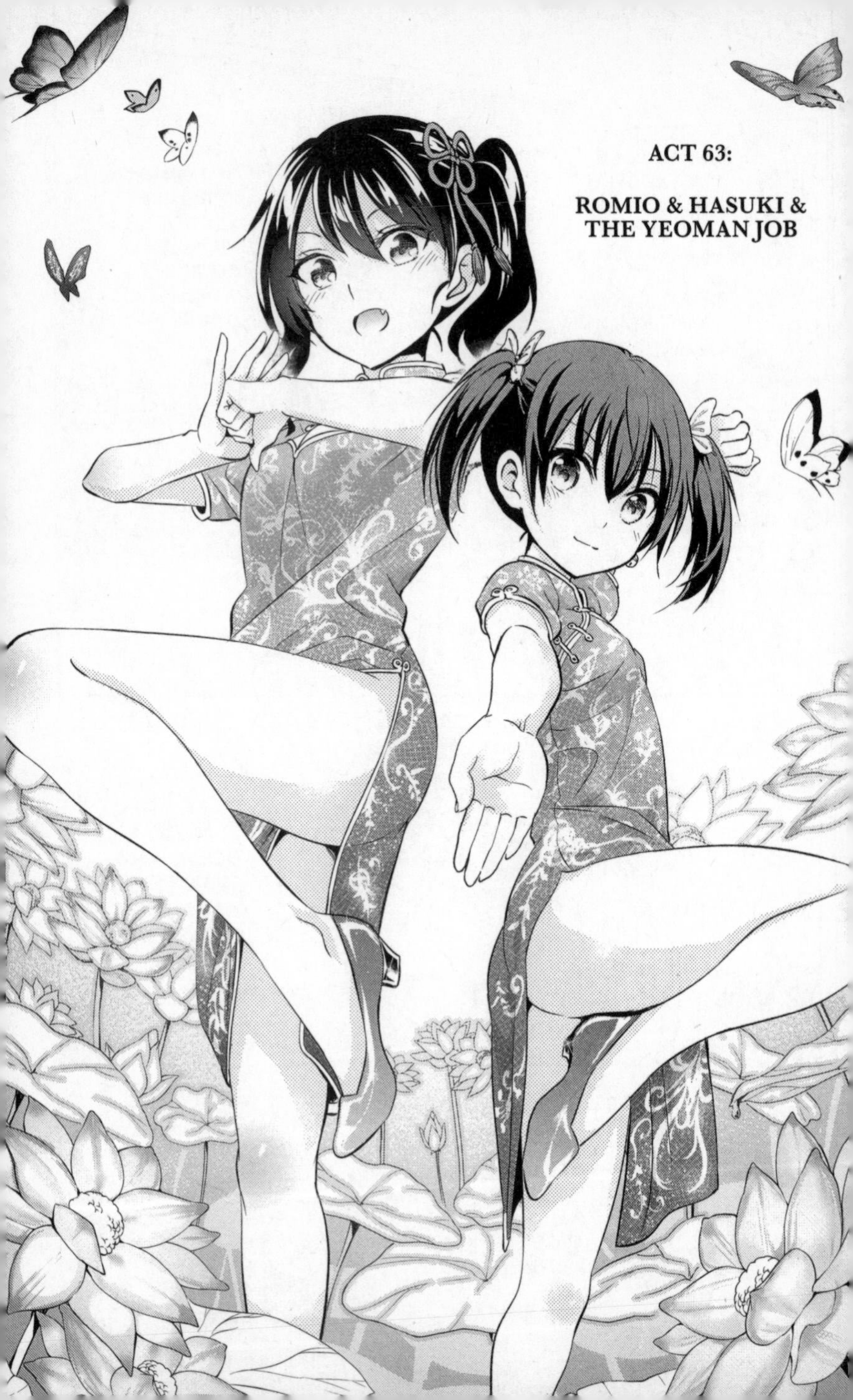

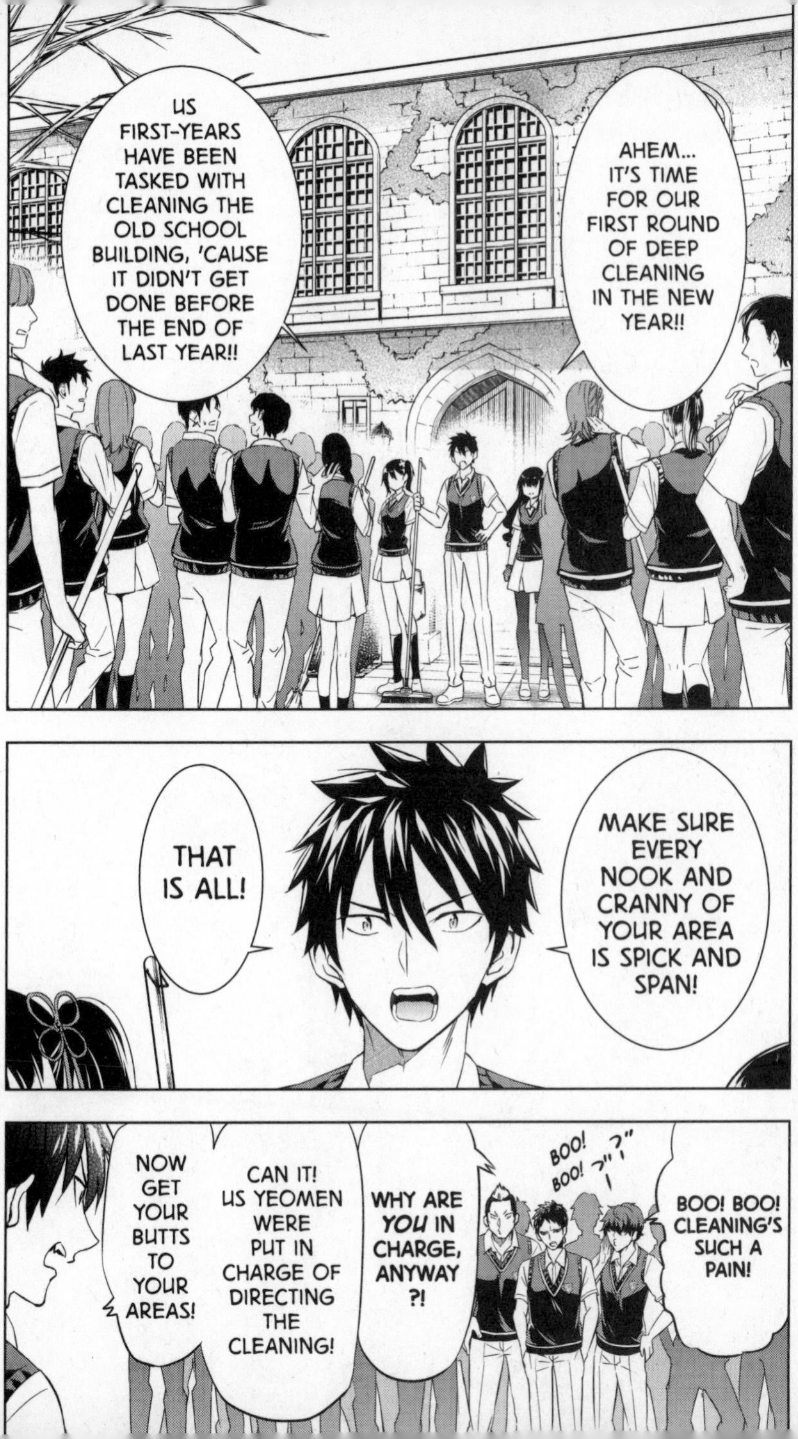
AHEM... IT'S TIME FOR OUR FIRST ROUND OF DEEP CLEANING IN THE NEW YEAR!!
US FIRST-YEARS HAVE BEEN TASKED WITH CLEANING THE OLD SCHOOL BUILDING, 'CAUSE IT DIDN'T GET DONE BEFORE THE END OF LAST YEAR!!
MAKE SURE EVERY NOOK AND CRANNY OF YOUR AREA IS SPICK AND SPAN!
THAT IS ALL!
BOO! BOO! CLEANING'S SUCH A PAIN!
BOO! BOO!
WHY ARE *YOU* IN CHARGE, ANYWAY?!
CAN IT! US YEOMEN WERE PUT IN CHARGE OF DIRECTING THE CLEANING!
NOW GET YOUR BUTTS TO YOUR AREAS!

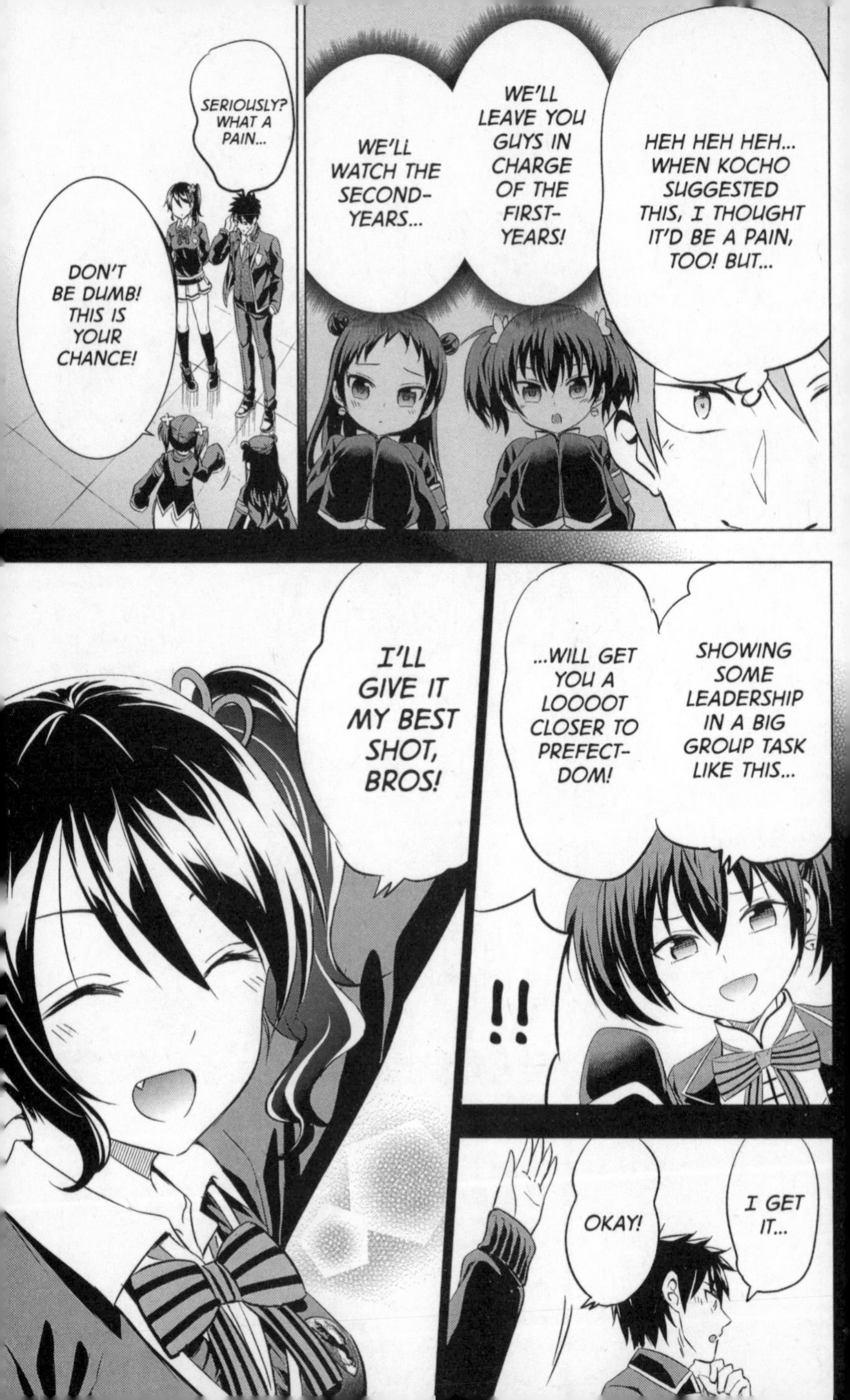
HEH HEH HEH... WHEN KOCHO SUGGESTED THIS, I THOUGHT IT'D BE A PAIN, TOO! BUT...
WE'LL LEAVE YOU GUYS IN CHARGE OF THE FIRST-YEARS!
WE'LL WATCH THE SECOND-YEARS...
SERIOUSLY? WHAT A PAIN...
DON'T BE DUMB! THIS IS YOUR CHANCE!
SHOWING SOME LEADERSHIP IN A BIG GROUP TASK LIKE THIS...
...WILL GET YOU A LOOOOT CLOSER TO PREFECT-DOM!
!!
I GET IT...
OKAY!
I'LL GIVE IT MY BEST SHOT, BROS!

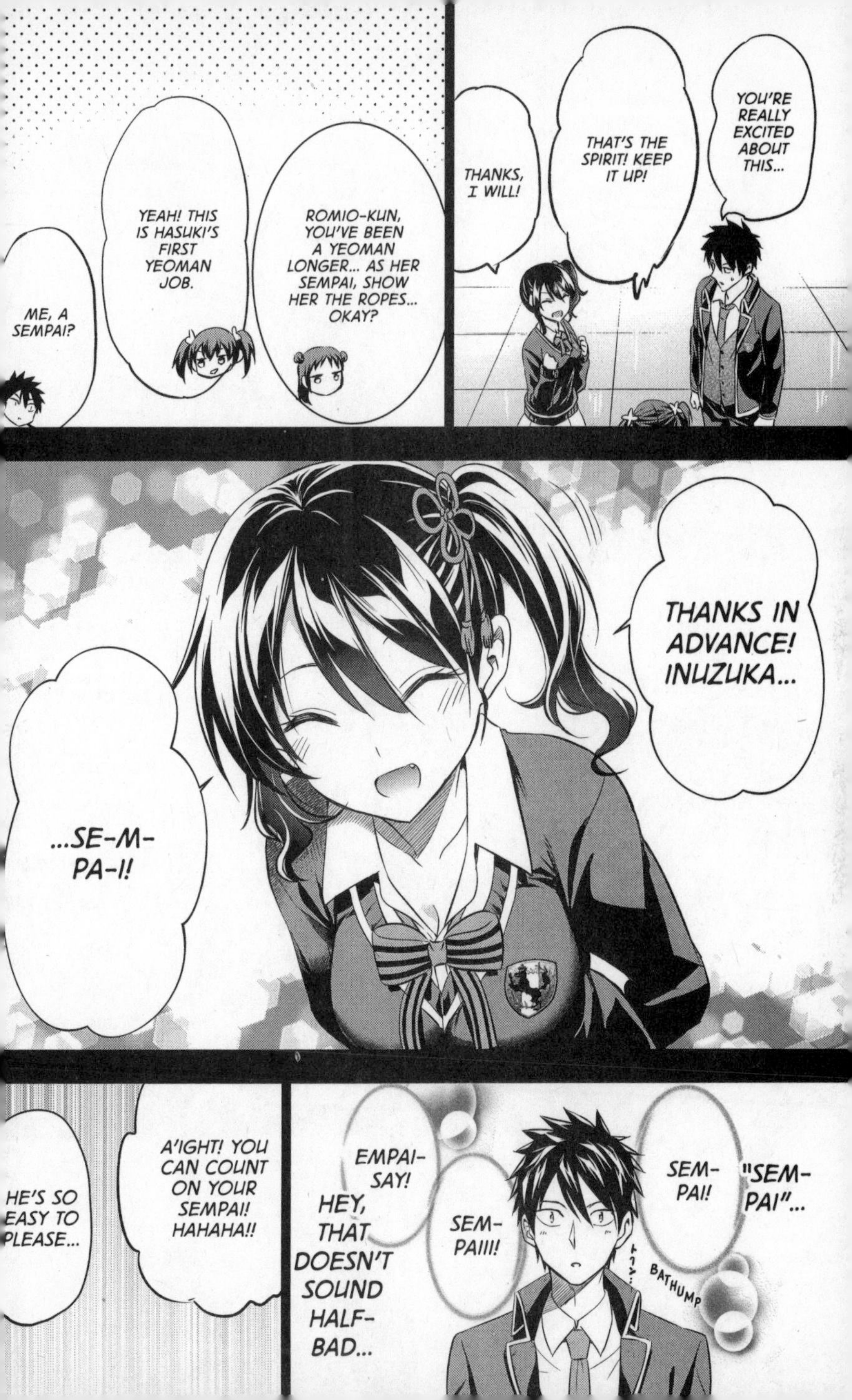
YOU'RE REALLY EXCITED ABOUT THIS...
THAT'S THE SPIRIT! KEEP IT UP!
THANKS, I WILL!
ROMIO-KUN, YOU'VE BEEN A YEOMAN LONGER... AS HER SEMPAI, SHOW HER THE ROPES... OKAY?
YEAH! THIS IS HASUKI'S FIRST YEOMAN JOB.
ME, A SEMPAI?
THANKS IN ADVANCE! INUZUKA...
...SE-M-PA-I!
"SEM-PAI"...
SEM-PAI!
EMPAI-SAY!
SEM-PAIII!
HEY, THAT DOESN'T SOUND HALF-BAD...
BATHUMP
A'IGHT! YOU CAN COUNT ON YOUR SEMPAI! HAHAHA!!
HE'S SO EASY TO PLEASE...

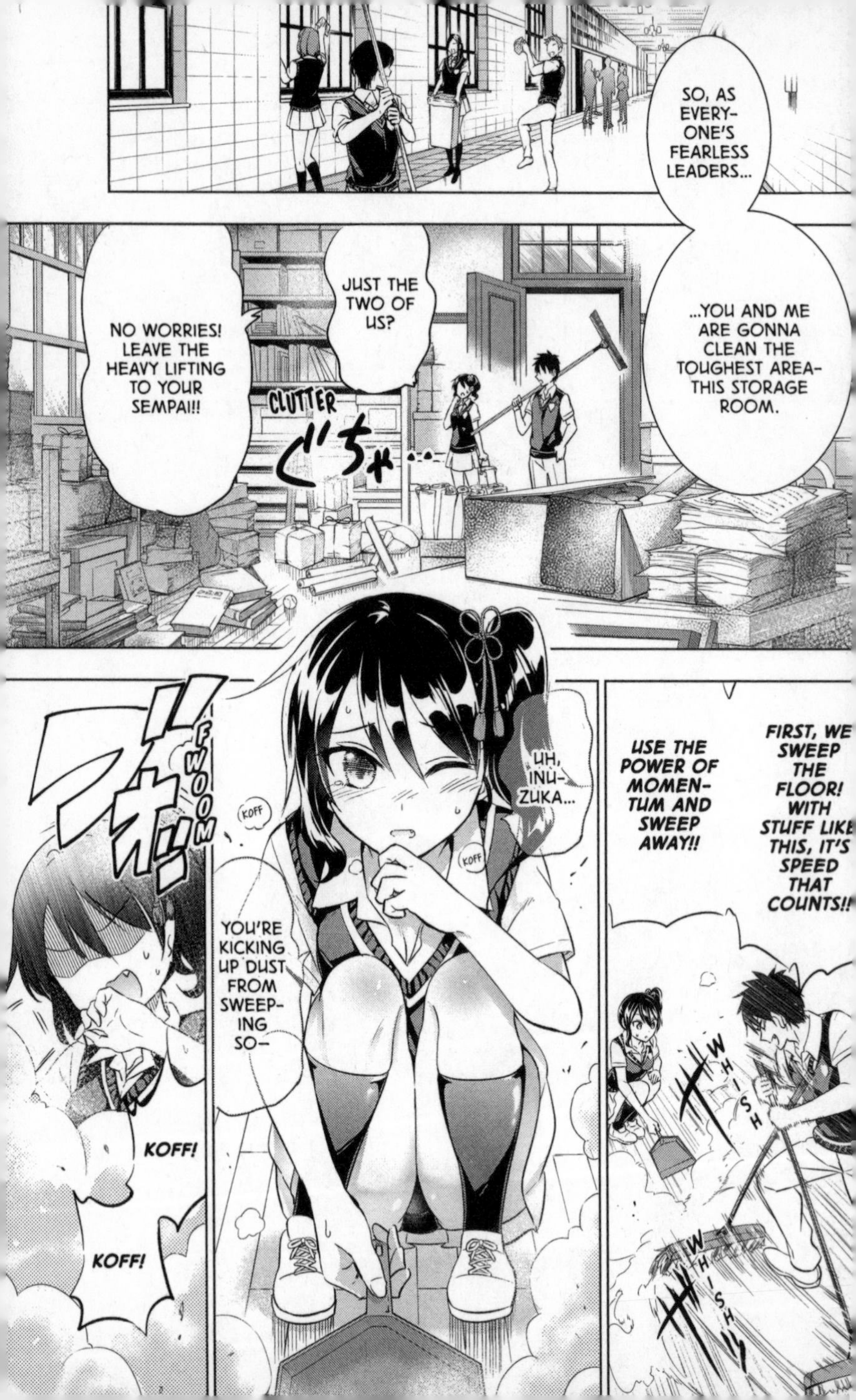
SO, AS EVERYONE'S FEARLESS LEADERS...
...YOU AND ME ARE GONNA CLEAN THE TOUGHEST AREA-THIS STORAGE ROOM.
JUST THE TWO OF US?
CLUTTER
NO WORRIES! LEAVE THE HEAVY LIFTING TO YOUR SEMPAI!!
FIRST, WE SWEEP THE FLOOR! WITH STUFF LIKE THIS, IT'S SPEED THAT COUNTS!!
USE THE POWER OF MOMENTUM AND SWEEP AWAY!!
WHISH
WHISH
UH, INUZUKA...
KOFF
KOFF
YOU'RE KICKING UP DUST FROM SWEEPING SO—
FWOOOM
KOFF!
KOFF!

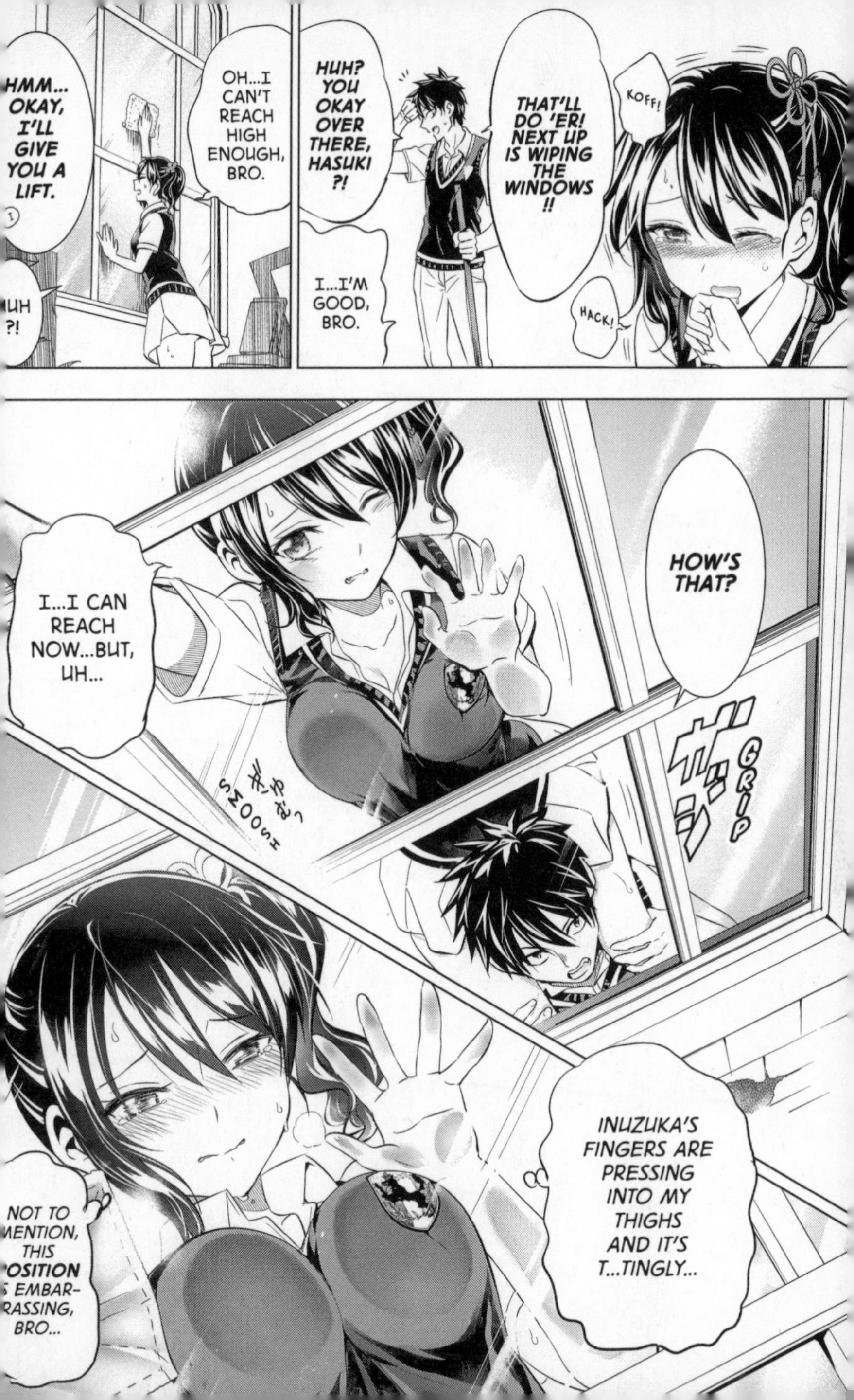
KOFF!
THAT'LL DO 'ER! NEXT UP IS WIPING THE WINDOWS !!
HACK!
HUH? YOU OKAY OVER THERE, HASUKI ?!
I...I'M GOOD, BRO.
OH...I CAN'T REACH HIGH ENOUGH, BRO.
HMM... OKAY, I'LL GIVE YOU A LIFT.
UH ?!
HOW'S THAT?
GRIP
I...I CAN REACH NOW...BUT, UH...
SWOOSH
INUZUKA'S FINGERS ARE PRESSING INTO MY THIGHS AND IT'S T...TINGLY...
NOT TO MENTION, THIS OSITION S EMBAR-RASSING, BRO...

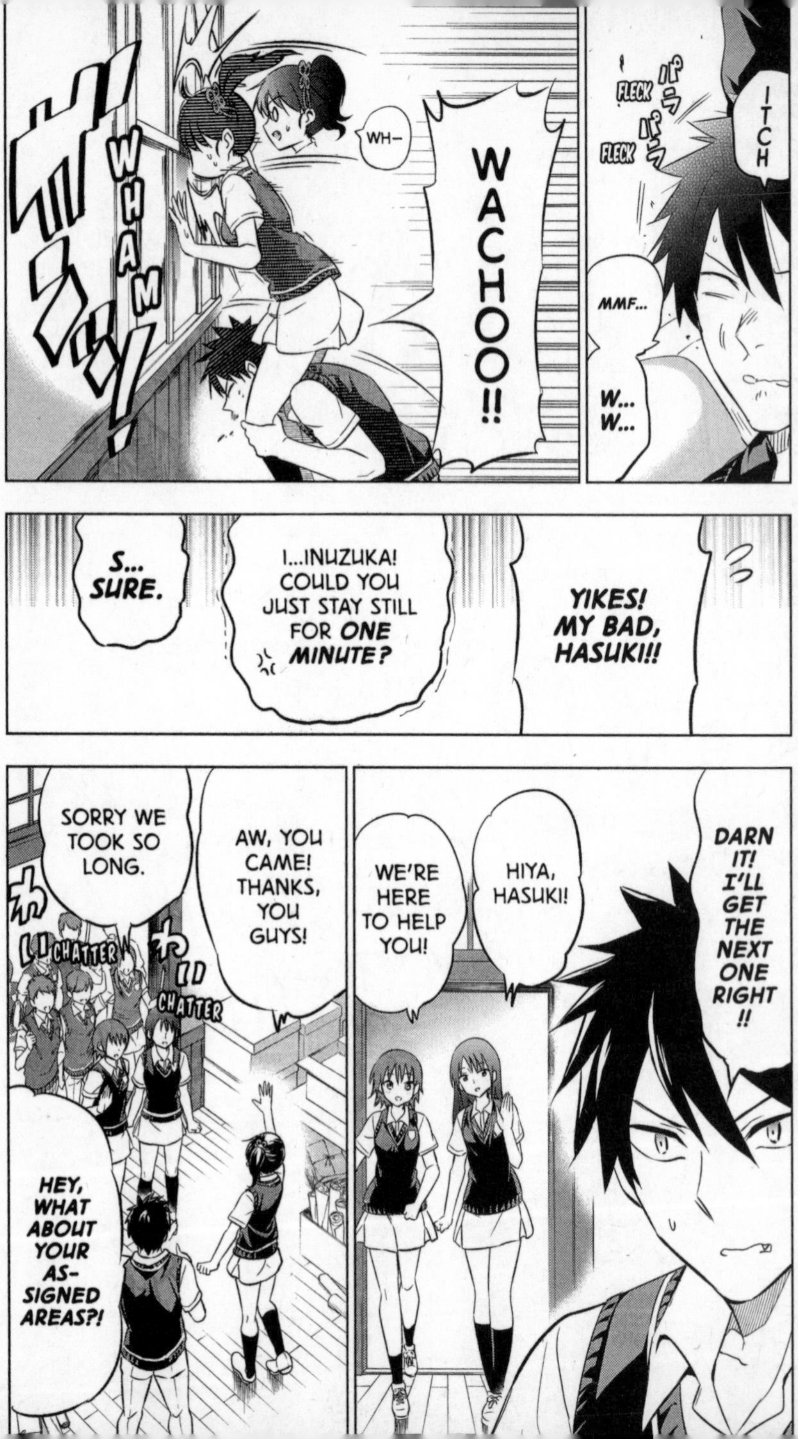
ITCH
FLECK
FLECK
MMF...
W... W...
WACHOO!!
WH–
WHAM
YIKES! MY BAD, HASUKI!!
I...INUZUKA! COULD YOU JUST STAY STILL FOR ONE MINUTE?
S... SURE.
DARN IT! I'LL GET THE NEXT ONE RIGHT!!
HIYA, HASUKI!
WE'RE HERE TO HELP YOU!
AW, YOU CAME! THANKS, YOU GUYS!
SORRY WE TOOK SO LONG.
CHATTER
CHATTER
HEY, WHAT ABOUT YOUR AS-SIGNED AREAS?!

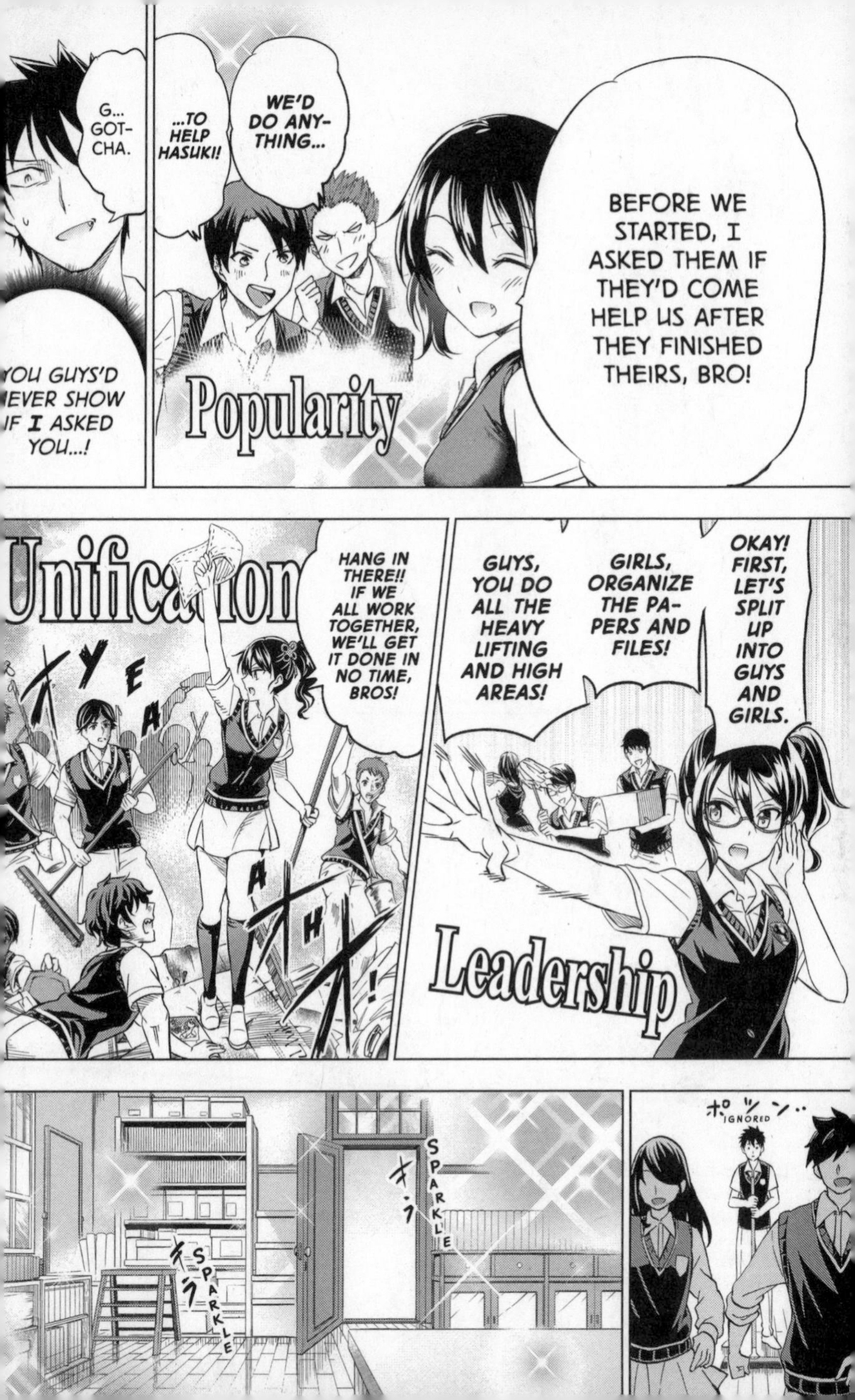
BEFORE WE STARTED, I ASKED THEM IF THEY'D COME HELP US AFTER THEY FINISHED THEIRS, BRO!
WE'D DO ANY-THING...
...TO HELP HASUKI!
Popularity
G... GOT-CHA.
YOU GUYS'D NEVER SHOW IF I ASKED YOU...!
OKAY! FIRST, LET'S SPLIT UP INTO GUYS AND GIRLS.
GIRLS, ORGANIZE THE PA-PERS AND FILES!
GUYS, YOU DO ALL THE HEAVY LIFTING AND HIGH AREAS!
Leadership
HANG IN THERE!! IF WE ALL WORK TOGETHER, WE'LL GET IT DONE IN NO TIME, BROS!
Unification
YEAAH!
IGNORED
SPARKLE
SPARKLE

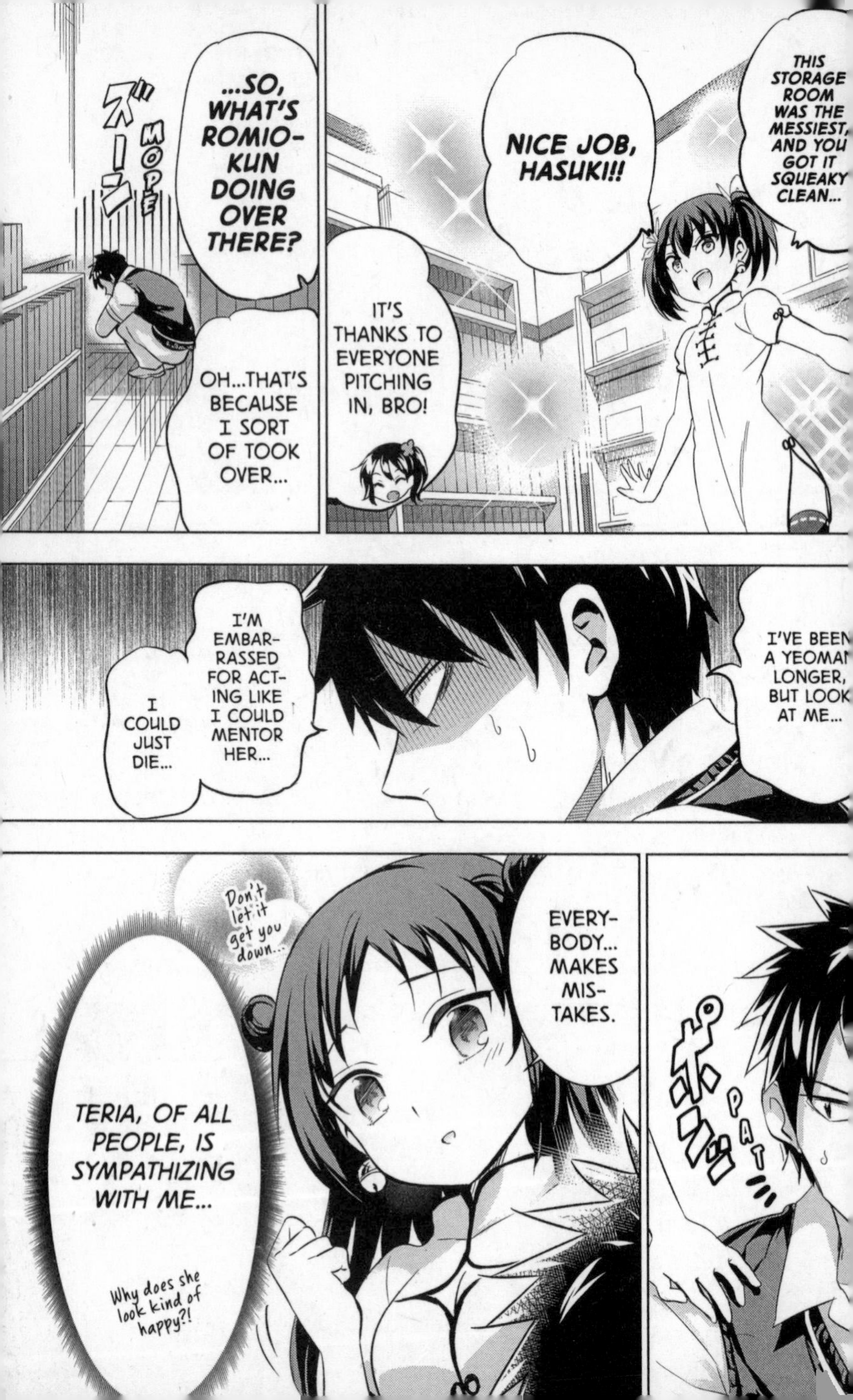
THIS STORAGE ROOM WAS THE MESSIEST, AND YOU GOT IT SQUEAKY CLEAN...
NICE JOB, HASUKI!!
IT'S THANKS TO EVERYONE PITCHING IN, BRO!
...SO, WHAT'S ROMIO-KUN DOING OVER THERE?
MOPE
OH...THAT'S BECAUSE I SORT OF TOOK OVER...
I'VE BEEN A YEOMAN LONGER, BUT LOOK AT ME...
I'M EMBARRASSED FOR ACTING LIKE I COULD MENTOR HER...
I COULD JUST DIE...
PAT
EVERYBODY... MAKES MISTAKES.
Don't let it get you down...
TERIA, OF ALL PEOPLE, IS SYMPATHIZING WITH ME...
Why does she look kind of happy?!

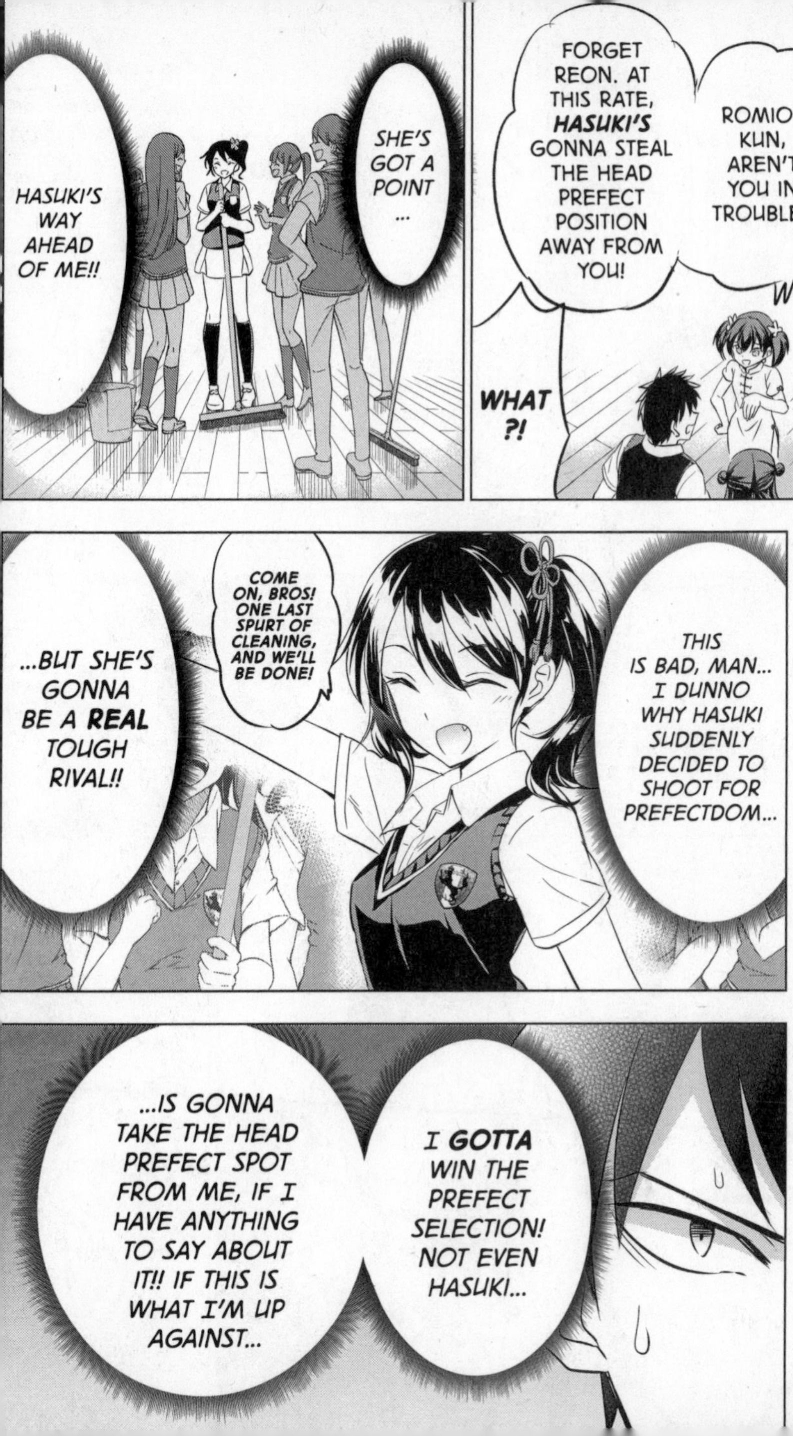
ROMIO-KUN, AREN'T YOU IN TROUBLE?
FORGET REON. AT THIS RATE, **HASUKI'S** GONNA STEAL THE HEAD PREFECT POSITION AWAY FROM YOU!
WHAT ?!
SHE'S GOT A POINT ...
HASUKI'S WAY AHEAD OF ME!!
THIS IS BAD, MAN... I DUNNO WHY HASUKI SUDDENLY DECIDED TO SHOOT FOR PREFECTDOM...
COME ON, BROS! ONE LAST SPURT OF CLEANING, AND WE'LL BE DONE!
...BUT SHE'S GONNA BE A **REAL** TOUGH RIVAL!!
I **GOTTA** WIN THE PREFECT SELECTION! NOT EVEN HASUKI...
...IS GONNA TAKE THE HEAD PREFECT SPOT FROM ME, IF I HAVE ANYTHING TO SAY ABOUT IT!! IF THIS IS WHAT I'M UP AGAINST...

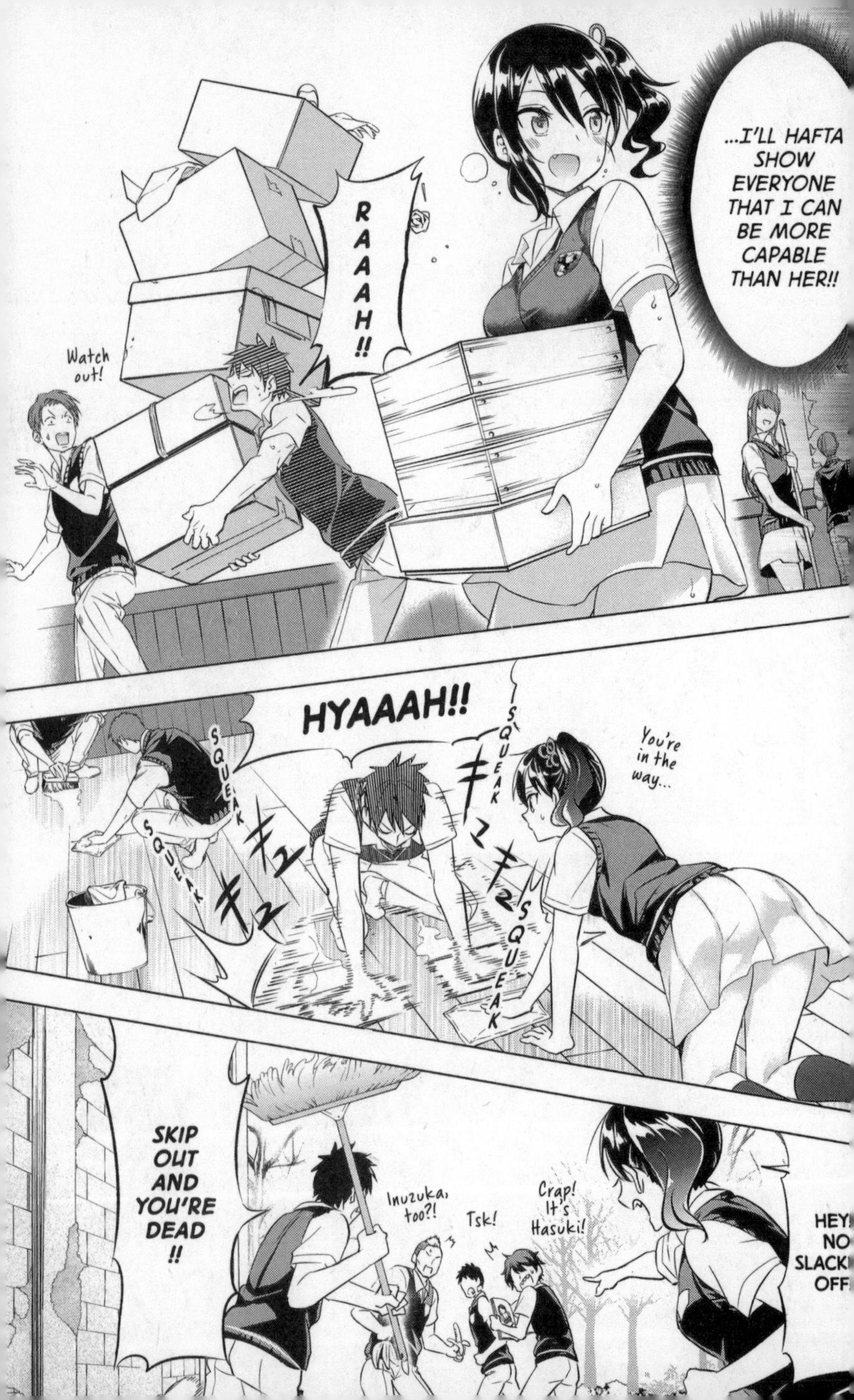
...I'LL HAFTA SHOW EVERYONE THAT I CAN BE MORE CAPABLE THAN HER!!
RAAAAH!!
Watch out!
You're in the way...
SQUEAK
SQUEAK
HYAAAH!!
SQUEAK
SQUEAK
HEY! NO SLACKI OFF
Crap! It's Hasuki!
Tsk!
Inuzuka, too?!
SKIP OUT AND YOU'RE DEAD!!

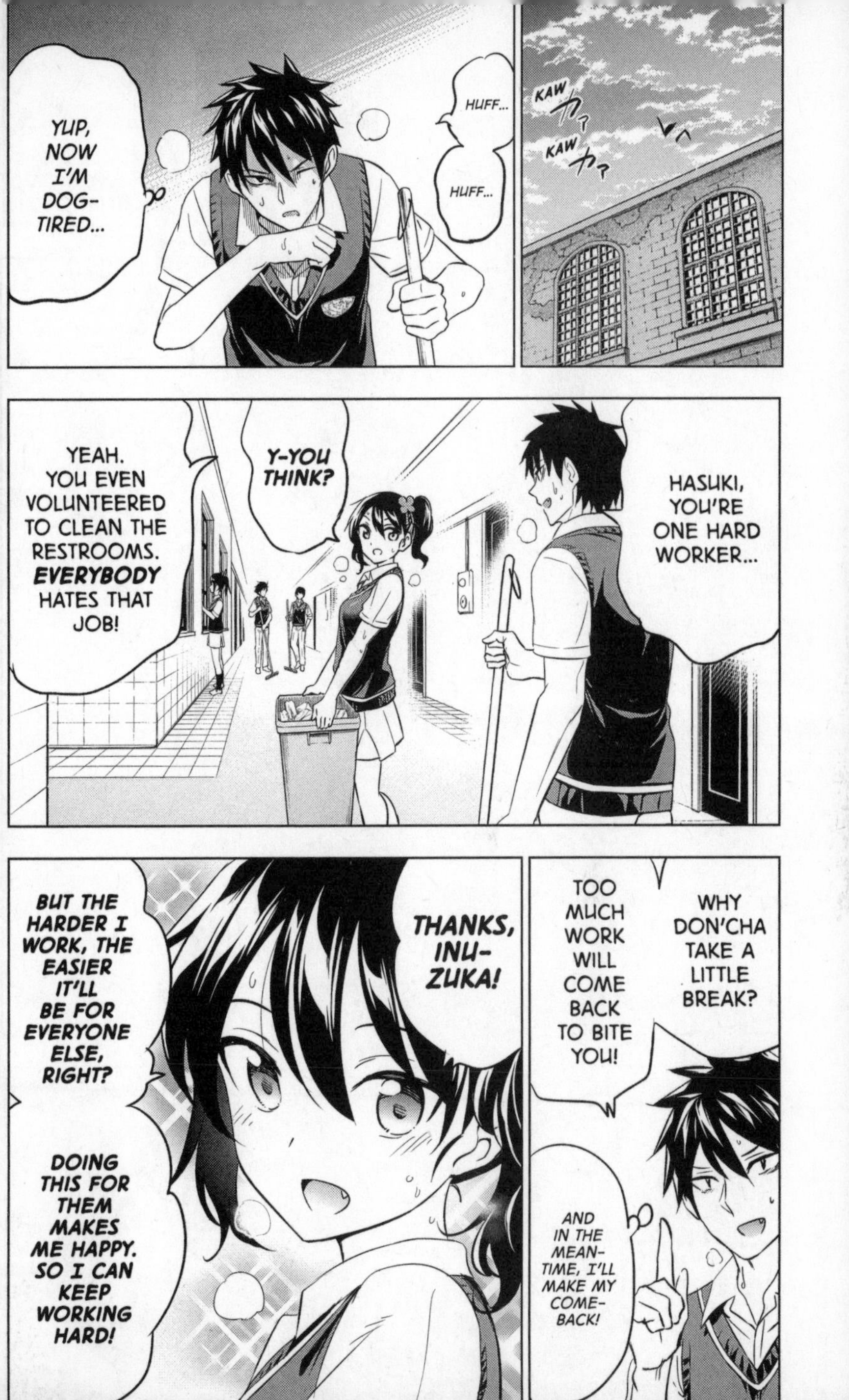
KAW
KAW
HUFF...
HUFF...
YUP, NOW I'M DOG-TIRED...
HASUKI, YOU'RE ONE HARD WORKER...
Y-YOU THINK?
YEAH. YOU EVEN VOLUNTEERED TO CLEAN THE RESTROOMS. EVERYBODY HATES THAT JOB!
WHY DON'CHA TAKE A LITTLE BREAK?
TOO MUCH WORK WILL COME BACK TO BITE YOU!
AND IN THE MEAN-TIME, I'LL MAKE MY COME-BACK!
THANKS, INU-ZUKA!
BUT THE HARDER I WORK, THE EASIER IT'LL BE FOR EVERYONE ELSE, RIGHT?
DOING THIS FOR THEM MAKES ME HAPPY. SO I CAN KEEP WORKING HARD!

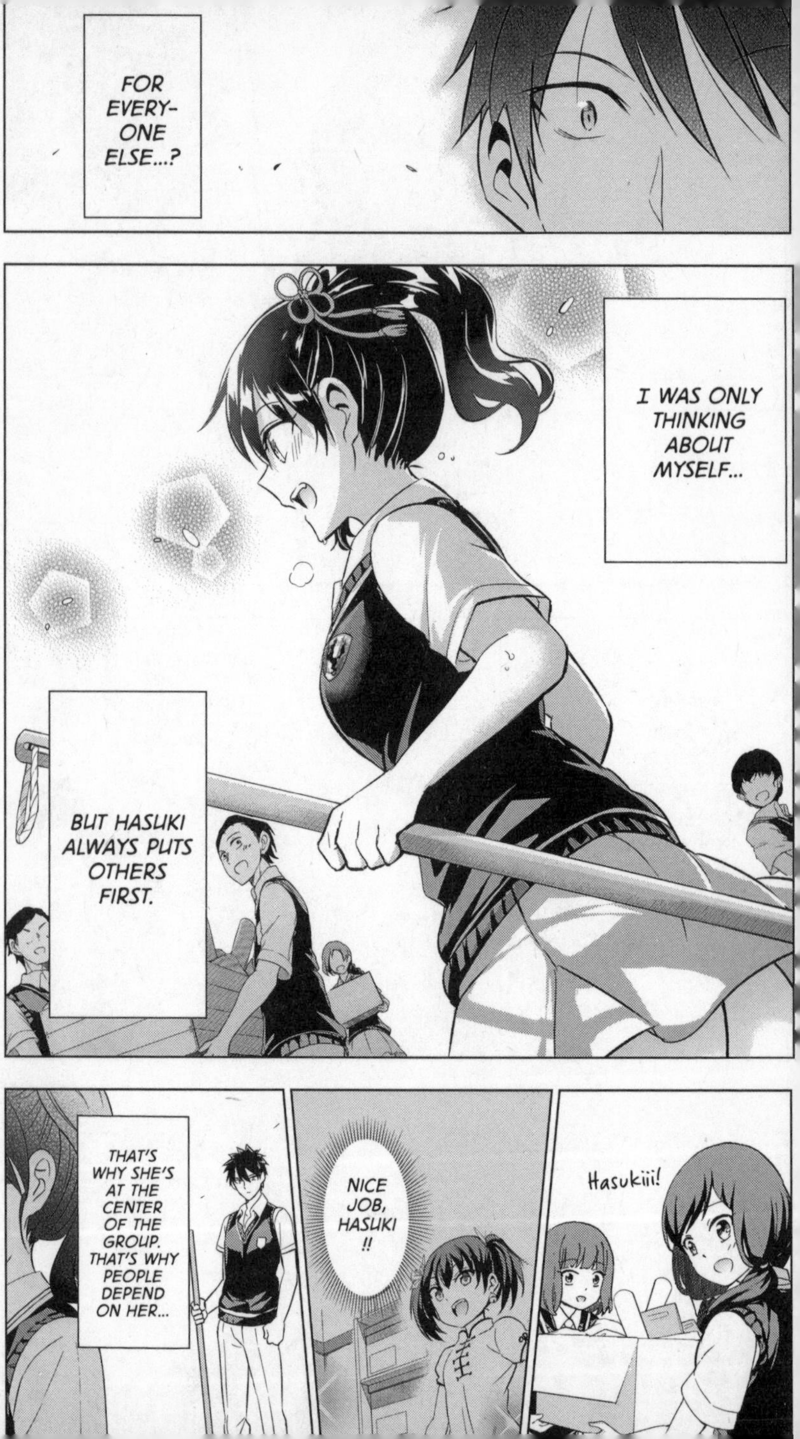
FOR EVERY-ONE ELSE...?
I WAS ONLY THINKING ABOUT MYSELF...
BUT HASUKI ALWAYS PUTS OTHERS FIRST.
Hasukiii!
NICE JOB, HASUKI !!
THAT'S WHY SHE'S AT THE CENTER OF THE GROUP. THAT'S WHY PEOPLE DEPEND ON HER...

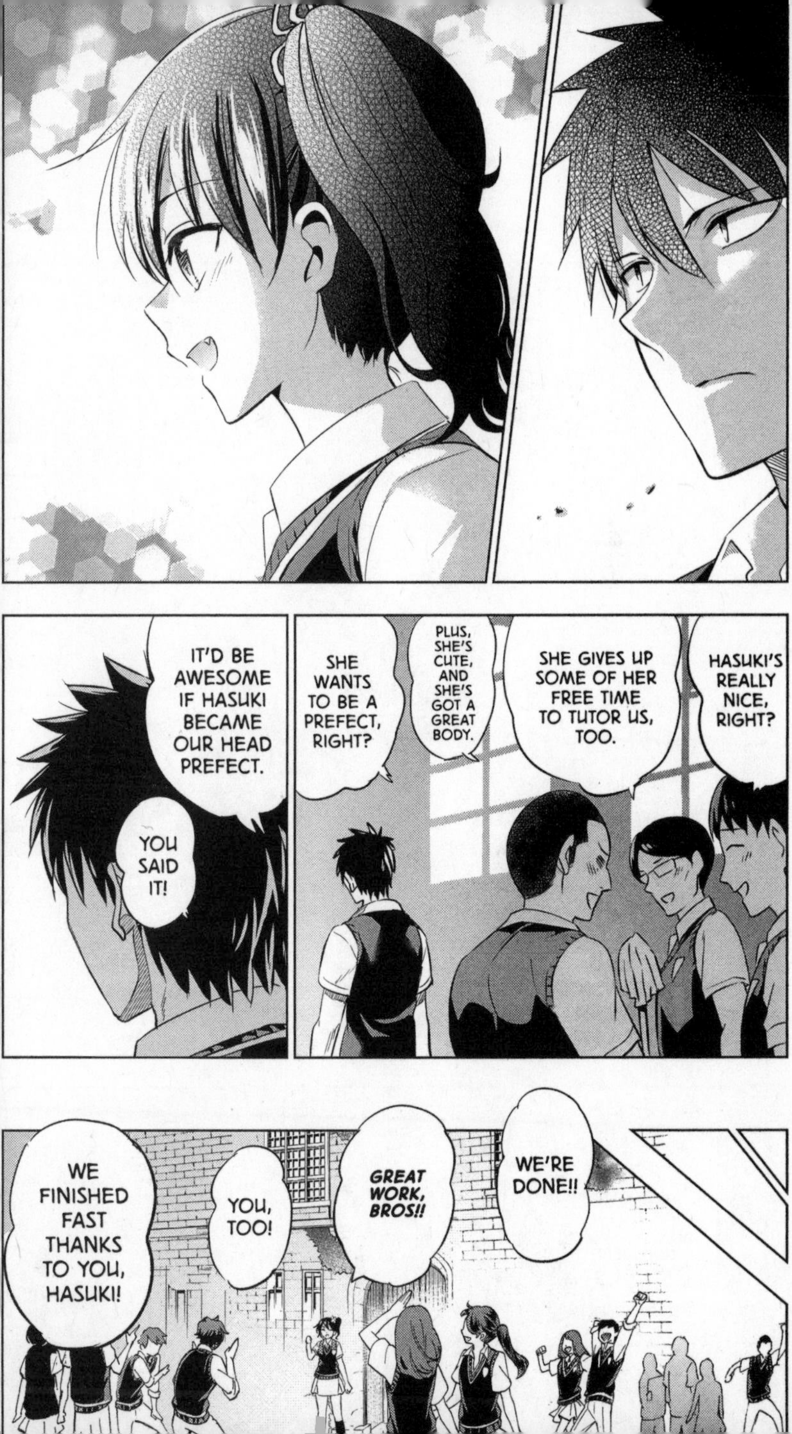
HASUKI'S REALLY NICE, RIGHT?
SHE GIVES UP SOME OF HER FREE TIME TO TUTOR US, TOO.
PLUS, SHE'S CUTE, AND SHE'S GOT A GREAT BODY.
SHE WANTS TO BE A PREFECT, RIGHT?
IT'D BE AWESOME IF HASUKI BECAME OUR HEAD PREFECT.
YOU SAID IT!
WE'RE DONE!!
GREAT WORK, BROS!!
YOU, TOO!
WE FINISHED FAST THANKS TO YOU, HASUKI!

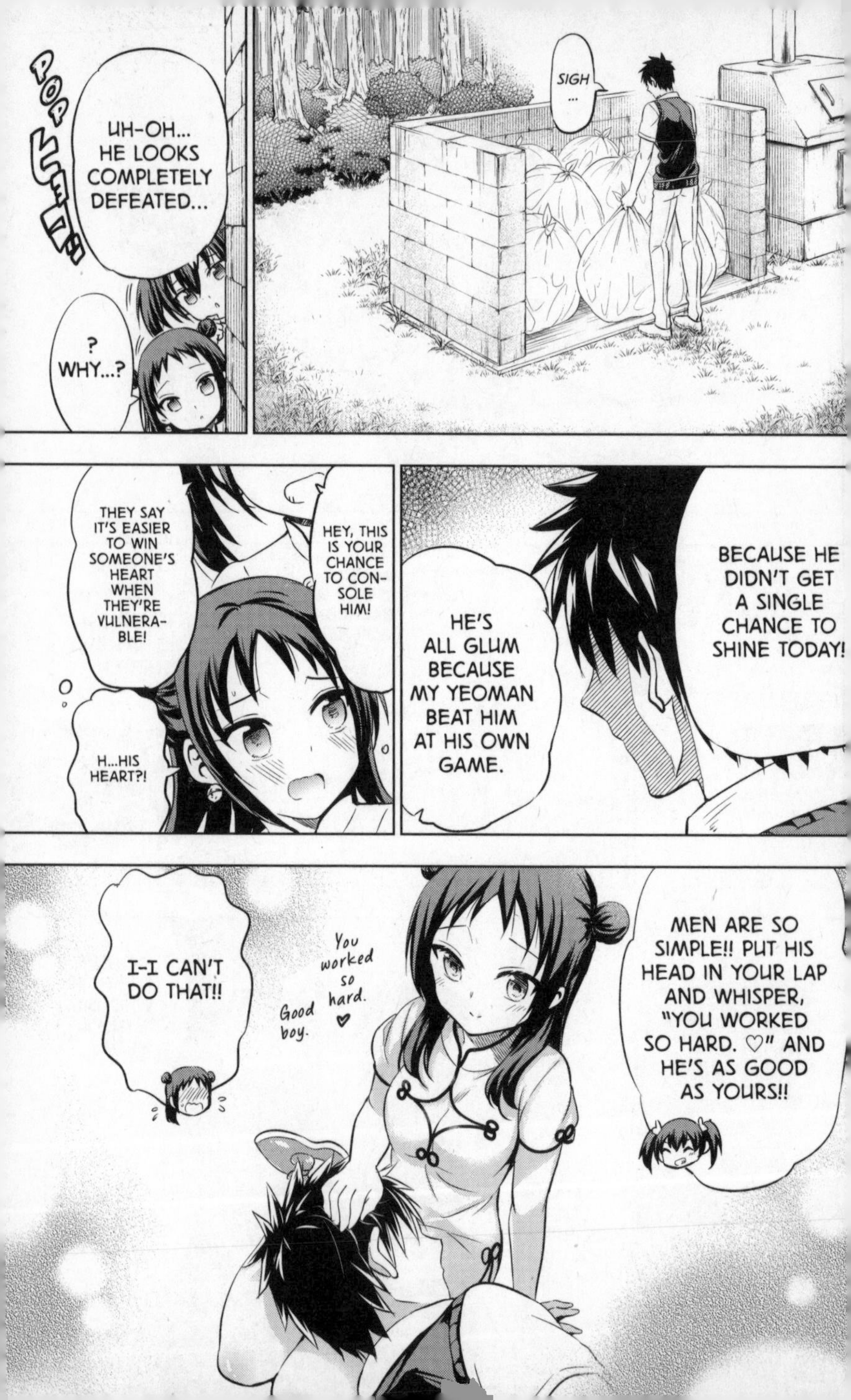
SIGH...
UH-OH... HE LOOKS COMPLETELY DEFEATED...
? WHY...?
BECAUSE HE DIDN'T GET A SINGLE CHANCE TO SHINE TODAY!
HE'S ALL GLUM BECAUSE MY YEOMAN BEAT HIM AT HIS OWN GAME.
HEY, THIS IS YOUR CHANCE TO CON-SOLE HIM!
THEY SAY IT'S EASIER TO WIN SOMEONE'S HEART WHEN THEY'RE VULNERA-BLE!
H...HIS HEART?!
MEN ARE SO SIMPLE!! PUT HIS HEAD IN YOUR LAP AND WHISPER, "YOU WORKED SO HARD. ♡" AND HE'S AS GOOD AS YOURS!!
You worked so hard. ♡
Good boy.
I-I CAN'T DO THAT!!

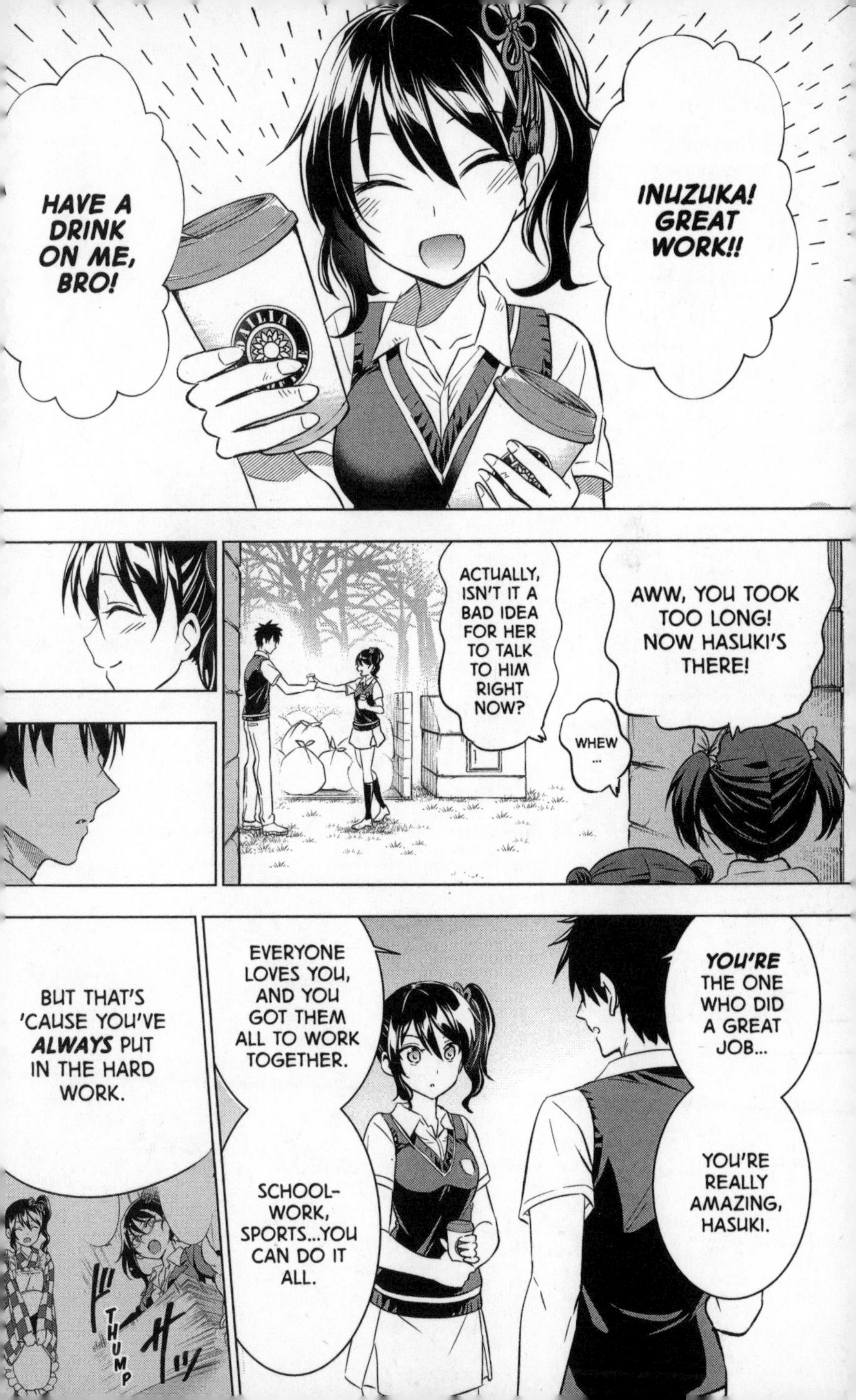
INUZUKA! GREAT WORK!!
HAVE A DRINK ON ME, BRO!
AWW, YOU TOOK TOO LONG! NOW HASUKI'S THERE!
ACTUALLY, ISN'T IT A BAD IDEA FOR HER TO TALK TO HIM RIGHT NOW?
WHEW ...
YOU'RE THE ONE WHO DID A GREAT JOB...
YOU'RE REALLY AMAZING, HASUKI.
EVERYONE LOVES YOU, AND YOU GOT THEM ALL TO WORK TOGETHER.
SCHOOL-WORK, SPORTS...YOU CAN DO IT ALL.
BUT THAT'S 'CAUSE YOU'VE ALWAYS PUT IN THE HARD WORK.
THUMP

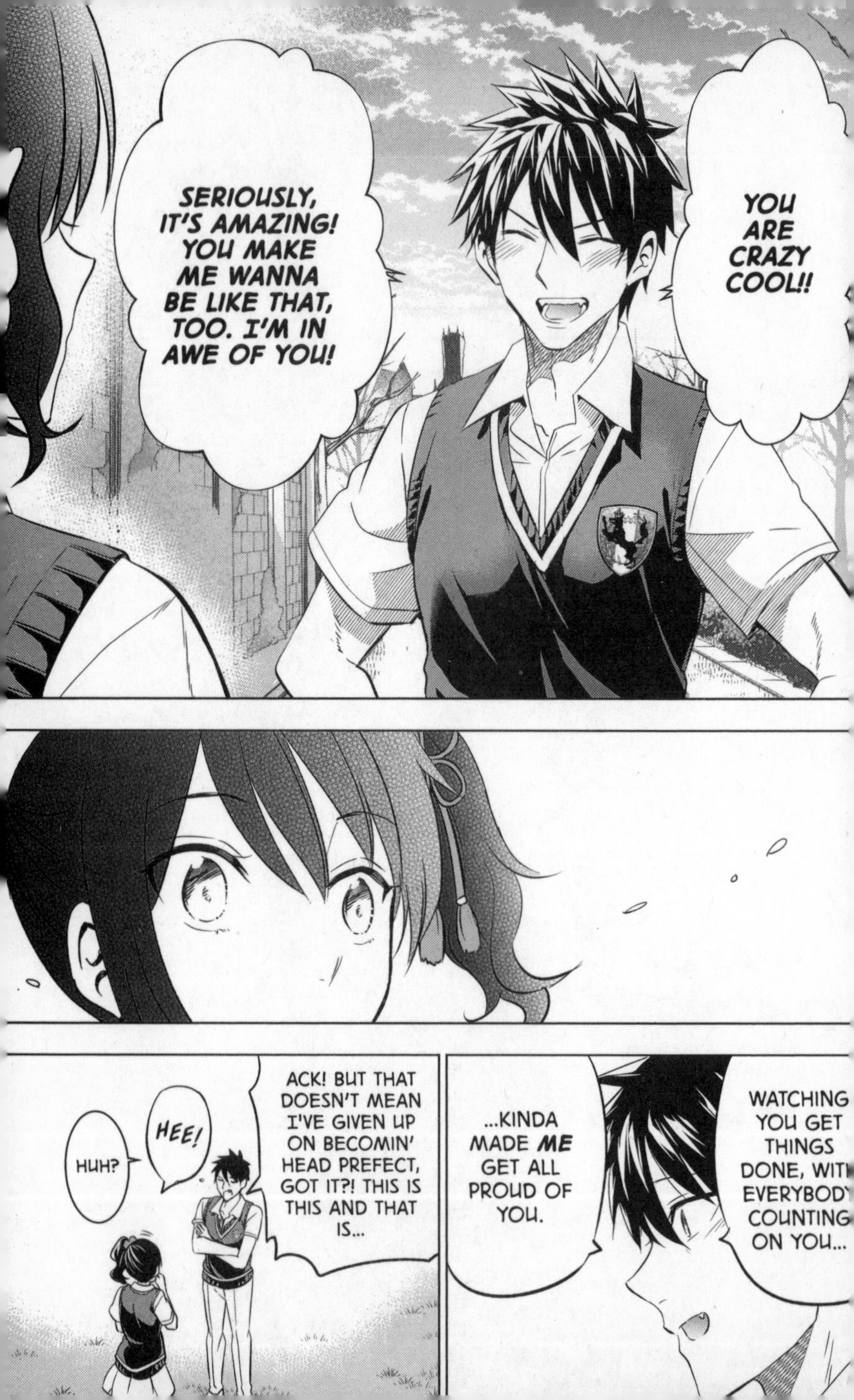
YOU ARE CRAZY COOL!!
SERIOUSLY, IT'S AMAZING! YOU MAKE ME WANNA BE LIKE THAT, TOO. I'M IN AWE OF YOU!
WATCHING YOU GET THINGS DONE, WIT EVERYBOD COUNTING ON YOU...
...KINDA MADE *ME* GET ALL PROUD OF YOU.
ACK! BUT THAT DOESN'T MEAN I'VE GIVEN UP ON BECOMIN' HEAD PREFECT, GOT IT?! THIS IS THIS AND THAT IS...
HEE!
HUH?

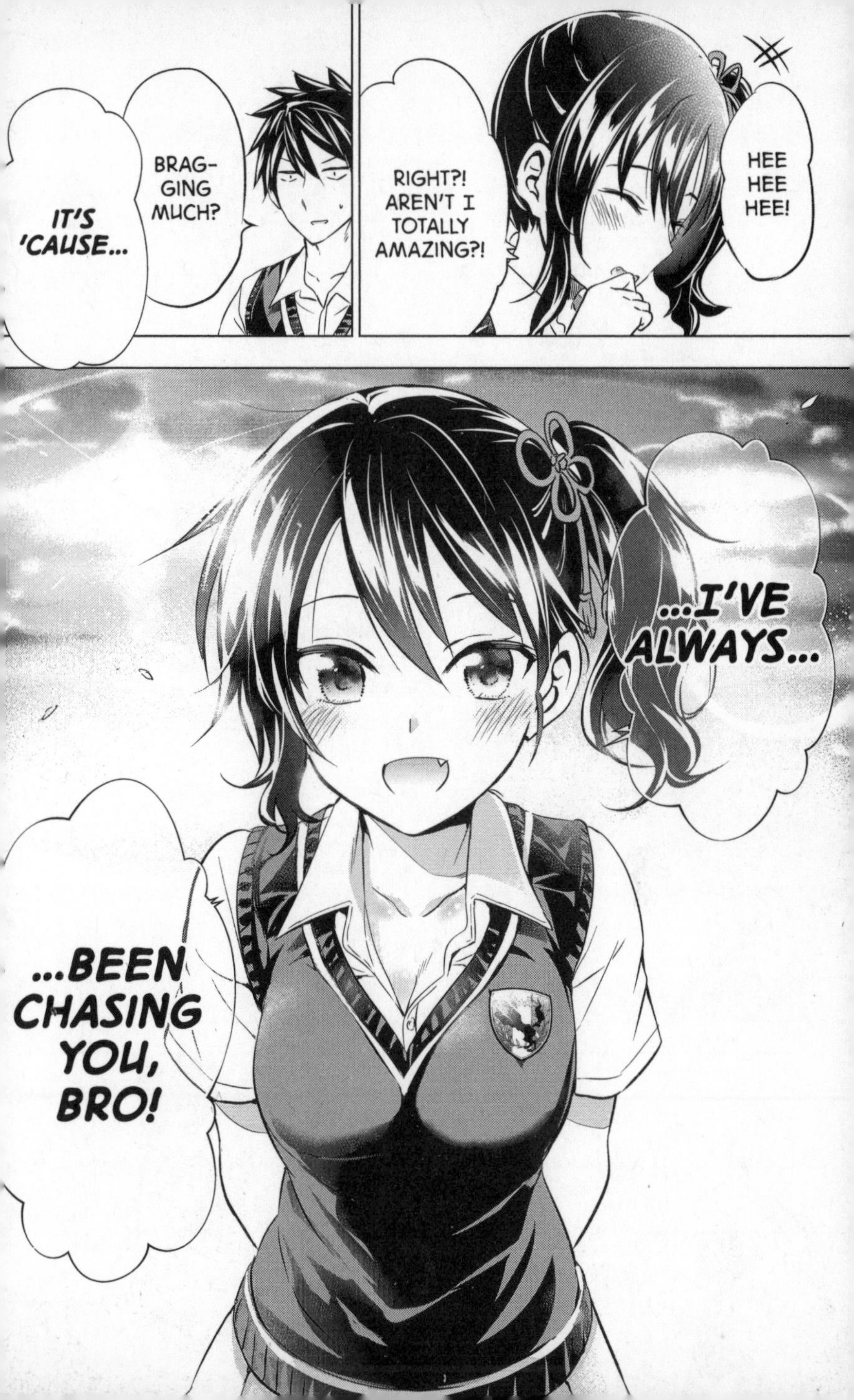
HEE HEE HEE!
RIGHT?! AREN'T I TOTALLY AMAZING?!
BRAG-GING MUCH?
IT'S 'CAUSE...
...I'VE ALWAYS...
...BEEN CHASING YOU, BRO!

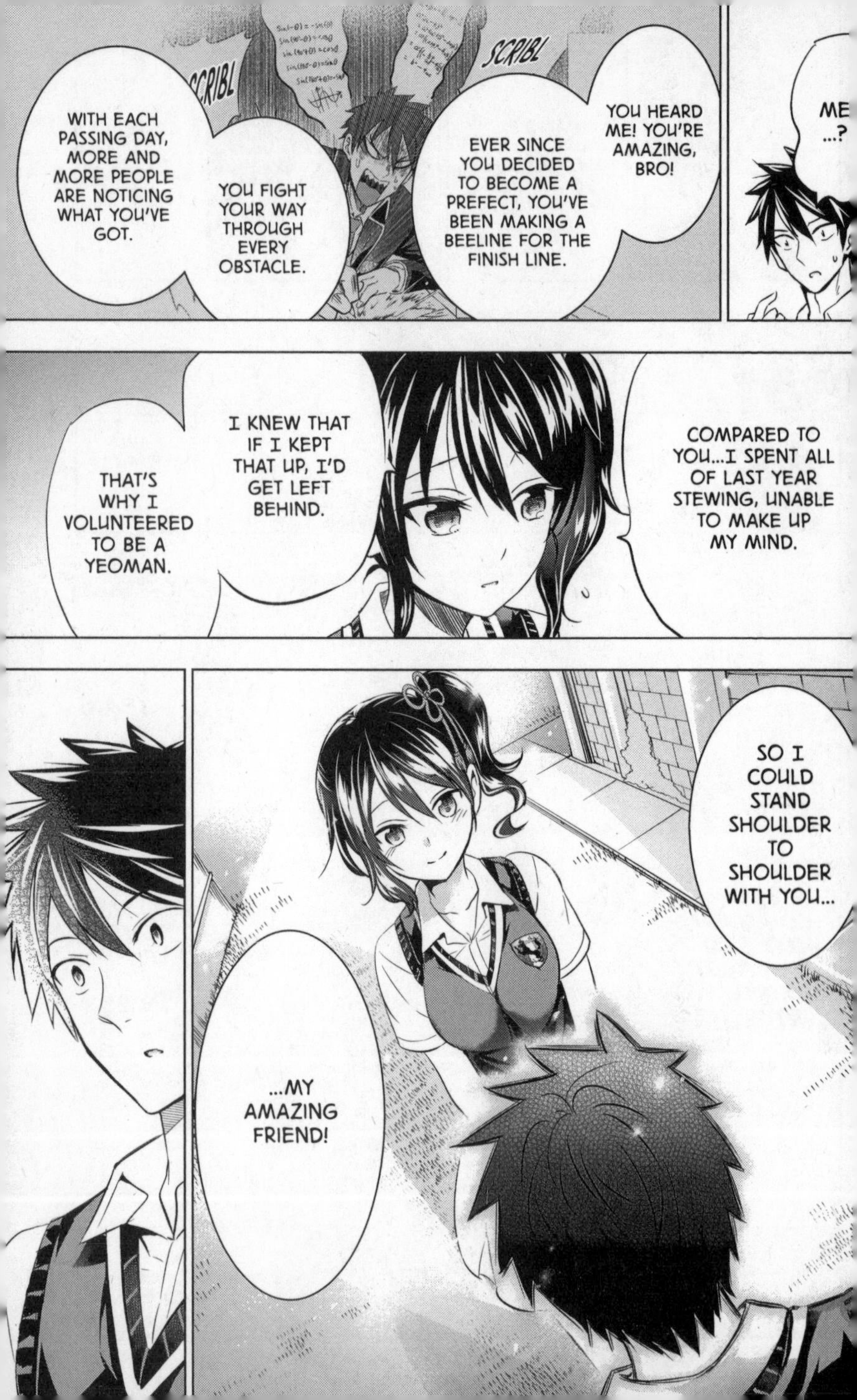
ME ...?
YOU HEARD ME! YOU'RE AMAZING, BRO!
SCRIBL
EVER SINCE YOU DECIDED TO BECOME A PREFECT, YOU'VE BEEN MAKING A BEELINE FOR THE FINISH LINE.
YOU FIGHT YOUR WAY THROUGH EVERY OBSTACLE.
SCRIBL
WITH EACH PASSING DAY, MORE AND MORE PEOPLE ARE NOTICING WHAT YOU'VE GOT.
COMPARED TO YOU...I SPENT ALL OF LAST YEAR STEWING, UNABLE TO MAKE UP MY MIND.
I KNEW THAT IF I KEPT THAT UP, I'D GET LEFT BEHIND.
THAT'S WHY I VOLUNTEERED TO BE A YEOMAN.
SO I COULD STAND SHOULDER TO SHOULDER WITH YOU...
...MY AMAZING FRIEND!

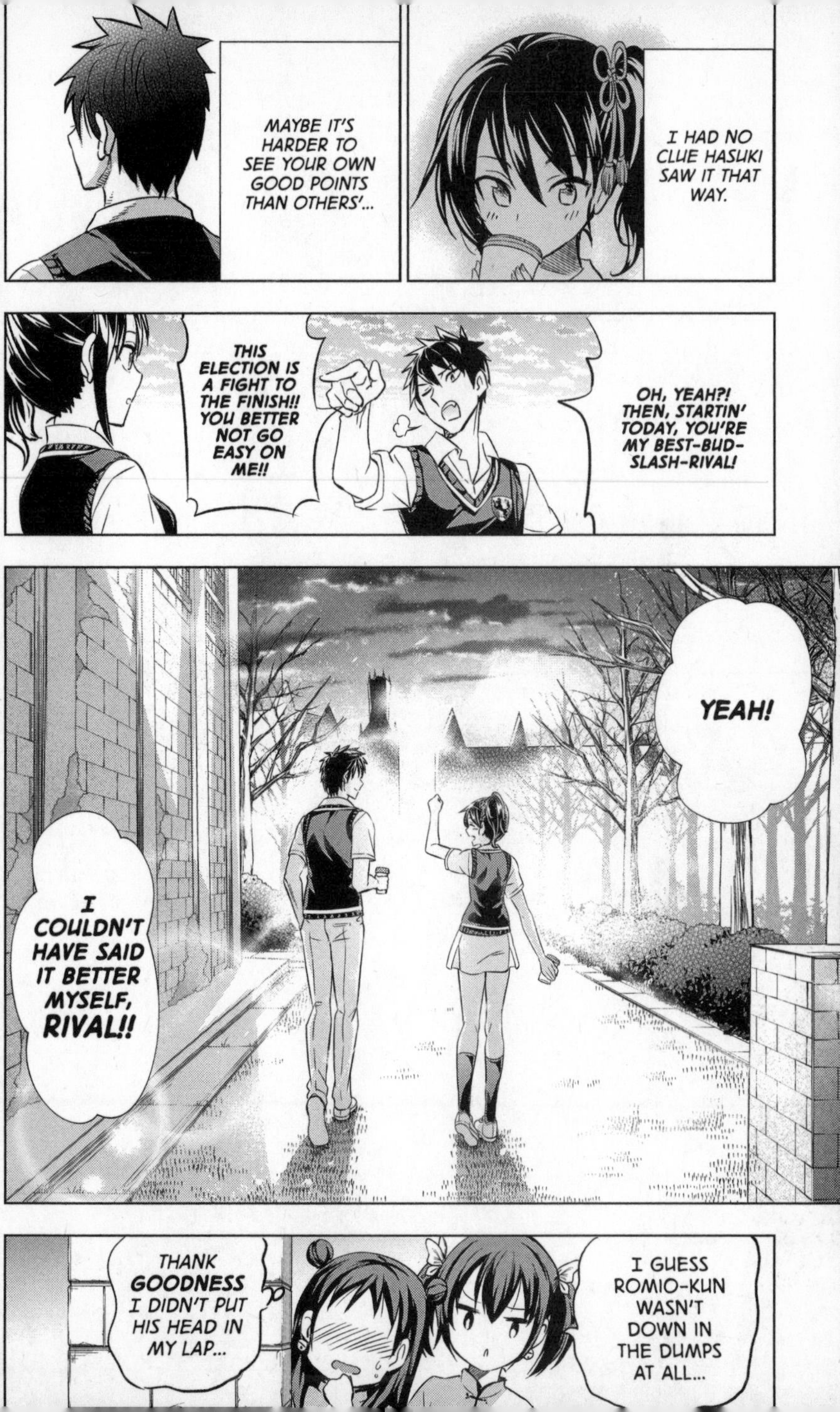
I HAD NO CLUE HASUKI SAW IT THAT WAY.
MAYBE IT'S HARDER TO SEE YOUR OWN GOOD POINTS THAN OTHERS'...
OH, YEAH?! THEN, STARTIN' TODAY, YOU'RE MY BEST-BUD-SLASH-RIVAL!
THIS ELECTION IS A FIGHT TO THE FINISH!! YOU BETTER NOT GO EASY ON ME!!
YEAH!
I COULDN'T HAVE SAID IT BETTER MYSELF, RIVAL!!
I GUESS ROMIO-KUN WASN'T DOWN IN THE DUMPS AT ALL...
THANK GOODNESS I DIDN'T PUT HIS HEAD IN MY LAP...

ACT 64:

ROMIO & PRINCESS CHAR & COFFEE I

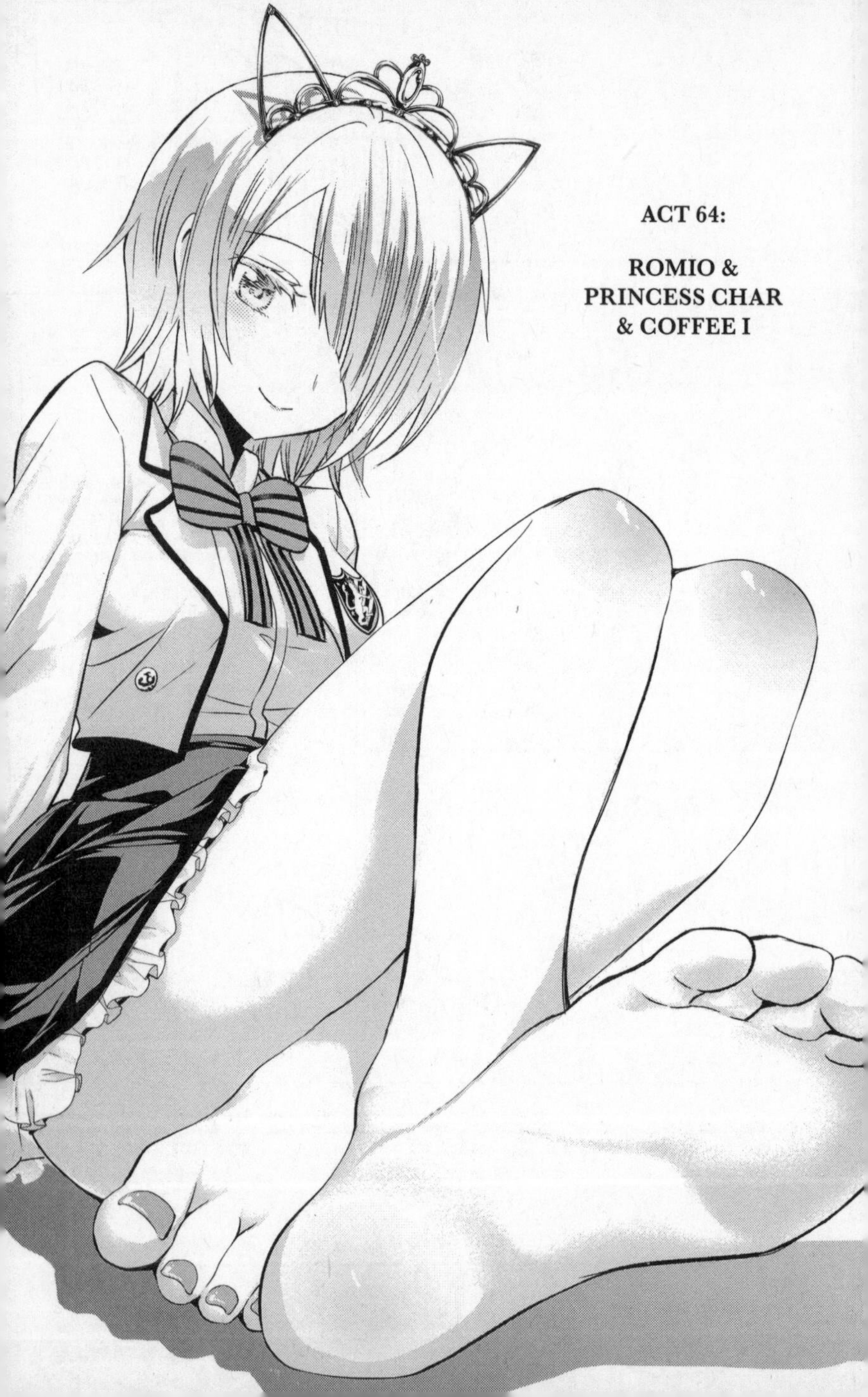

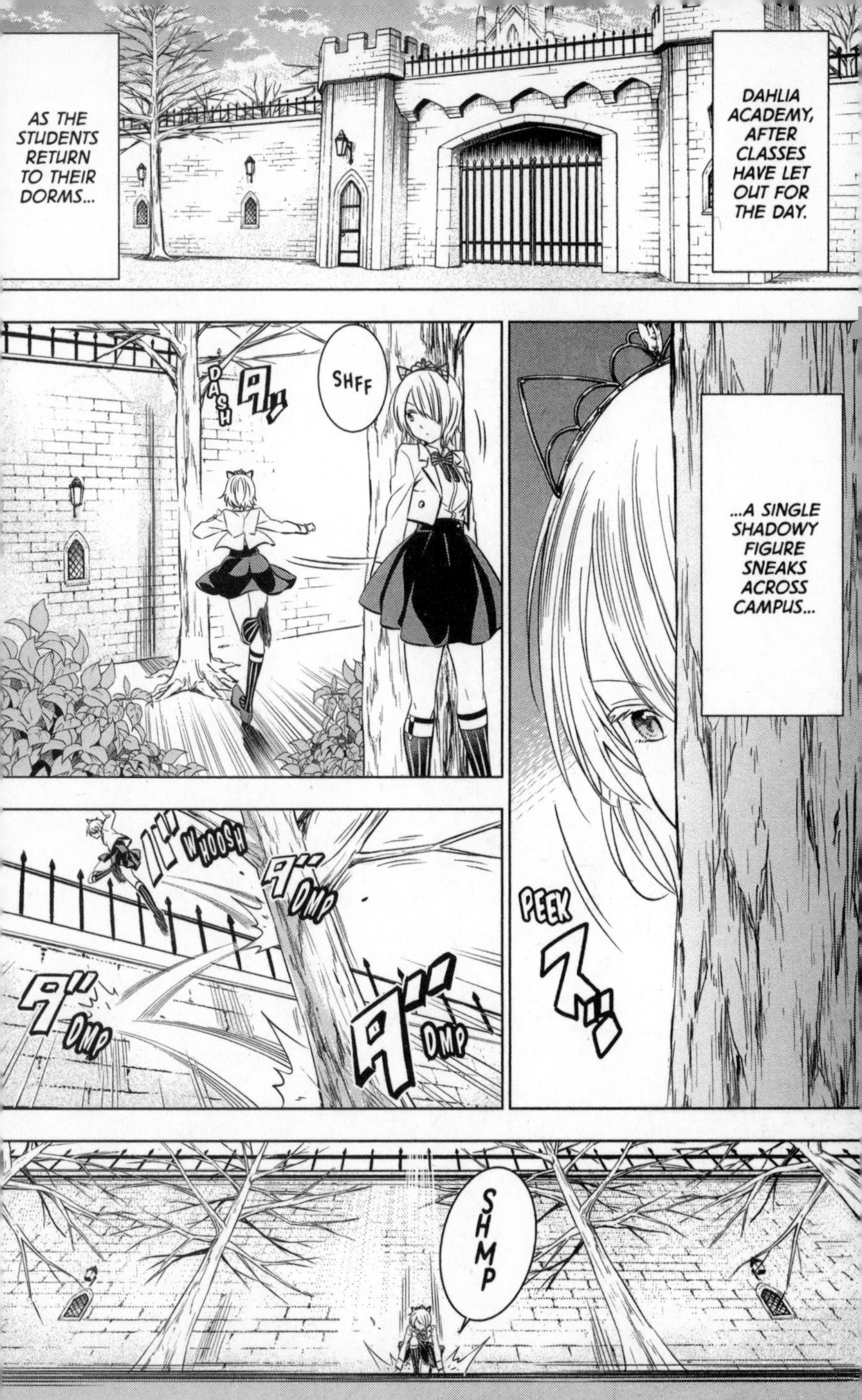
DAHLIA ACADEMY, AFTER CLASSES HAVE LET OUT FOR THE DAY.
AS THE STUDENTS RETURN TO THEIR DORMS...
...A SINGLE SHADOWY FIGURE SNEAKS ACROSS CAMPUS...
PEEK
SHFF
DASH
WHOOSH
DOMP
DOMP
DOMP
SHMP

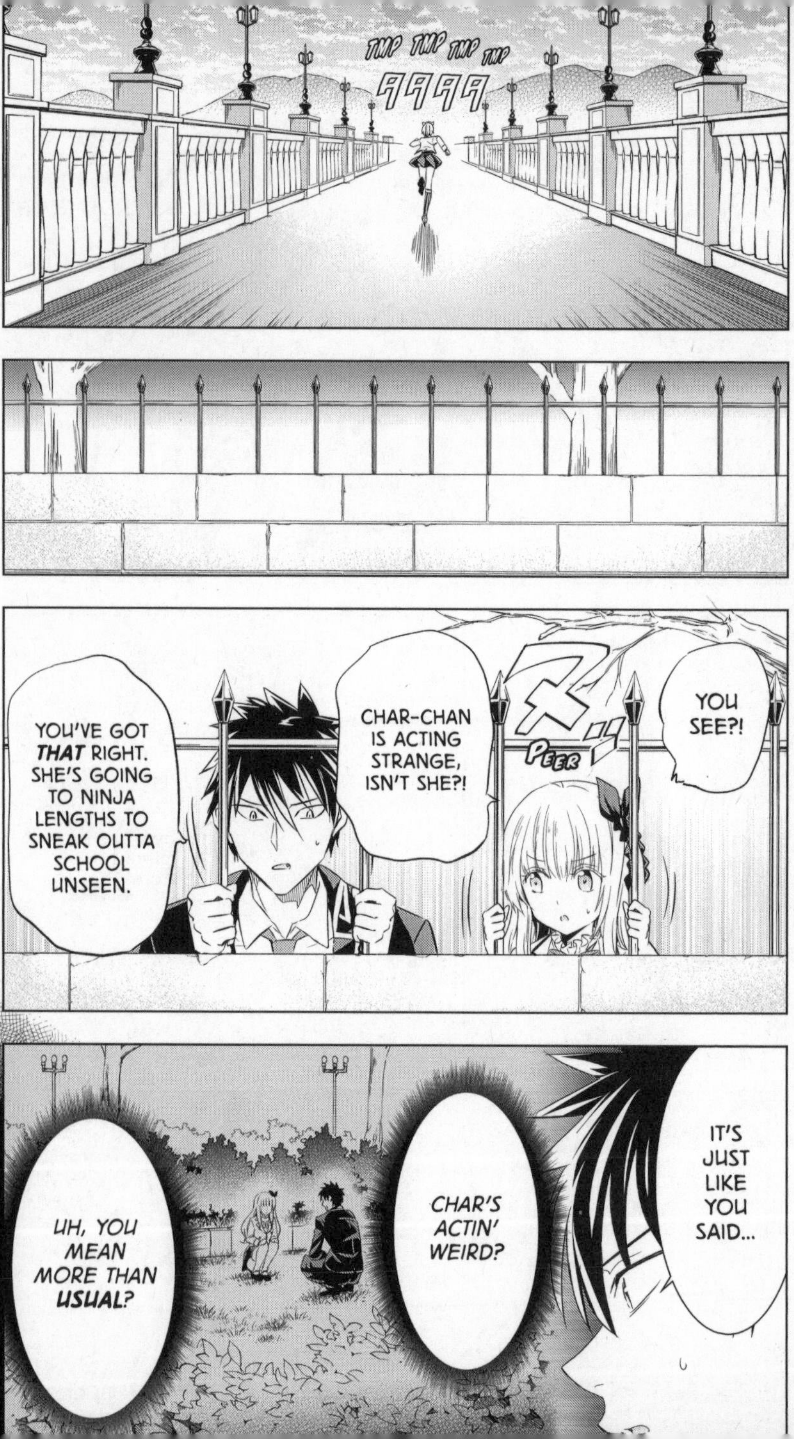
TMP TMP TMP TMP
YOU SEE?!
PEER
CHAR-CHAN IS ACTING STRANGE, ISN'T SHE?!
YOU'VE GOT **THAT** RIGHT. SHE'S GOING TO NINJA LENGTHS TO SNEAK OUTTA SCHOOL UNSEEN.
IT'S JUST LIKE YOU SAID...
CHAR'S ACTIN' WEIRD?
*UH, YOU MEAN MORE THAN **USUAL**?*

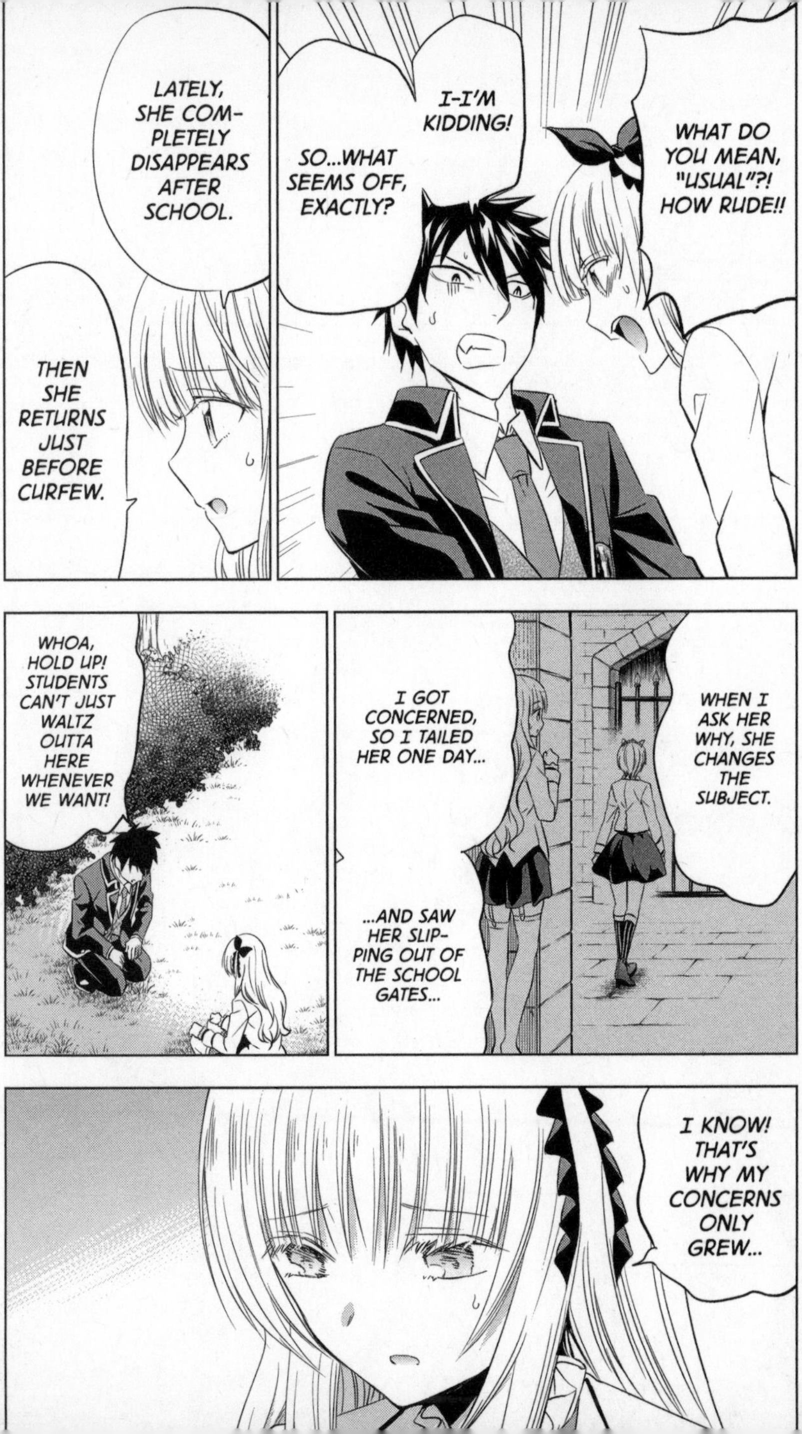
WHAT DO YOU MEAN, "USUAL"?! HOW RUDE!!
I-I'M KIDDING!
SO...WHAT SEEMS OFF, EXACTLY?
LATELY, SHE COMPLETELY DISAPPEARS AFTER SCHOOL.
THEN SHE RETURNS JUST BEFORE CURFEW.
WHEN I ASK HER WHY, SHE CHANGES THE SUBJECT.
I GOT CONCERNED, SO I TAILED HER ONE DAY...
...AND SAW HER SLIPPING OUT OF THE SCHOOL GATES...
WHOA, HOLD UP! STUDENTS CAN'T JUST WALTZ OUTTA HERE WHENEVER WE WANT!
I KNOW! THAT'S WHY MY CONCERNS ONLY GREW...

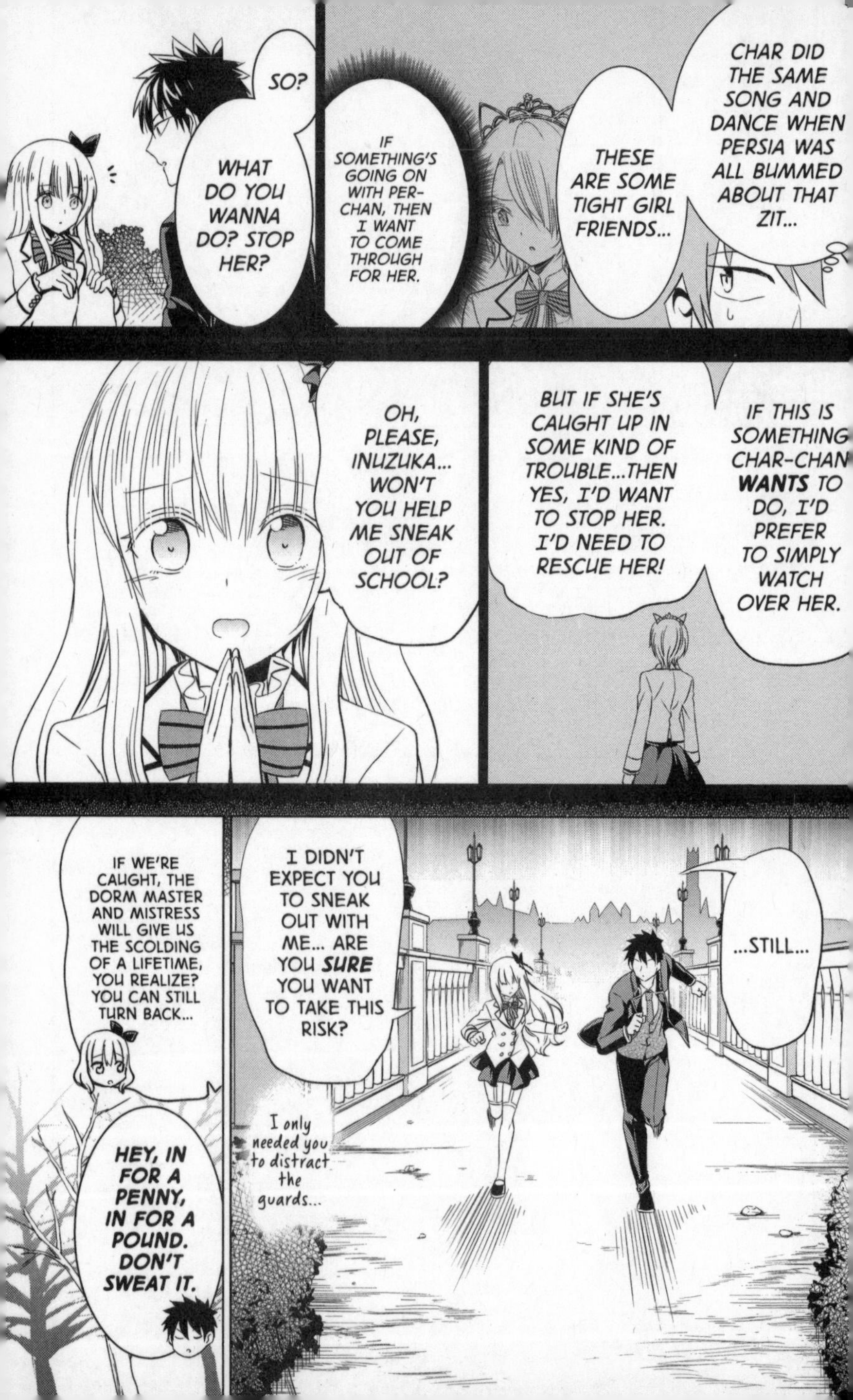
CHAR DID THE SAME SONG AND DANCE WHEN PERSIA WAS ALL BUMMED ABOUT THAT ZIT...
THESE ARE SOME TIGHT GIRL FRIENDS...
IF SOMETHING'S GOING ON WITH PER-CHAN, THEN I WANT TO COME THROUGH FOR HER.
SO?
WHAT DO YOU WANNA DO? STOP HER?
IF THIS IS SOMETHING CHAR-CHAN **WANTS** TO DO, I'D PREFER TO SIMPLY WATCH OVER HER.
BUT IF SHE'S CAUGHT UP IN SOME KIND OF TROUBLE...THEN YES, I'D WANT TO STOP HER. I'D NEED TO RESCUE HER!
OH, PLEASE, INUZUKA... WON'T YOU HELP ME SNEAK OUT OF SCHOOL?
...STILL...
I DIDN'T EXPECT YOU TO SNEAK OUT WITH ME... ARE YOU ***SURE*** YOU WANT TO TAKE THIS RISK?
I only needed you to distract the guards...
IF WE'RE CAUGHT, THE DORM MASTER AND MISTRESS WILL GIVE US THE SCOLDING OF A LIFETIME, YOU REALIZE? YOU CAN STILL TURN BACK...
HEY, IN FOR A PENNY, IN FOR A POUND. DON'T SWEAT IT.

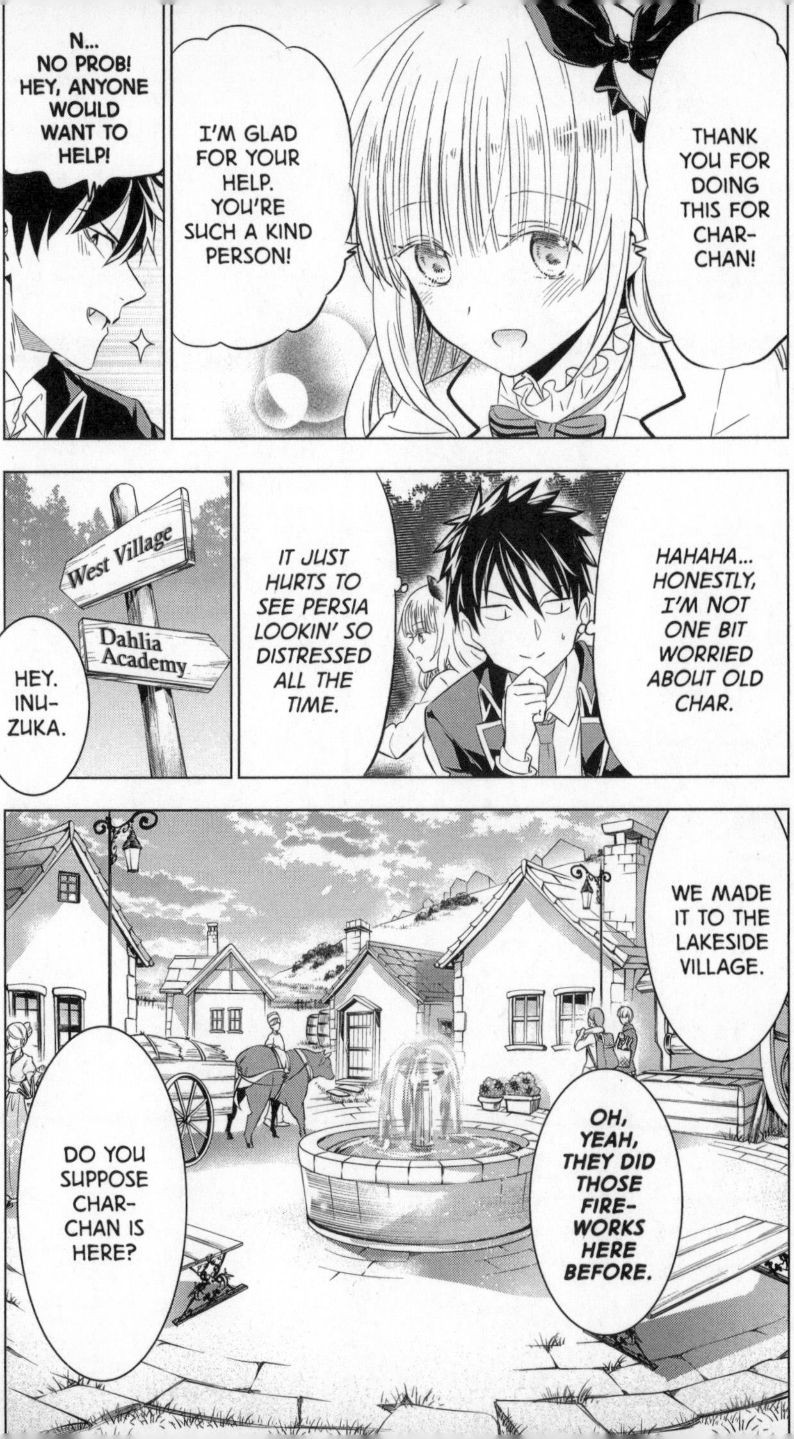
THANK YOU FOR DOING THIS FOR CHAR-CHAN!
I'M GLAD FOR YOUR HELP. YOU'RE SUCH A KIND PERSON!
N... NO PROB! HEY, ANYONE WOULD WANT TO HELP!
HAHAHA... HONESTLY, I'M NOT ONE BIT WORRIED ABOUT OLD CHAR.
IT JUST HURTS TO SEE PERSIA LOOKIN' SO DISTRESSED ALL THE TIME.
West Village
Dahlia Academy
HEY. INU-ZUKA.
WE MADE IT TO THE LAKESIDE VILLAGE.
OH, YEAH, THEY DID THOSE FIRE-WORKS HERE BEFORE.
DO YOU SUPPOSE CHAR-CHAN IS HERE?

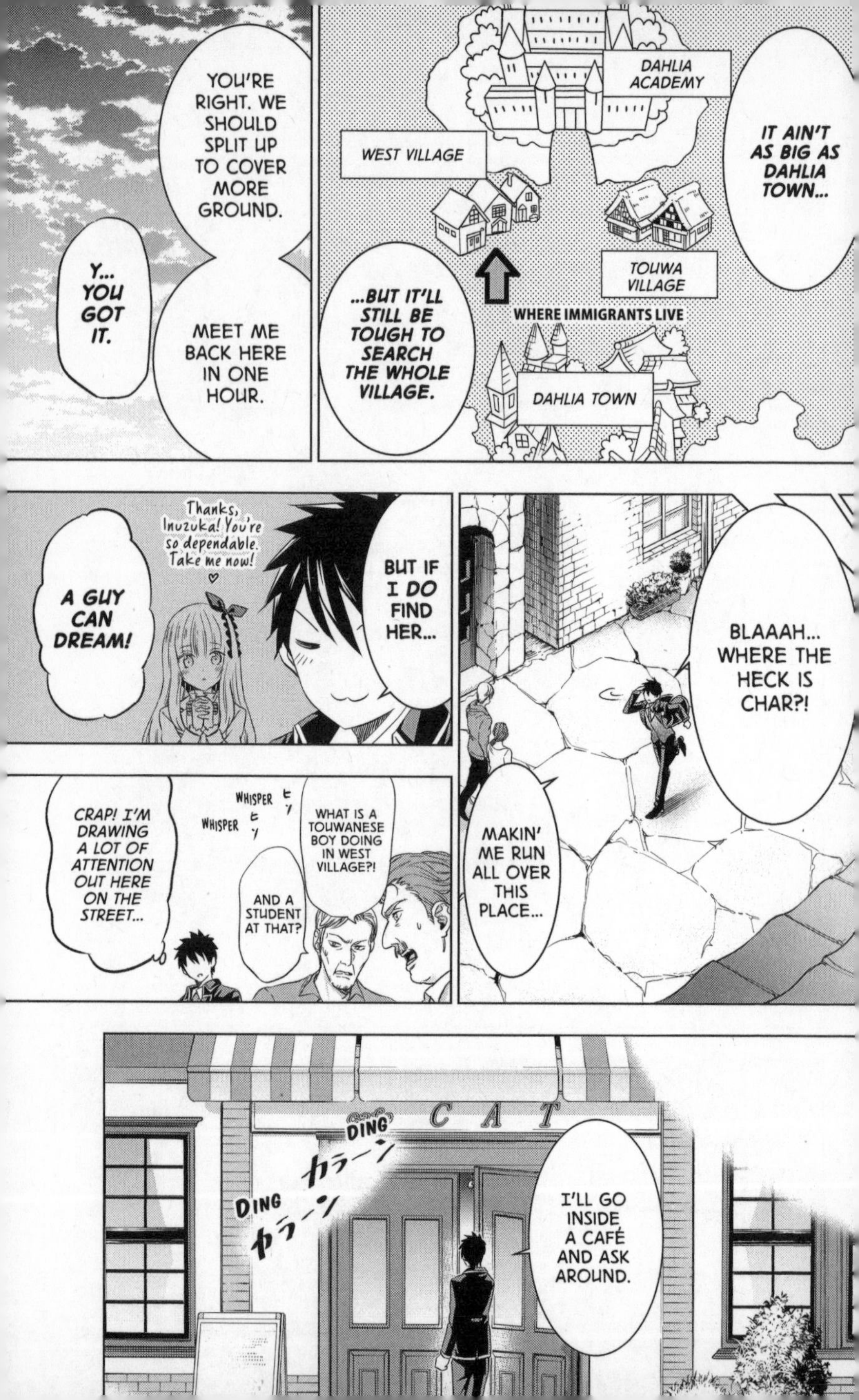
IT AIN'T AS BIG AS DAHLIA TOWN...
DAHLIA ACADEMY
WEST VILLAGE
TOUWA VILLAGE
WHERE IMMIGRANTS LIVE
DAHLIA TOWN
...BUT IT'LL STILL BE TOUGH TO SEARCH THE WHOLE VILLAGE.
YOU'RE RIGHT. WE SHOULD SPLIT UP TO COVER MORE GROUND.
MEET ME BACK HERE IN ONE HOUR.
Y... YOU GOT IT.
BLAAAH... WHERE THE HECK IS CHAR?!
MAKIN' ME RUN ALL OVER THIS PLACE...
BUT IF I DO FIND HER...
Thanks, Inuzuka! You're so dependable. Take me now! ♡
A GUY CAN DREAM!
WHAT IS A TOUWANESE BOY DOING IN WEST VILLAGE?!
WHISPER ヒソ
WHISPER ヒソ
AND A STUDENT AT THAT?
CRAP! I'M DRAWING A LOT OF ATTENTION OUT HERE ON THE STREET...
I'LL GO INSIDE A CAFÉ AND ASK AROUND.
CAT
DING カラーン
DING カラーン

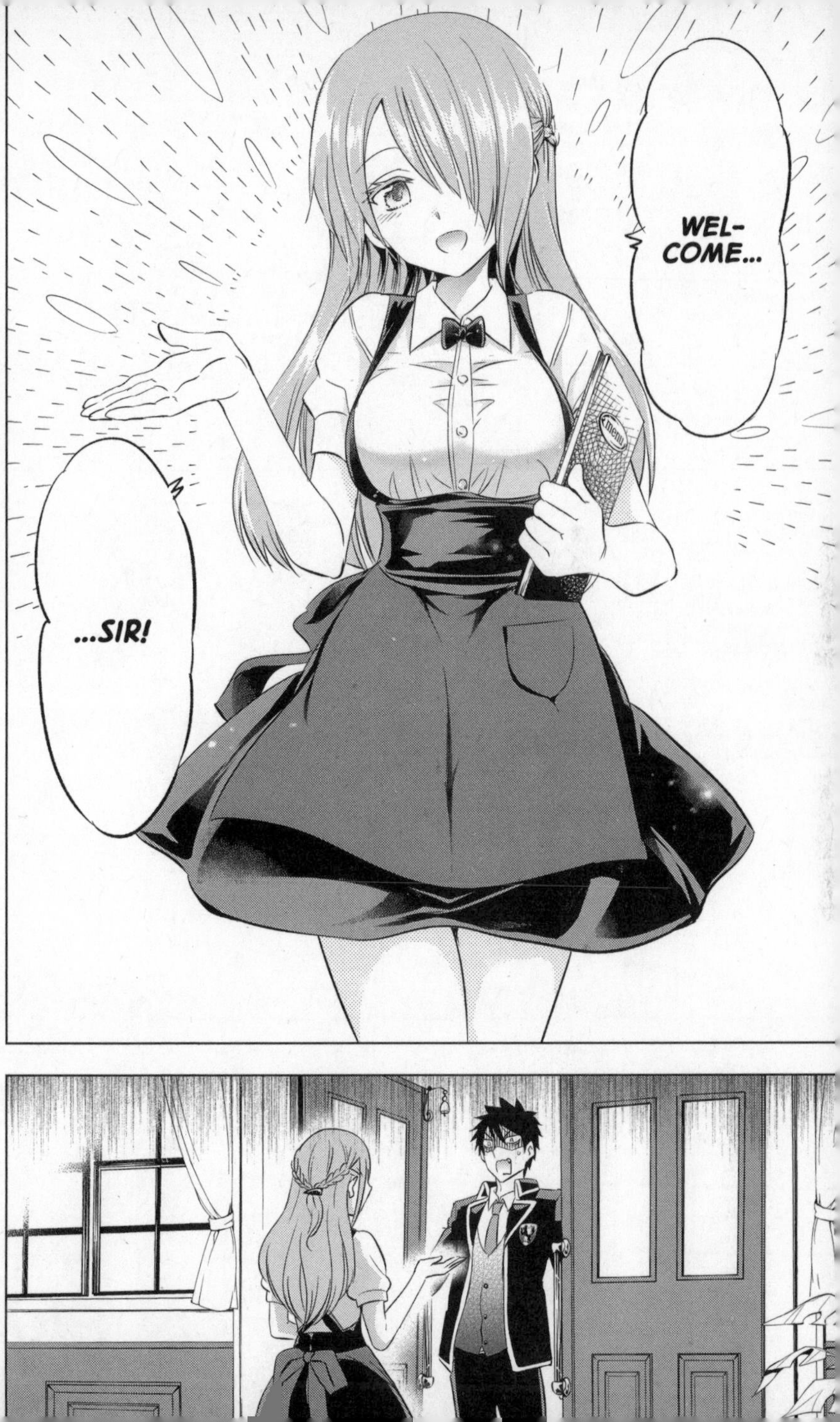
WEL-
COME...
...SIR!

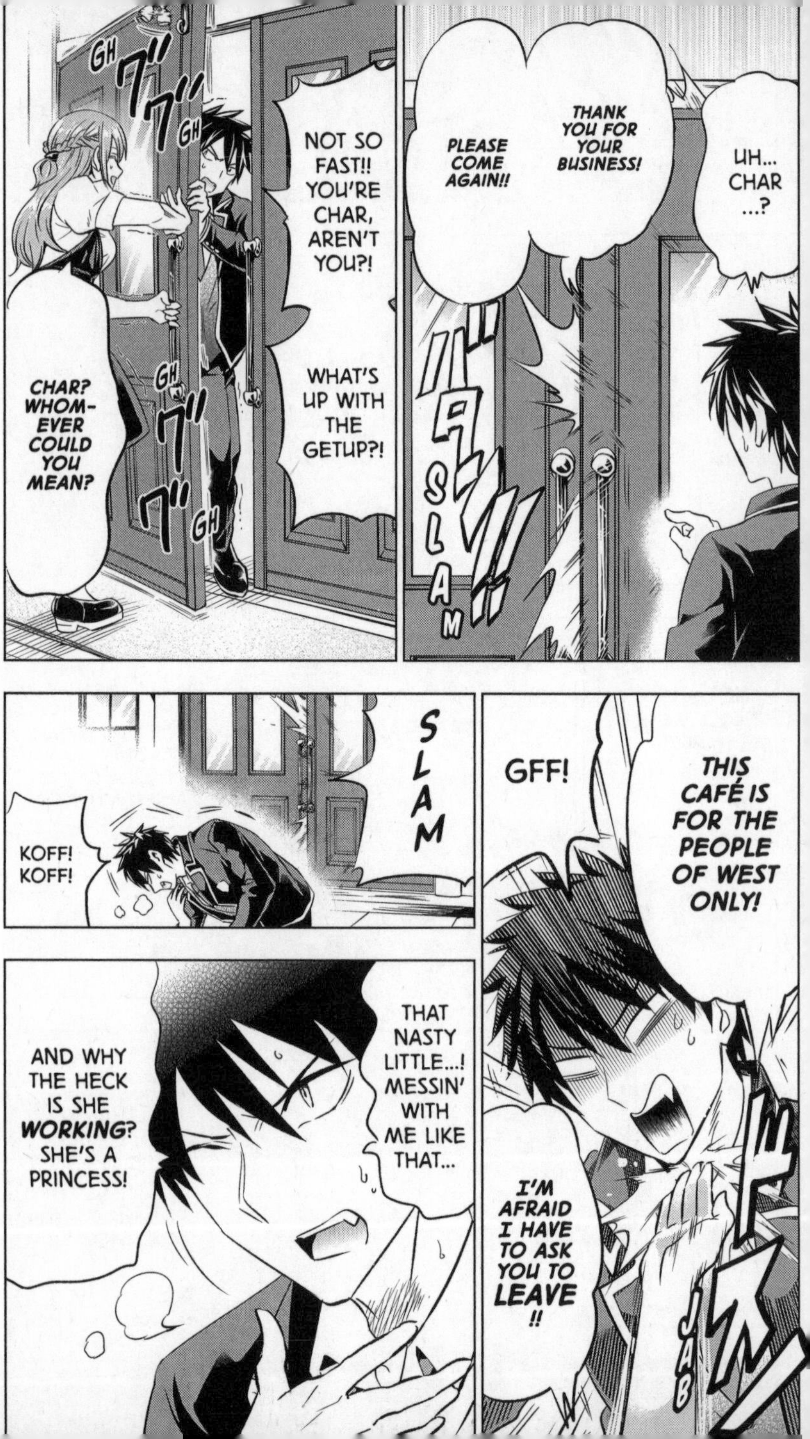
UH... CHAR ...?
THANK YOU FOR YOUR BUSINESS!
PLEASE COME AGAIN!!
SLAM
NOT SO FAST!! YOU'RE CHAR, AREN'T YOU?!
WHAT'S UP WITH THE GETUP?!
GH
GH
GH
GH
CHAR? WHOM-EVER COULD YOU MEAN?
THIS CAFÉ IS FOR THE PEOPLE OF WEST ONLY!
GFF!
I'M AFRAID I HAVE TO ASK YOU TO LEAVE!!
JAB
SLAM
KOFF! KOFF!
THAT NASTY LITTLE...! MESSIN' WITH ME LIKE THAT...
AND WHY THE HECK IS SHE WORKING? SHE'S A PRINCESS!

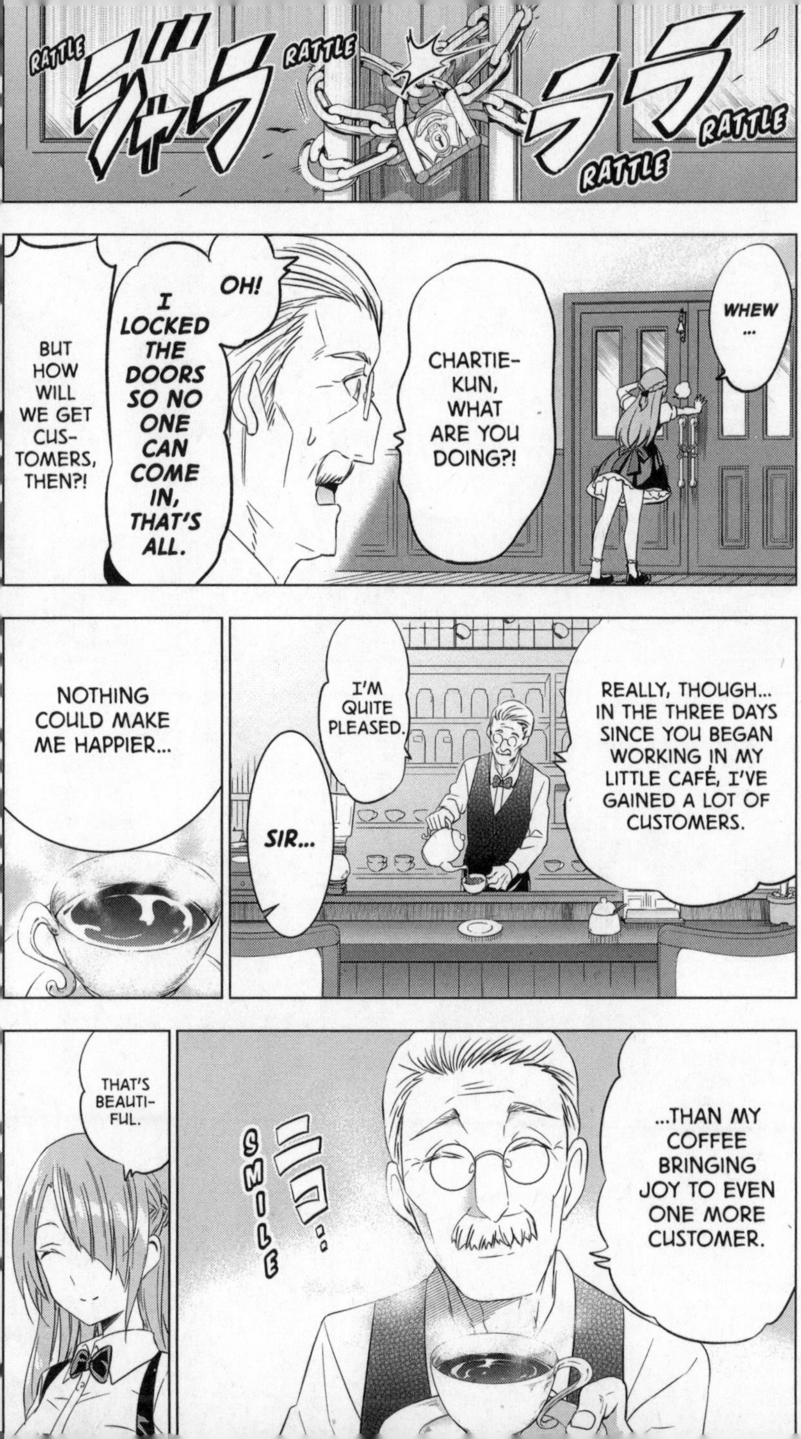
RATTLE
ジャラ
RATTLE
ララ
RATTLE
RATTLE
WHEW...
CHARTIE-KUN, WHAT ARE YOU DOING?!
OH! I LOCKED THE DOORS SO NO ONE CAN COME IN, THAT'S ALL.
BUT HOW WILL WE GET CUSTOMERS, THEN?!
REALLY, THOUGH... IN THE THREE DAYS SINCE YOU BEGAN WORKING IN MY LITTLE CAFÉ, I'VE GAINED A LOT OF CUSTOMERS.
I'M QUITE PLEASED.
SIR...
NOTHING COULD MAKE ME HAPPIER...
...THAN MY COFFEE BRINGING JOY TO EVEN ONE MORE CUSTOMER.
ニコ..
SMILE
THAT'S BEAUTIFUL.

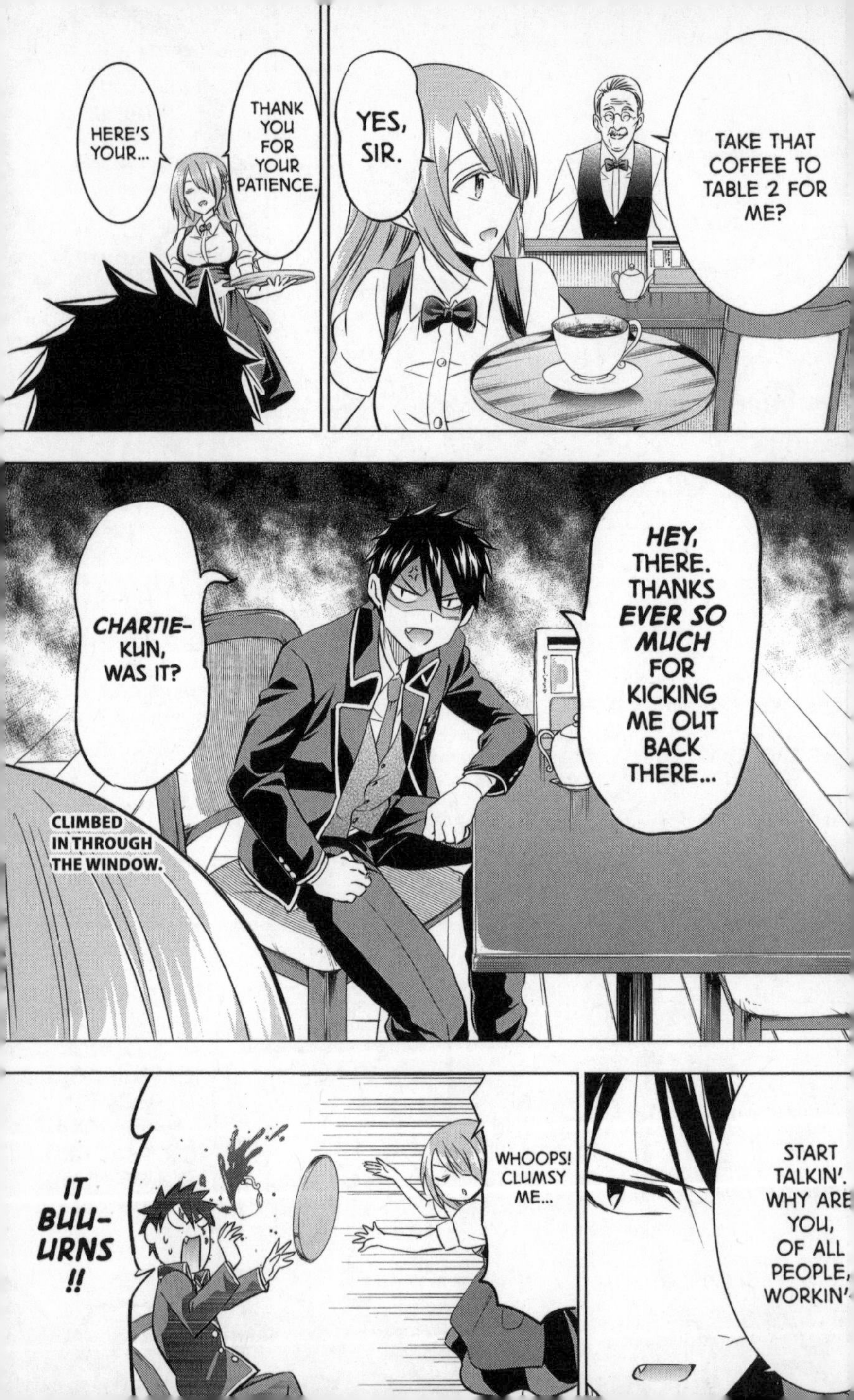
TAKE THAT COFFEE TO TABLE 2 FOR ME?
YES, SIR.
THANK YOU FOR YOUR PATIENCE.
HERE'S YOUR...
HEY, THERE. THANKS *EVER SO MUCH* FOR KICKING ME OUT BACK THERE...
*CHARTIE-*KUN, WAS IT?
CLIMBED IN THROUGH THE WINDOW.
START TALKIN'. WHY ARE YOU, OF ALL PEOPLE, WORKIN'
WHOOPS! CLUMSY ME...
IT BUU-URNS!!

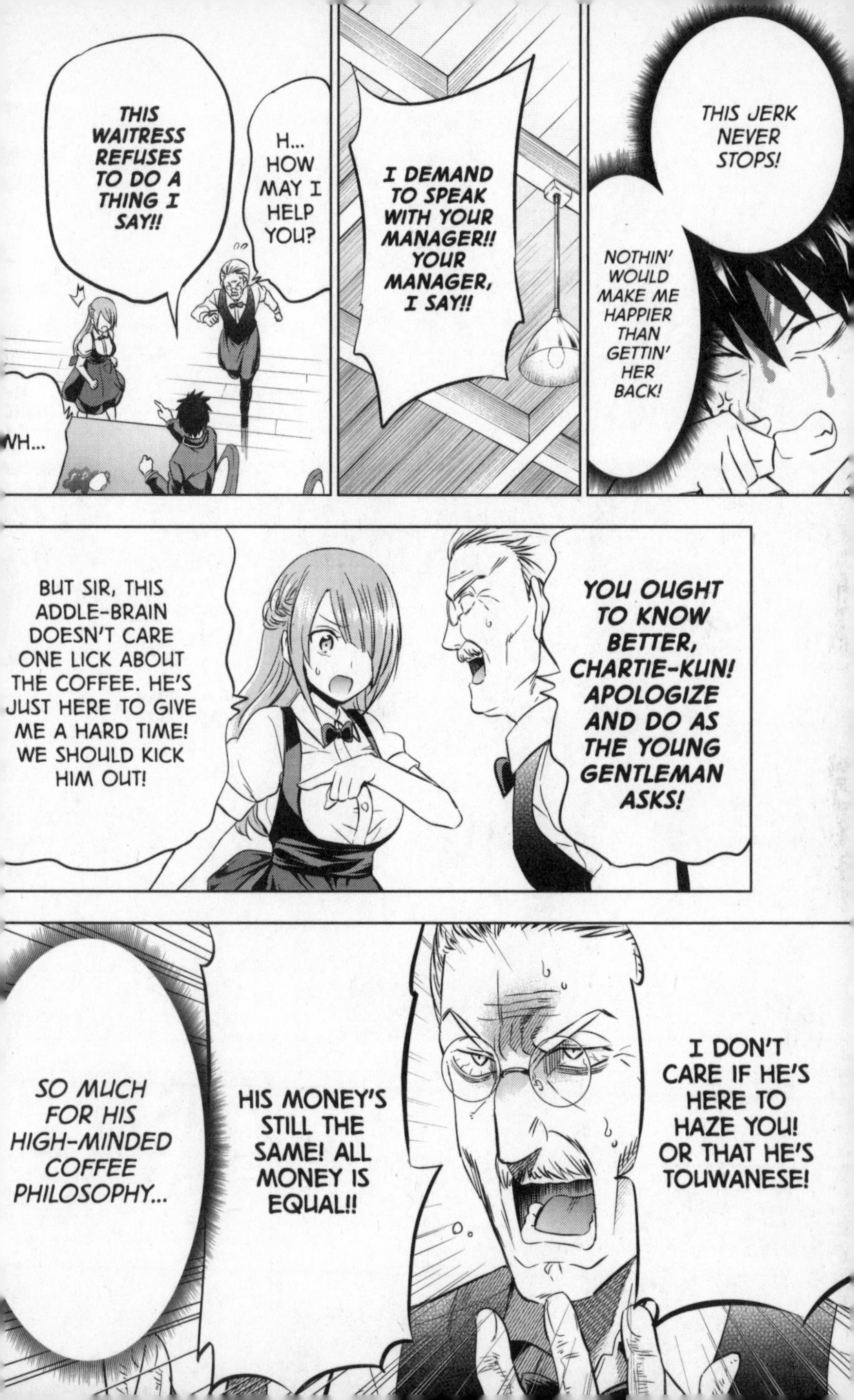
THIS JERK NEVER STOPS!
NOTHIN' WOULD MAKE ME HAPPIER THAN GETTIN' HER BACK!
I DEMAND TO SPEAK WITH YOUR MANAGER!! YOUR MANAGER, I SAY!!
H... HOW MAY I HELP YOU?
THIS WAITRESS REFUSES TO DO A THING I SAY!!
WH...
YOU OUGHT TO KNOW BETTER, CHARTIE-KUN! APOLOGIZE AND DO AS THE YOUNG GENTLEMAN ASKS!
BUT SIR, THIS ADDLE-BRAIN DOESN'T CARE ONE LICK ABOUT THE COFFEE. HE'S JUST HERE TO GIVE ME A HARD TIME! WE SHOULD KICK HIM OUT!
I DON'T CARE IF HE'S HERE TO HAZE YOU! OR THAT HE'S TOUWANESE!
HIS MONEY'S STILL THE SAME! ALL MONEY IS EQUAL!!
SO MUCH FOR HIS HIGH-MINDED COFFEE PHILOSOPHY...

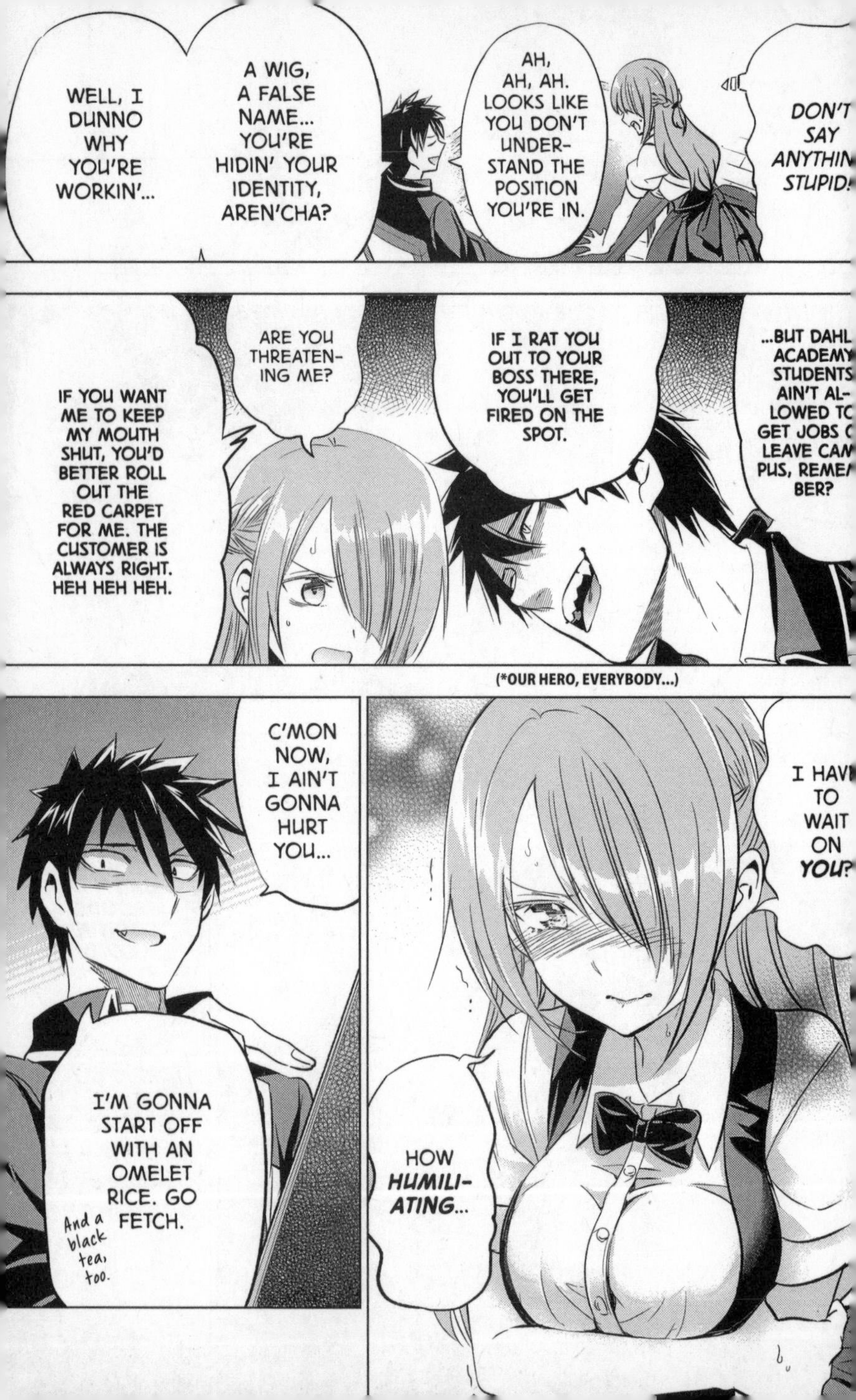
DON'T SAY ANYTHIN STUPID!
AH, AH, AH. LOOKS LIKE YOU DON'T UNDER- STAND THE POSITION YOU'RE IN.
A WIG, A FALSE NAME... YOU'RE HIDIN' YOUR IDENTITY, AREN'CHA?
WELL, I DUNNO WHY YOU'RE WORKIN'...
...BUT DAHL ACADEMY STUDENTS AIN'T AL- LOWED TO GET JOBS LEAVE CAM PUS, REME BER?
IF I RAT YOU OUT TO YOUR BOSS THERE, YOU'LL GET FIRED ON THE SPOT.
ARE YOU THREATEN- ING ME?
IF YOU WANT ME TO KEEP MY MOUTH SHUT, YOU'D BETTER ROLL OUT THE RED CARPET FOR ME. THE CUSTOMER IS ALWAYS RIGHT. HEH HEH HEH.
(*OUR HERO, EVERYBODY...)
I HAV TO WAIT ON *YOU*?
HOW *HUMILI- ATING*...
C'MON NOW, I AIN'T GONNA HURT YOU...
I'M GONNA START OFF WITH AN OMELET RICE. GO FETCH.
And a black tea, too.

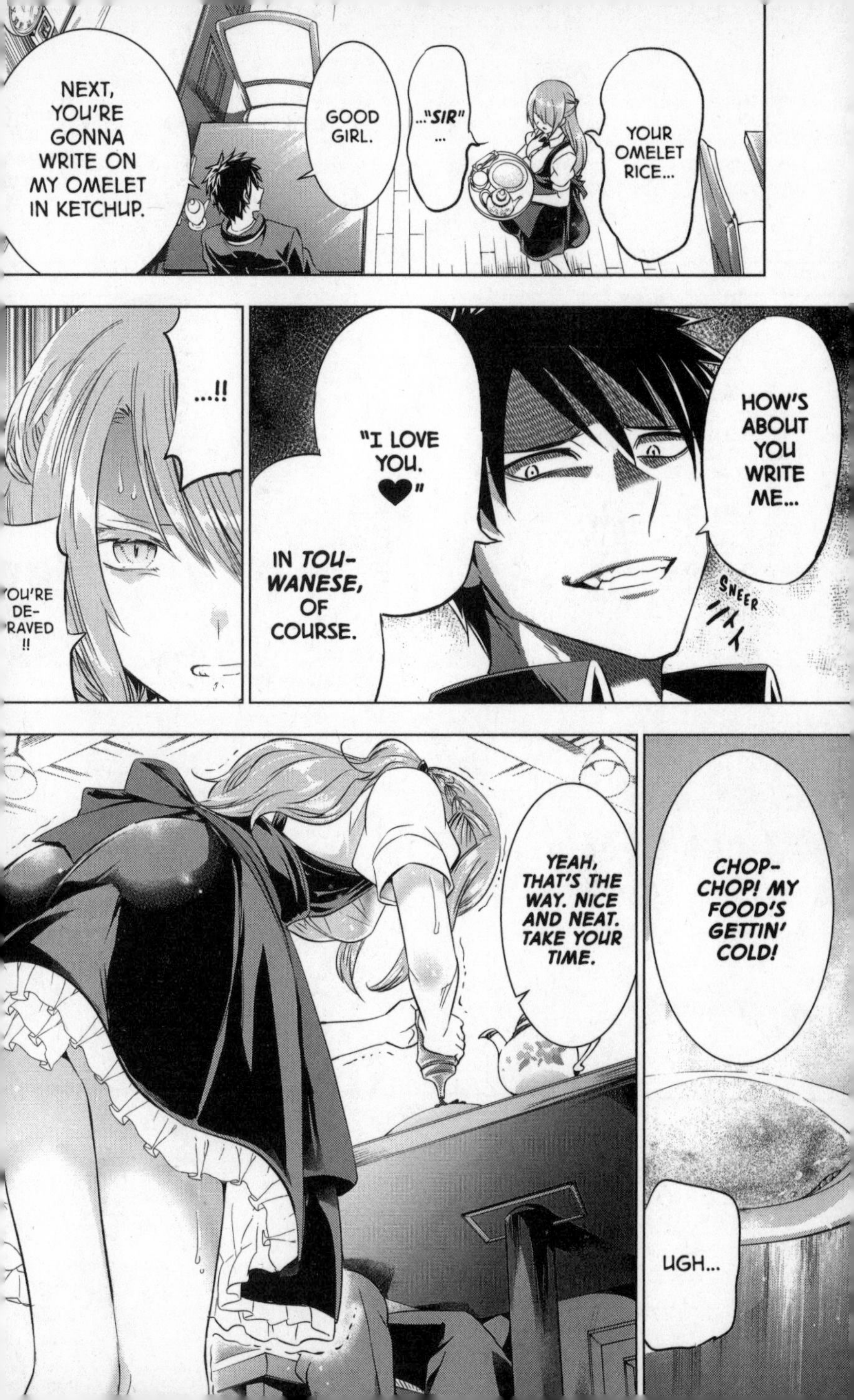
YOUR OMELET RICE...
..."SIR" ...
GOOD GIRL.
NEXT, YOU'RE GONNA WRITE ON MY OMELET IN KETCHUP.
HOW'S ABOUT YOU WRITE ME...
SNEER
"I LOVE YOU. ♥"
IN TOU-WANESE, OF COURSE.
...!!
OU'RE DE-RAVED !!
CHOP-CHOP! MY FOOD'S GETTIN' COLD!
UGH...
YEAH, THAT'S THE WAY. NICE AND NEAT. TAKE YOUR TIME.

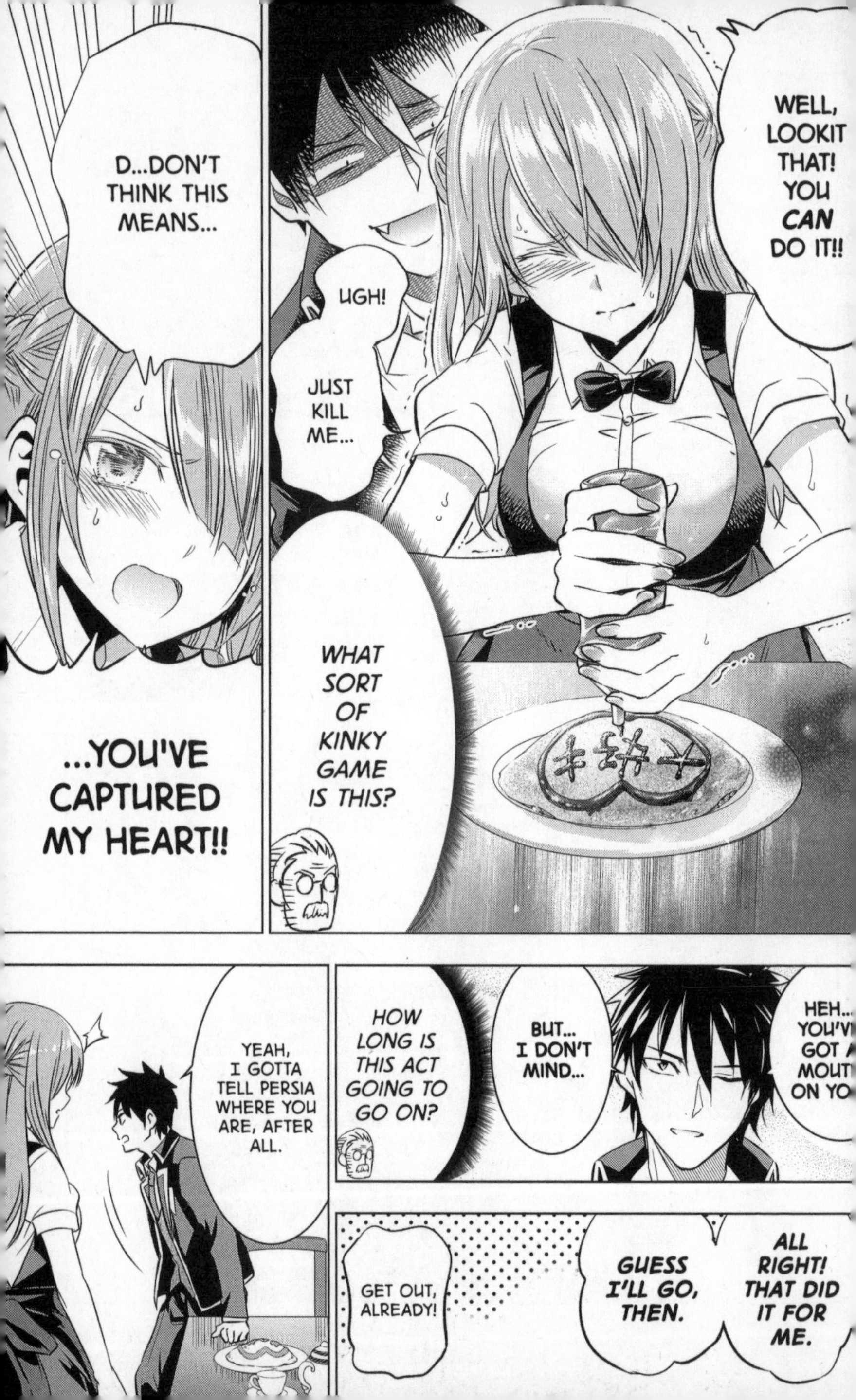
WELL, LOOKIT THAT! YOU CAN DO IT!!
UGH!
JUST KILL ME...
WHAT SORT OF KINKY GAME IS THIS?
D...DON'T THINK THIS MEANS...
...YOU'VE CAPTURED MY HEART!!
HEH... YOU'V GOT A MOUT ON YO
BUT... I DON'T MIND...
HOW LONG IS THIS ACT GOING TO GO ON?
ALL RIGHT! THAT DID IT FOR ME.
GUESS I'LL GO, THEN.
GET OUT, ALREADY!
YEAH, I GOTTA TELL PERSIA WHERE YOU ARE, AFTER ALL.

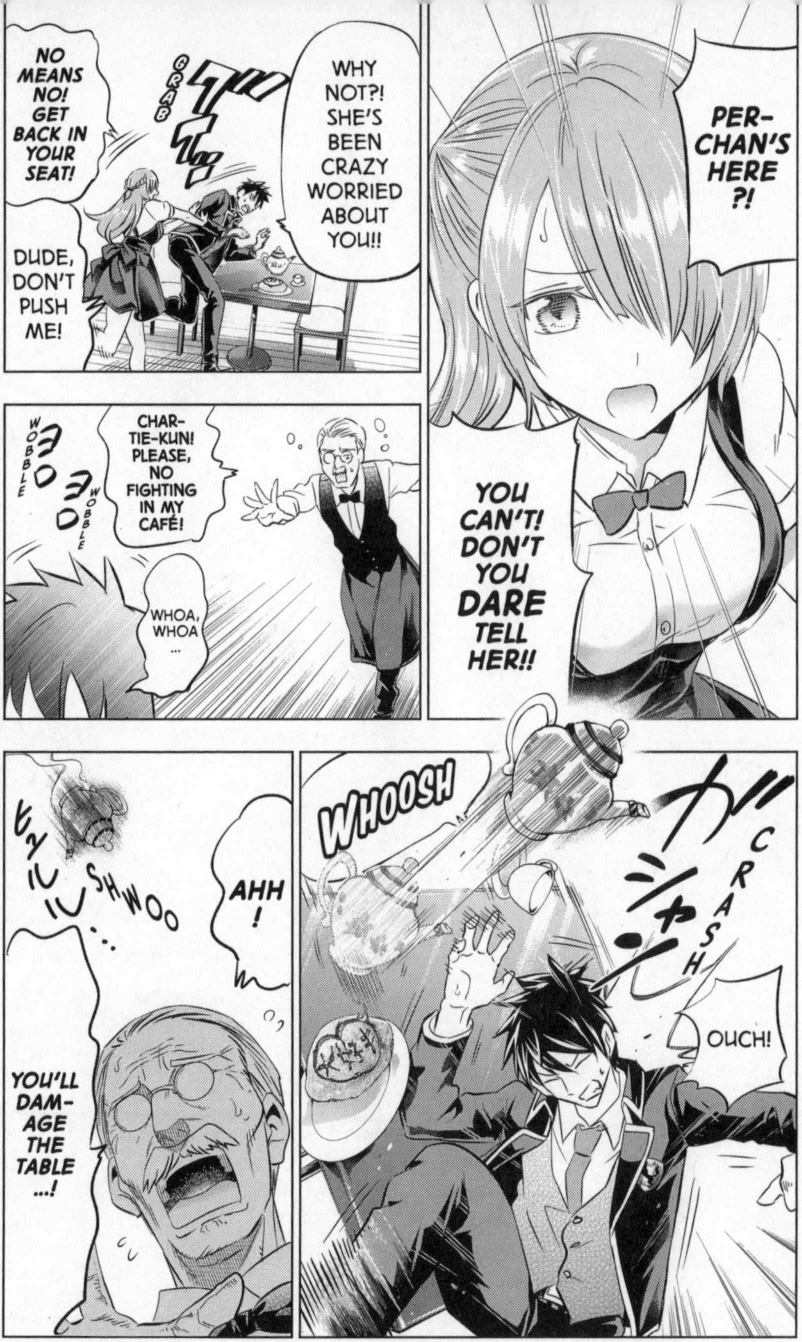
PER-CHAN'S HERE?!
YOU CAN'T! DON'T YOU DARE TELL HER!!
WHY NOT?! SHE'S BEEN CRAZY WORRIED ABOUT YOU!!
GRAB
NO MEANS NO! GET BACK IN YOUR SEAT!
DUDE, DON'T PUSH ME!
CHAR-TIE-KUN! PLEASE, NO FIGHTING IN MY CAFÉ!
WOBBLE
WOBBLE
WHOA, WHOA ...
WHOOSH
CRASH
OUCH!
AHH!
SHWOO...
YOU'LL DAM-AGE THE TABLE ...!

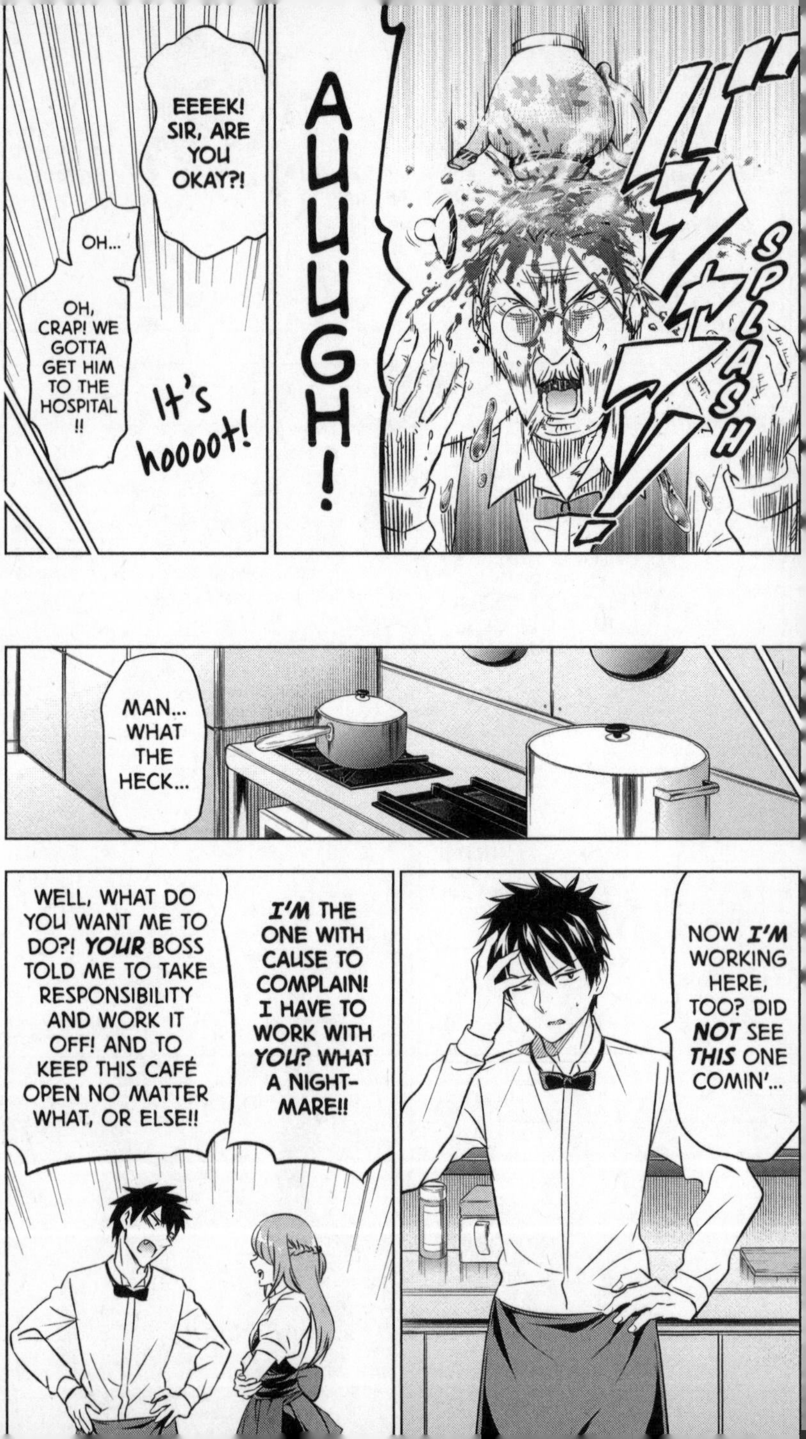
SPLASH
AUUUGH!
EEEEK! SIR, ARE YOU OKAY?!
OH...
It's hoooot!
OH, CRAP! WE GOTTA GET HIM TO THE HOSPITAL!!
MAN... WHAT THE HECK...
NOW I'M WORKING HERE, TOO? DID NOT SEE THIS ONE COMIN'...
I'M THE ONE WITH CAUSE TO COMPLAIN! I HAVE TO WORK WITH YOU? WHAT A NIGHTMARE!!
WELL, WHAT DO YOU WANT ME TO DO?! YOUR BOSS TOLD ME TO TAKE RESPONSIBILITY AND WORK IT OFF! AND TO KEEP THIS CAFÉ OPEN NO MATTER WHAT, OR ELSE!!

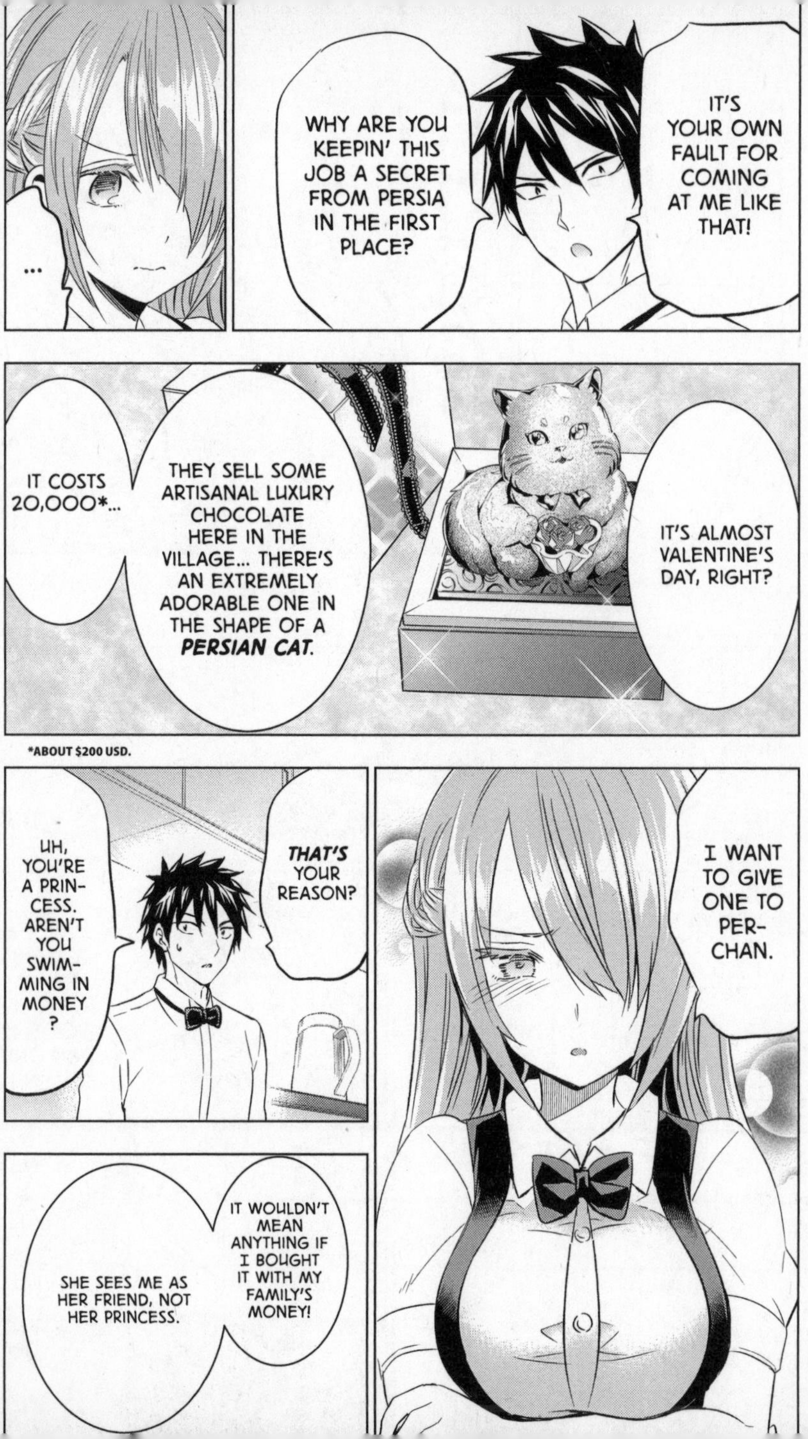
IT'S YOUR OWN FAULT FOR COMING AT ME LIKE THAT!
WHY ARE YOU KEEPIN' THIS JOB A SECRET FROM PERSIA IN THE FIRST PLACE?
...
IT'S ALMOST VALENTINE'S DAY, RIGHT?
THEY SELL SOME ARTISANAL LUXURY CHOCOLATE HERE IN THE VILLAGE... THERE'S AN EXTREMELY ADORABLE ONE IN THE SHAPE OF A ***PERSIAN CAT***.
IT COSTS 20,000*...
I WANT TO GIVE ONE TO PER-CHAN.
THAT'S YOUR REASON?
UH, YOU'RE A PRINCESS. AREN'T YOU SWIMMING IN MONEY?
IT WOULDN'T MEAN ANYTHING IF I BOUGHT IT WITH MY FAMILY'S MONEY!
SHE SEES ME AS HER FRIEND, NOT HER PRINCESS.

*ABOUT $200 USD.

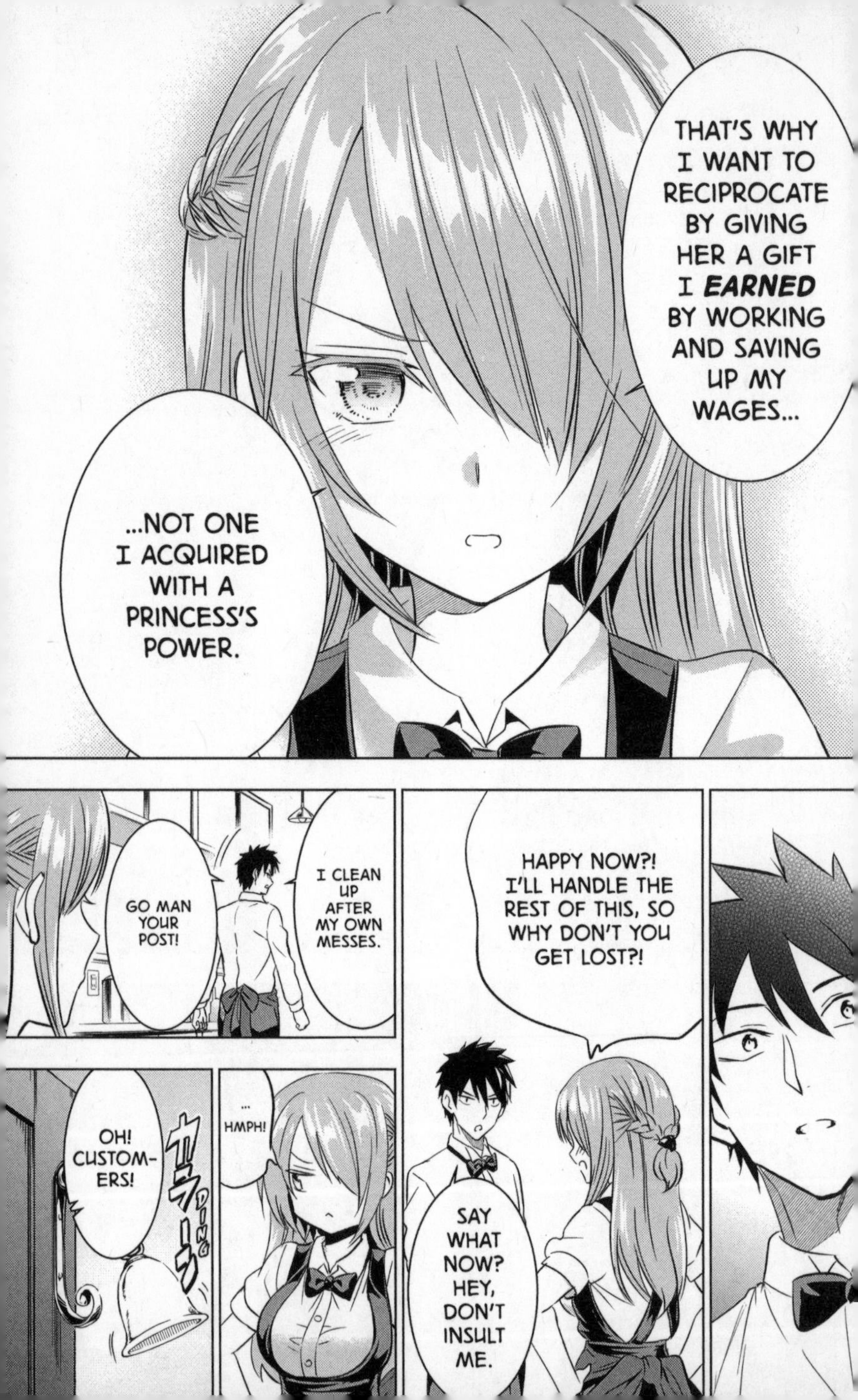
THAT'S WHY I WANT TO RECIPROCATE BY GIVING HER A GIFT I ***EARNED*** BY WORKING AND SAVING UP MY WAGES...
...NOT ONE I ACQUIRED WITH A PRINCESS'S POWER.
HAPPY NOW?! I'LL HANDLE THE REST OF THIS, SO WHY DON'T YOU GET LOST?!
SAY WHAT NOW? HEY, DON'T INSULT ME.
I CLEAN UP AFTER MY OWN MESSES.
GO MAN YOUR POST!
...HMPH!
DING
OH! CUSTOM-ERS!

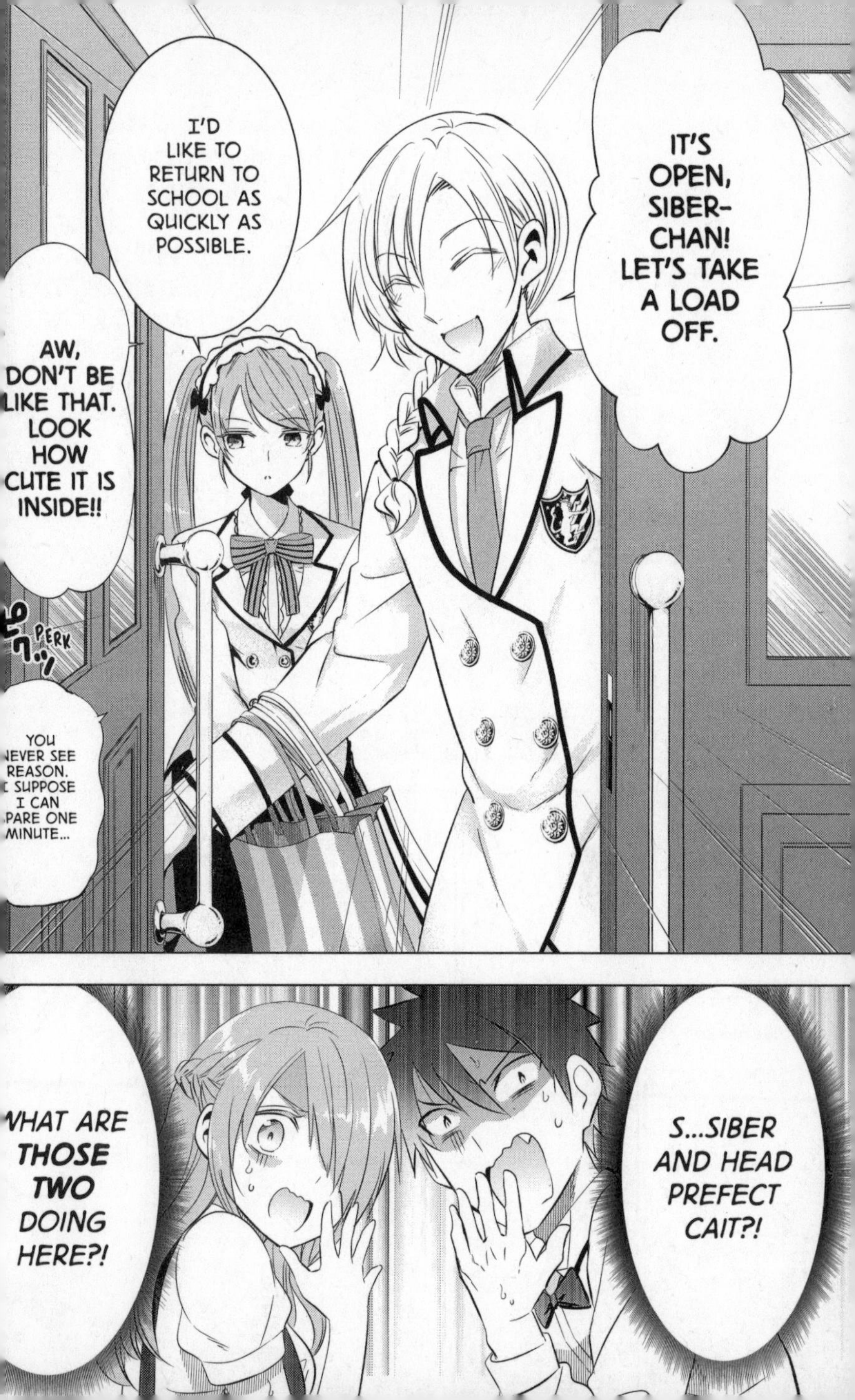
IT'S OPEN, SIBER-CHAN! LET'S TAKE A LOAD OFF.
I'D LIKE TO RETURN TO SCHOOL AS QUICKLY AS POSSIBLE.
AW, DON'T BE LIKE THAT. LOOK HOW CUTE IT IS INSIDE!!
PERK
YOU NEVER SEE REASON. I SUPPOSE I CAN SPARE ONE MINUTE...
S...SIBER AND HEAD PREFECT CAIT?!
WHAT ARE THOSE TWO DOING HERE?!

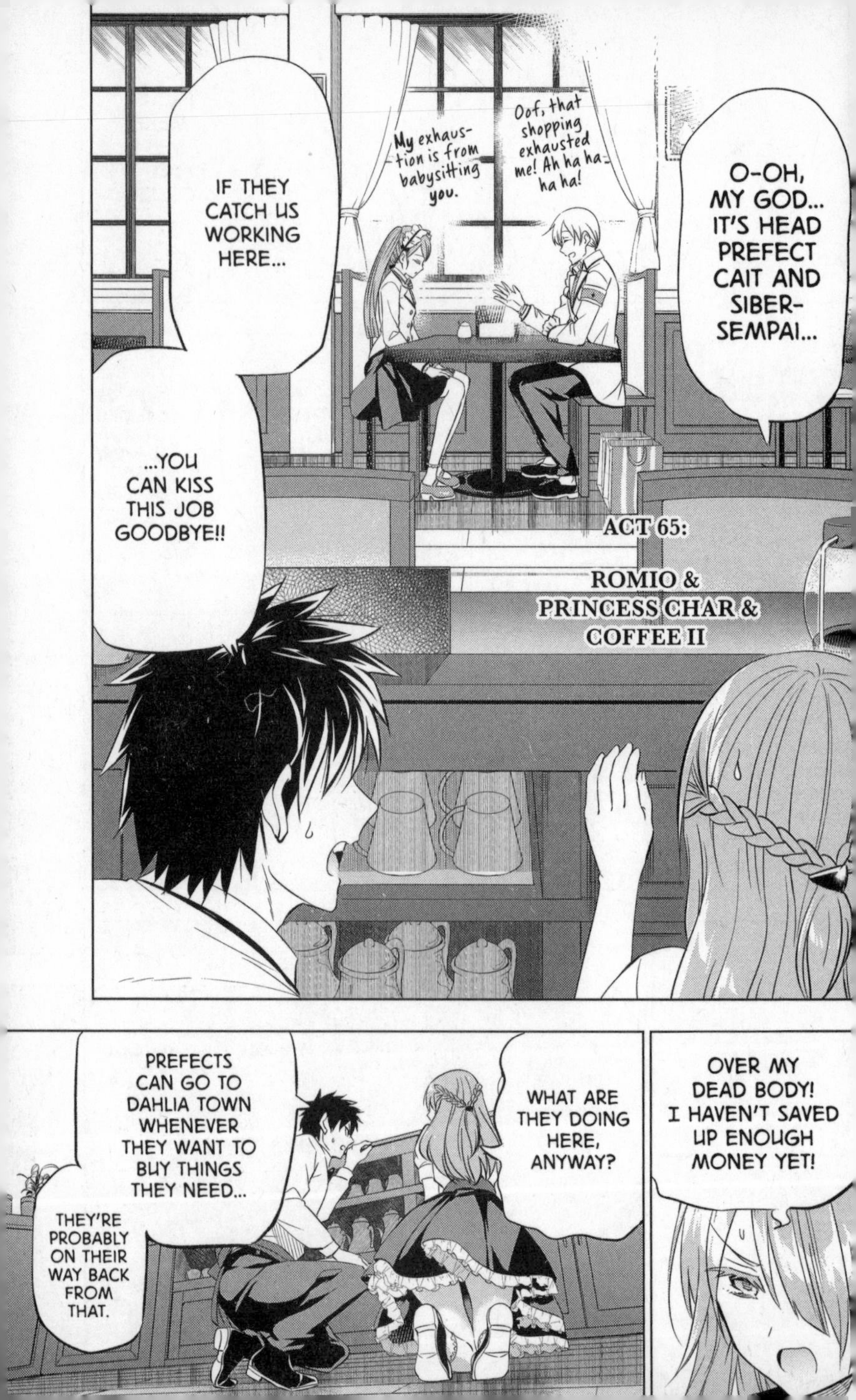
O-OH, MY GOD... IT'S HEAD PREFECT CAIT AND SIBER-SEMPAI...
Oof, that shopping exhausted me! Ah ha ha ha ha!
My exhaustion is from babysitting you.
ACT 65:
ROMIO & PRINCESS CHAR & COFFEE II
IF THEY CATCH US WORKING HERE...
...YOU CAN KISS THIS JOB GOODBYE!!
OVER MY DEAD BODY! I HAVEN'T SAVED UP ENOUGH MONEY YET!
WHAT ARE THEY DOING HERE, ANYWAY?
PREFECTS CAN GO TO DAHLIA TOWN WHENEVER THEY WANT TO BUY THINGS THEY NEED...
THEY'RE PROBABLY ON THEIR WAY BACK FROM THAT.

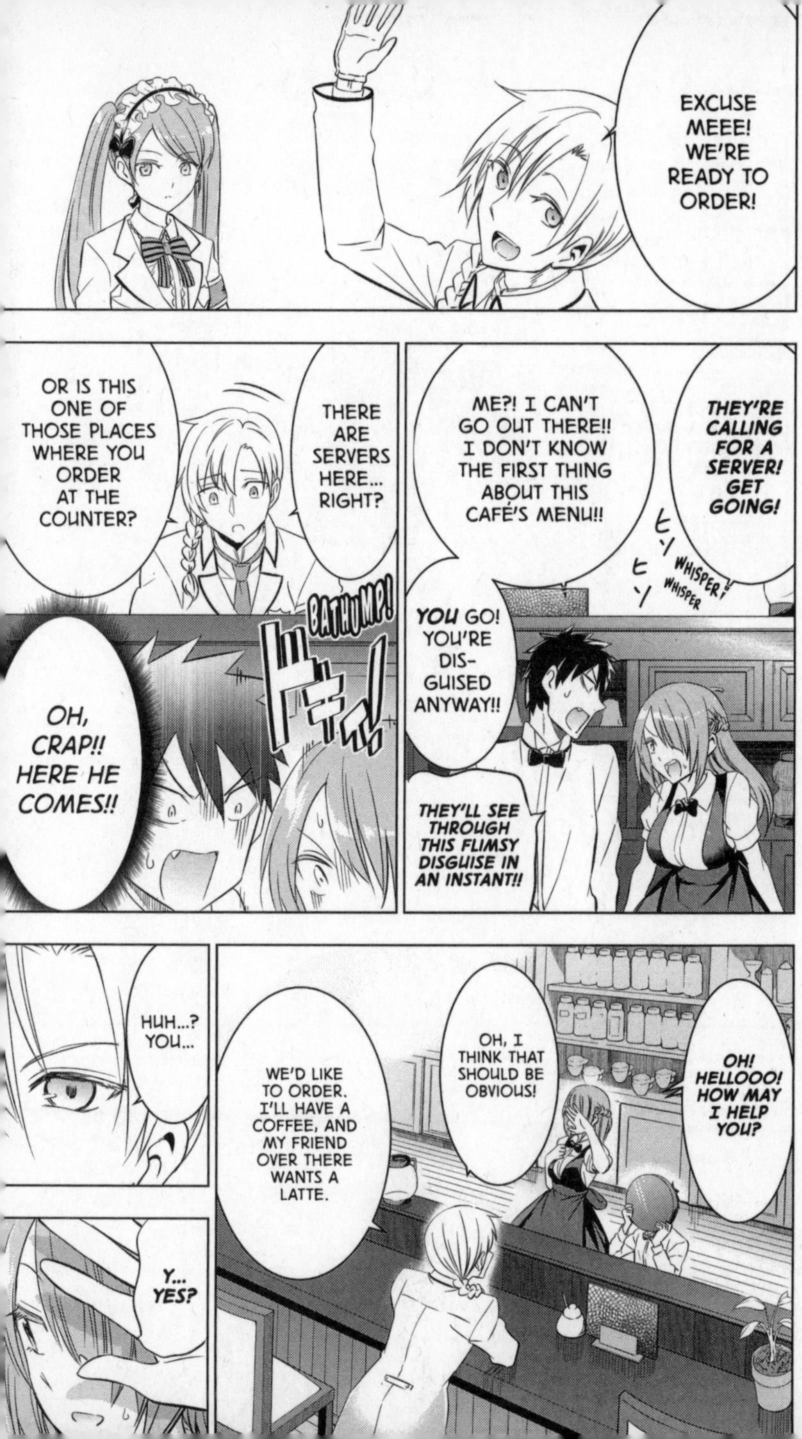
EXCUSE MEEE! WE'RE READY TO ORDER!
THEY'RE CALLING FOR A SERVER! GET GOING!
ME?! I CAN'T GO OUT THERE!! I DON'T KNOW THE FIRST THING ABOUT THIS CAFÉ'S MENU!!
ヒソ ヒソ
WHISPER WHISPER
YOU GO! YOU'RE DIS-GUISED ANYWAY!!
THEY'LL SEE THROUGH THIS FLIMSY DISGUISE IN AN INSTANT!!
THERE ARE SERVERS HERE... RIGHT?
OR IS THIS ONE OF THOSE PLACES WHERE YOU ORDER AT THE COUNTER?
BATHUMP!
OH, CRAP!! HERE HE COMES!!
OH! HELLOOO! HOW MAY I HELP YOU?
OH, I THINK THAT SHOULD BE OBVIOUS!
WE'D LIKE TO ORDER. I'LL HAVE A COFFEE, AND MY FRIEND OVER THERE WANTS A LATTE.
HUH...? YOU...
Y... YES?

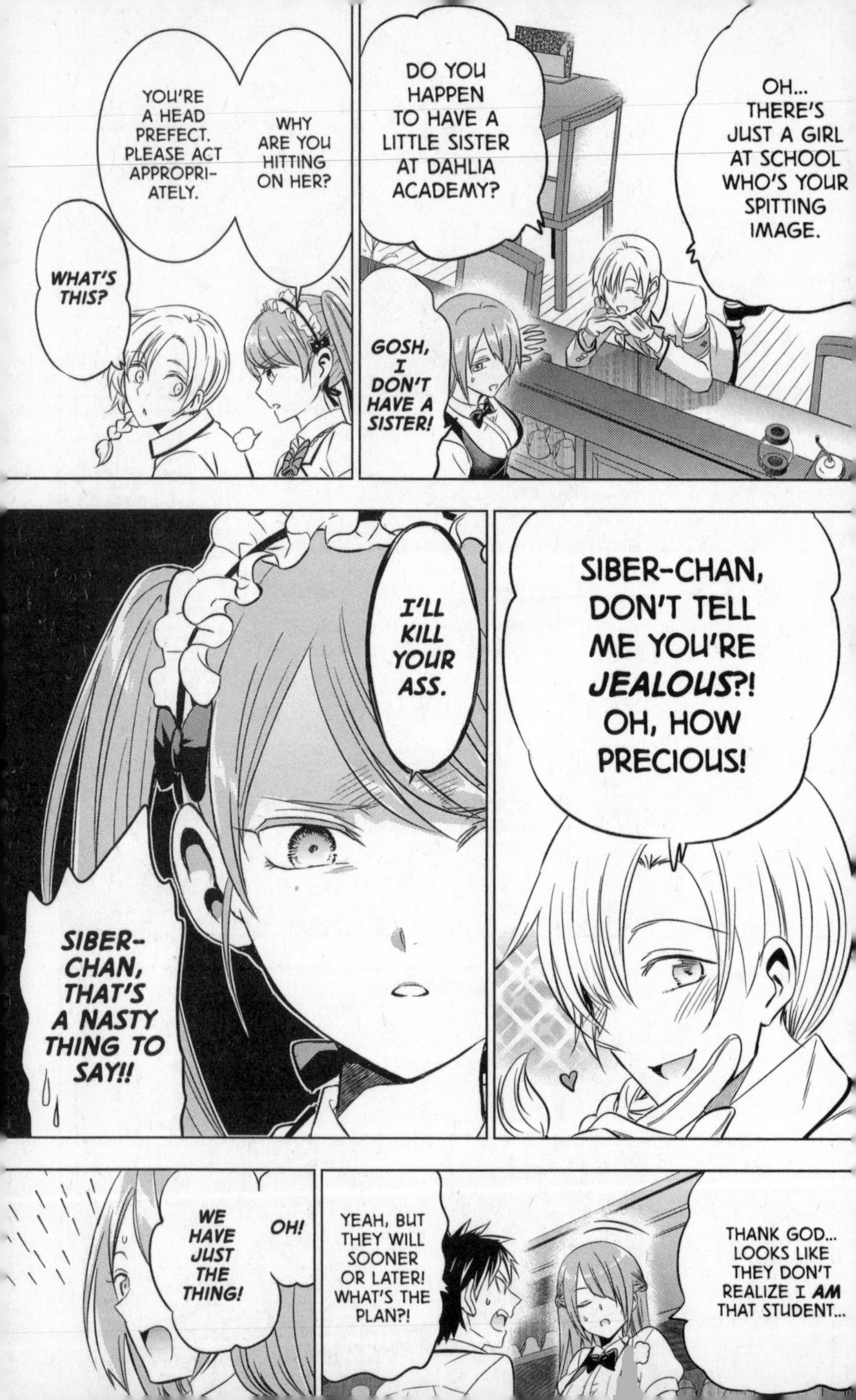
OH... THERE'S JUST A GIRL AT SCHOOL WHO'S YOUR SPITTING IMAGE.
DO YOU HAPPEN TO HAVE A LITTLE SISTER AT DAHLIA ACADEMY?
GOSH, I DON'T HAVE A SISTER!
WHY ARE YOU HITTING ON HER?
YOU'RE A HEAD PREFECT. PLEASE ACT APPROPRI-ATELY.
WHAT'S THIS?
SIBER-CHAN, DON'T TELL ME YOU'RE *JEALOUS*?! OH, HOW PRECIOUS!
I'LL KILL YOUR ASS.
SIBER-CHAN, THAT'S A NASTY THING TO SAY!!
THANK GOD... LOOKS LIKE THEY DON'T REALIZE I *AM* THAT STUDENT...
YEAH, BUT THEY WILL SOONER OR LATER! WHAT'S THE PLAN?!
OH! WE HAVE JUST THE THING!

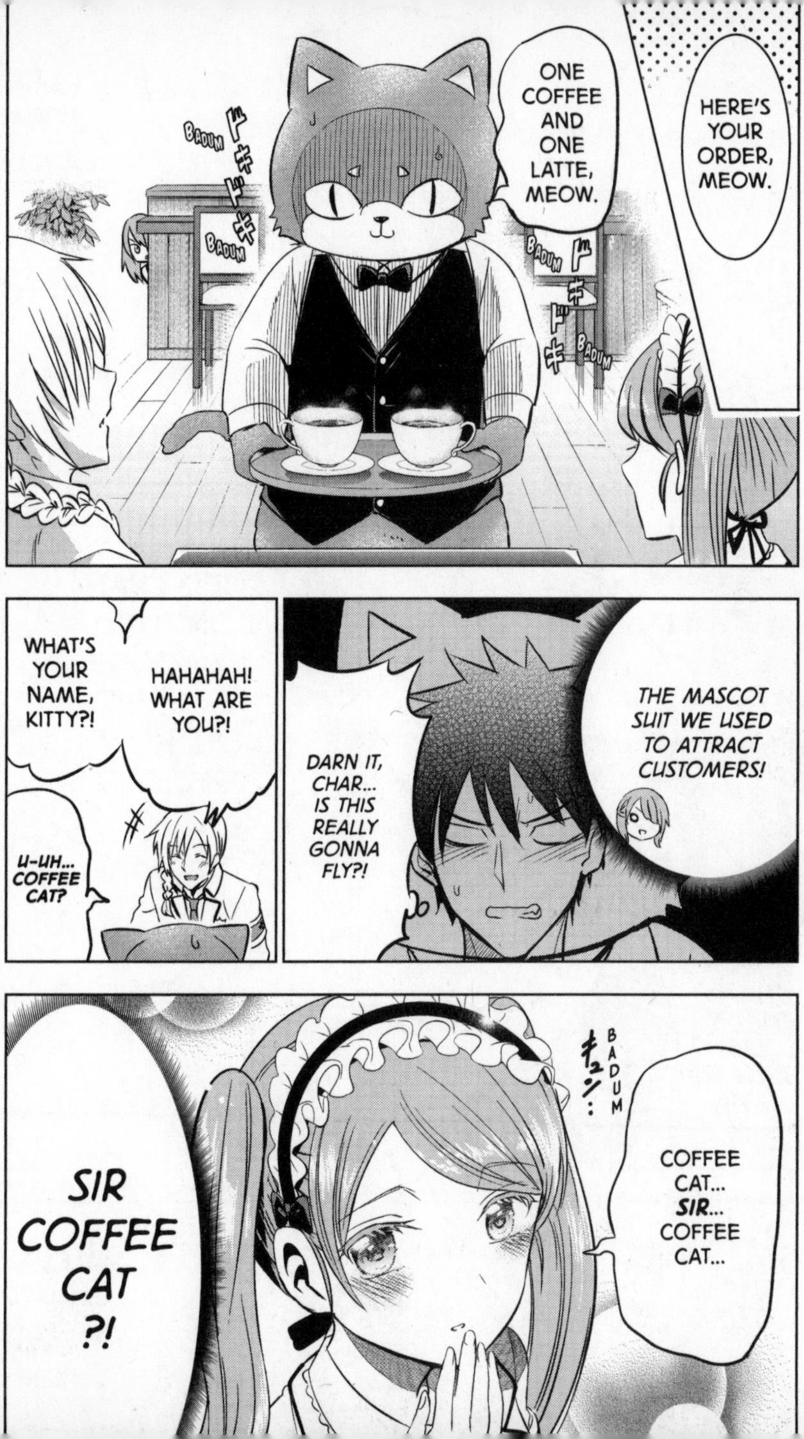
HERE'S YOUR ORDER, MEOW.
ONE COFFEE AND ONE LATTE, MEOW.
BADUM
BADUM
BADUM
BADUM
THE MASCOT SUIT WE USED TO ATTRACT CUSTOMERS!
DARN IT, CHAR... IS THIS REALLY GONNA FLY?!
HAHAHAH! WHAT ARE YOU?!
WHAT'S YOUR NAME, KITTY?!
U-UH... COFFEE CAT?
BADUM
COFFEE CAT... **SIR**... COFFEE CAT...
SIR COFFEE CAT ?!

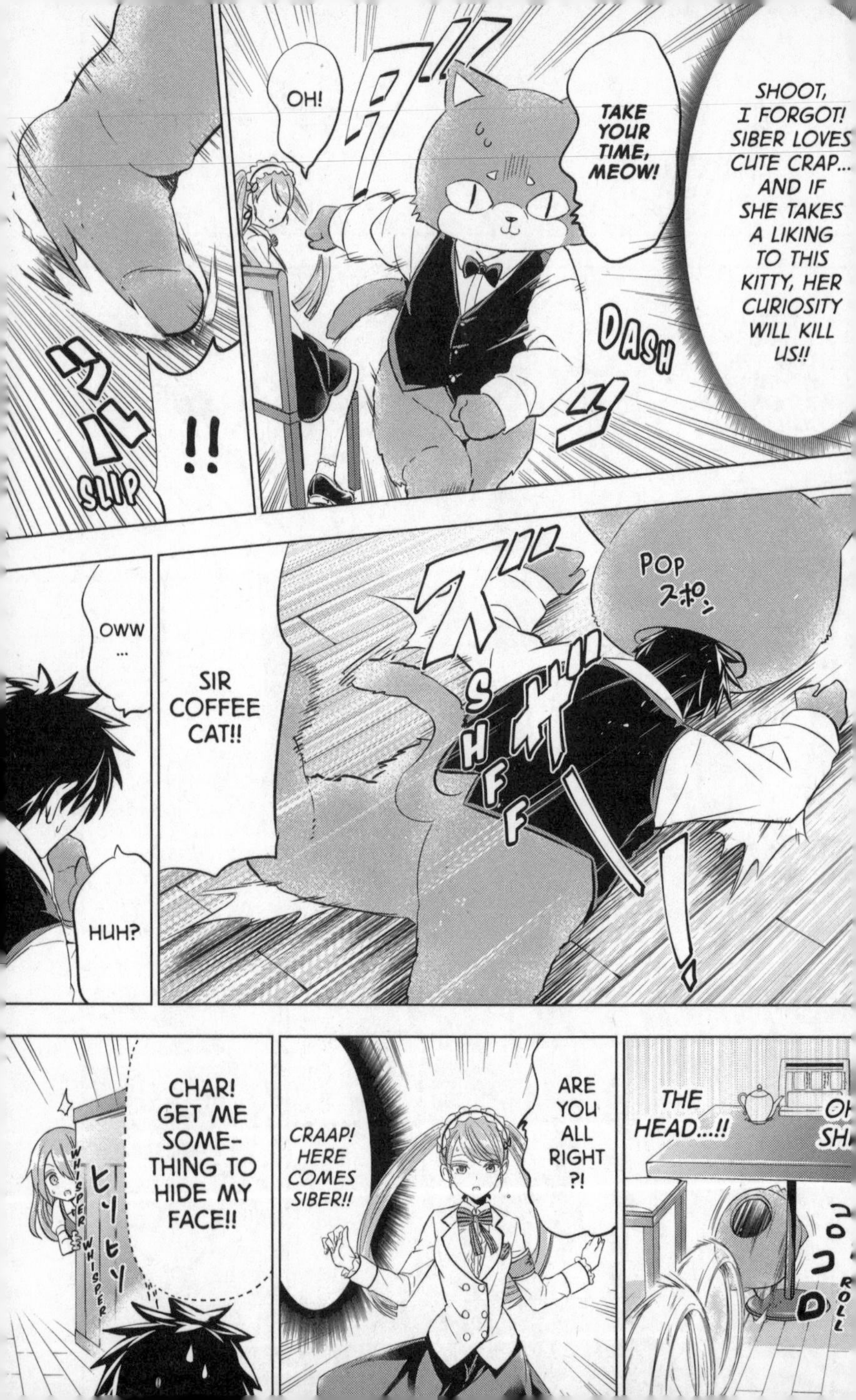
SHOOT, I FORGOT! SIBER LOVES CUTE CRAP... AND IF SHE TAKES A LIKING TO THIS KITTY, HER CURIOSITY WILL KILL US!!
TAKE YOUR TIME, MEOW!
DASH
OH!
SLIP
!!
POP
スポン
SHFF
SIR COFFEE CAT!!
OWW ...
HUH?
THE HEAD...!!
OH SH
ROLL
ARE YOU ALL RIGHT?!
CRAAP! HERE COMES SIBER!!
CHAR! GET ME SOME-THING TO HIDE MY FACE!!
WHISPER WHISPER

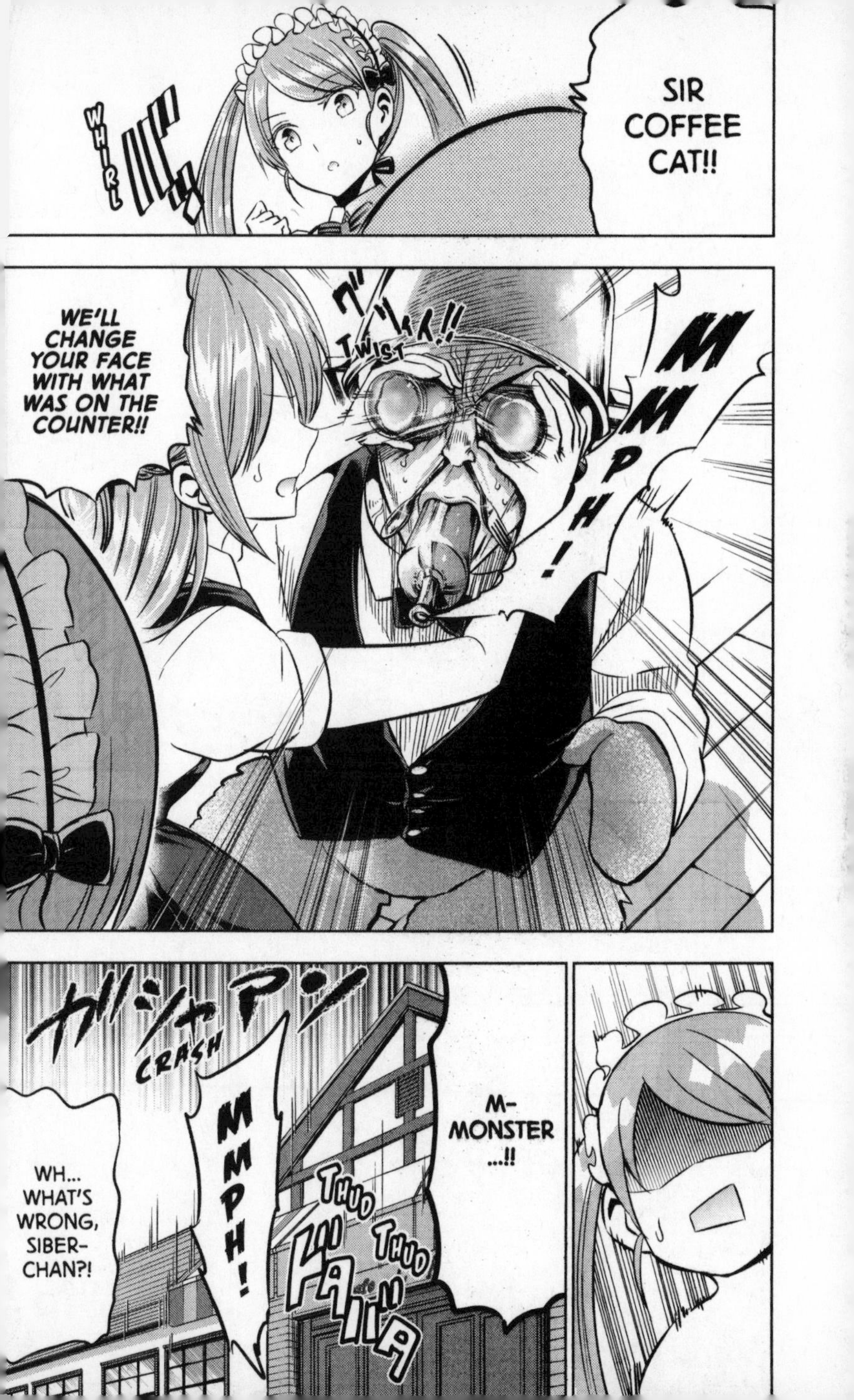
SIR COFFEE CAT!!
WHIRL
MMMPH!
TWIST
WE'LL CHANGE YOUR FACE WITH WHAT WAS ON THE COUNTER!!
CRASH
M-MONSTER ...!!
MMMPH!
THUD THUD
WH... WHAT'S WRONG, SIBER-CHAN?!

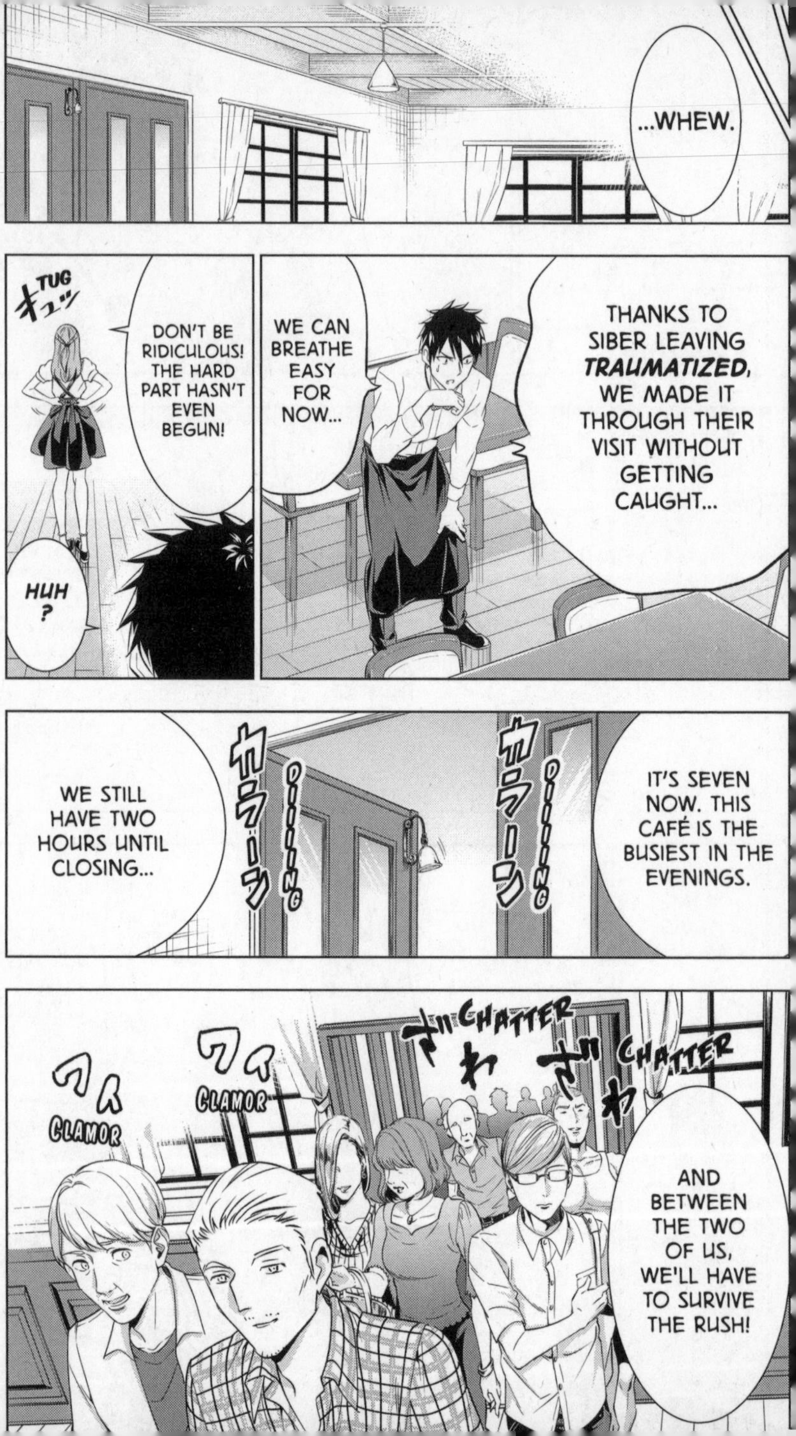
...WHEW.
THANKS TO SIBER LEAVING *TRAUMATIZED*, WE MADE IT THROUGH THEIR VISIT WITHOUT GETTING CAUGHT...
WE CAN BREATHE EASY FOR NOW...
キュッ TUG
DON'T BE RIDICULOUS! THE HARD PART HASN'T EVEN BEGUN!
HUH?
IT'S SEVEN NOW. THIS CAFÉ IS THE BUSIEST IN THE EVENINGS.
カラーン DIIIING
カラーン DIIIING
WE STILL HAVE TWO HOURS UNTIL CLOSING...
ざわ CHATTER
ざわ CHATTER
AND BETWEEN THE TWO OF US, WE'LL HAVE TO SURVIVE THE RUSH!
ワイ CLAMOR
ワイ CLAMOR

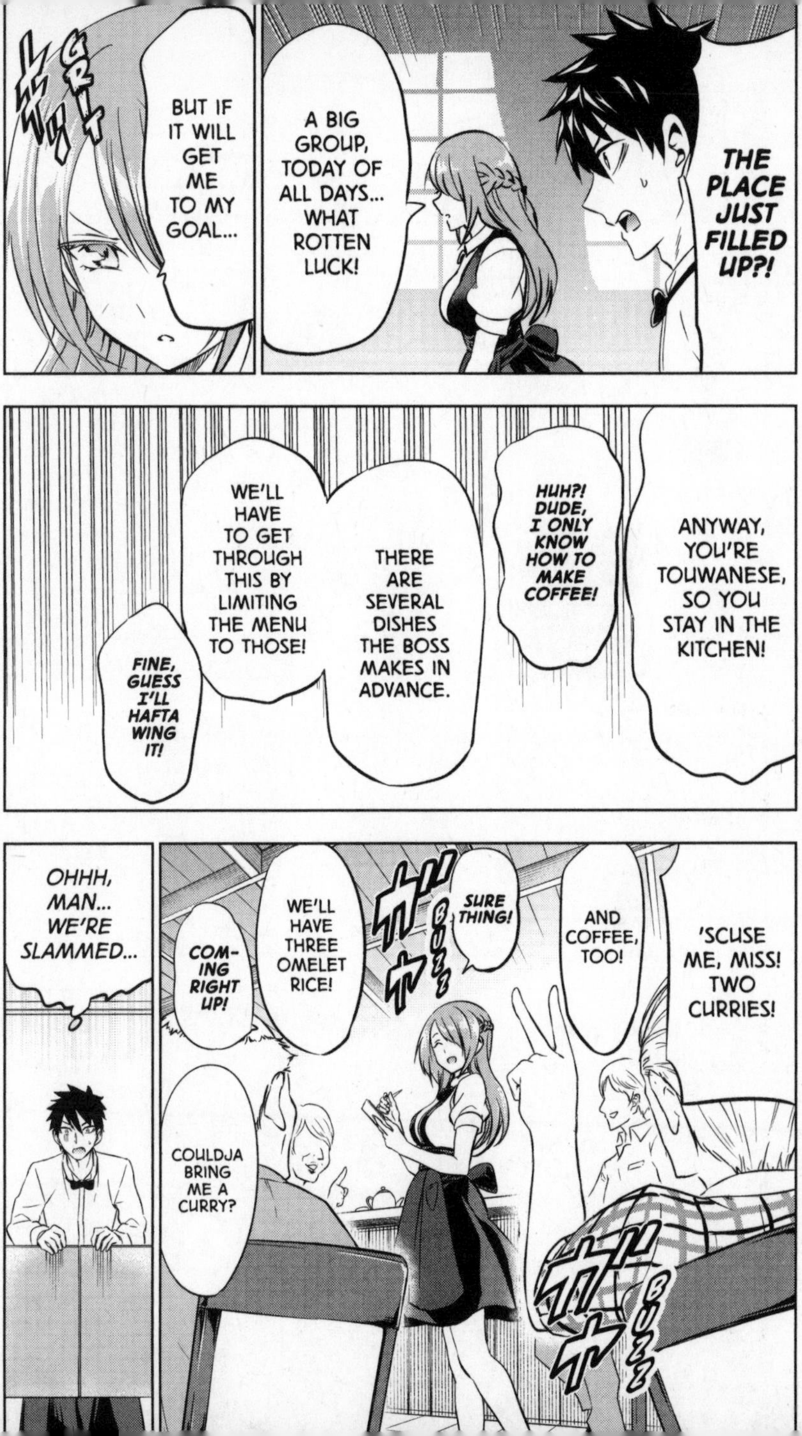
THE PLACE JUST FILLED UP?!
A BIG GROUP, TODAY OF ALL DAYS... WHAT ROTTEN LUCK!
GRIT
BUT IF IT WILL GET ME TO MY GOAL...
ANYWAY, YOU'RE TOUWANESE, SO YOU STAY IN THE KITCHEN!
HUH?! DUDE, I ONLY KNOW HOW TO MAKE COFFEE!
THERE ARE SEVERAL DISHES THE BOSS MAKES IN ADVANCE.
WE'LL HAVE TO GET THROUGH THIS BY LIMITING THE MENU TO THOSE!
FINE, GUESS I'LL HAFTA WING IT!
'SCUSE ME, MISS! TWO CURRIES!
AND COFFEE, TOO!
SURE THING!
BUZZ
WE'LL HAVE THREE OMELET RICE!
COM-ING RIGHT UP!
COULDJA BRING ME A CURRY?
BUZZ
OHHH, MAN... WE'RE SLAMMED...

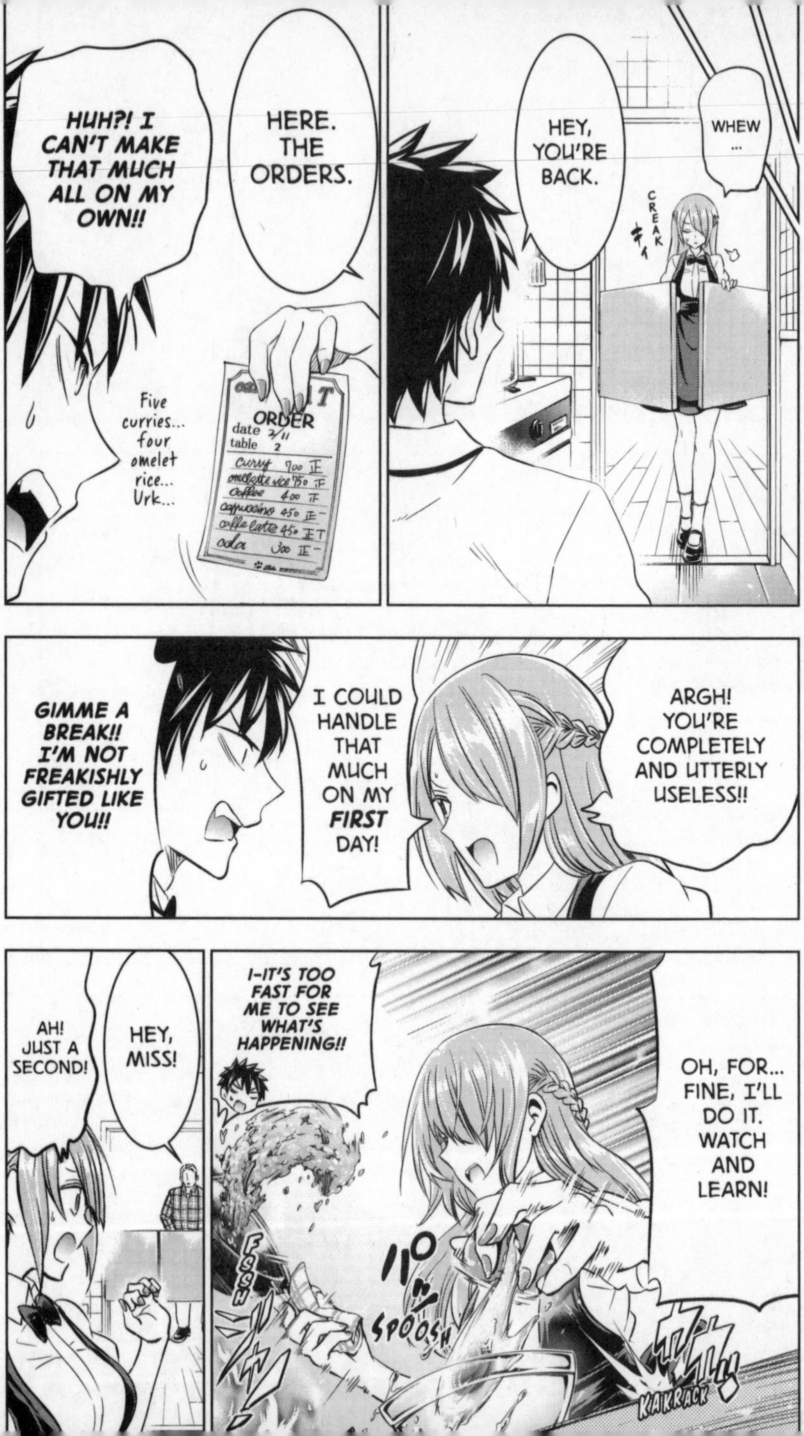
WHEW ...
CREAK
キィ
HEY, YOU'RE BACK.
HERE. THE ORDERS.
HUH?! I CAN'T MAKE THAT MUCH ALL ON MY OWN!!
ORDER
date 2/11
table 2
curry 700
omelette rice 750
coffee 400
cappuccino 450
caffe latte 450
cola 300
Five curries... four omelet rice... Urk...
ARGH! YOU'RE COMPLETELY AND UTTERLY USELESS!!
I COULD HANDLE THAT MUCH ON MY FIRST DAY!
GIMME A BREAK!! I'M NOT FREAKISHLY GIFTED LIKE YOU!!
OH, FOR... FINE, I'LL DO IT. WATCH AND LEARN!
I-IT'S TOO FAST FOR ME TO SEE WHAT'S HAPPENING!!
FSSH
SPOOSH
KAKRACK
HEY, MISS!
AH! JUST A SECOND!

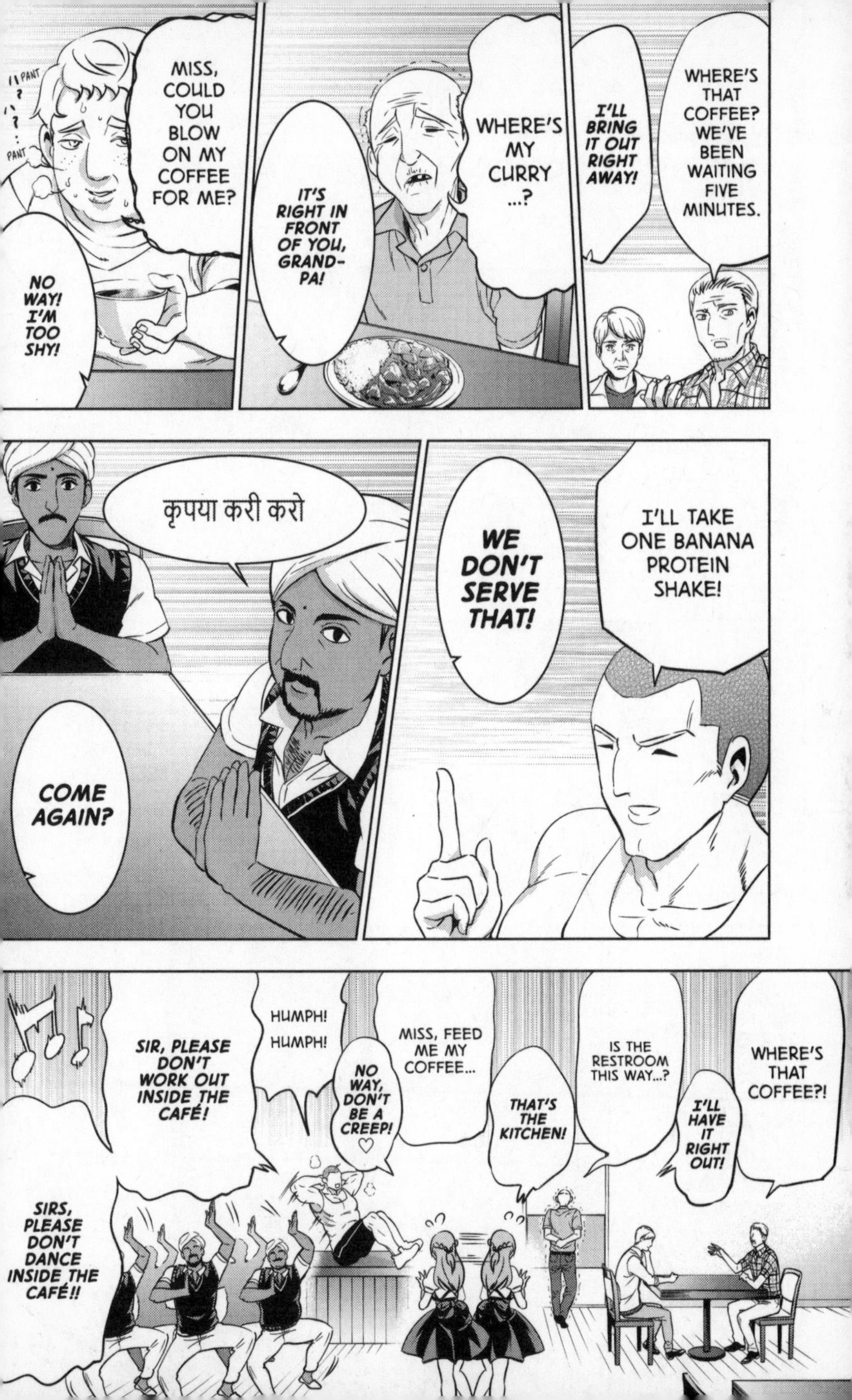
WHERE'S THAT COFFEE? WE'VE BEEN WAITING FIVE MINUTES.
I'LL BRING IT OUT RIGHT AWAY!
WHERE'S MY CURRY ...?
IT'S RIGHT IN FRONT OF YOU, GRAND-PA!
PANT
PANT
MISS, COULD YOU BLOW ON MY COFFEE FOR ME?
NO WAY! I'M TOO SHY!
I'LL TAKE ONE BANANA PROTEIN SHAKE!
WE DON'T SERVE THAT!
कृपया करी करो
COME AGAIN?
WHERE'S THAT COFFEE?!
I'LL HAVE IT RIGHT OUT!
IS THE RESTROOM THIS WAY...?
THAT'S THE KITCHEN!
MISS, FEED ME MY COFFEE...
NO WAY, DON'T BE A CREEP! ♡
HUMPH! HUMPH!
SIR, PLEASE DON'T WORK OUT INSIDE THE CAFÉ!
SIRS, PLEASE DON'T DANCE INSIDE THE CAFÉ!!

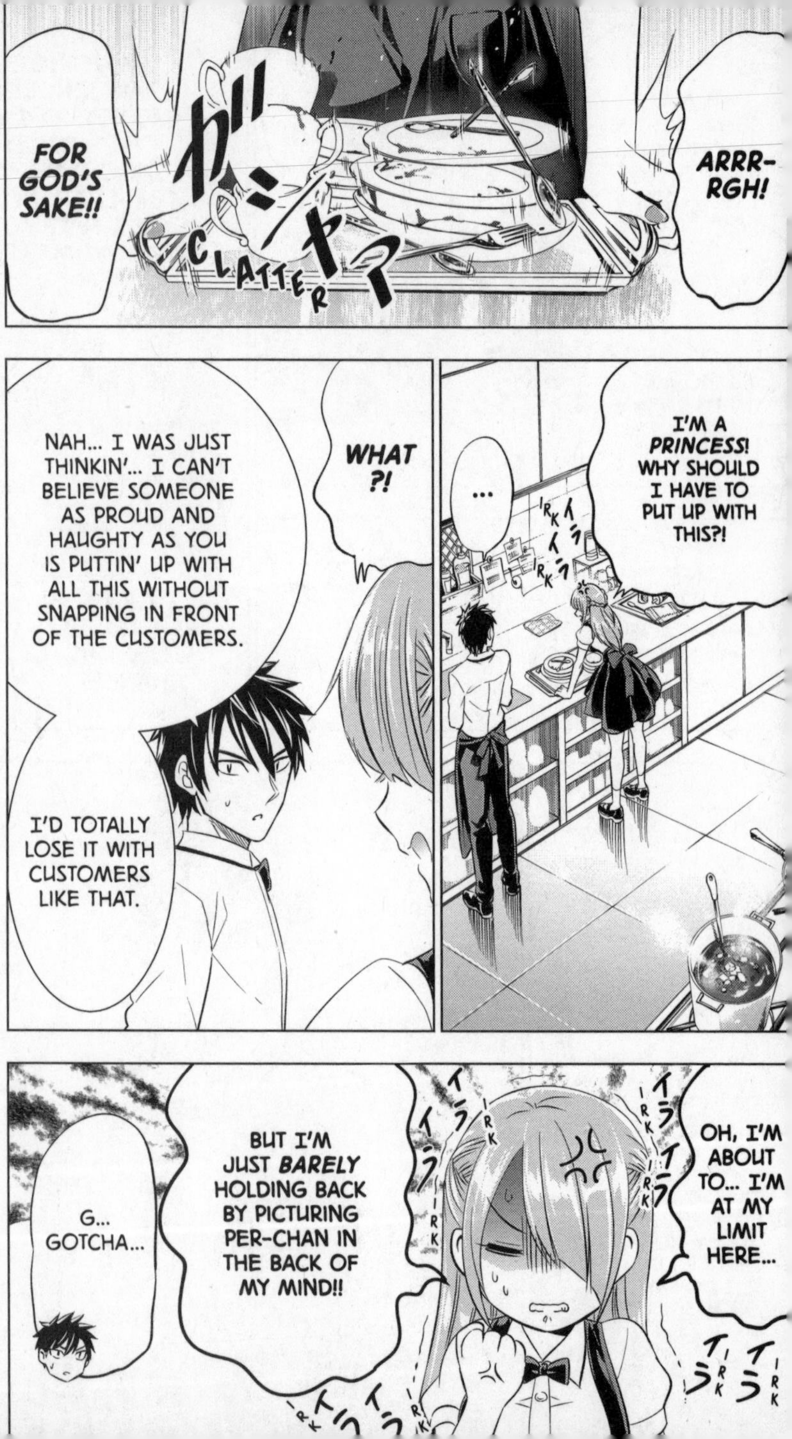
ARRR-RGH!
CLATTER
FOR GOD'S SAKE!!
I'M A PRINCESS! WHY SHOULD I HAVE TO PUT UP WITH THIS?!
IRK IRK
...
WHAT?!
NAH... I WAS JUST THINKIN'... I CAN'T BELIEVE SOMEONE AS PROUD AND HAUGHTY AS YOU IS PUTTIN' UP WITH ALL THIS WITHOUT SNAPPING IN FRONT OF THE CUSTOMERS.
I'D TOTALLY LOSE IT WITH CUSTOMERS LIKE THAT.
OH, I'M ABOUT TO... I'M AT MY LIMIT HERE...
IRK IRK IRK IRK IRK IRK
BUT I'M JUST BARELY HOLDING BACK BY PICTURING PER-CHAN IN THE BACK OF MY MIND!!
G... GOTCHA...

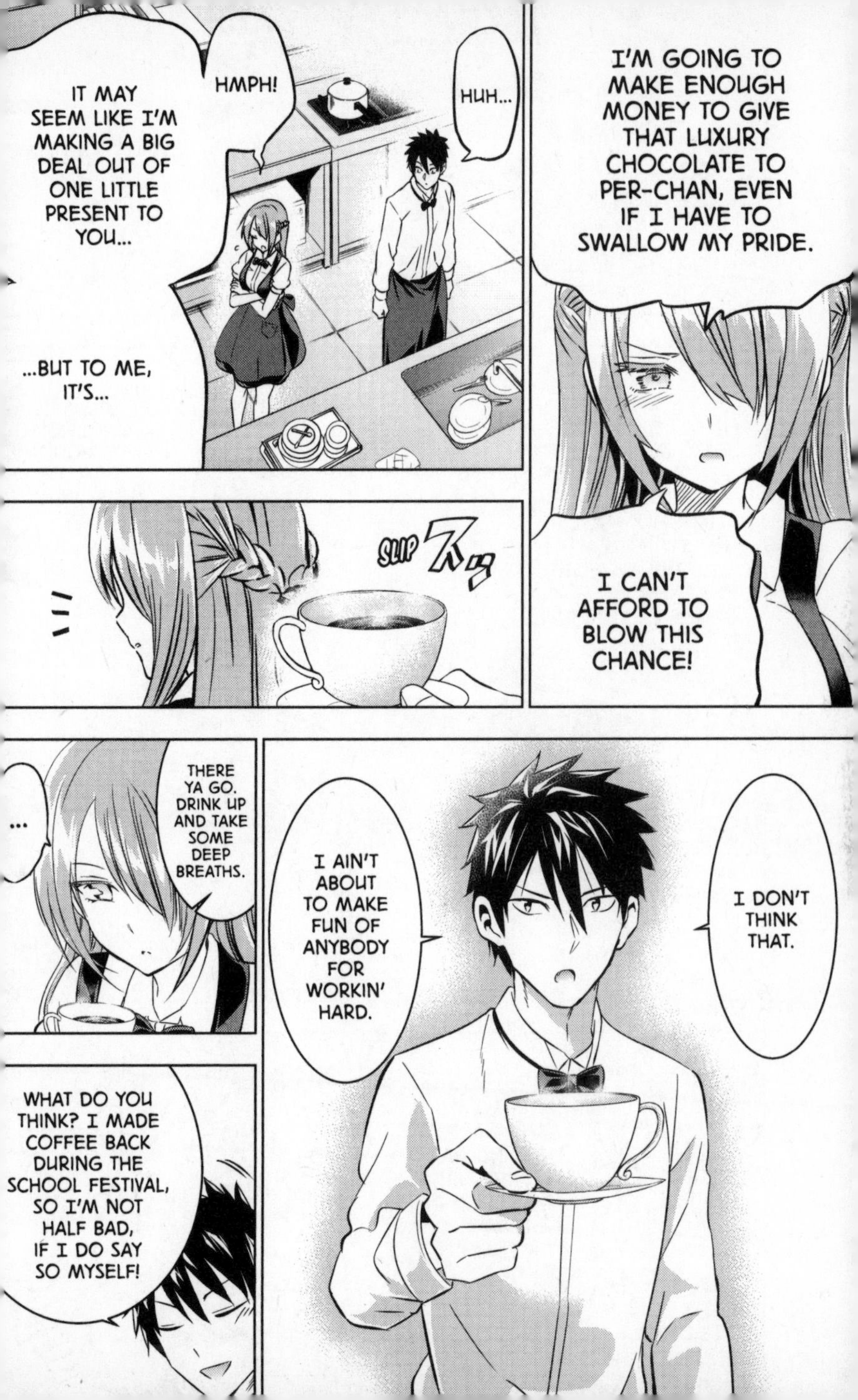
I'M GOING TO MAKE ENOUGH MONEY TO GIVE THAT LUXURY CHOCOLATE TO PER-CHAN, EVEN IF I HAVE TO SWALLOW MY PRIDE.
I CAN'T AFFORD TO BLOW THIS CHANCE!
HUH...
HMPH!
IT MAY SEEM LIKE I'M MAKING A BIG DEAL OUT OF ONE LITTLE PRESENT TO YOU...
...BUT TO ME, IT'S...
SLIP
I DON'T THINK THAT.
I AIN'T ABOUT TO MAKE FUN OF ANYBODY FOR WORKIN' HARD.
THERE YA GO. DRINK UP AND TAKE SOME DEEP BREATHS.
...
WHAT DO YOU THINK? I MADE COFFEE BACK DURING THE SCHOOL FESTIVAL, SO I'M NOT HALF BAD, IF I DO SAY SO MYSELF!

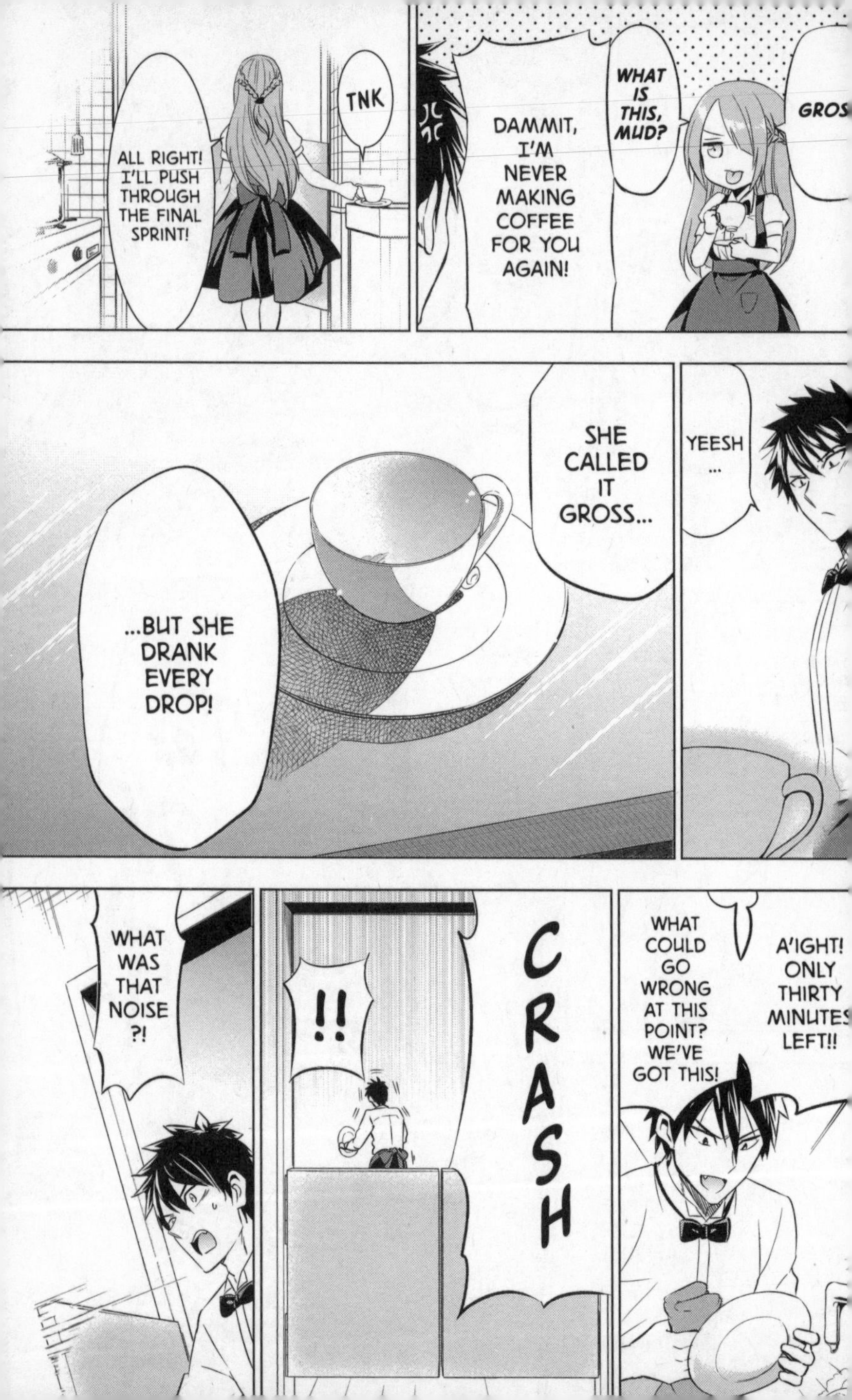
GROS
WHAT IS THIS, MUD?
DAMMIT, I'M NEVER MAKING COFFEE FOR YOU AGAIN!
TNK
ALL RIGHT! I'LL PUSH THROUGH THE FINAL SPRINT!
YEESH ...
SHE CALLED IT GROSS...
...BUT SHE DRANK EVERY DROP!
A'IGHT! ONLY THIRTY MINUTES LEFT!!
WHAT COULD GO WRONG AT THIS POINT? WE'VE GOT THIS!
CRASH
!!
WHAT WAS THAT NOISE ?!

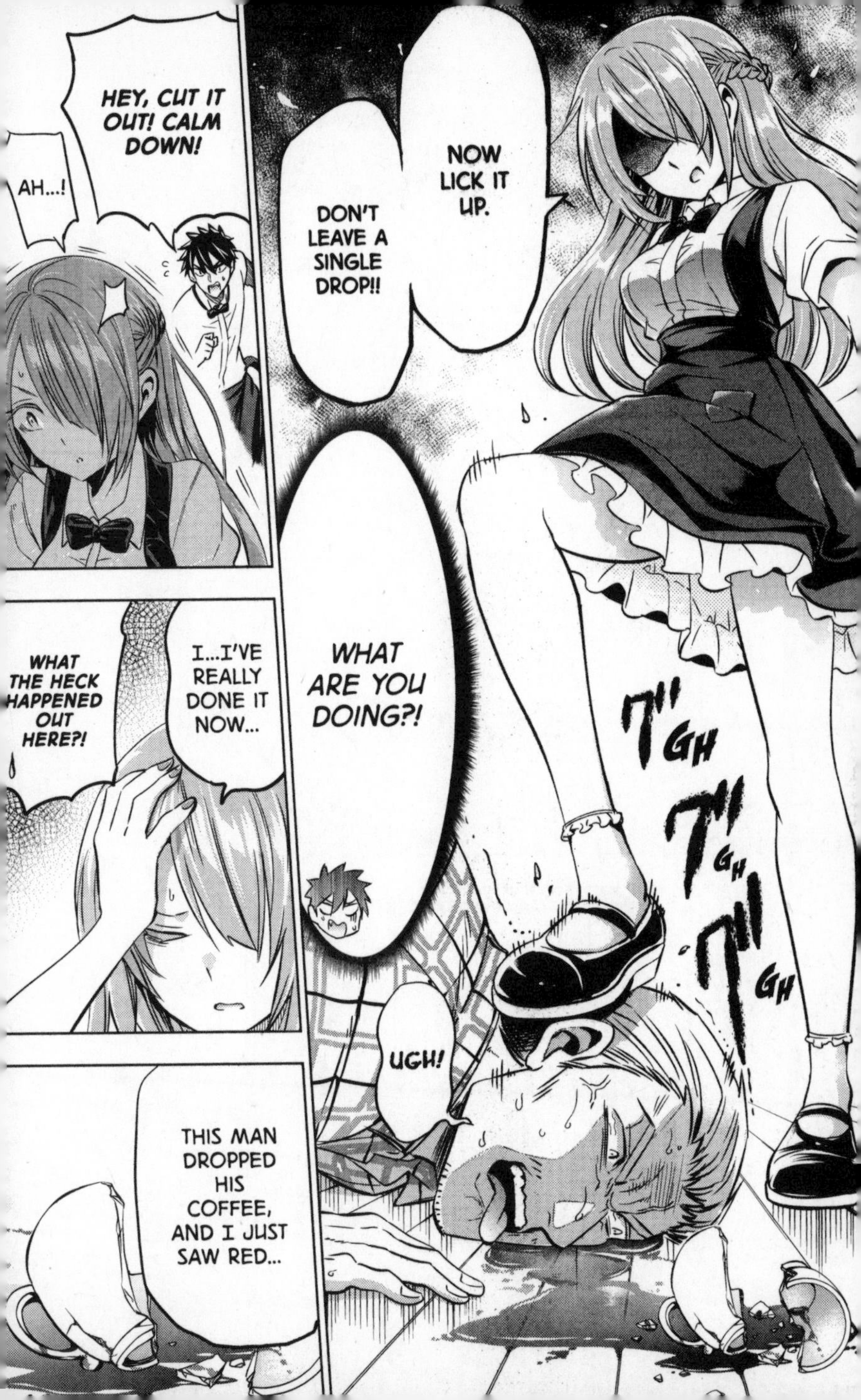
NOW LICK IT UP.
DON'T LEAVE A SINGLE DROP!!
WHAT ARE YOU DOING?!
GH GH GH
UGH!
HEY, CUT IT OUT! CALM DOWN!
AH...!
I...I'VE REALLY DONE IT NOW...
WHAT THE HECK HAPPENED OUT HERE?!
THIS MAN DROPPED HIS COFFEE, AND I JUST SAW RED...

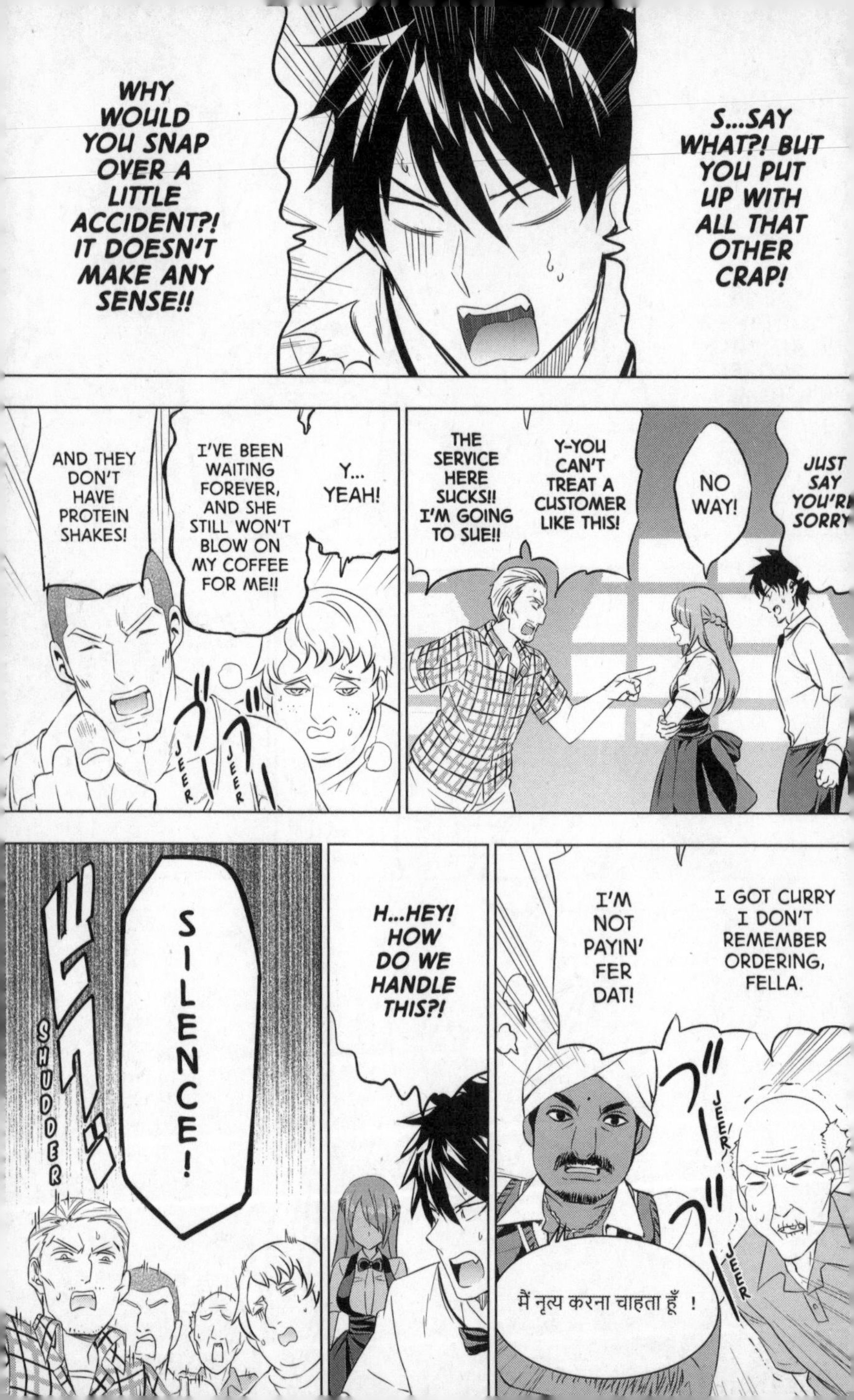
S...SAY WHAT?! BUT YOU PUT UP WITH ALL THAT OTHER CRAP!
WHY WOULD YOU SNAP OVER A LITTLE ACCIDENT?! IT DOESN'T MAKE ANY SENSE!!
JUST SAY YOU'R SORRY
NO WAY!
Y-YOU CAN'T TREAT A CUSTOMER LIKE THIS!
THE SERVICE HERE SUCKS!! I'M GOING TO SUE!!
Y... YEAH!
I'VE BEEN WAITING FOREVER, AND SHE STILL WON'T BLOW ON MY COFFEE FOR ME!!
AND THEY DON'T HAVE PROTEIN SHAKES!
JEER
JEER
I GOT CURRY I DON'T REMEMBER ORDERING, FELLA.
I'M NOT PAYIN' FER DAT!
JEER
JEER
मैं नृत्य करना चाहता हूँ !
H...HEY! HOW DO WE HANDLE THIS?!
SILENCE!
SHUDDER

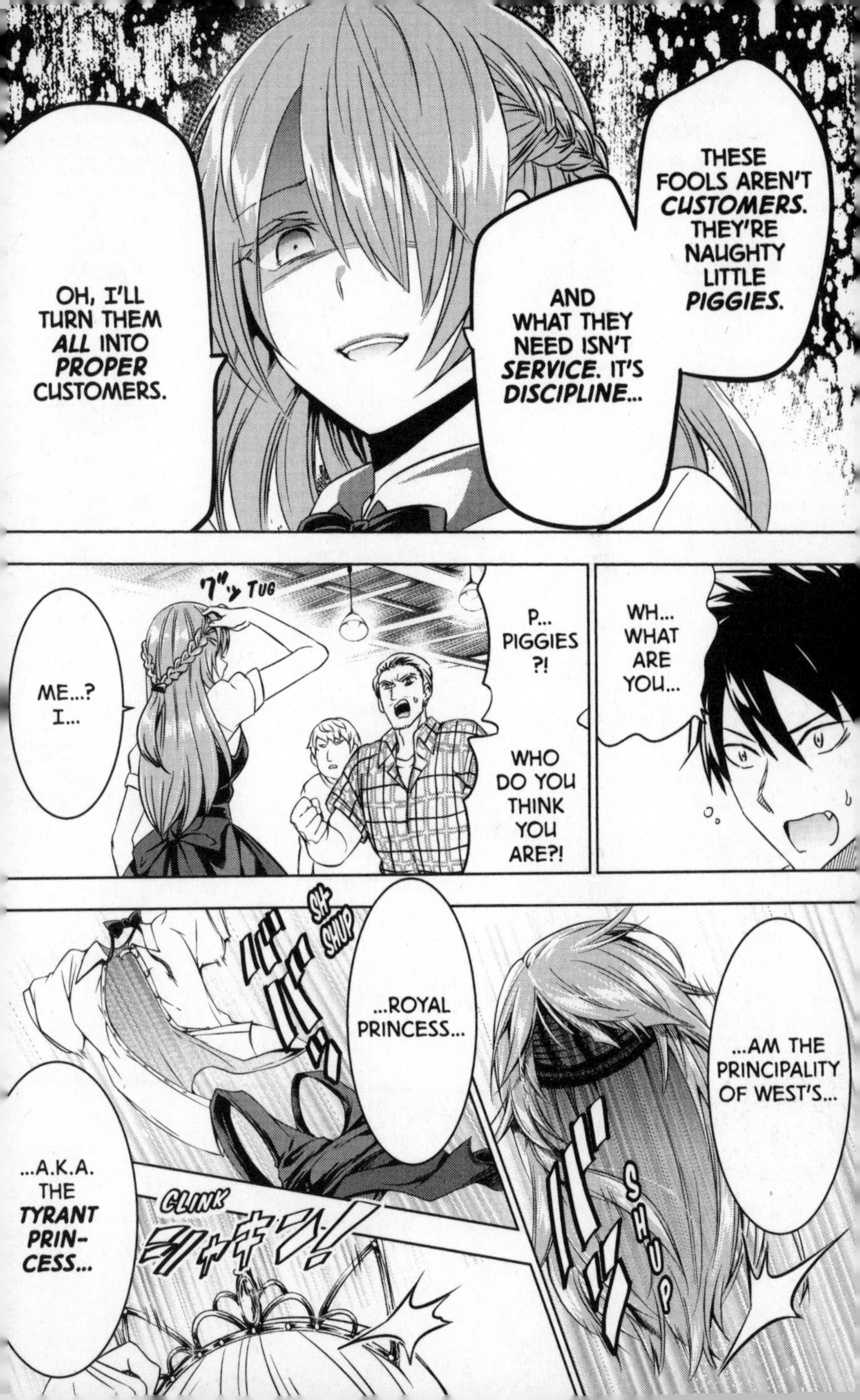
THESE FOOLS AREN'T CUSTOMERS. THEY'RE NAUGHTY LITTLE PIGGIES.
AND WHAT THEY NEED ISN'T SERVICE. IT'S DISCIPLINE...
OH, I'LL TURN THEM ALL INTO PROPER CUSTOMERS.
WH... WHAT ARE YOU...
P... PIGGIES?!
WHO DO YOU THINK YOU ARE?!
TUG
ME...? I...
...AM THE PRINCIPALITY OF WEST'S...
SHUP
...ROYAL PRINCESS...
SH SHUP
...A.K.A. THE TYRANT PRINCESS...
CLINK

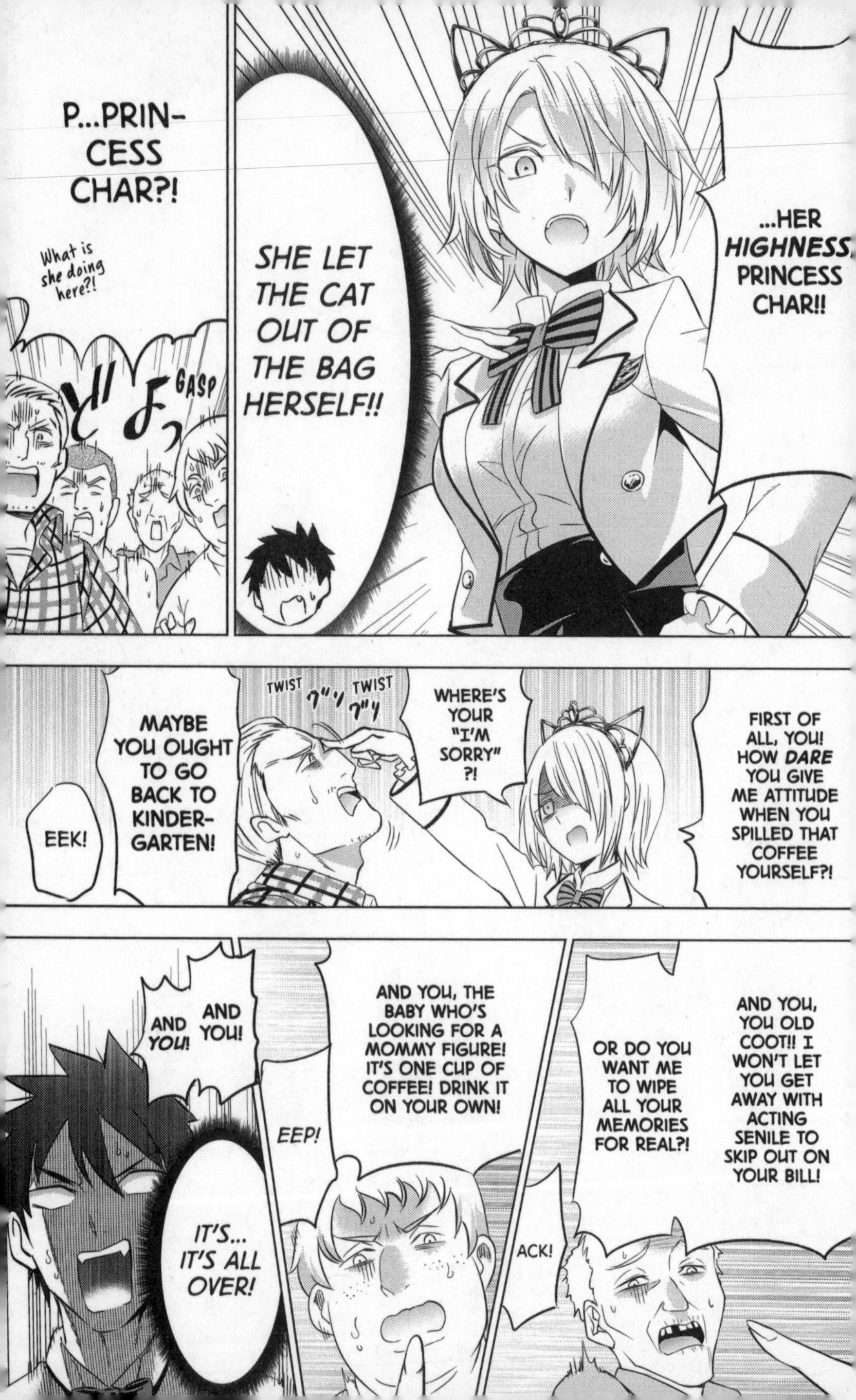

...HER HIGHNESS, PRINCESS CHAR!!
SHE LET THE CAT OUT OF THE BAG HERSELF!!
P...PRIN-CESS CHAR?!
What is she doing here?!
GASP
FIRST OF ALL, YOU! HOW DARE YOU GIVE ME ATTITUDE WHEN YOU SPILLED THAT COFFEE YOURSELF?!
WHERE'S YOUR "I'M SORRY" ?!
TWIST TWIST
MAYBE YOU OUGHT TO GO BACK TO KINDER-GARTEN!
EEK!
AND YOU, YOU OLD COOT!! I WON'T LET YOU GET AWAY WITH ACTING SENILE TO SKIP OUT ON YOUR BILL!
OR DO YOU WANT ME TO WIPE ALL YOUR MEMORIES FOR REAL?!
ACK!
AND YOU, THE BABY WHO'S LOOKING FOR A MOMMY FIGURE! IT'S ONE CUP OF COFFEE! DRINK IT ON YOUR OWN!
EEP!
AND YOU!
AND YOU!
IT'S... IT'S ALL OVER!

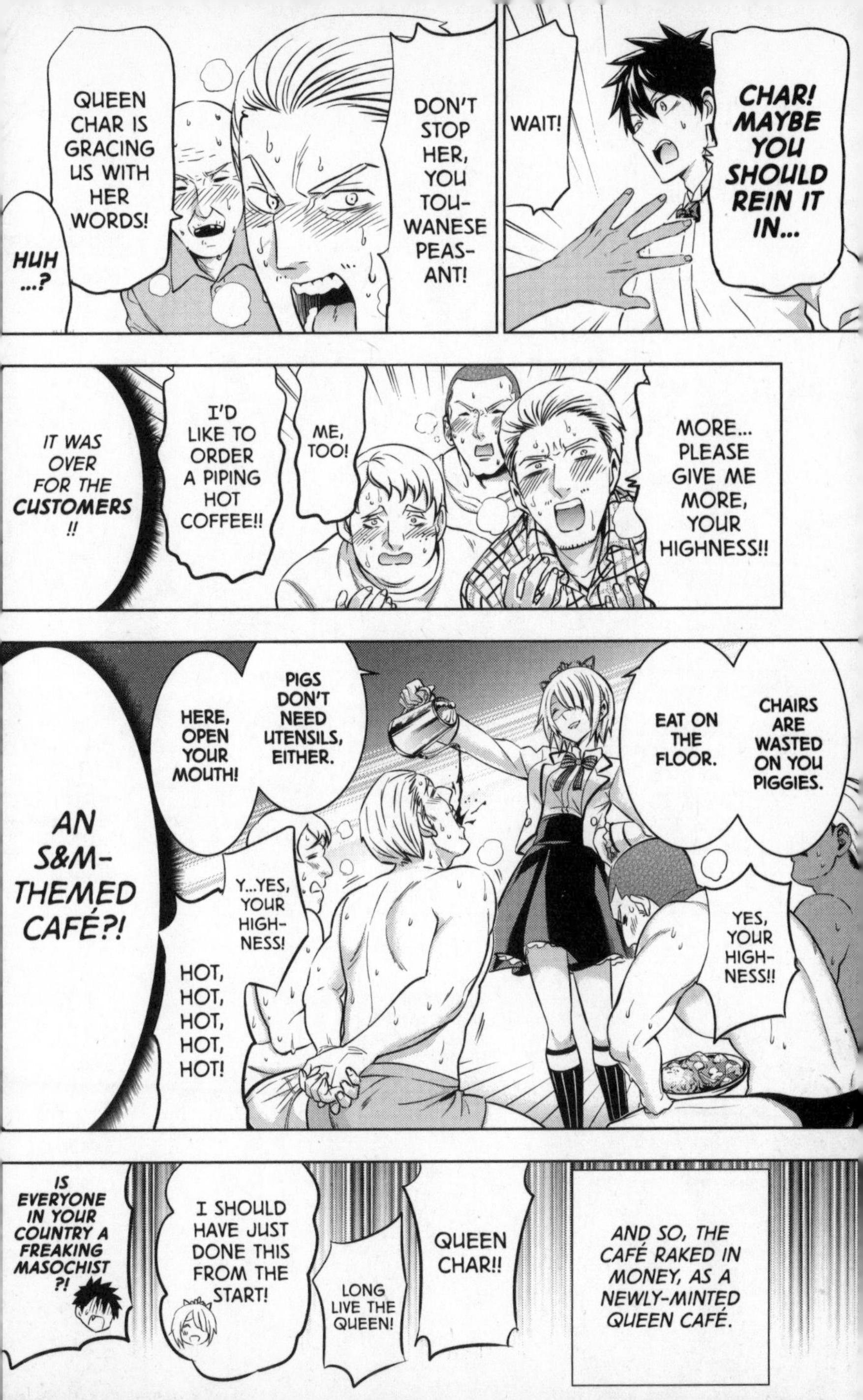
CHAR! MAYBE YOU SHOULD REIN IT IN...
WAIT!
DON'T STOP HER, YOU TOU-WANESE PEAS-ANT!
QUEEN CHAR IS GRACING US WITH HER WORDS!
HUH ...?
MORE... PLEASE GIVE ME MORE, YOUR HIGHNESS!!
ME, TOO!
I'D LIKE TO ORDER A PIPING HOT COFFEE!!
IT WAS OVER FOR THE CUSTOMERS!!
CHAIRS ARE WASTED ON YOU PIGGIES.
EAT ON THE FLOOR.
PIGS DON'T NEED UTENSILS, EITHER.
HERE, OPEN YOUR MOUTH!
YES, YOUR HIGH-NESS!!
Y...YES, YOUR HIGH-NESS!
HOT, HOT, HOT, HOT, HOT!
AN S&M-THEMED CAFÉ?!
AND SO, THE CAFÉ RAKED IN MONEY, AS A NEWLY-MINTED QUEEN CAFÉ.
QUEEN CHAR!!
LONG LIVE THE QUEEN!
I SHOULD HAVE JUST DONE THIS FROM THE START!
IS EVERYONE IN YOUR COUNTRY A FREAKING MASOCHIST?!

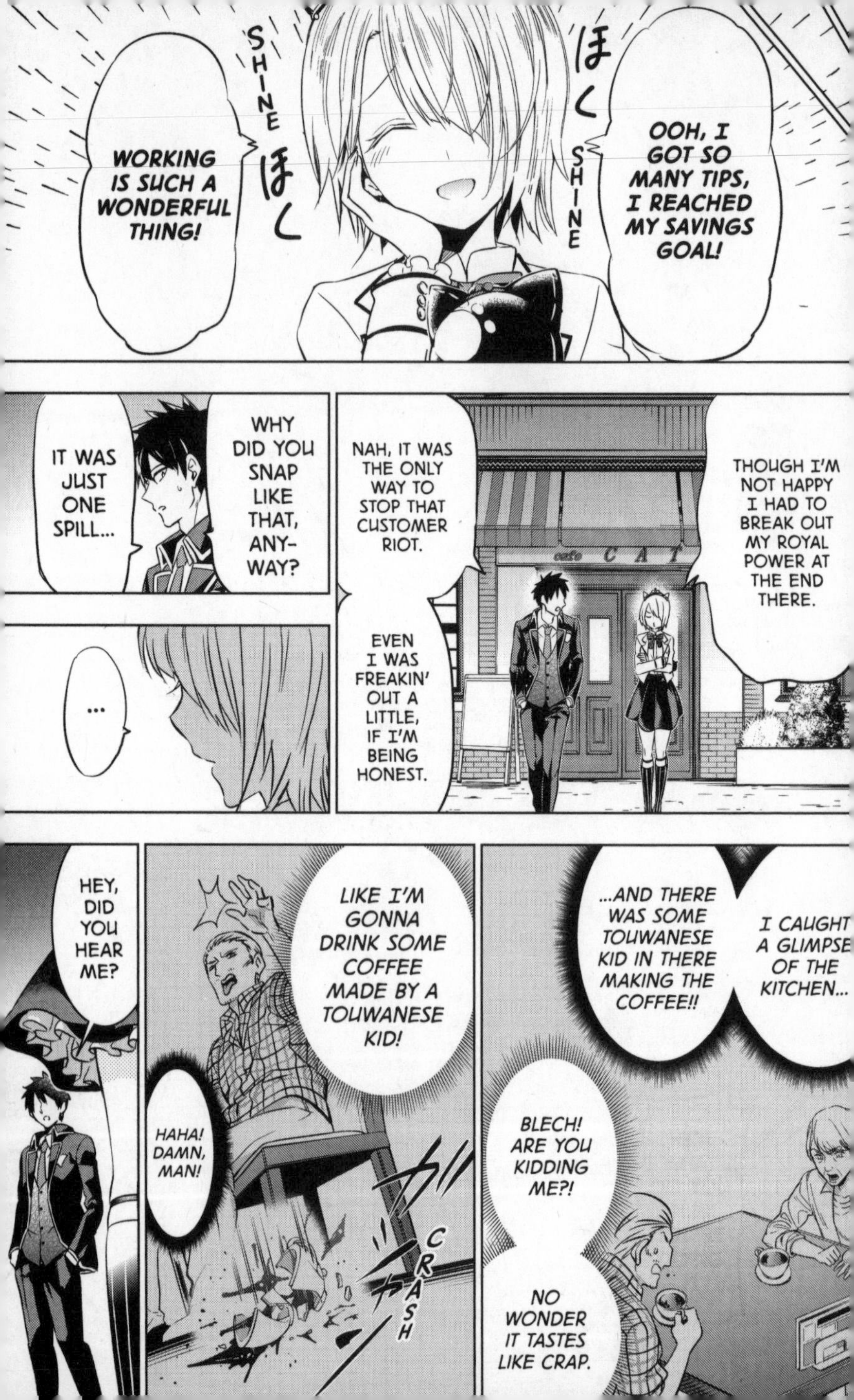
OOH, I GOT SO MANY TIPS, I REACHED MY SAVINGS GOAL!
ほく SHINE
SHINE ほし
WORKING IS SUCH A WONDERFUL THING!
THOUGH I'M NOT HAPPY I HAD TO BREAK OUT MY ROYAL POWER AT THE END THERE.
NAH, IT WAS THE ONLY WAY TO STOP THAT CUSTOMER RIOT.
EVEN I WAS FREAKIN' OUT A LITTLE, IF I'M BEING HONEST.
cafe CAT
WHY DID YOU SNAP LIKE THAT, ANYWAY?
IT WAS JUST ONE SPILL...
...
I CAUGHT A GLIMPSE OF THE KITCHEN...
...AND THERE WAS SOME TOUWANESE KID IN THERE MAKING THE COFFEE!!
BLECH! ARE YOU KIDDING ME?!
NO WONDER IT TASTES LIKE CRAP.
LIKE I'M GONNA DRINK SOME COFFEE MADE BY A TOUWANESE KID!
HAHA! DAMN, MAN!
CRASH
HEY, DID YOU HEAR ME?

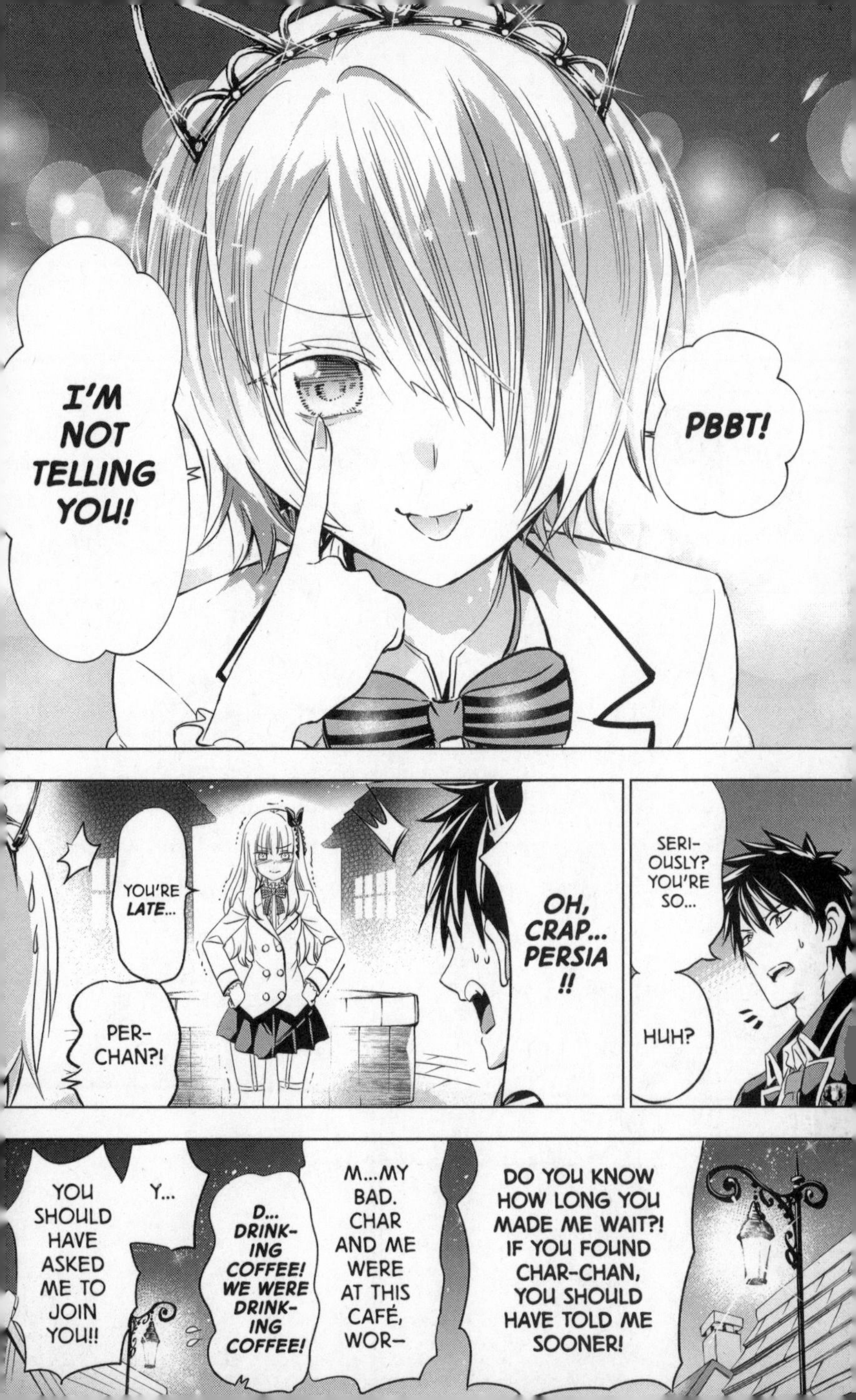
I'M NOT TELLING YOU!
PBBT!
SERI-OUSLY? YOU'RE SO...
HUH?
OH, CRAP... PERSIA!!
YOU'RE LATE...
PER-CHAN?!
DO YOU KNOW HOW LONG YOU MADE ME WAIT?! IF YOU FOUND CHAR-CHAN, YOU SHOULD HAVE TOLD ME SOONER!
M...MY BAD. CHAR AND ME WERE AT THIS CAFÉ, WOR–
D... DRINK-ING COFFEE! WE WERE DRINK-ING COFFEE!
Y...
YOU SHOULD HAVE ASKED ME TO JOIN YOU!!

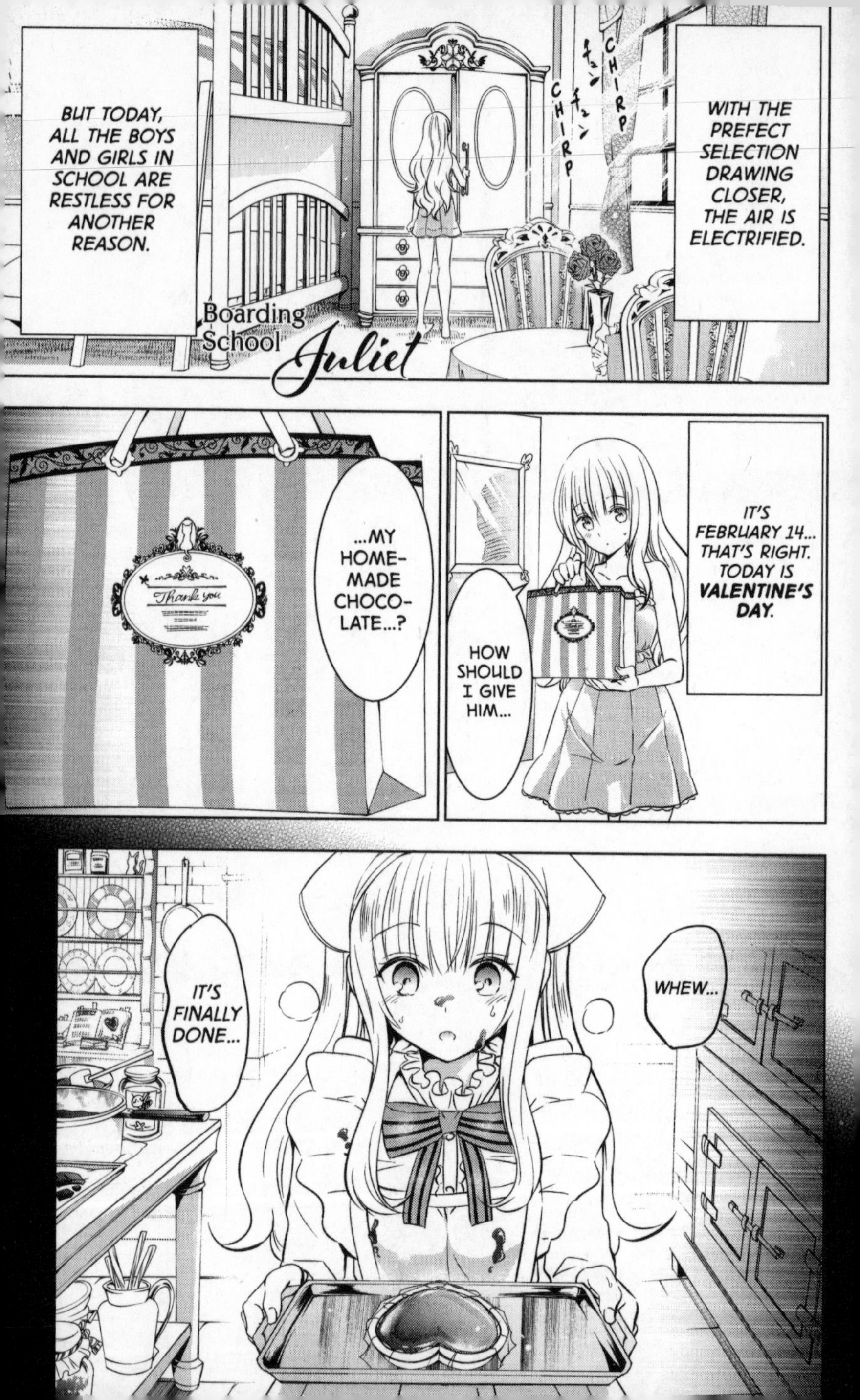

WITH THE PREFECT SELECTION DRAWING CLOSER, THE AIR IS ELECTRIFIED.
CHIRP
CHIRP
BUT TODAY, ALL THE BOYS AND GIRLS IN SCHOOL ARE RESTLESS FOR ANOTHER REASON.
Boarding School Juliet
IT'S FEBRUARY 14... THAT'S RIGHT. TODAY IS **VALENTINE'S DAY.**
HOW SHOULD I GIVE HIM...
...MY HOME-MADE CHOCO-LATE...?
Thank you
WHEW...
IT'S FINALLY DONE...

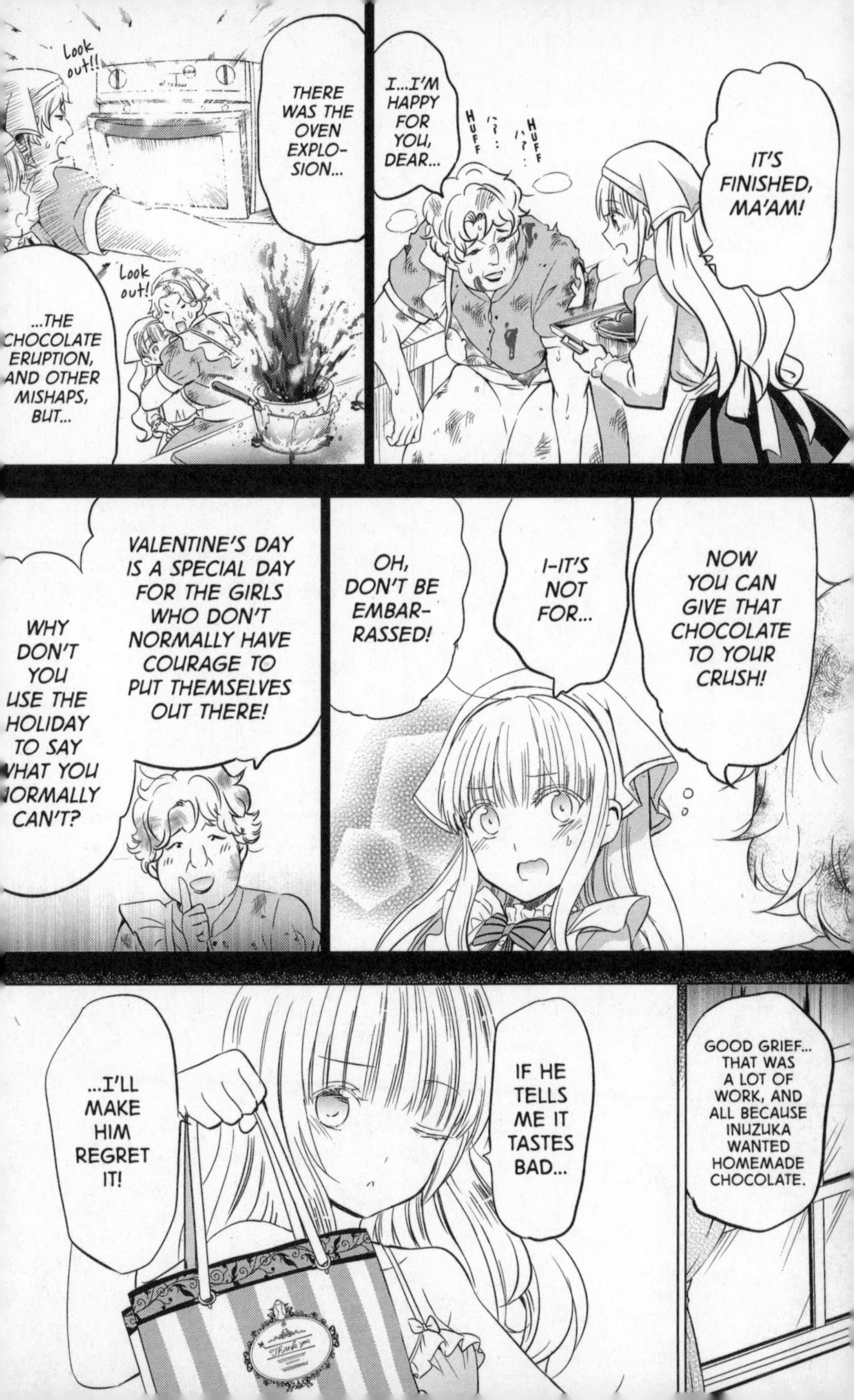
IT'S FINISHED, MA'AM!
HUFF HUFF
I...I'M HAPPY FOR YOU, DEAR...
THERE WAS THE OVEN EXPLOSION...
Look out!!
Look out!
...THE CHOCOLATE ERUPTION, AND OTHER MISHAPS, BUT...
NOW YOU CAN GIVE THAT CHOCOLATE TO YOUR CRUSH!
I-IT'S NOT FOR...
OH, DON'T BE EMBARRASSED!
VALENTINE'S DAY IS A SPECIAL DAY FOR THE GIRLS WHO DON'T NORMALLY HAVE COURAGE TO PUT THEMSELVES OUT THERE!
WHY DON'T YOU USE THE HOLIDAY TO SAY WHAT YOU NORMALLY CAN'T?
GOOD GRIEF... THAT WAS A LOT OF WORK, AND ALL BECAUSE INUZUKA WANTED HOMEMADE CHOCOLATE.
IF HE TELLS ME IT TASTES BAD...
...I'LL MAKE HIM REGRET IT!

ACT 66: VALENTINE'S DAY & JULIET I

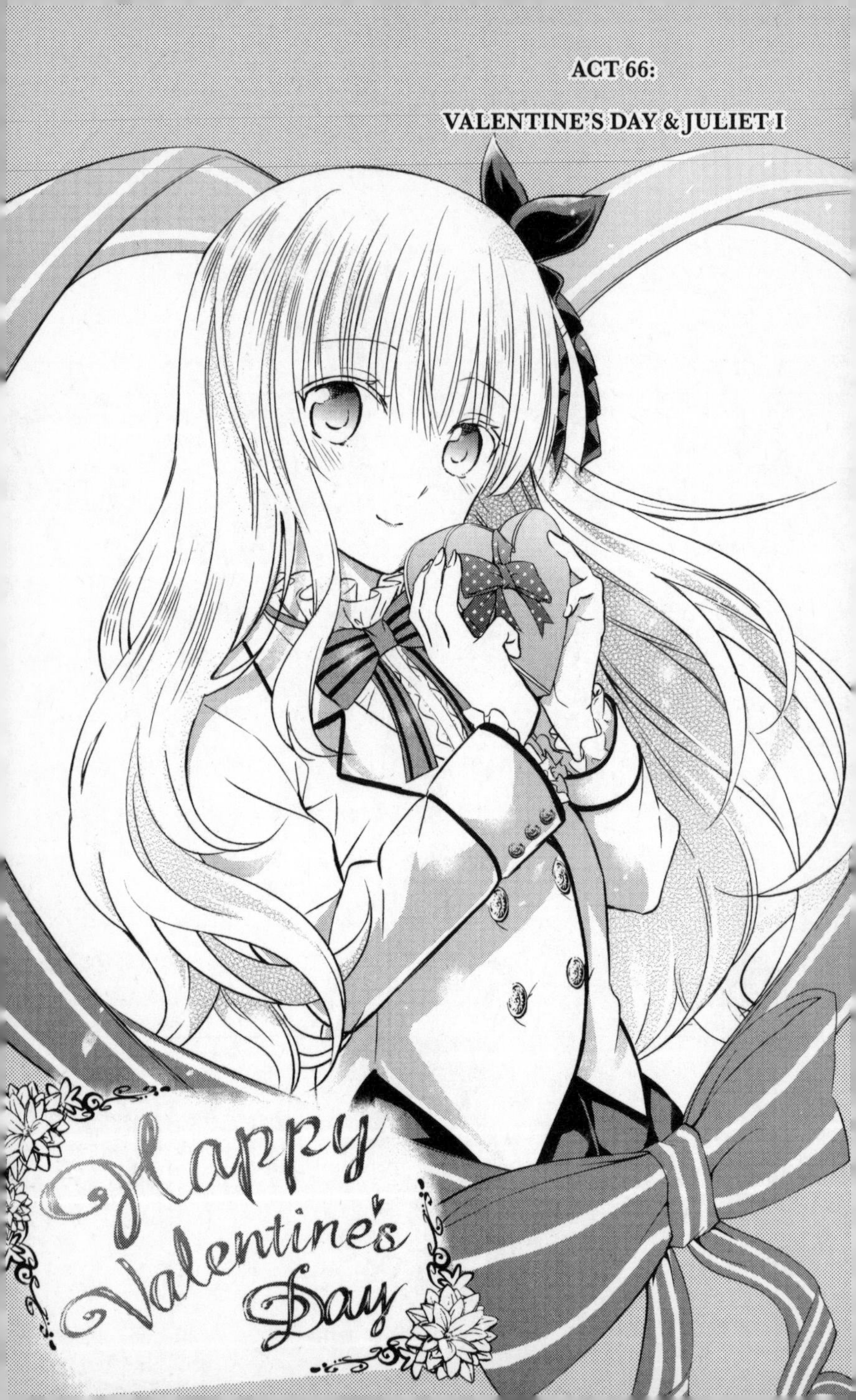
Happy Valentine's Day

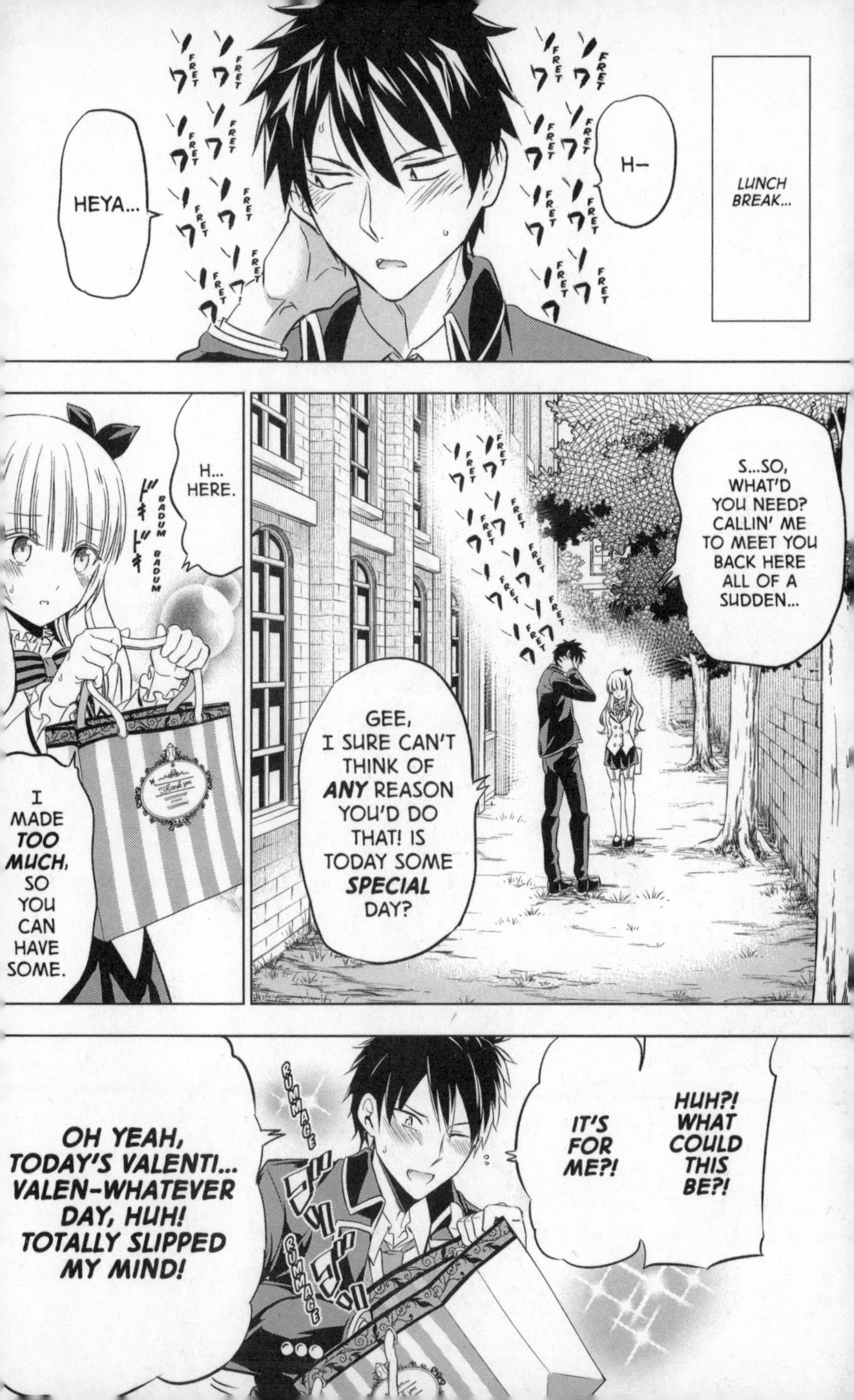
LUNCH BREAK...
H–
FRET FRET FRET FRET
HEYA...
S...SO, WHAT'D YOU NEED? CALLIN' ME TO MEET YOU BACK HERE ALL OF A SUDDEN...
FRET FRET FRET
GEE, I SURE CAN'T THINK OF **ANY** REASON YOU'D DO THAT! IS TODAY SOME **SPECIAL** DAY?
H... HERE.
BADUM BADUM
I MADE **TOO MUCH,** SO YOU CAN HAVE SOME.
HUH?! WHAT COULD THIS BE?!
IT'S FOR ME?!
RUMMAGE RUMMAGE
OH YEAH, TODAY'S VALENTI... VALEN-WHATEVER DAY, HUH! TOTALLY SLIPPED MY MIND!

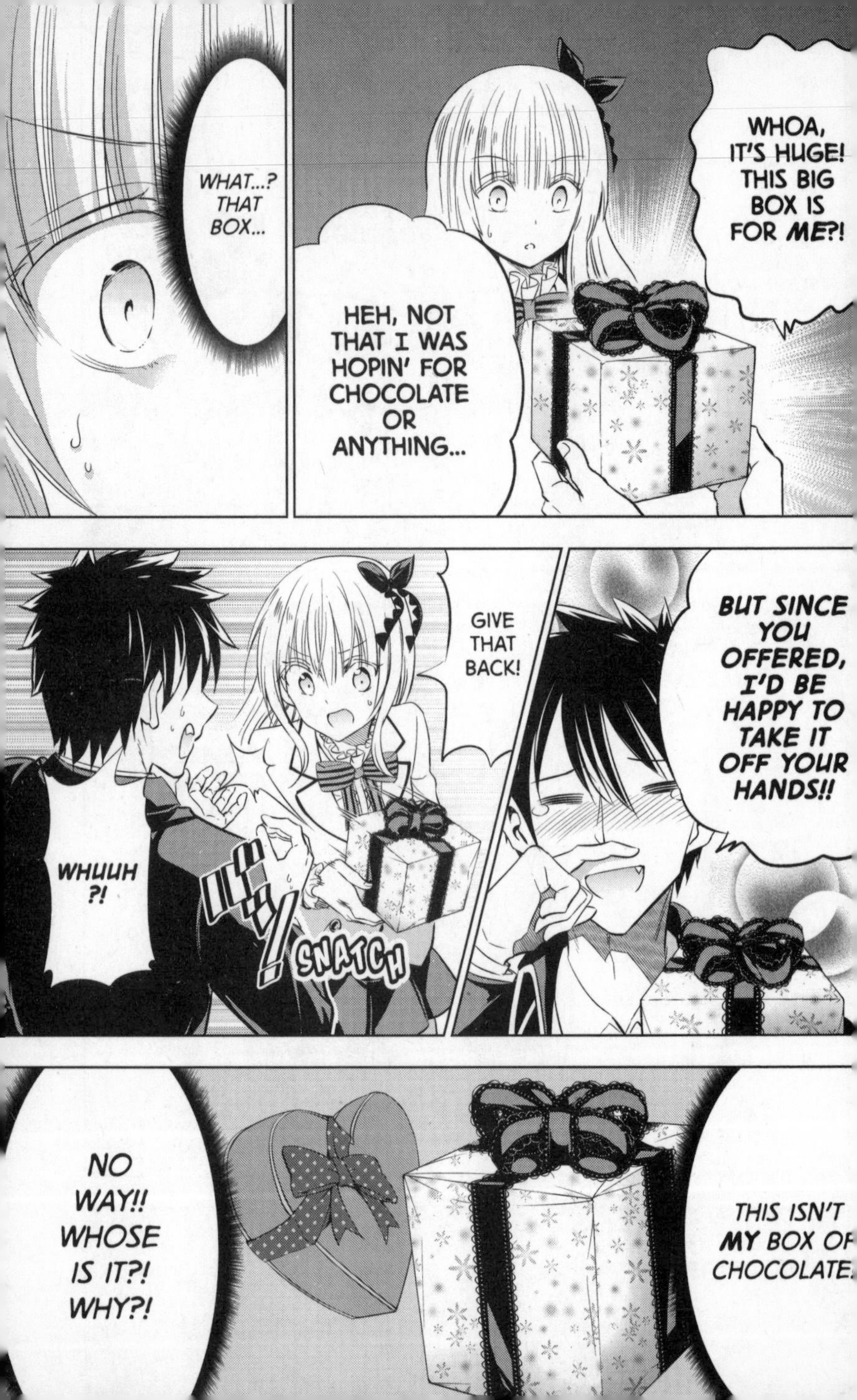
WHOA, IT'S HUGE! THIS BIG BOX IS FOR *ME*?!
HEH, NOT THAT I WAS HOPIN' FOR CHOCOLATE OR ANYTHING...
WHAT...? THAT BOX...
BUT SINCE YOU OFFERED, I'D BE HAPPY TO TAKE IT OFF YOUR HANDS!!
GIVE THAT BACK!
SNATCH
WHUUH ?!
THIS ISN'T **MY** BOX OF CHOCOLATE.
NO WAY!! WHOSE IS IT?! WHY?!

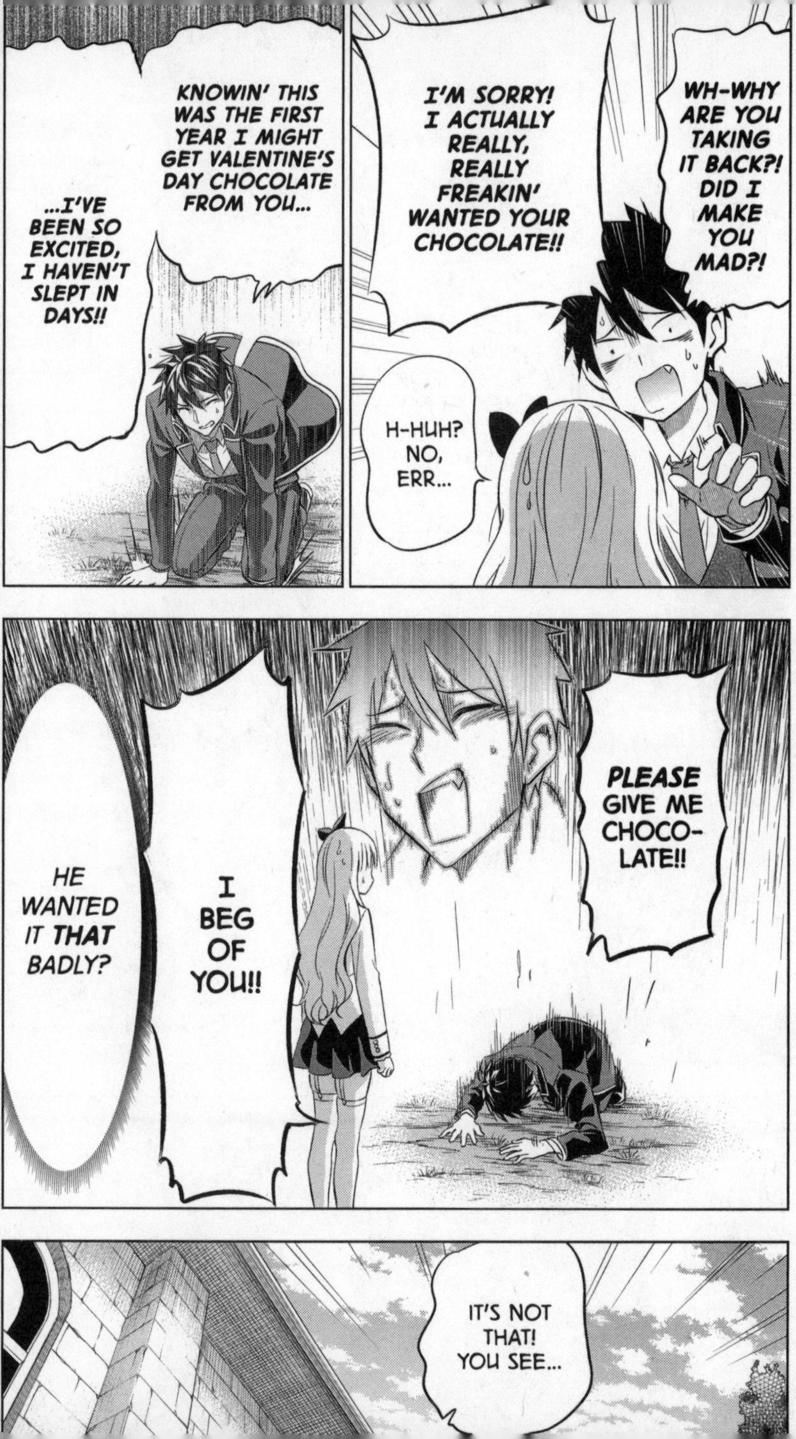
WH-WHY ARE YOU TAKING IT BACK?! DID I MAKE YOU MAD?!
I'M SORRY! I ACTUALLY REALLY, REALLY FREAKIN' WANTED YOUR CHOCOLATE!!
H-HUH? NO, ERR...
KNOWIN' THIS WAS THE FIRST YEAR I MIGHT GET VALENTINE'S DAY CHOCOLATE FROM YOU...
...I'VE BEEN SO EXCITED, I HAVEN'T SLEPT IN DAYS!!
PLEASE GIVE ME CHOCO-LATE!!
I BEG OF YOU!!
HE WANTED IT **THAT** BADLY?
IT'S NOT THAT! YOU SEE...

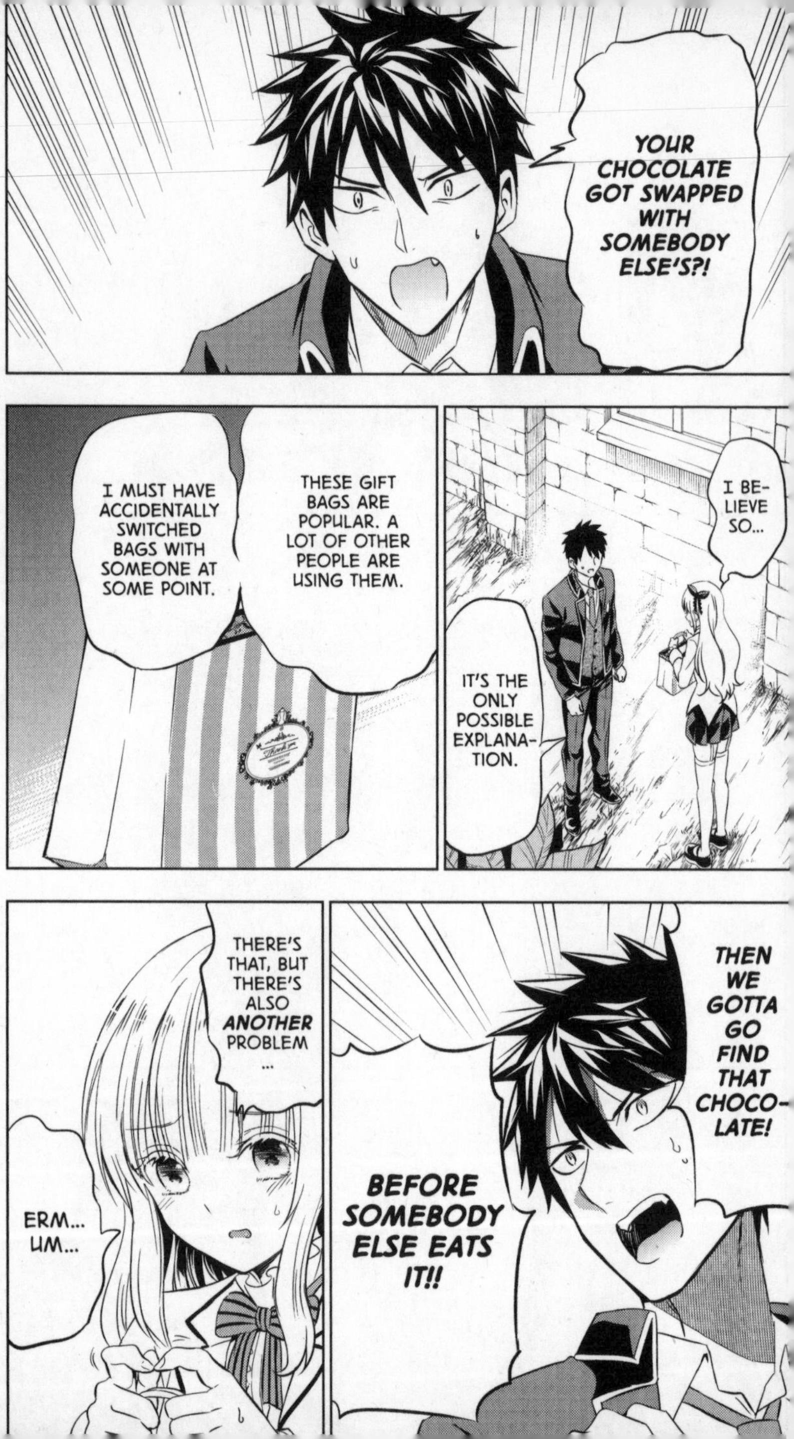
YOUR CHOCOLATE GOT SWAPPED WITH SOMEBODY ELSE'S?!
I BE-LIEVE SO...
IT'S THE ONLY POSSIBLE EXPLANA-TION.
THESE GIFT BAGS ARE POPULAR. A LOT OF OTHER PEOPLE ARE USING THEM.
I MUST HAVE ACCIDENTALLY SWITCHED BAGS WITH SOMEONE AT SOME POINT.
THEN WE GOTTA GO FIND THAT CHOCO-LATE!
BEFORE SOMEBODY ELSE EATS IT!!
THERE'S THAT, BUT THERE'S ALSO ANOTHER PROBLEM ...
ERM... UM...

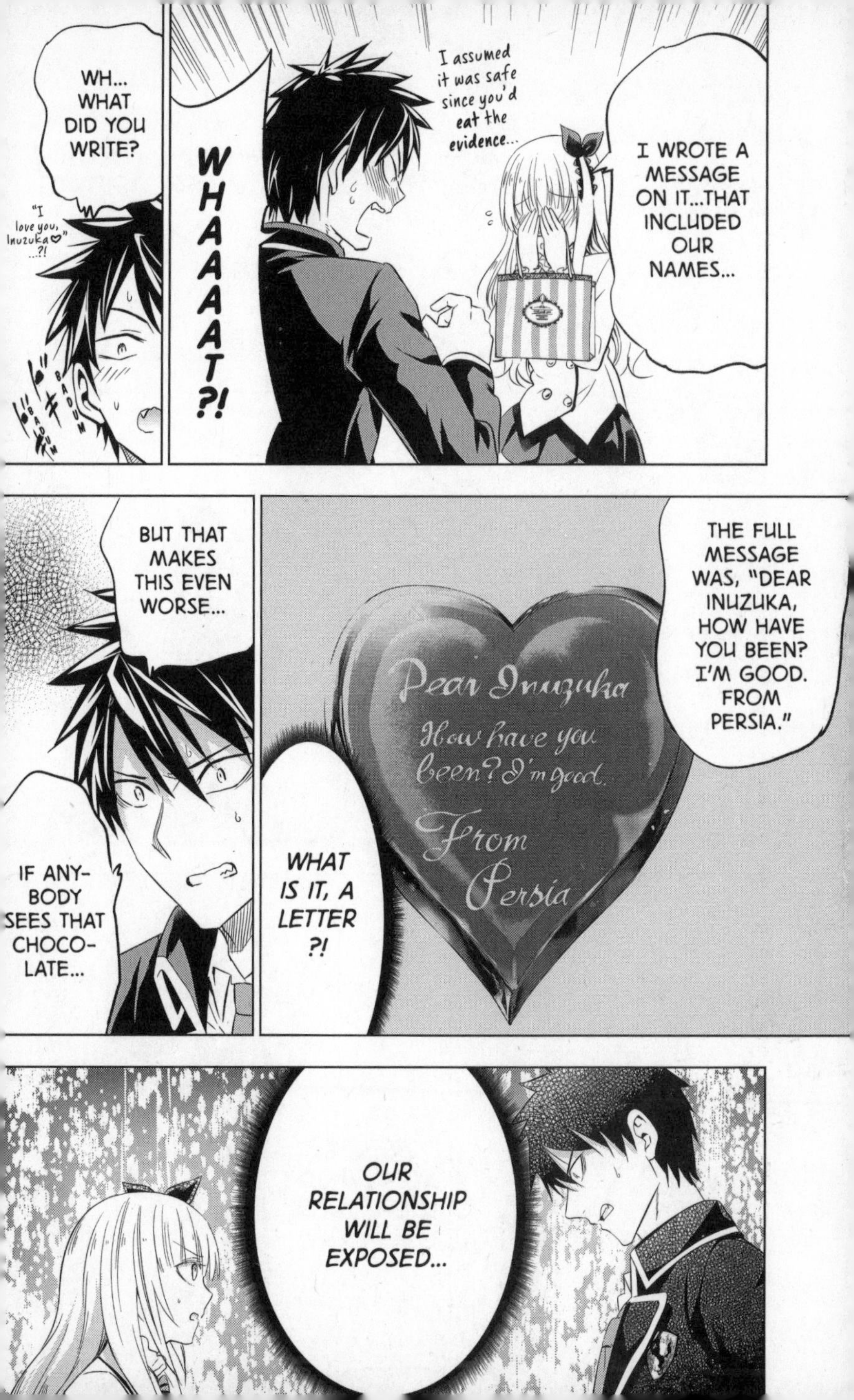
I WROTE A MESSAGE ON IT...THAT INCLUDED OUR NAMES...
I assumed it was safe since you'd eat the evidence...
WHAAAAAT?!
WH... WHAT DID YOU WRITE?
"I love you, Inuzuka♡" ...?!
BADUM
BADUM
THE FULL MESSAGE WAS, "DEAR INUZUKA, HOW HAVE YOU BEEN? I'M GOOD. FROM PERSIA."
Dear Inuzuka
How have you been? I'm good.
From Persia
WHAT IS IT, A LETTER ?!
BUT THAT MAKES THIS EVEN WORSE...
IF ANY-BODY SEES THAT CHOCO-LATE...
OUR RELATIONSHIP WILL BE EXPOSED...

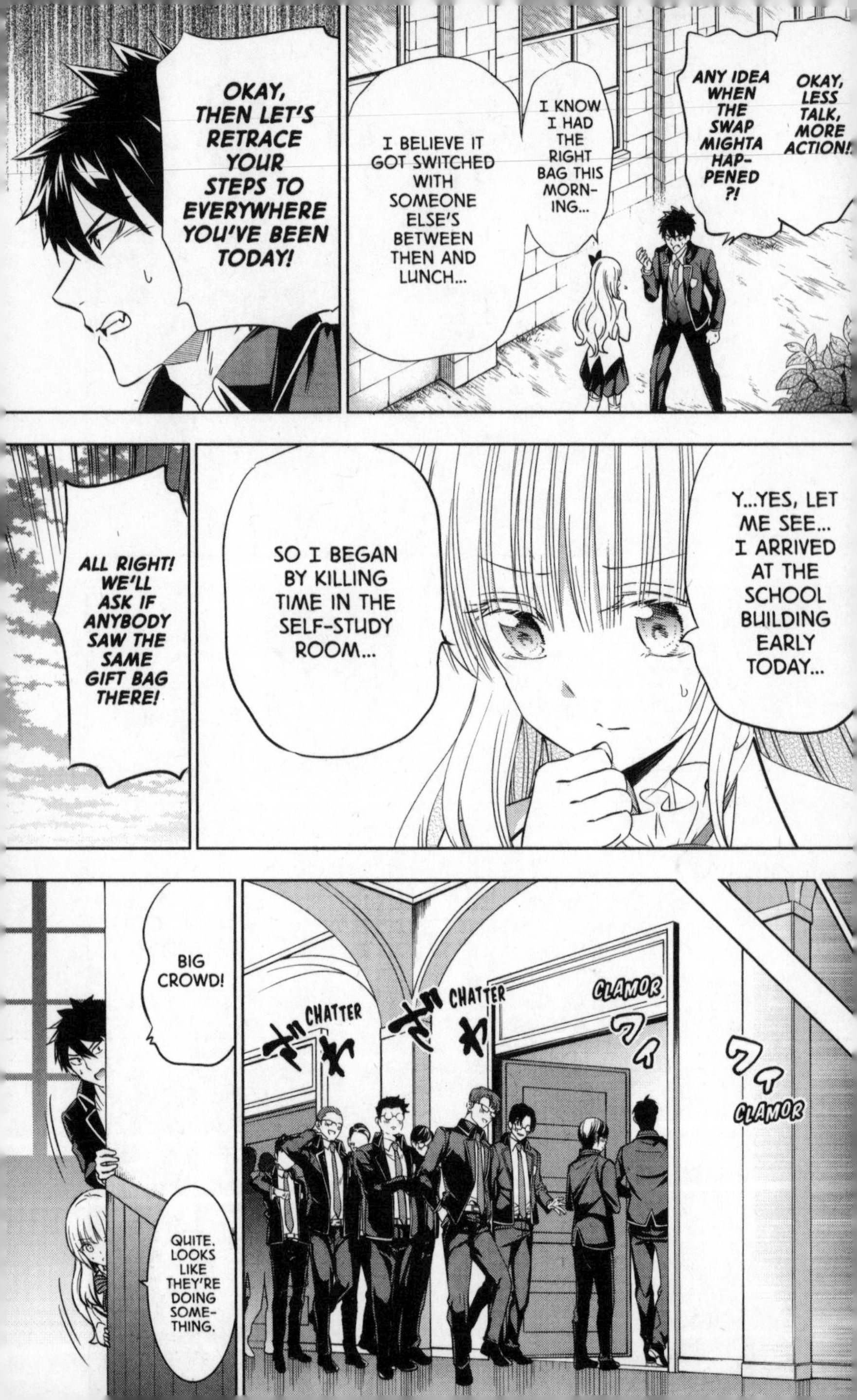
OKAY, LESS TALK, MORE ACTION!
ANY IDEA WHEN THE SWAP MIGHTA HAP-PENED ?!
I KNOW I HAD THE RIGHT BAG THIS MORN-ING...
I BELIEVE IT GOT SWITCHED WITH SOMEONE ELSE'S BETWEEN THEN AND LUNCH...
OKAY, THEN LET'S RETRACE YOUR STEPS TO EVERYWHERE YOU'VE BEEN TODAY!
Y...YES, LET ME SEE... I ARRIVED AT THE SCHOOL BUILDING EARLY TODAY...
SO I BEGAN BY KILLING TIME IN THE SELF-STUDY ROOM...
ALL RIGHT! WE'LL ASK IF ANYBODY SAW THE SAME GIFT BAG THERE!
CLAMOR
CLAMOR
CHATTER
CHATTER
BIG CROWD!
QUITE. LOOKS LIKE THEY'RE DOING SOME-THING.

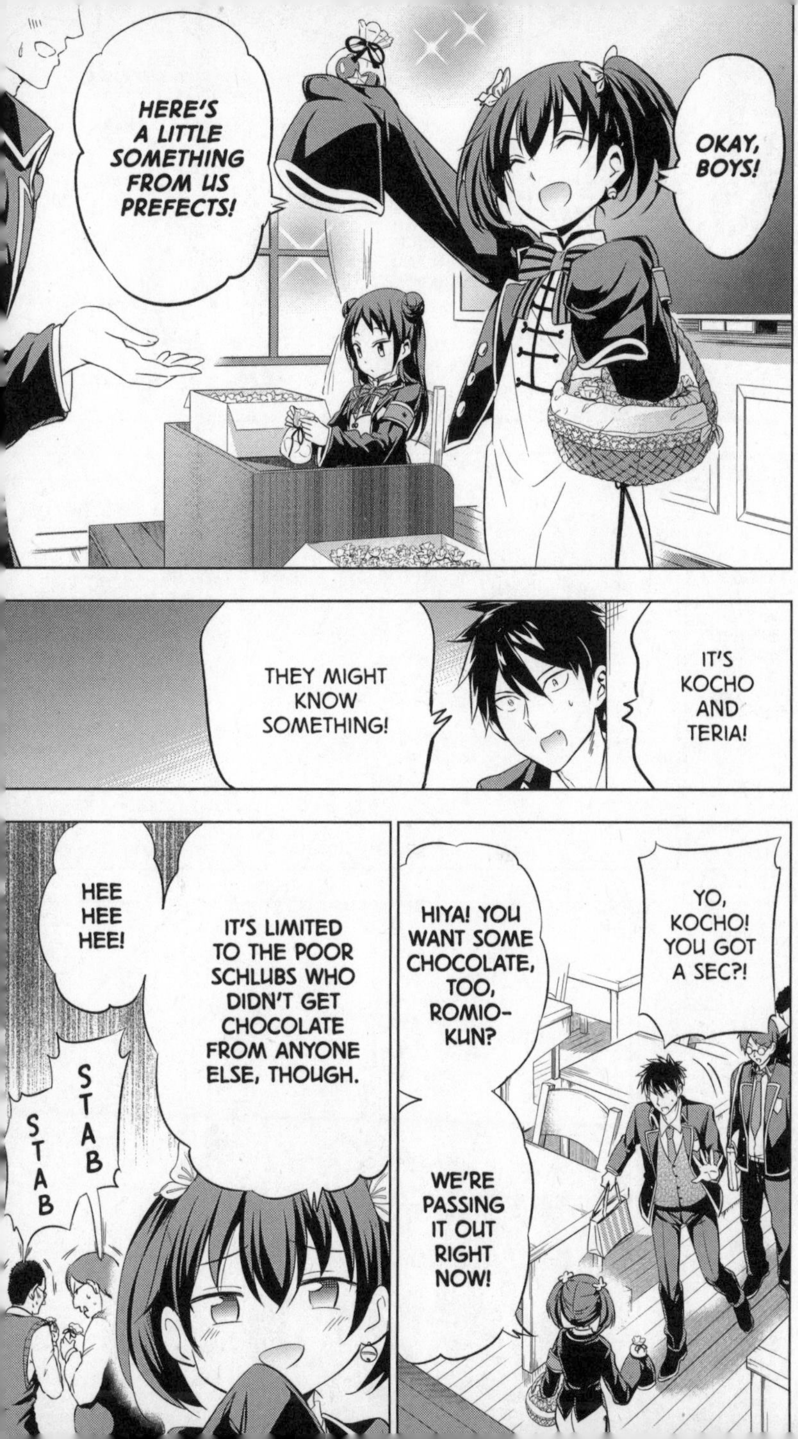
OKAY, BOYS!
HERE'S A LITTLE SOMETHING FROM US PREFECTS!
IT'S KOCHO AND TERIA!
THEY MIGHT KNOW SOMETHING!
YO, KOCHO! YOU GOT A SEC?!
HIYA! YOU WANT SOME CHOCOLATE, TOO, ROMIO-KUN?
WE'RE PASSING IT OUT RIGHT NOW!
IT'S LIMITED TO THE POOR SCHLUBS WHO DIDN'T GET CHOCOLATE FROM ANYONE ELSE, THOUGH.
HEE HEE HEE!
STAB
STAB

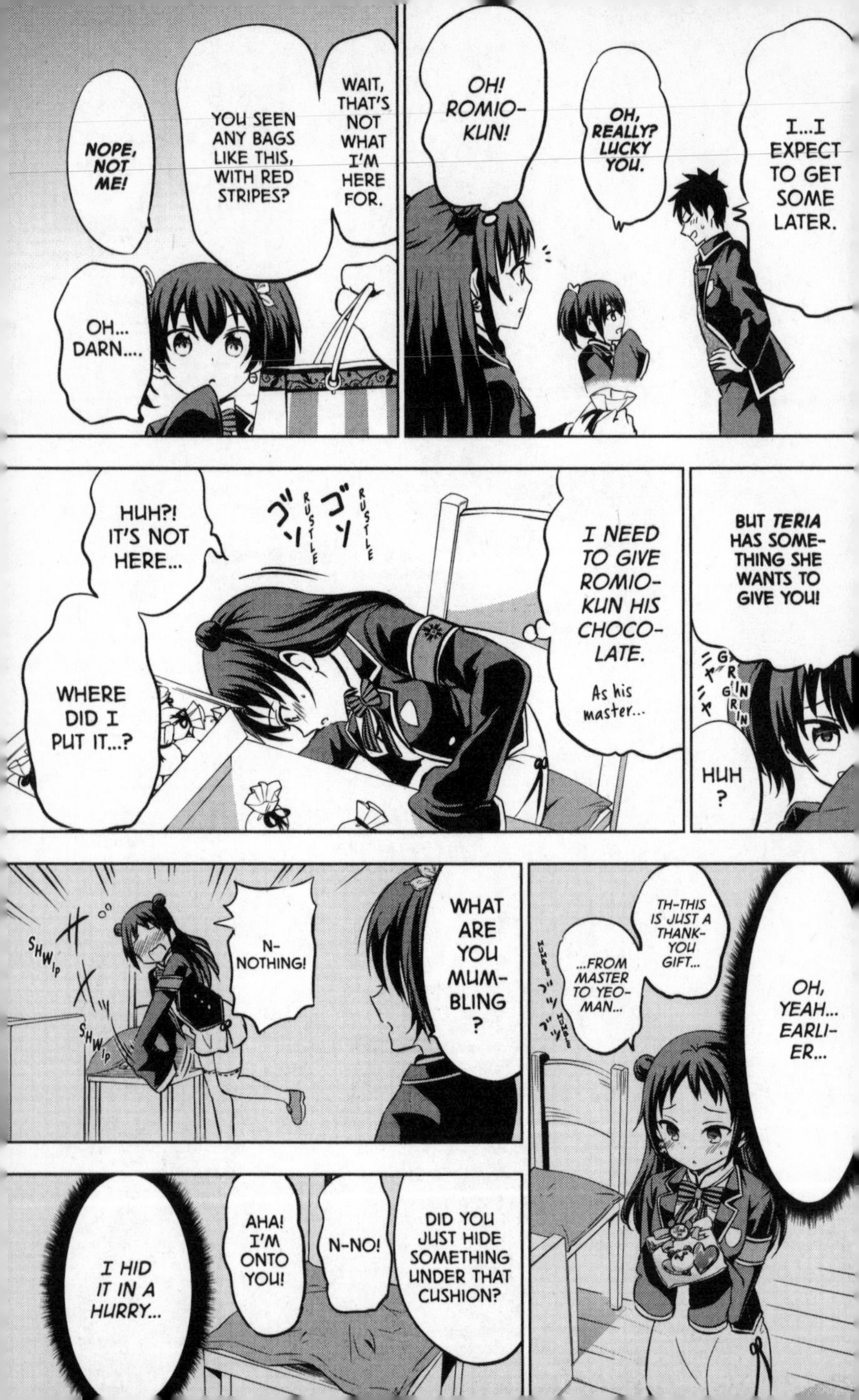

I...I EXPECT TO GET SOME LATER.
OH, REALLY? LUCKY YOU.
OH! ROMIO-KUN!
WAIT, THAT'S NOT WHAT I'M HERE FOR.
YOU SEEN ANY BAGS LIKE THIS, WITH RED STRIPES?
NOPE, NOT ME!
OH... DARN....
BUT TERIA HAS SOMETHING SHE WANTS TO GIVE YOU!
GRIN GRIN
HUH?
I NEED TO GIVE ROMIO-KUN HIS CHOCOLATE.
As his master...
RUSTLE RUSTLE
HUH?! IT'S NOT HERE...
WHERE DID I PUT IT...?
OH, YEAH... EARLIER...
TH-THIS IS JUST A THANK-YOU GIFT...
...FROM MASTER TO YEOMAN...
MUMBLE MUMBLE
WHAT ARE YOU MUMBLING?
N-NOTHING!
SHWIP SHWIP
DID YOU JUST HIDE SOMETHING UNDER THAT CUSHION?
N-NO!
AHA! I'M ONTO YOU!
I HID IT IN A HURRY...

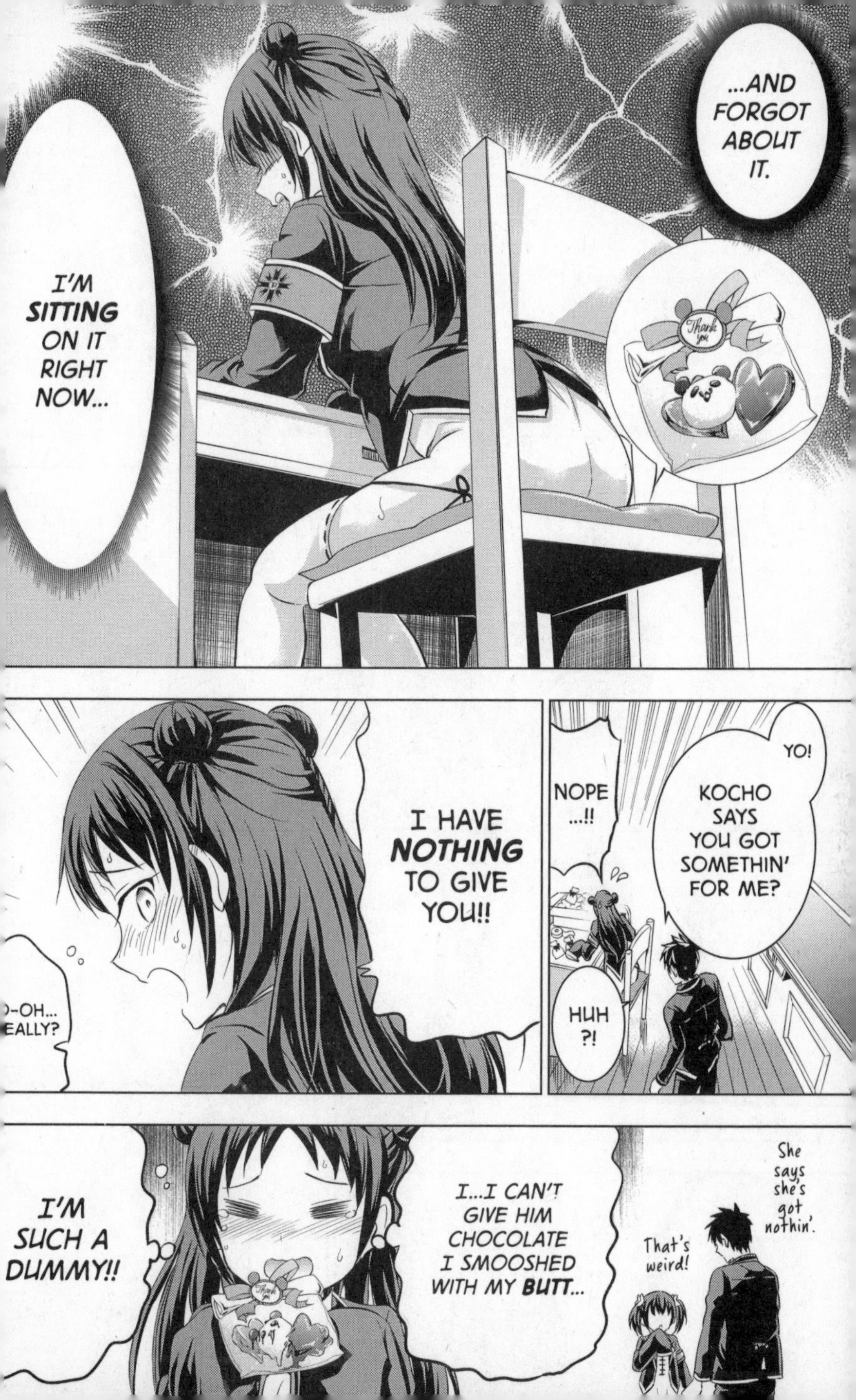
...AND FORGOT ABOUT IT.
I'M SITTING ON IT RIGHT NOW...
Thank you
YO!
KOCHO SAYS YOU GOT SOMETHIN' FOR ME?
NOPE ...!!
HUH ?!
I HAVE NOTHING TO GIVE YOU!!
-OH... EALLY?
She says she's got nothin'.
That's weird!
I...I CAN'T GIVE HIM CHOCOLATE I SMOOSHED WITH MY BUTT...
I'M SUCH A DUMMY!!

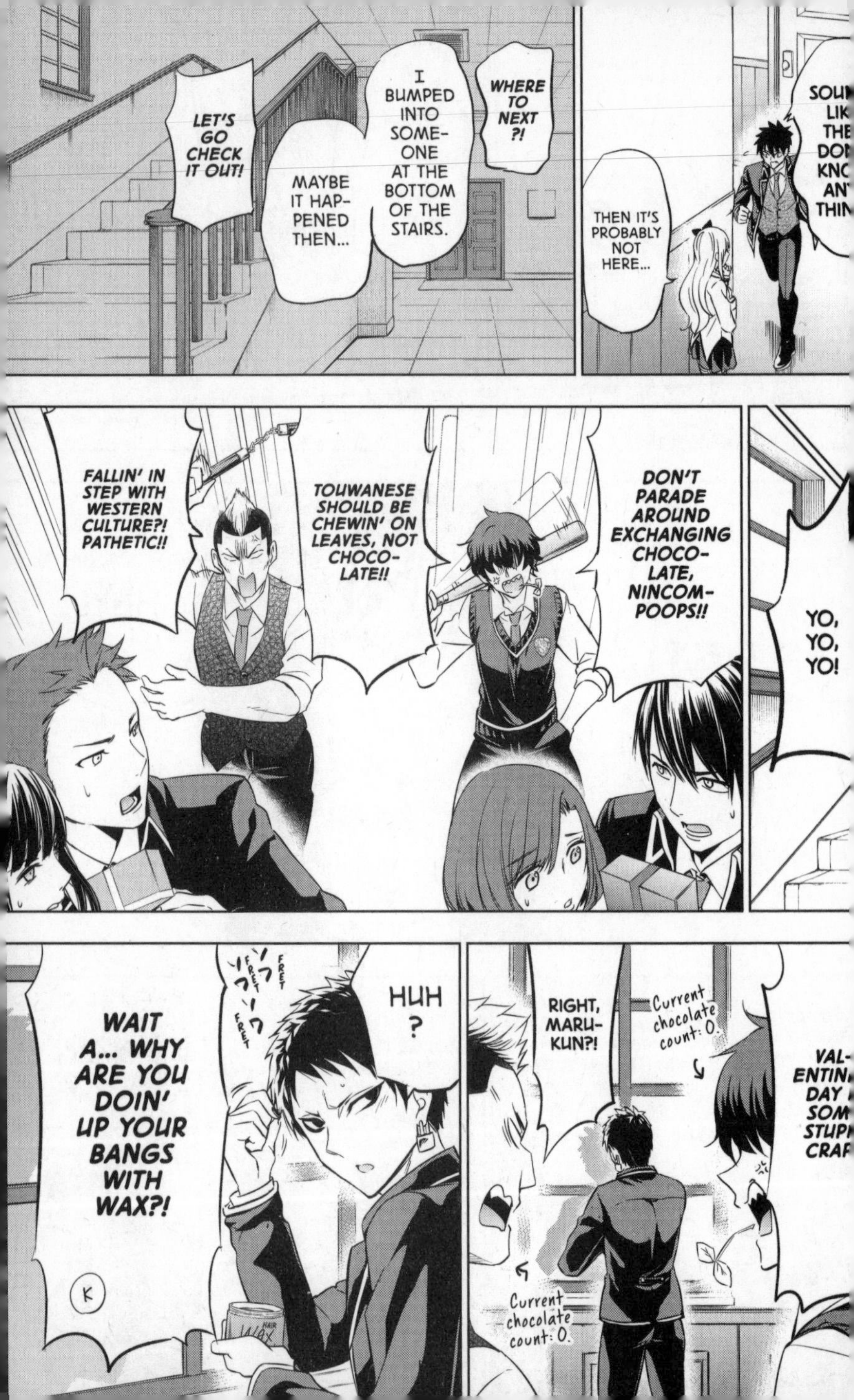

THEN IT'S PROBABLY NOT HERE...
WHERE TO NEXT?!
I BUMPED INTO SOMEONE AT THE BOTTOM OF THE STAIRS.
MAYBE IT HAPPENED THEN...
LET'S GO CHECK IT OUT!
YO, YO, YO!
DON'T PARADE AROUND EXCHANGING CHOCOLATE, NINCOMPOOPS!!
TOUWANESE SHOULD BE CHEWIN' ON LEAVES, NOT CHOCOLATE!!
FALLIN' IN STEP WITH WESTERN CULTURE?! PATHETIC!!
Current chocolate count: 0.
RIGHT, MARU-KUN?!
Current chocolate count: 0.
HUH?
FRET FRET FRET
WAIT A... WHY ARE YOU DOIN' UP YOUR BANGS WITH WAX?!
K
HAIR WAX

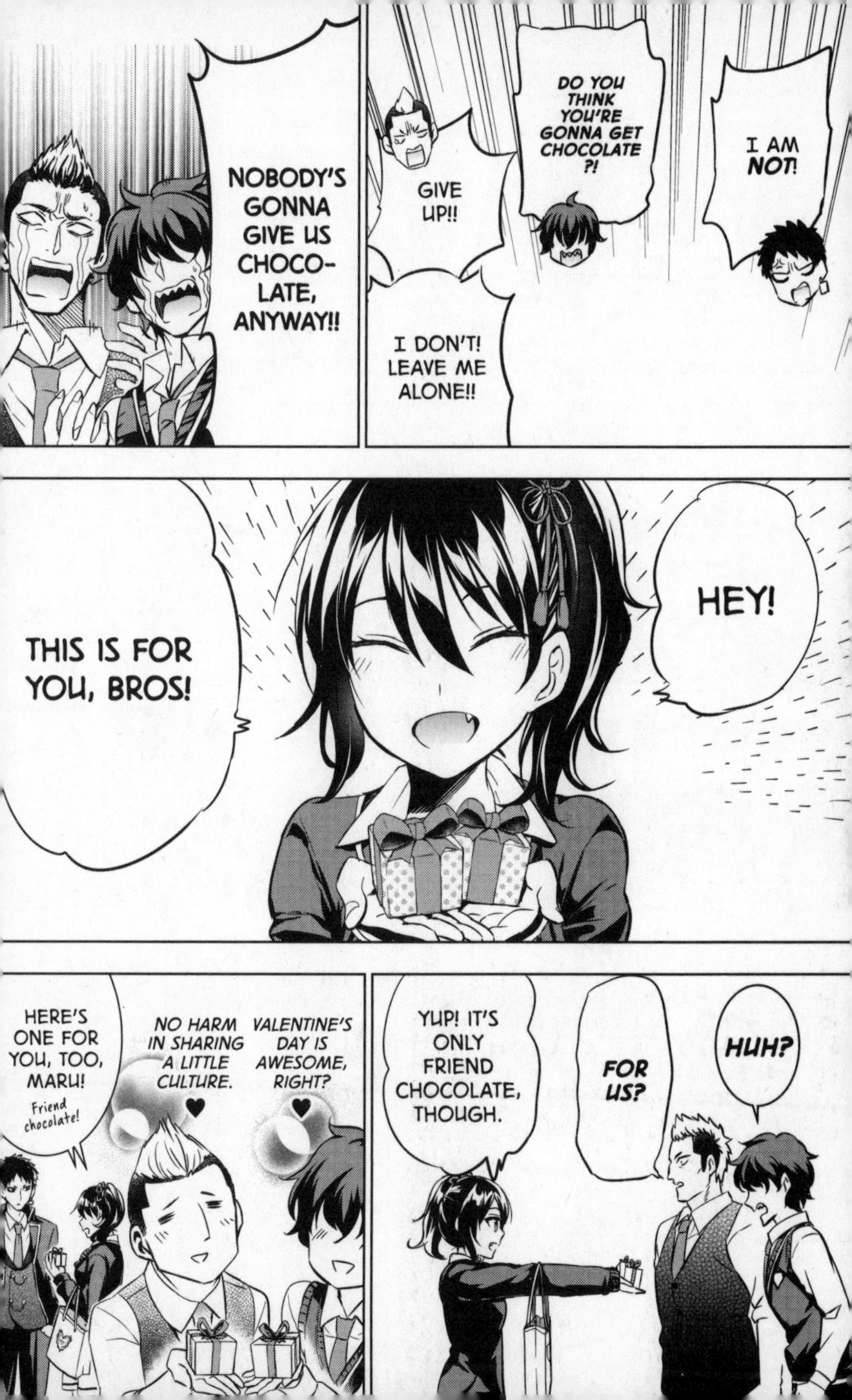
I AM NOT!
DO YOU THINK YOU'RE GONNA GET CHOCOLATE ?!
GIVE UP!!
I DON'T! LEAVE ME ALONE!!
NOBODY'S GONNA GIVE US CHOCO-LATE, ANYWAY!!
HEY!
THIS IS FOR YOU, BROS!
HUH?
FOR US?
YUP! IT'S ONLY FRIEND CHOCOLATE, THOUGH.
VALENTINE'S DAY IS AWESOME, RIGHT?
NO HARM IN SHARING A LITTLE CULTURE.
HERE'S ONE FOR YOU, TOO, MARU!
Friend chocolate!

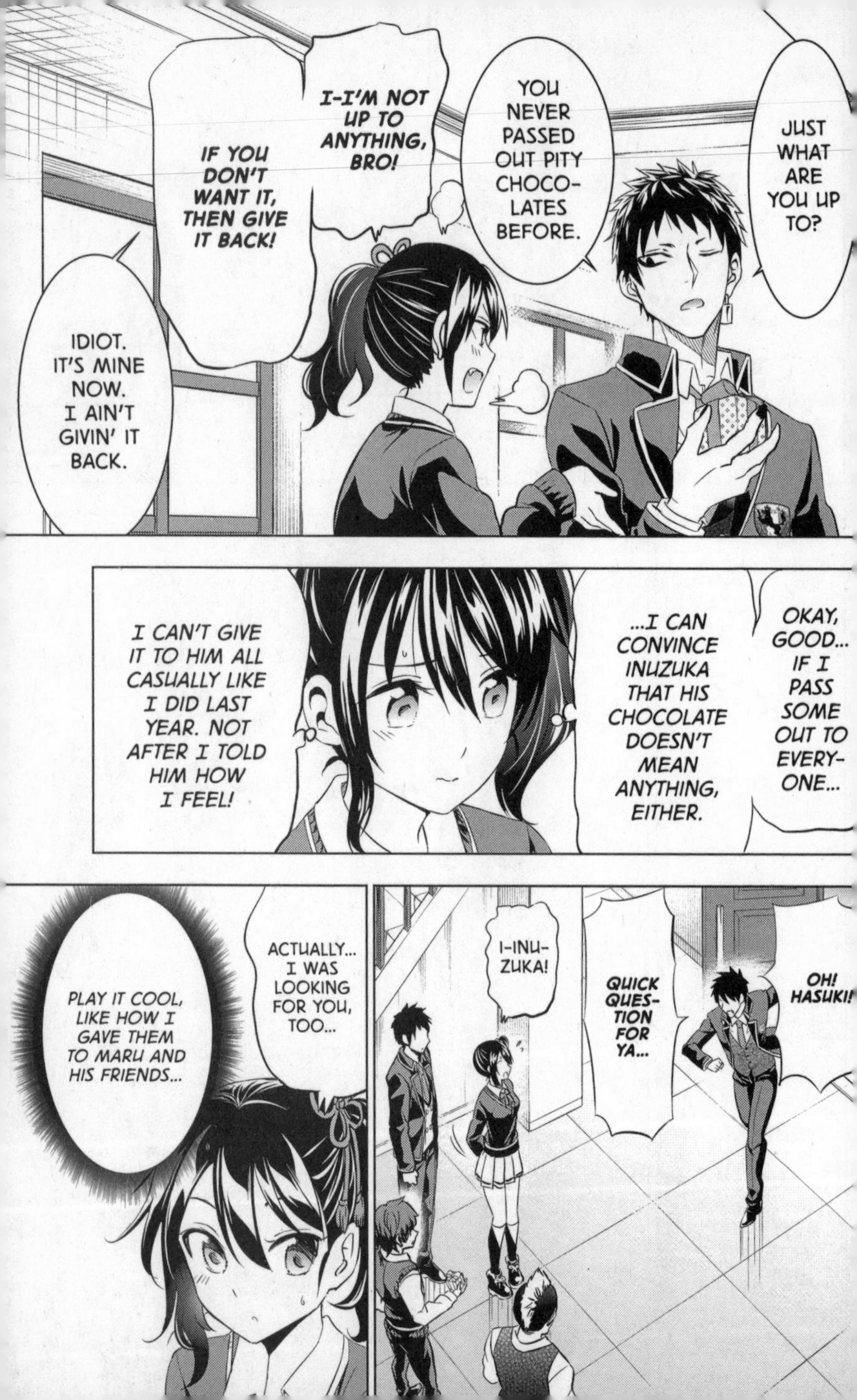
JUST WHAT ARE YOU UP TO?
YOU NEVER PASSED OUT PITY CHOCO-LATES BEFORE.
I-I'M NOT UP TO ANYTHING, BRO!
IF YOU DON'T WANT IT, THEN GIVE IT BACK!
IDIOT. IT'S MINE NOW. I AIN'T GIVIN' IT BACK.
OKAY, GOOD... IF I PASS SOME OUT TO EVERY-ONE...
...I CAN CONVINCE INUZUKA THAT HIS CHOCOLATE DOESN'T MEAN ANYTHING, EITHER.
I CAN'T GIVE IT TO HIM ALL CASUALLY LIKE I DID LAST YEAR. NOT AFTER I TOLD HIM HOW I FEEL!
OH! HASUKI!
QUICK QUES-TION FOR YA...
I-INU-ZUKA!
ACTUALLY... I WAS LOOKING FOR YOU, TOO...
PLAY IT COOL, LIKE HOW I GAVE THEM TO MARU AND HIS FRIENDS...

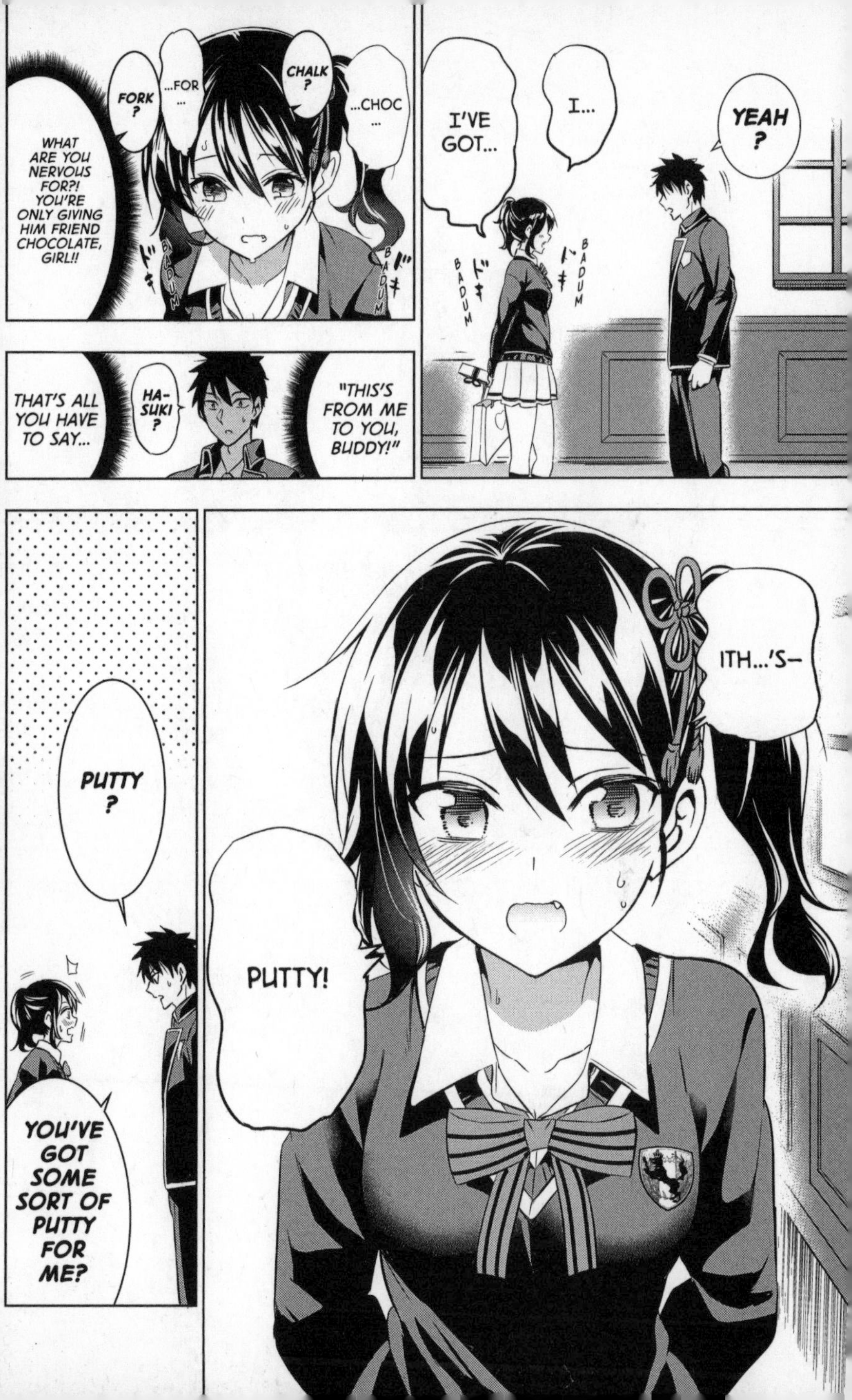
YEAH?
I...
I'VE GOT...
BADUM
BADUM
...CHOC ...
CHALK?
...FOR ...
FORK?
WHAT ARE YOU NERVOUS FOR?! YOU'RE ONLY GIVING HIM FRIEND CHOCOLATE, GIRL!!
BADUM
BADUM
"THIS'S FROM ME TO YOU, BUDDY!"
HA-SUKI?
THAT'S ALL YOU HAVE TO SAY...
ITH...'S—
PUTTY!
PUTTY?
YOU'VE GOT SOME SORT OF PUTTY FOR ME?

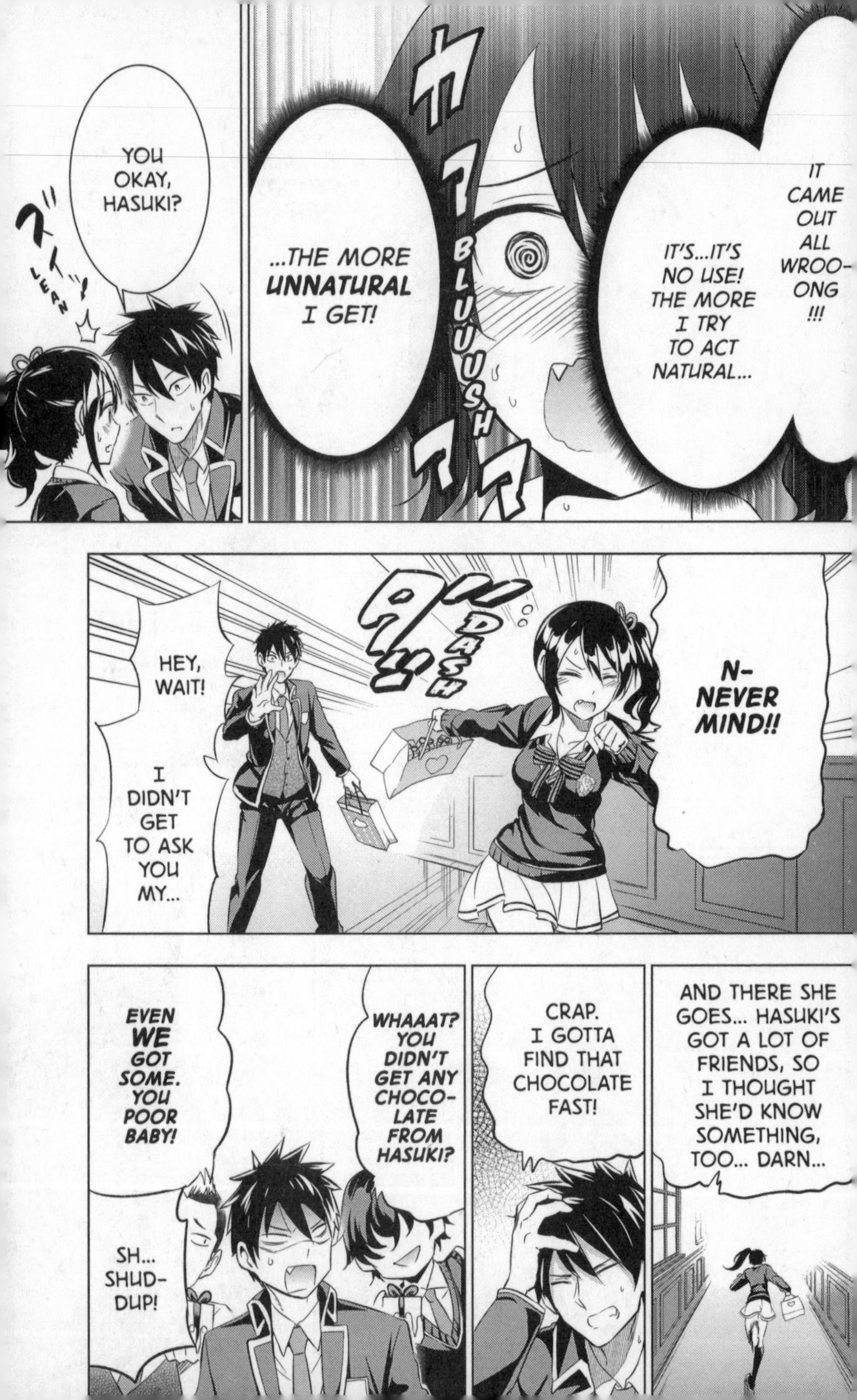
IT CAME OUT ALL WROO-ONG!!!
IT'S...IT'S NO USE! THE MORE I TRY TO ACT NATURAL...
...THE MORE UNNATURAL I GET!
BLUUUSH
YOU OKAY, HASUKI?
LEAN
N-NEVER MIND!!
DASH
HEY, WAIT!
I DIDN'T GET TO ASK YOU MY...
AND THERE SHE GOES... HASUKI'S GOT A LOT OF FRIENDS, SO I THOUGHT SHE'D KNOW SOMETHING, TOO... DARN...
CRAP. I GOTTA FIND THAT CHOCOLATE FAST!
WHAAAT? YOU DIDN'T GET ANY CHOCO-LATE FROM HASUKI?
EVEN WE GOT SOME. YOU POOR BABY!
SH... SHUD-DUP!

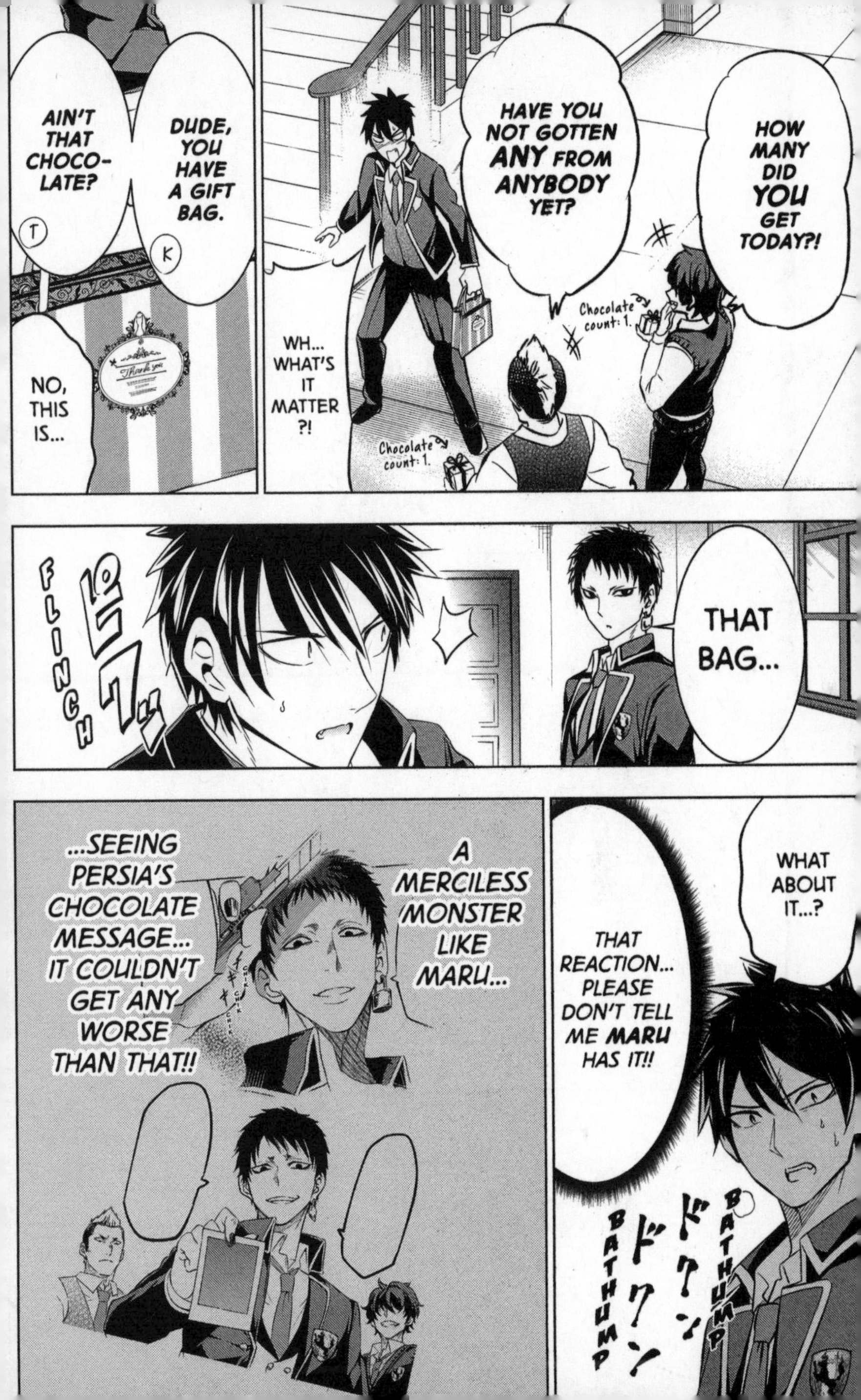
HOW MANY DID YOU GET TODAY?!
HAVE YOU NOT GOTTEN ANY FROM ANYBODY YET?
Chocolate count: 1.
WH... WHAT'S IT MATTER?!
Chocolate count: 1.
DUDE, YOU HAVE A GIFT BAG.
AIN'T THAT CHOCOLATE?
NO, THIS IS...
THAT BAG...
FLINCH
WHAT ABOUT IT...?
THAT REACTION... PLEASE DON'T TELL ME MARU HAS IT!!
BATHUMP
BATHUMP
A MERCILESS MONSTER LIKE MARU...
...SEEING PERSIA'S CHOCOLATE MESSAGE... IT COULDN'T GET ANY WORSE THAN THAT!!

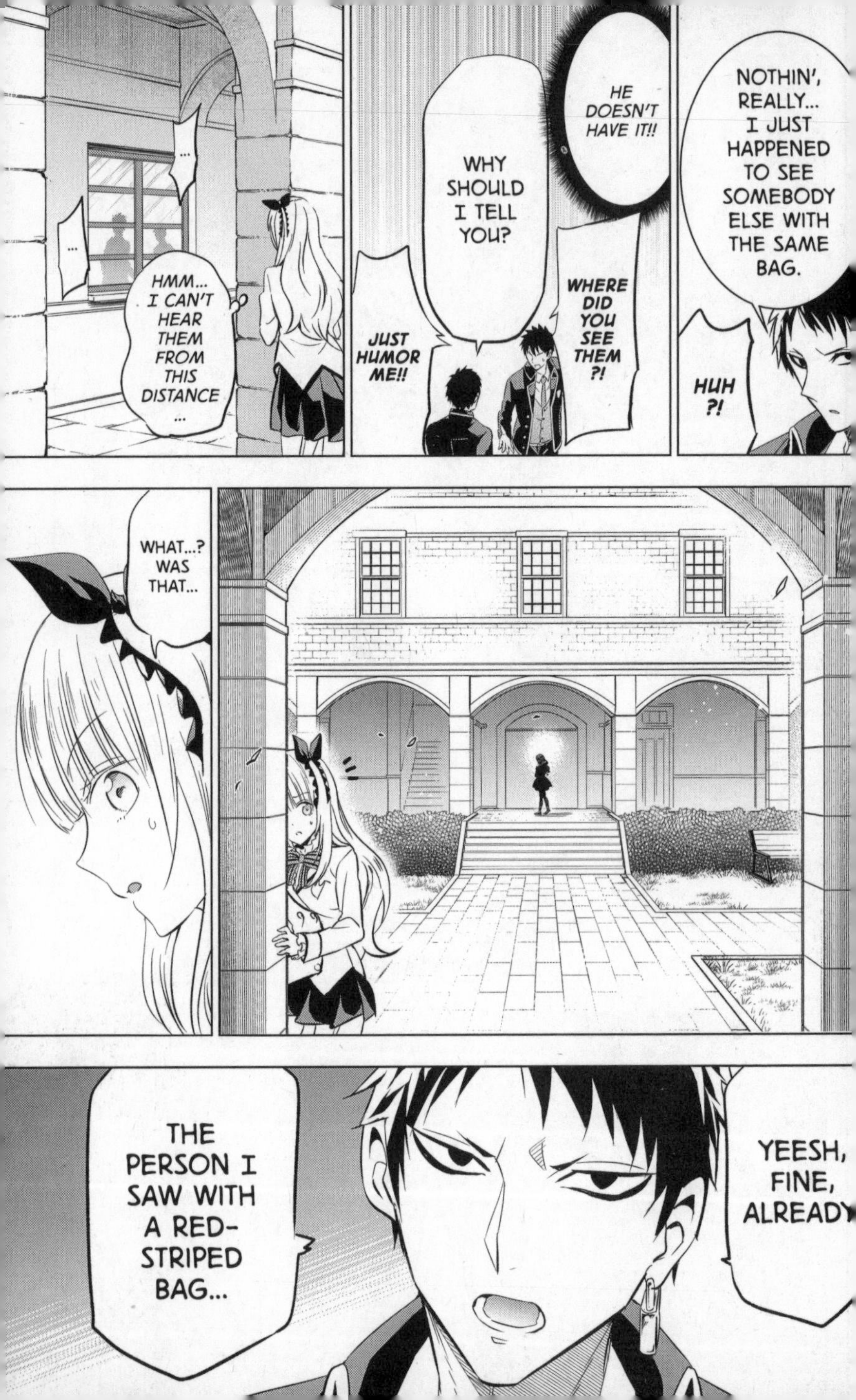
NOTHIN', REALLY... I JUST HAPPENED TO SEE SOMEBODY ELSE WITH THE SAME BAG.
HUH ?!
HE DOESN'T HAVE IT!!
WHERE DID YOU SEE THEM ?!
WHY SHOULD I TELL YOU?
JUST HUMOR ME!!
...
...
HMM... I CAN'T HEAR THEM FROM THIS DISTANCE ...
WHAT...? WAS THAT...
YEESH, FINE, ALREADY
THE PERSON I SAW WITH A RED-STRIPED BAG...

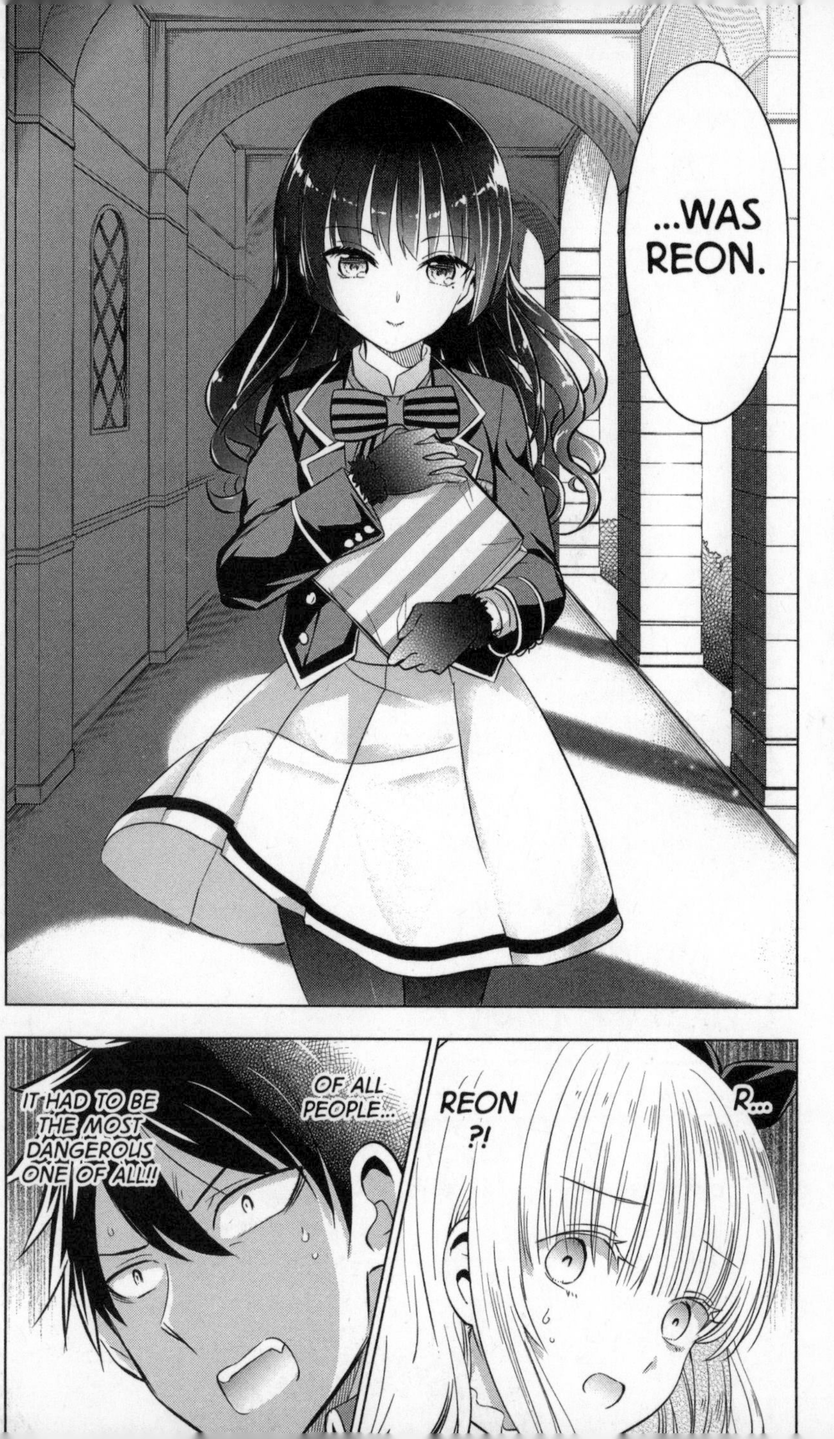
...WAS REON.
R...
REON?!
OF ALL PEOPLE...
IT HAD TO BE THE MOST DANGEROUS ONE OF ALL!!

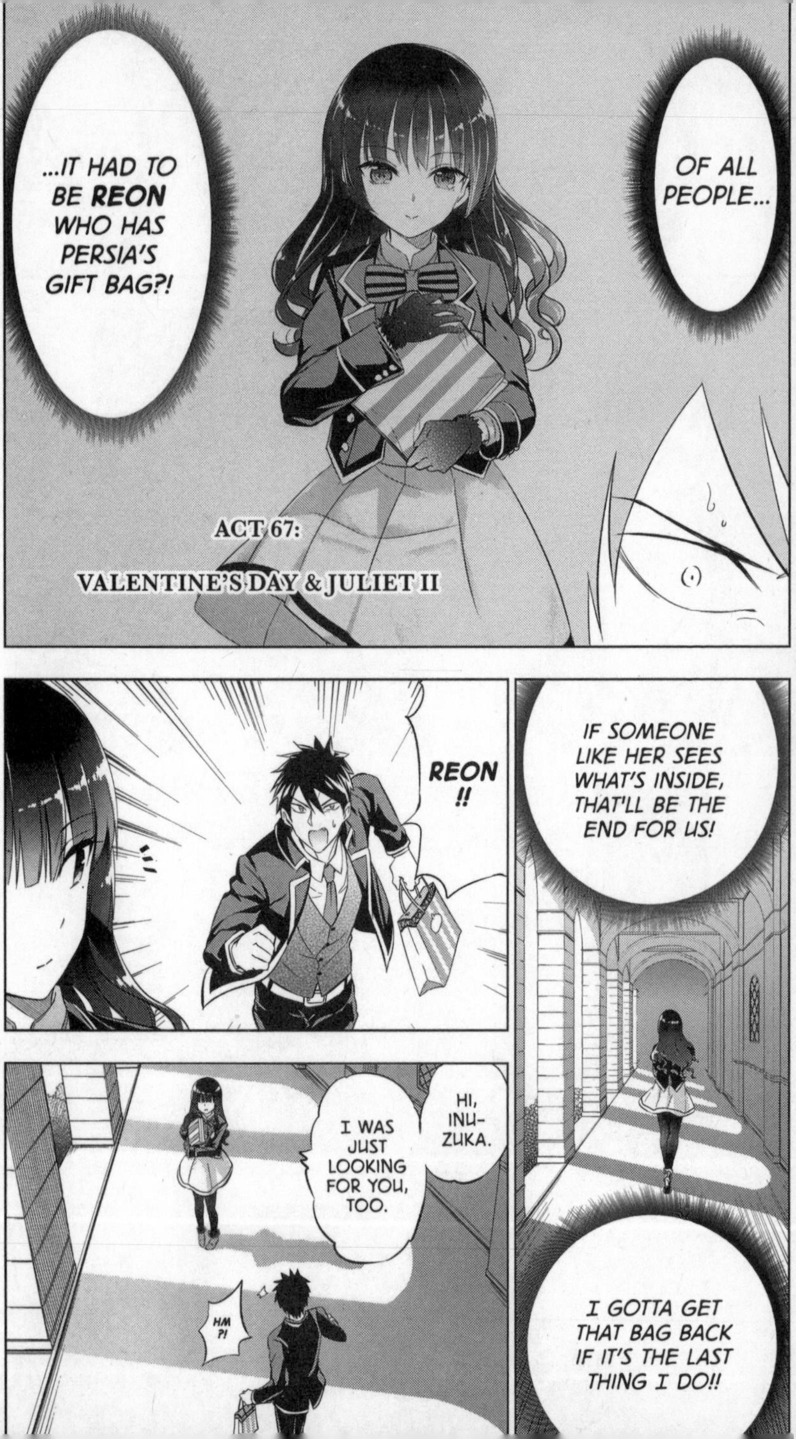
OF ALL PEOPLE...
...IT HAD TO BE REON WHO HAS PERSIA'S GIFT BAG?!
ACT 67:
VALENTINE'S DAY & JULIET II
IF SOMEONE LIKE HER SEES WHAT'S INSIDE, THAT'LL BE THE END FOR US!
I GOTTA GET THAT BAG BACK IF IT'S THE LAST THING I DO!!
REON !!
HI, INUZUKA.
I WAS JUST LOOKING FOR YOU, TOO.
HM ?!

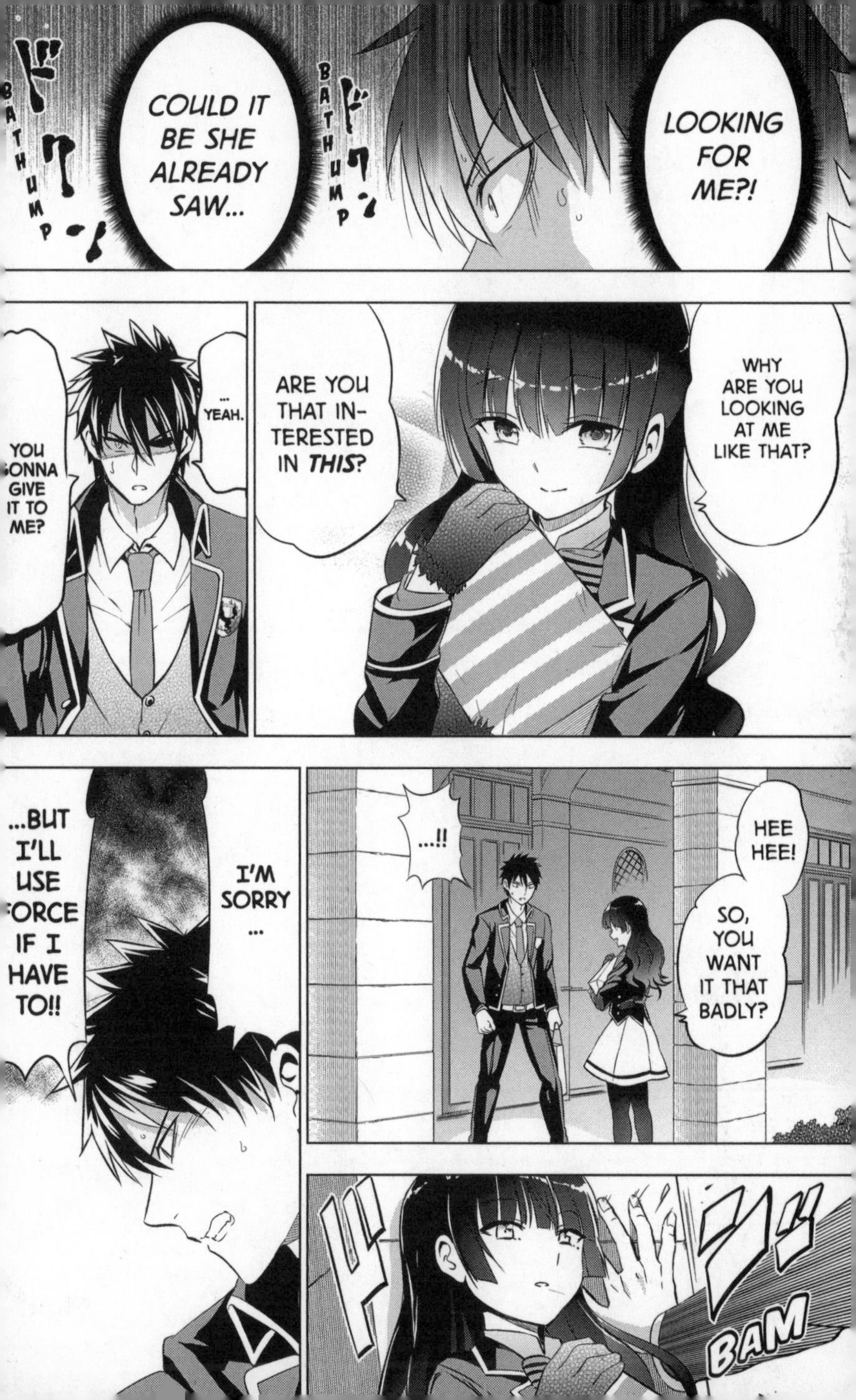
LOOKING FOR ME?!
BATHUMP
COULD IT BE SHE ALREADY SAW...
BATHUMP
WHY ARE YOU LOOKING AT ME LIKE THAT?
ARE YOU THAT INTERESTED IN *THIS*?
...YEAH.
YOU GONNA GIVE IT TO ME?
HEE HEE!
SO, YOU WANT IT THAT BADLY?
...!!
BAM
I'M SORRY...
...BUT I'LL USE FORCE IF I HAVE TO!!

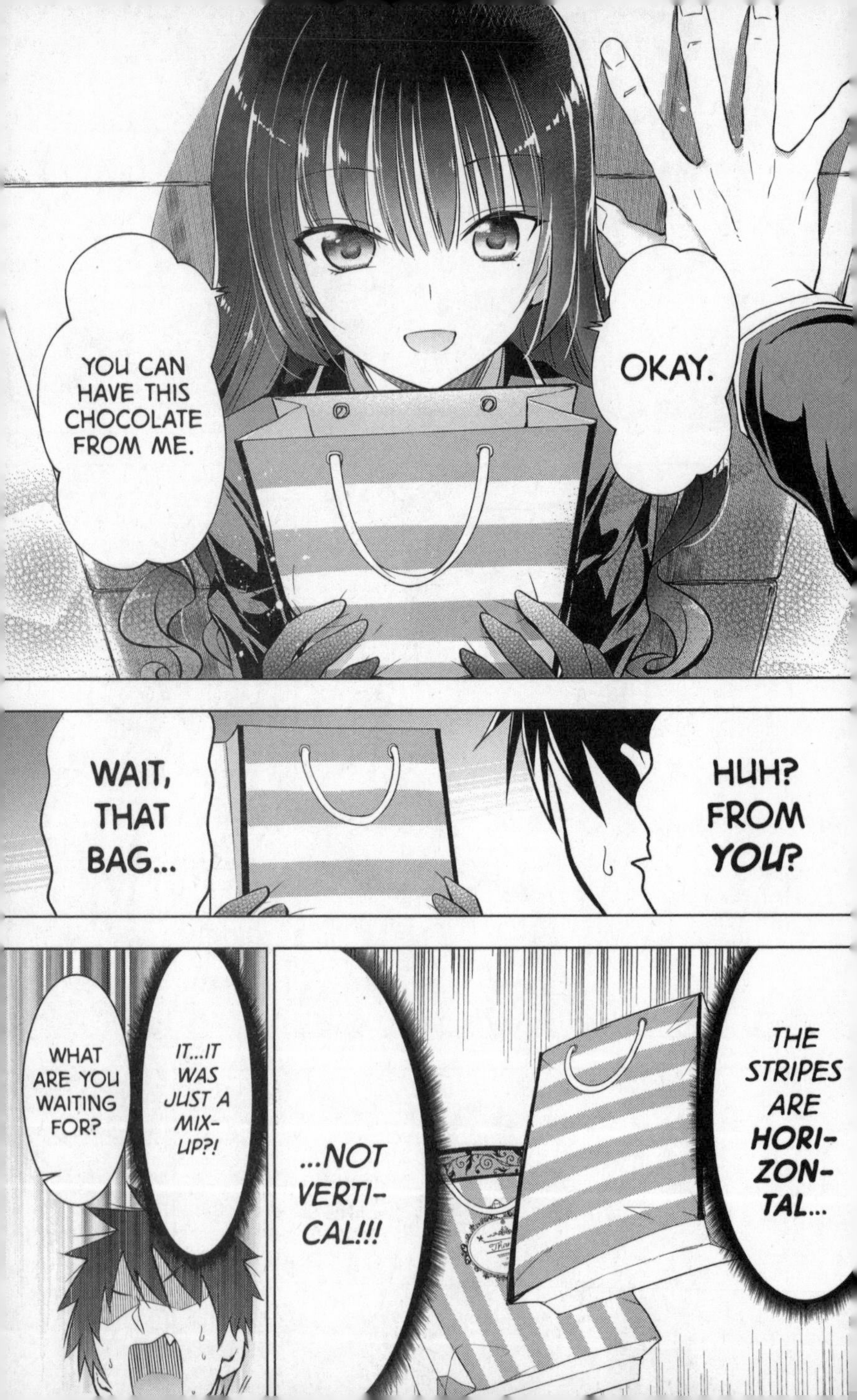
OKAY.
YOU CAN HAVE THIS CHOCOLATE FROM ME.
HUH? FROM *YOU*?
WAIT, THAT BAG...
THE STRIPES ARE HORIZONTAL...
...NOT VERTICAL!!!
IT...IT WAS JUST A MIX-UP?!
WHAT ARE YOU WAITING FOR?

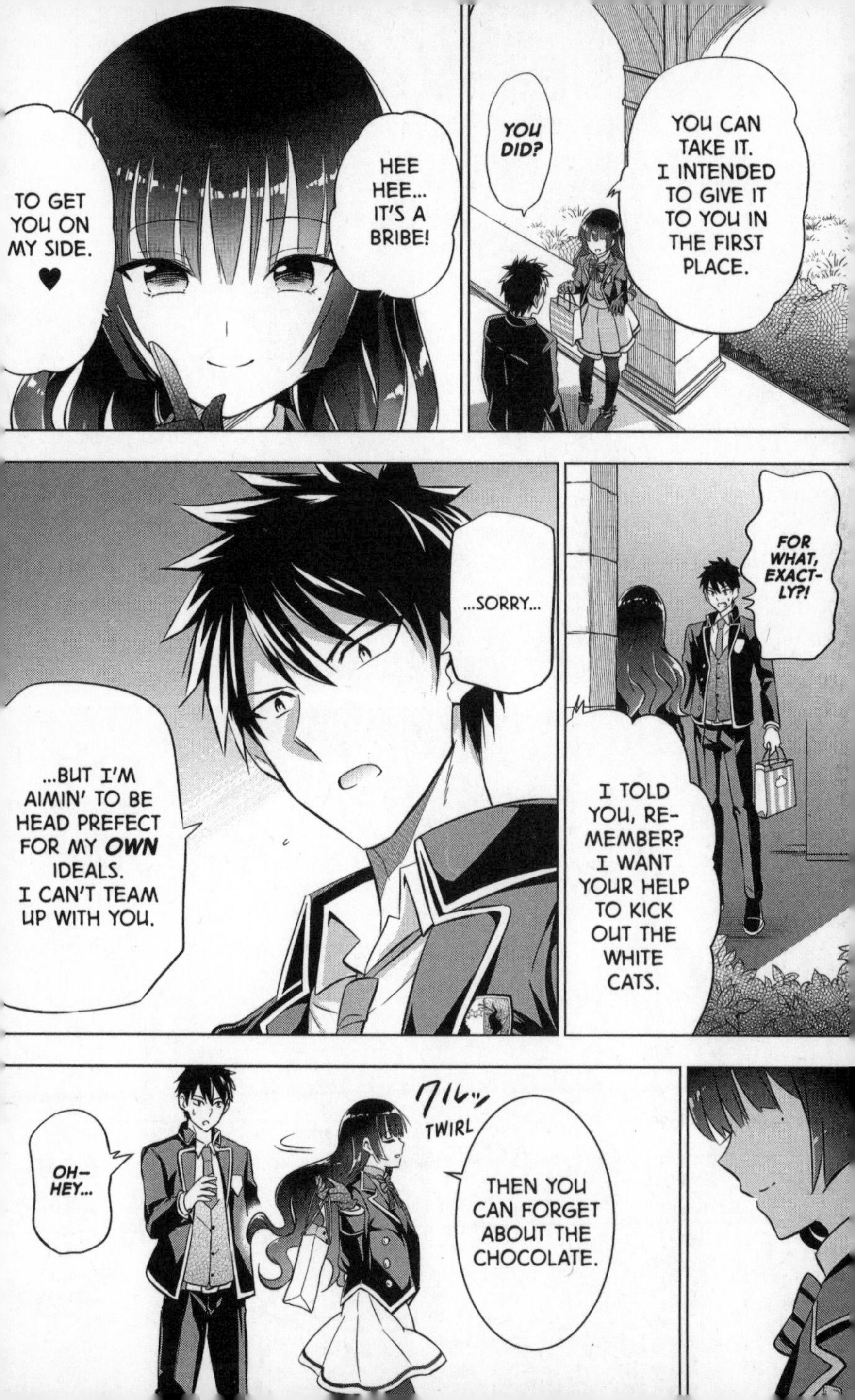
YOU CAN TAKE IT. I INTENDED TO GIVE IT TO YOU IN THE FIRST PLACE.
YOU DID?
HEE HEE... IT'S A BRIBE!
TO GET YOU ON MY SIDE. ♥
FOR WHAT, EXACTLY?!
I TOLD YOU, RE-MEMBER? I WANT YOUR HELP TO KICK OUT THE WHITE CATS.
...SORRY...
...BUT I'M AIMIN' TO BE HEAD PREFECT FOR MY OWN IDEALS. I CAN'T TEAM UP WITH YOU.
クルッ
TWIRL
THEN YOU CAN FORGET ABOUT THE CHOCOLATE.
OH— HEY...

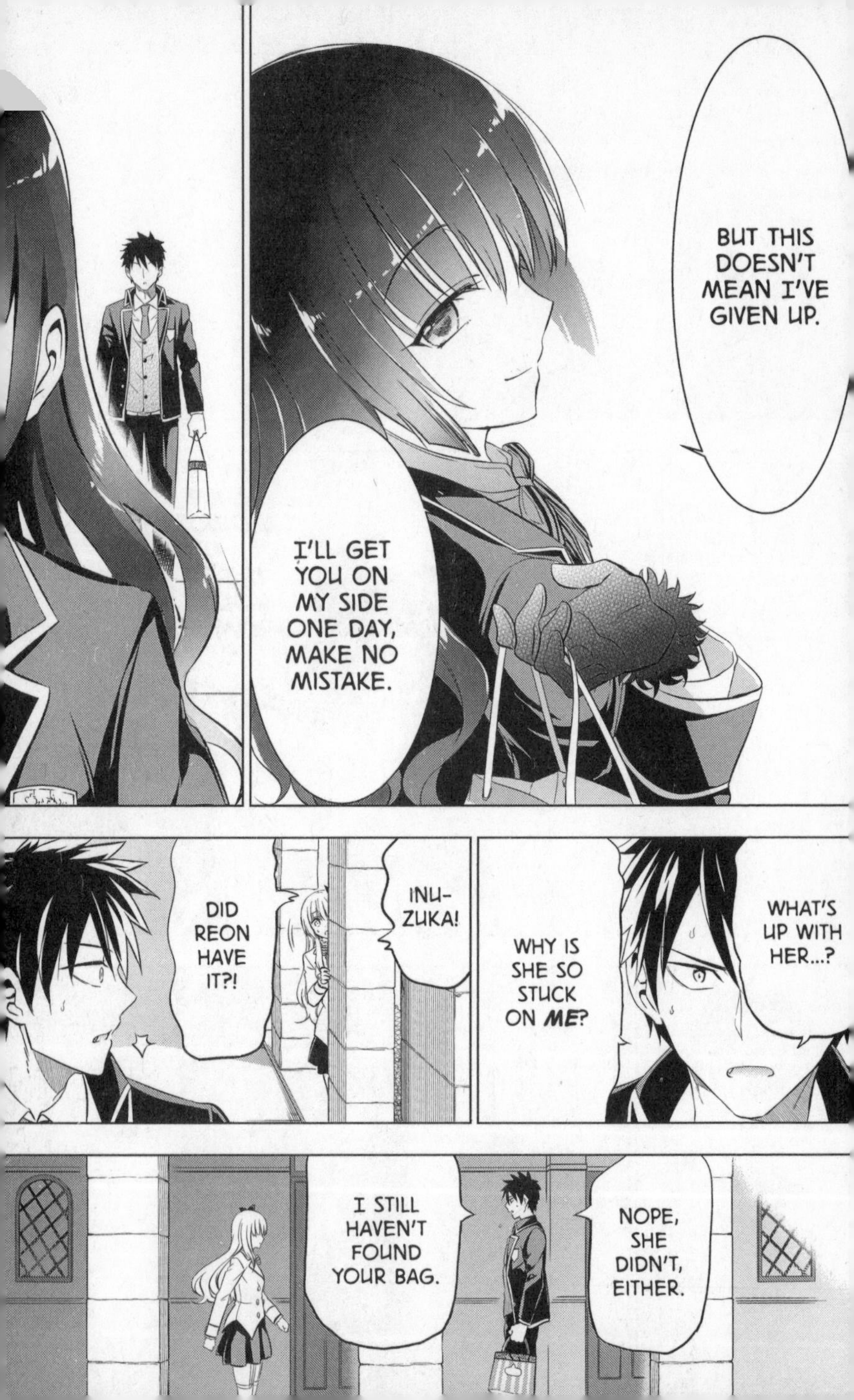
BUT THIS DOESN'T MEAN I'VE GIVEN UP.
I'LL GET YOU ON MY SIDE ONE DAY, MAKE NO MISTAKE.
WHAT'S UP WITH HER...?
WHY IS SHE SO STUCK ON *ME*?
INU-ZUKA!
DID REON HAVE IT?!
NOPE, SHE DIDN'T, EITHER.
I STILL HAVEN'T FOUND YOUR BAG.

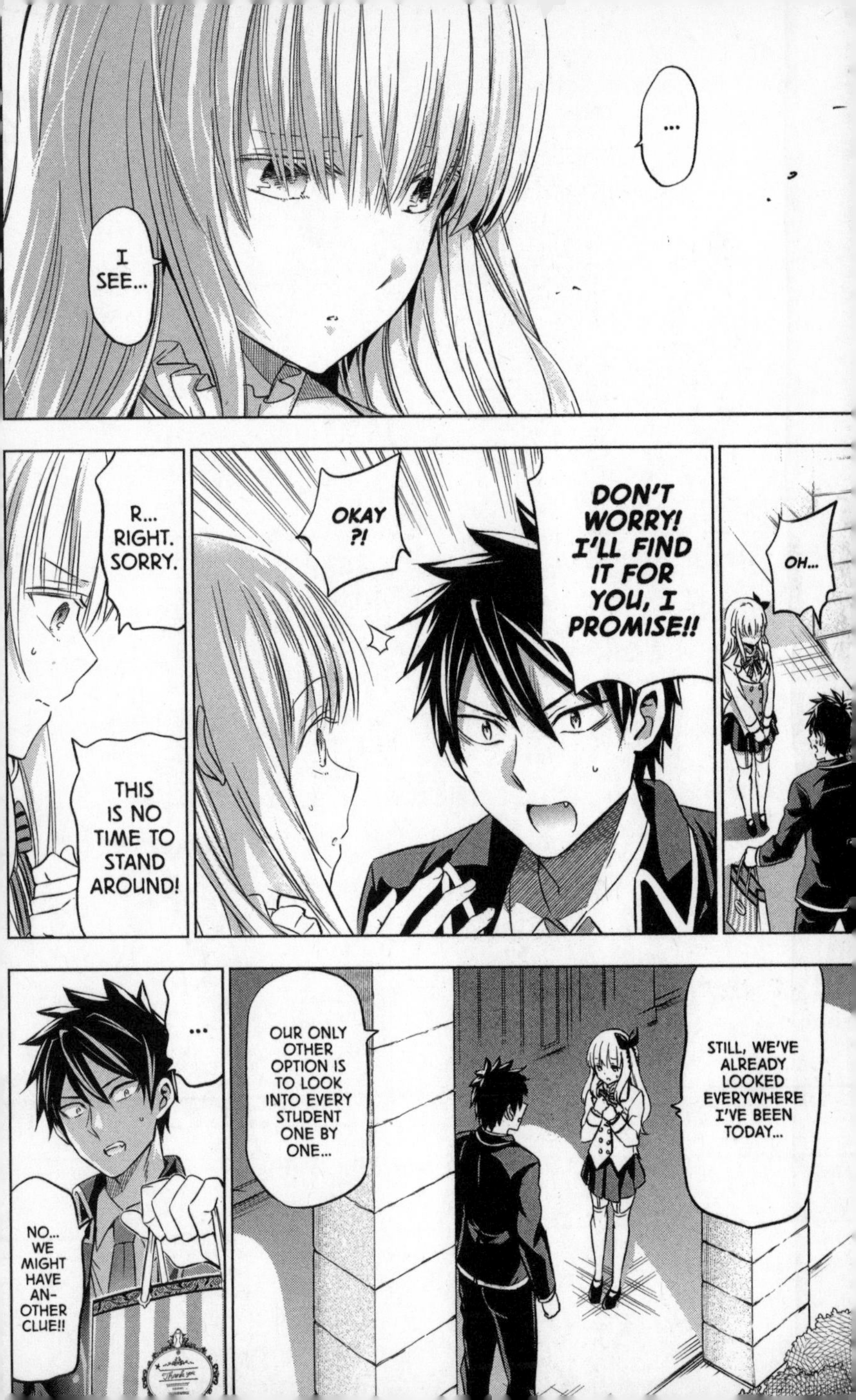
...
I SEE...
OH...
DON'T WORRY! I'LL FIND IT FOR YOU, I PROMISE!!
OKAY ?!
R... RIGHT. SORRY.
THIS IS NO TIME TO STAND AROUND!
STILL, WE'VE ALREADY LOOKED EVERYWHERE I'VE BEEN TODAY...
OUR ONLY OTHER OPTION IS TO LOOK INTO EVERY STUDENT ONE BY ONE...
...
NO... WE MIGHT HAVE AN-OTHER CLUE!!

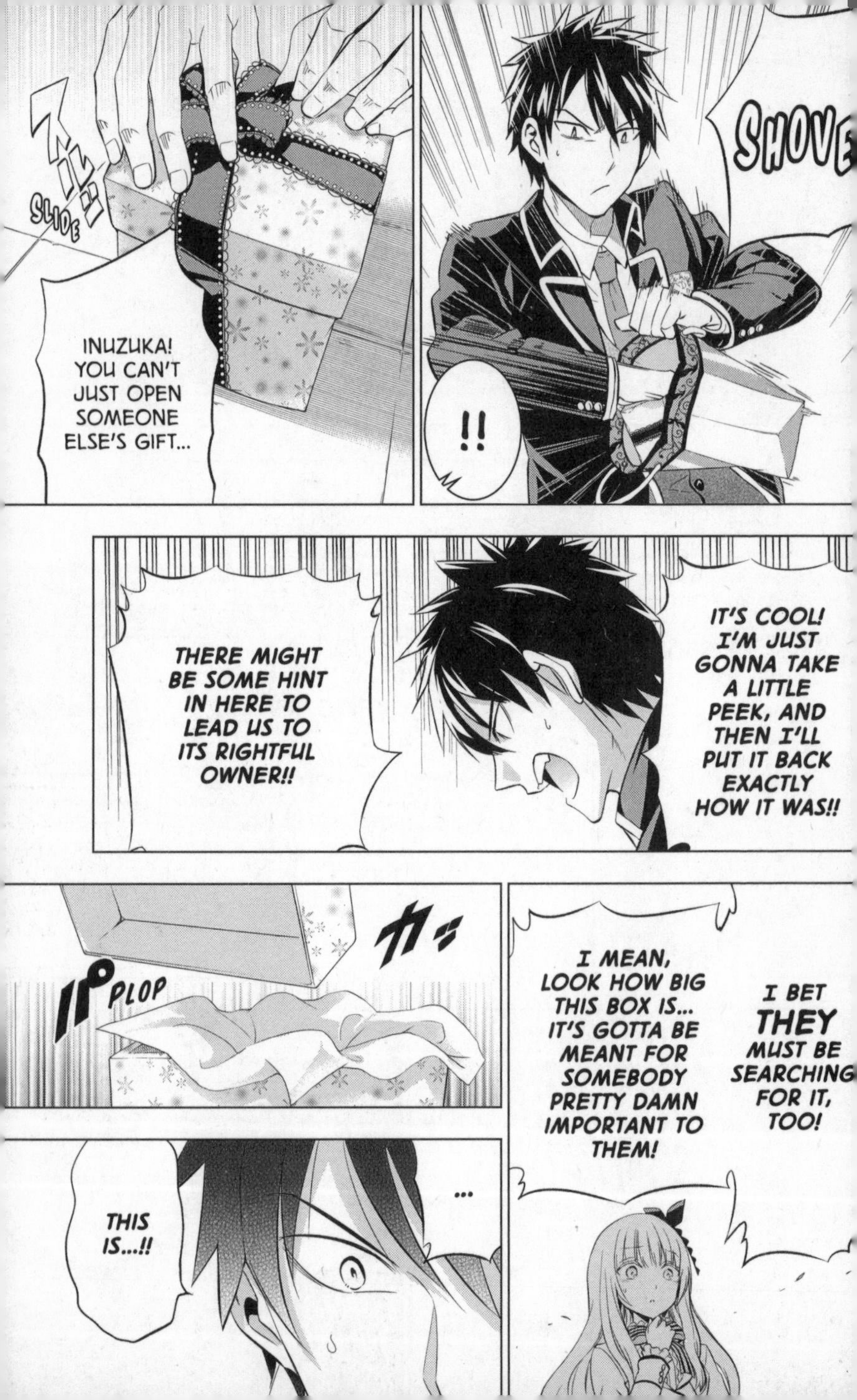
SHOVE
!!
SLIDE
INUZUKA! YOU CAN'T JUST OPEN SOMEONE ELSE'S GIFT...
IT'S COOL! I'M JUST GONNA TAKE A LITTLE PEEK, AND THEN I'LL PUT IT BACK EXACTLY HOW IT WAS!!
THERE MIGHT BE SOME HINT IN HERE TO LEAD US TO ITS RIGHTFUL OWNER!!
I BET THEY MUST BE SEARCHING FOR IT, TOO!
I MEAN, LOOK HOW BIG THIS BOX IS... IT'S GOTTA BE MEANT FOR SOMEBODY PRETTY DAMN IMPORTANT TO THEM!
PLOP
...
THIS IS...!!

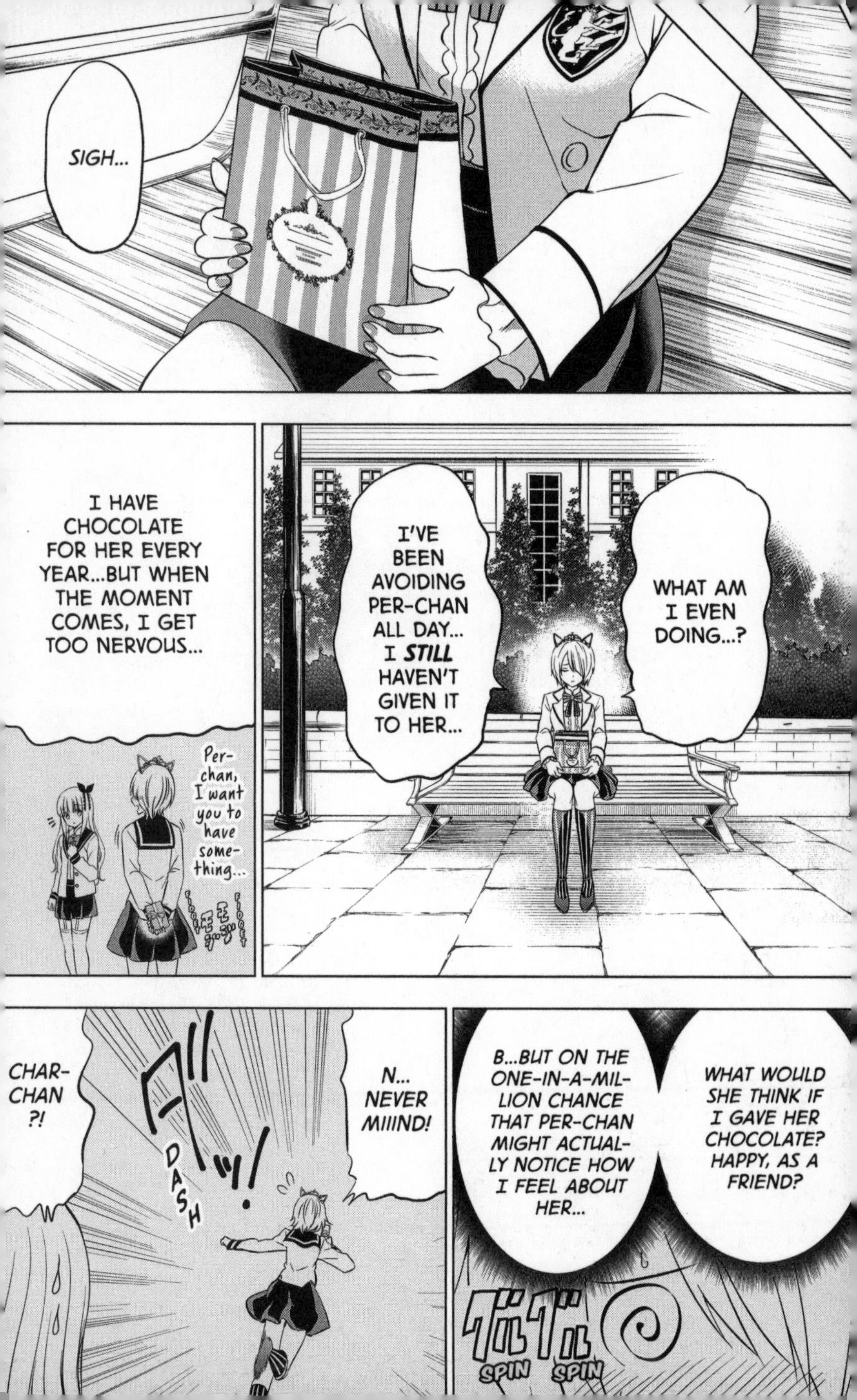
SIGH...
WHAT AM I EVEN DOING...?
I'VE BEEN AVOIDING PER-CHAN ALL DAY... I STILL HAVEN'T GIVEN IT TO HER...
I HAVE CHOCOLATE FOR HER EVERY YEAR...BUT WHEN THE MOMENT COMES, I GET TOO NERVOUS...
Per-chan, I want you to have some-thing...
FIDGET
FIDGET
WHAT WOULD SHE THINK IF I GAVE HER CHOCOLATE? HAPPY, AS A FRIEND?
B...BUT ON THE ONE-IN-A-MIL-LION CHANCE THAT PER-CHAN MIGHT ACTUAL-LY NOTICE HOW I FEEL ABOUT HER...
SPIN SPIN
N... NEVER MIIIND!
DASH
CHAR-CHAN ?!

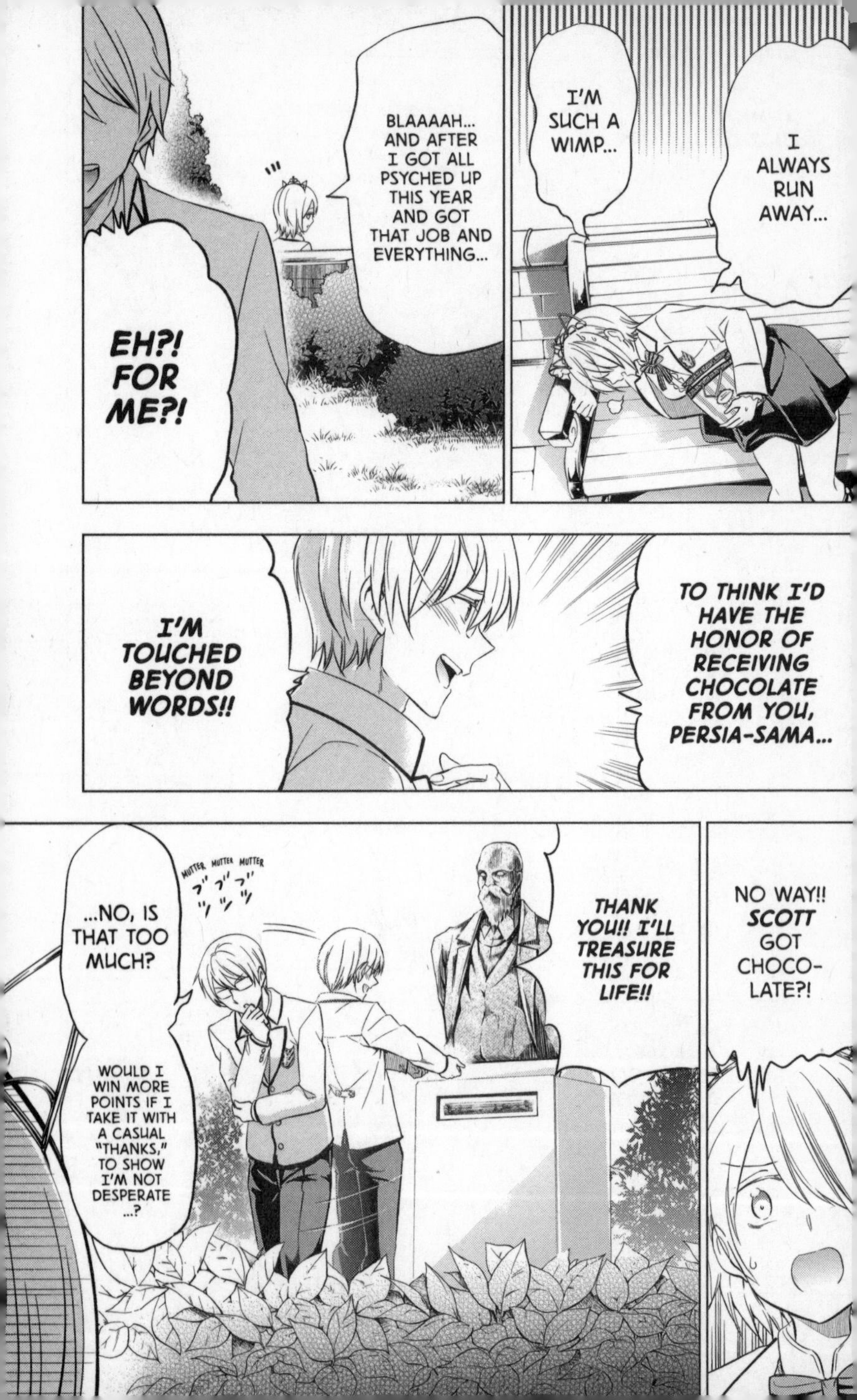
I ALWAYS RUN AWAY...
I'M SUCH A WIMP...
BLAAAAH... AND AFTER I GOT ALL PSYCHED UP THIS YEAR AND GOT THAT JOB AND EVERYTHING...
EH?! FOR ME?!
TO THINK I'D HAVE THE HONOR OF RECEIVING CHOCOLATE FROM YOU, PERSIA-SAMA...
I'M TOUCHED BEYOND WORDS!!
NO WAY!! SCOTT GOT CHOCO-LATE?!
THANK YOU!! I'LL TREASURE THIS FOR LIFE!!
MUTTER MUTTER MUTTER
...NO, IS THAT TOO MUCH?
WOULD I WIN MORE POINTS IF I TAKE IT WITH A CASUAL "THANKS," TO SHOW I'M NOT DESPERATE ...?

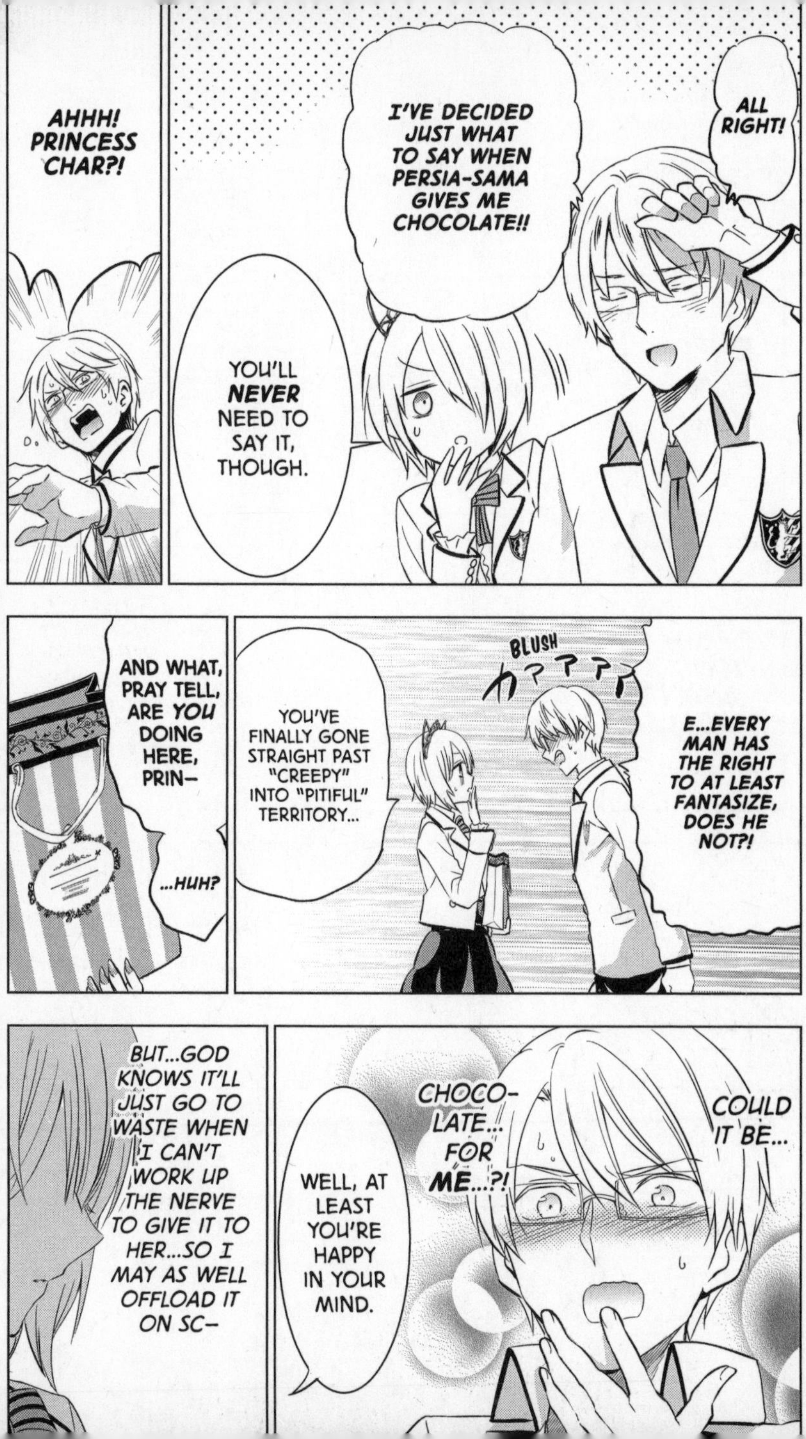
ALL RIGHT!
I'VE DECIDED JUST WHAT TO SAY WHEN PERSIA-SAMA GIVES ME CHOCOLATE!!
YOU'LL NEVER NEED TO SAY IT, THOUGH.
AHHH! PRINCESS CHAR?!
BLUSH
E...EVERY MAN HAS THE RIGHT TO AT LEAST FANTASIZE, DOES HE NOT?!
YOU'VE FINALLY GONE STRAIGHT PAST "CREEPY" INTO "PITIFUL" TERRITORY...
AND WHAT, PRAY TELL, ARE YOU DOING HERE, PRIN–
...HUH?
COULD IT BE...
CHOCO-LATE... FOR ME...?!
WELL, AT LEAST YOU'RE HAPPY IN YOUR MIND.
BUT...GOD KNOWS IT'LL JUST GO TO WASTE WHEN I CAN'T WORK UP THE NERVE TO GIVE IT TO HER...SO I MAY AS WELL OFFLOAD IT ON SC–

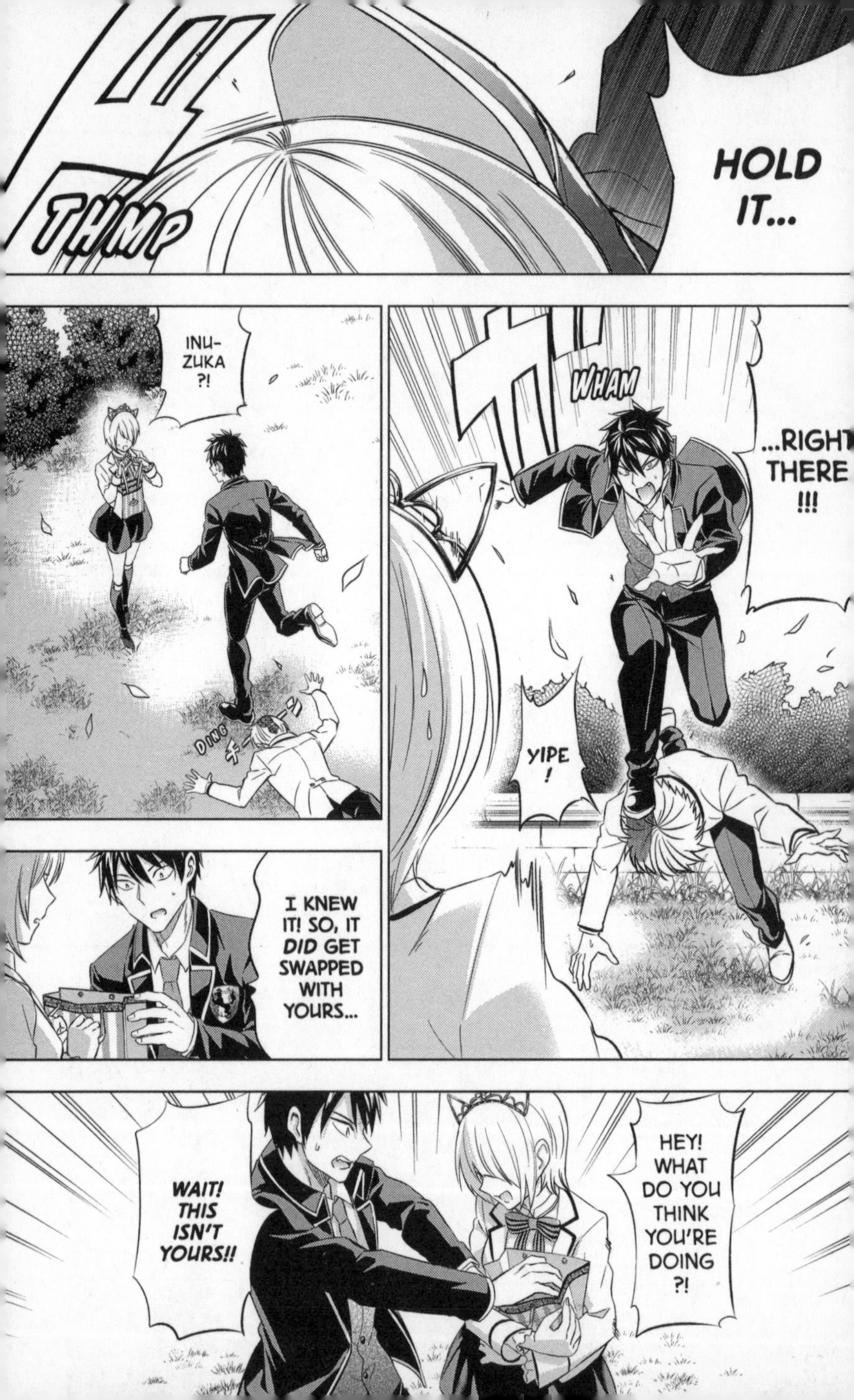
HOLD IT...
THMP
WHAM
...RIGHT THERE!!!
YIPE!
INU-ZUKA?!
DING
I KNEW IT! SO, IT *DID* GET SWAPPED WITH YOURS...
HEY! WHAT DO YOU THINK YOU'RE DOING?!
WAIT! THIS ISN'T YOURS!!

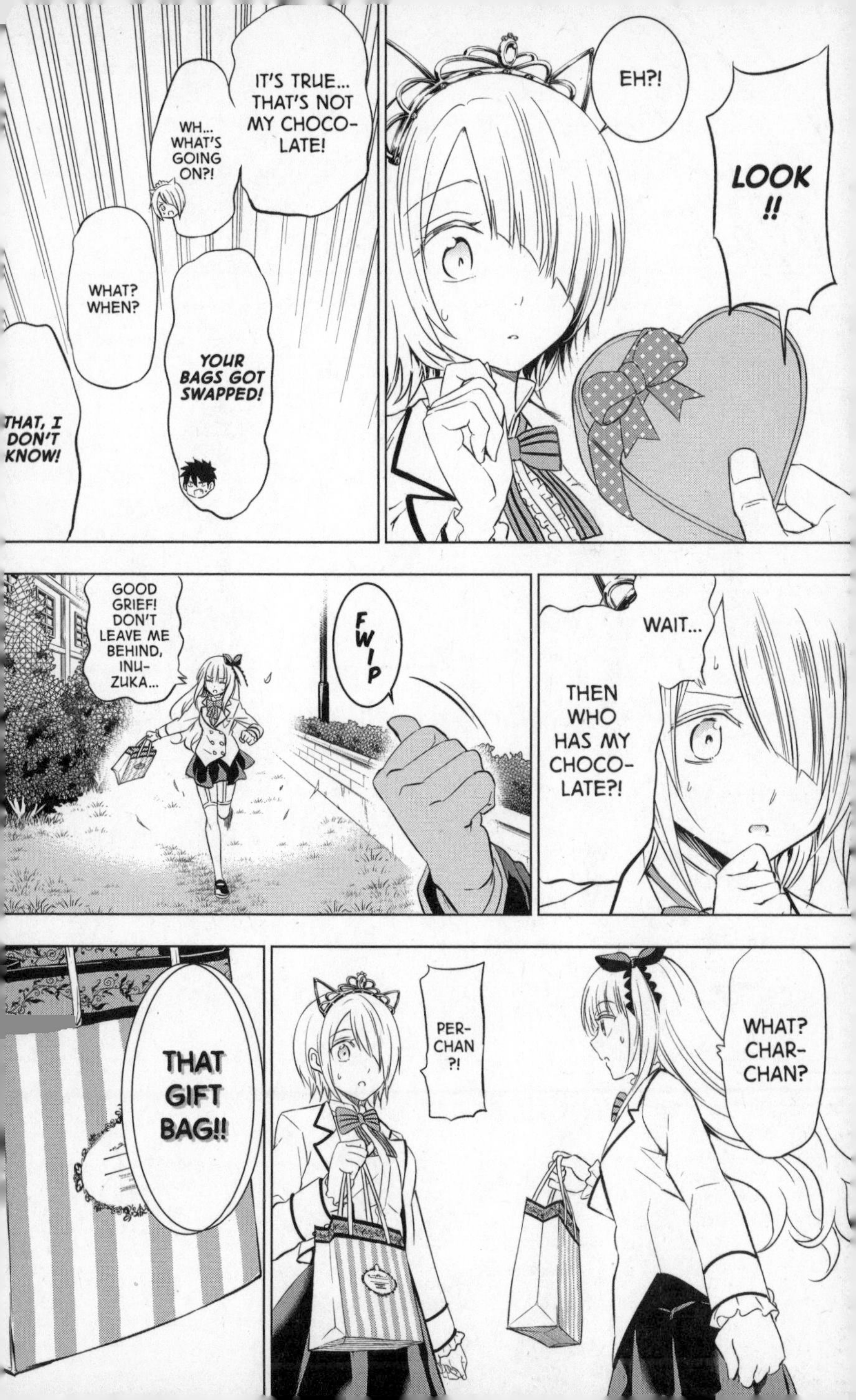
LOOK!!
EH?!
IT'S TRUE... THAT'S NOT MY CHOCOLATE!
WH... WHAT'S GOING ON?!
YOUR BAGS GOT SWAPPED!
WHAT? WHEN?
THAT, I DON'T KNOW!
WAIT...
THEN WHO HAS MY CHOCOLATE?!
FWIP
GOOD GRIEF! DON'T LEAVE ME BEHIND, INUZUKA...
WHAT? CHAR-CHAN?
PER-CHAN?!
THAT GIFT BAG!!

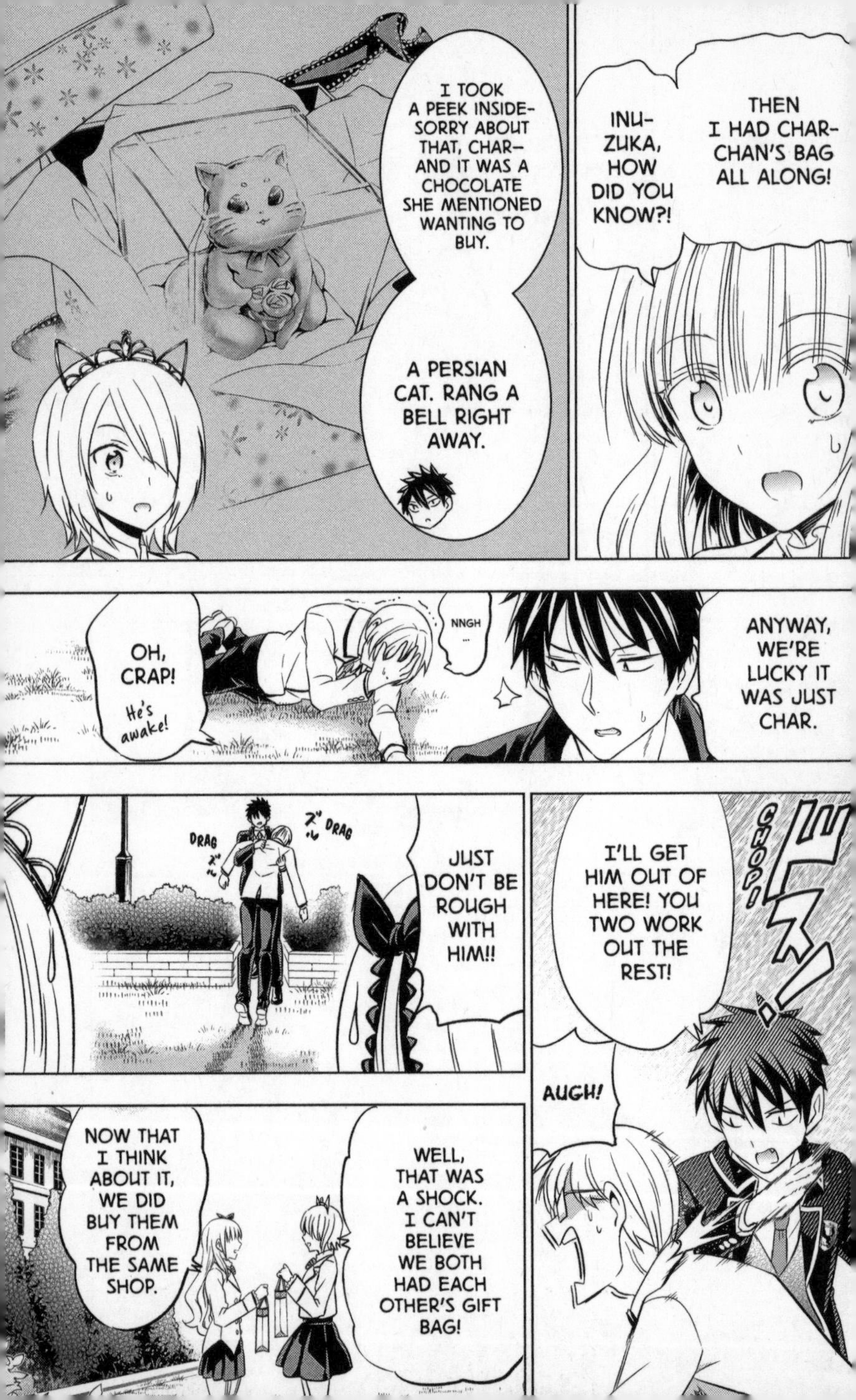
THEN I HAD CHAR-CHAN'S BAG ALL ALONG!
INU-ZUKA, HOW DID YOU KNOW?!
I TOOK A PEEK INSIDE-SORRY ABOUT THAT, CHAR-AND IT WAS A CHOCOLATE SHE MENTIONED WANTING TO BUY.
A PERSIAN CAT. RANG A BELL RIGHT AWAY.
ANYWAY, WE'RE LUCKY IT WAS JUST CHAR.
NNGH...
OH, CRAP!
He's awake!
CHOP!
I'LL GET HIM OUT OF HERE! YOU TWO WORK OUT THE REST!
AUGH!
JUST DON'T BE ROUGH WITH HIM!!
DRAG
DRAG
WELL, THAT WAS A SHOCK. I CAN'T BELIEVE WE BOTH HAD EACH OTHER'S GIFT BAG!
NOW THAT I THINK ABOUT IT, WE DID BUY THEM FROM THE SAME SHOP.

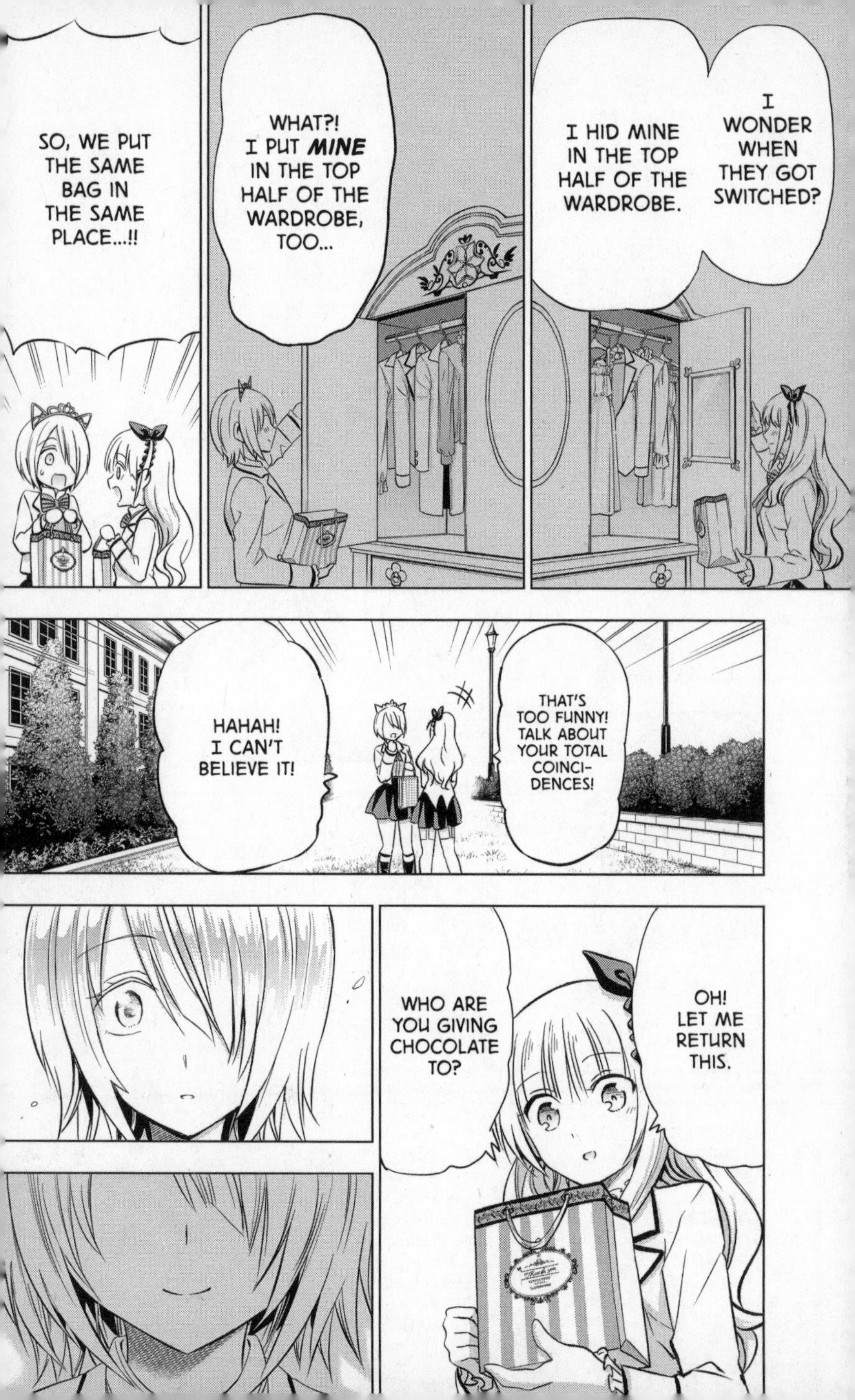
I WONDER WHEN THEY GOT SWITCHED?
I HID MINE IN THE TOP HALF OF THE WARDROBE.
WHAT?! I PUT *MINE* IN THE TOP HALF OF THE WARDROBE, TOO...
SO, WE PUT THE SAME BAG IN THE SAME PLACE...!!
THAT'S TOO FUNNY! TALK ABOUT YOUR TOTAL COINCI-DENCES!
HAHAH! I CAN'T BELIEVE IT!
OH! LET ME RETURN THIS.
WHO ARE YOU GIVING CHOCOLATE TO?

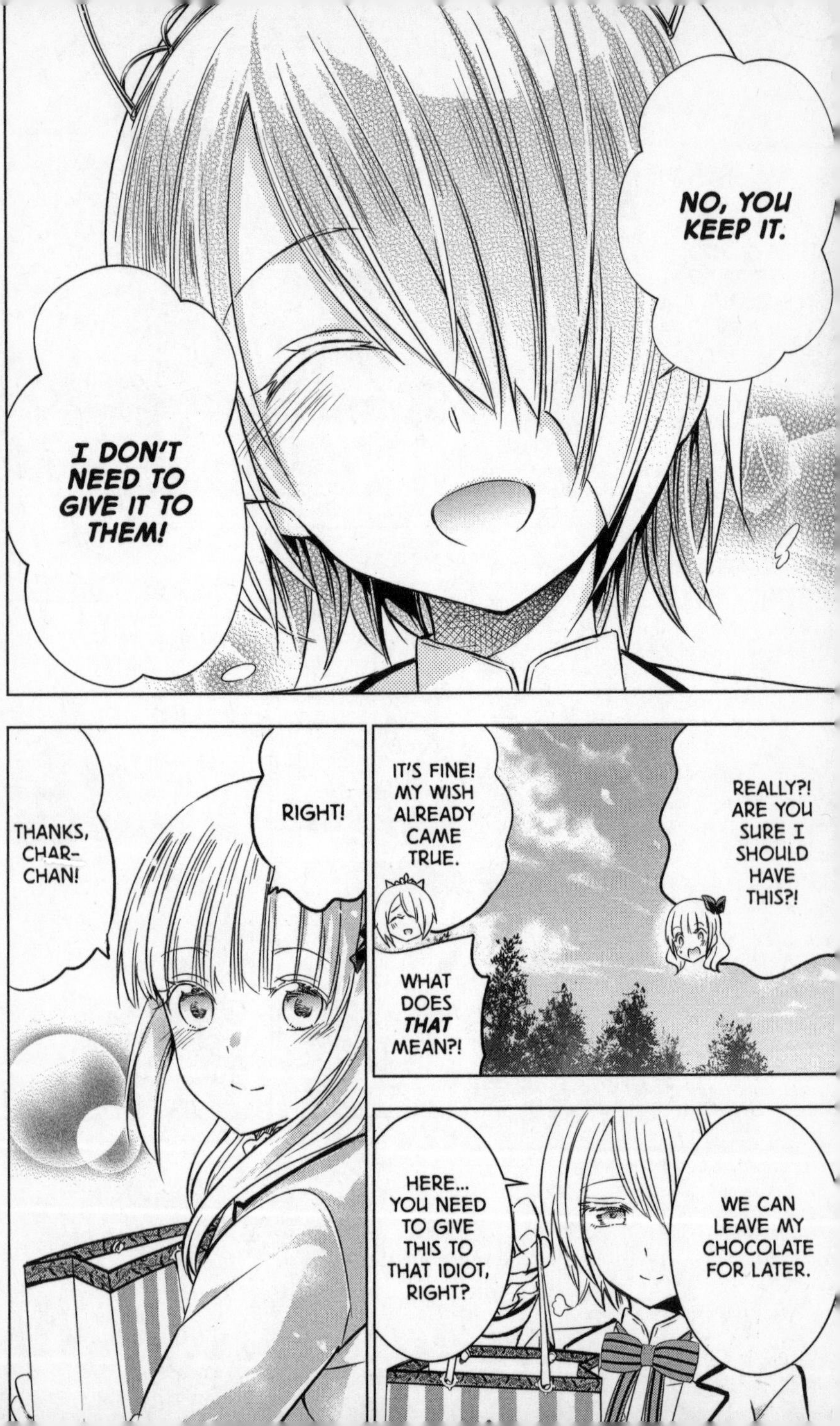
NO, YOU KEEP IT.
I DON'T NEED TO GIVE IT TO THEM!
REALLY?! ARE YOU SURE I SHOULD HAVE THIS?!
IT'S FINE! MY WISH ALREADY CAME TRUE.
WHAT DOES *THAT* MEAN?!
WE CAN LEAVE MY CHOCOLATE FOR LATER.
HERE... YOU NEED TO GIVE THIS TO THAT IDIOT, RIGHT?
RIGHT!
THANKS, CHAR-CHAN!

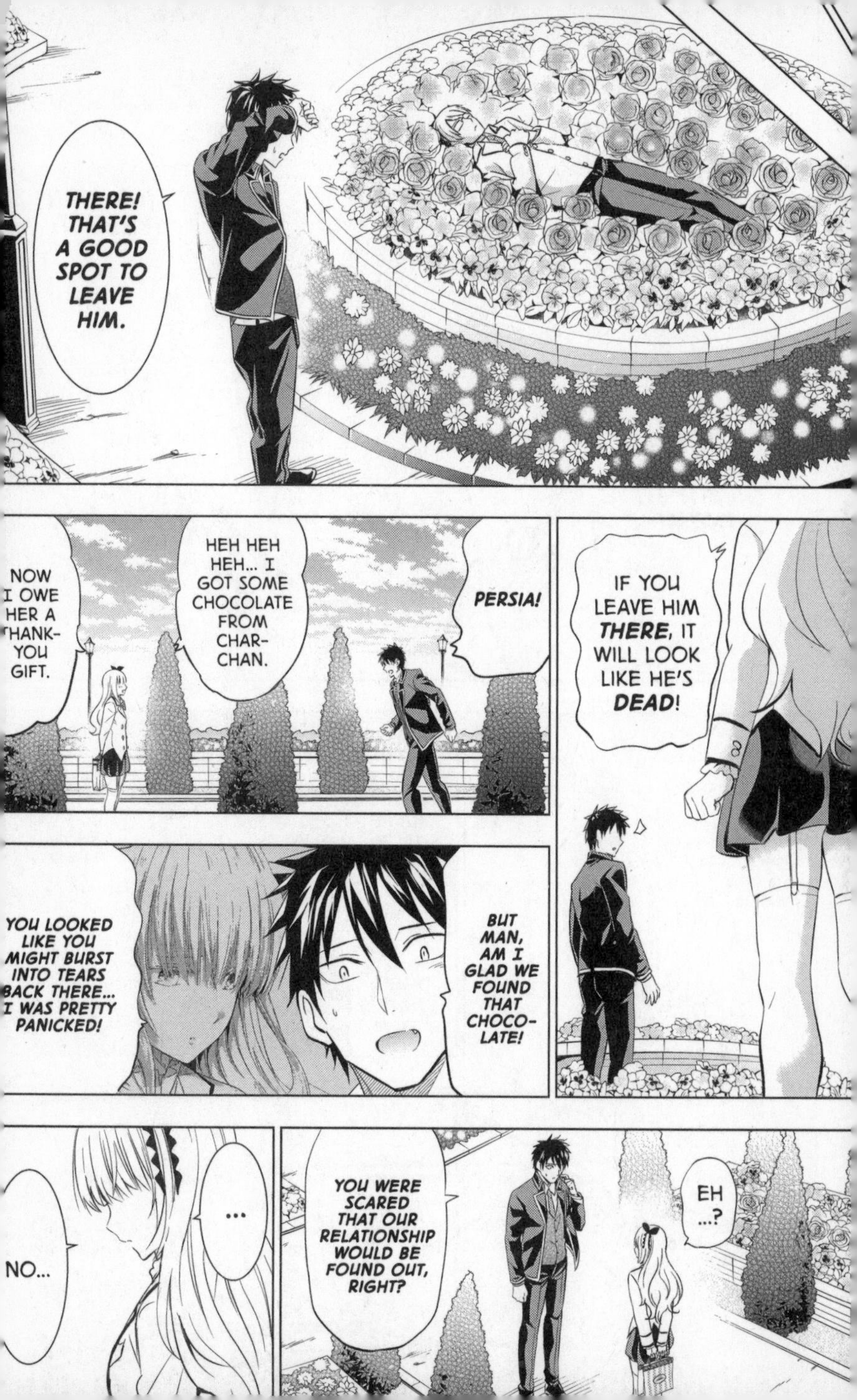

THERE! THAT'S A GOOD SPOT TO LEAVE HIM.
IF YOU LEAVE HIM THERE, IT WILL LOOK LIKE HE'S DEAD!
PERSIA!
HEH HEH HEH... I GOT SOME CHOCOLATE FROM CHAR-CHAN.
NOW I OWE HER A THANK-YOU GIFT.
BUT MAN, AM I GLAD WE FOUND THAT CHOCO-LATE!
YOU LOOKED LIKE YOU MIGHT BURST INTO TEARS BACK THERE... I WAS PRETTY PANICKED!
EH ...?
YOU WERE SCARED THAT OUR RELATIONSHIP WOULD BE FOUND OUT, RIGHT?
...
NO...

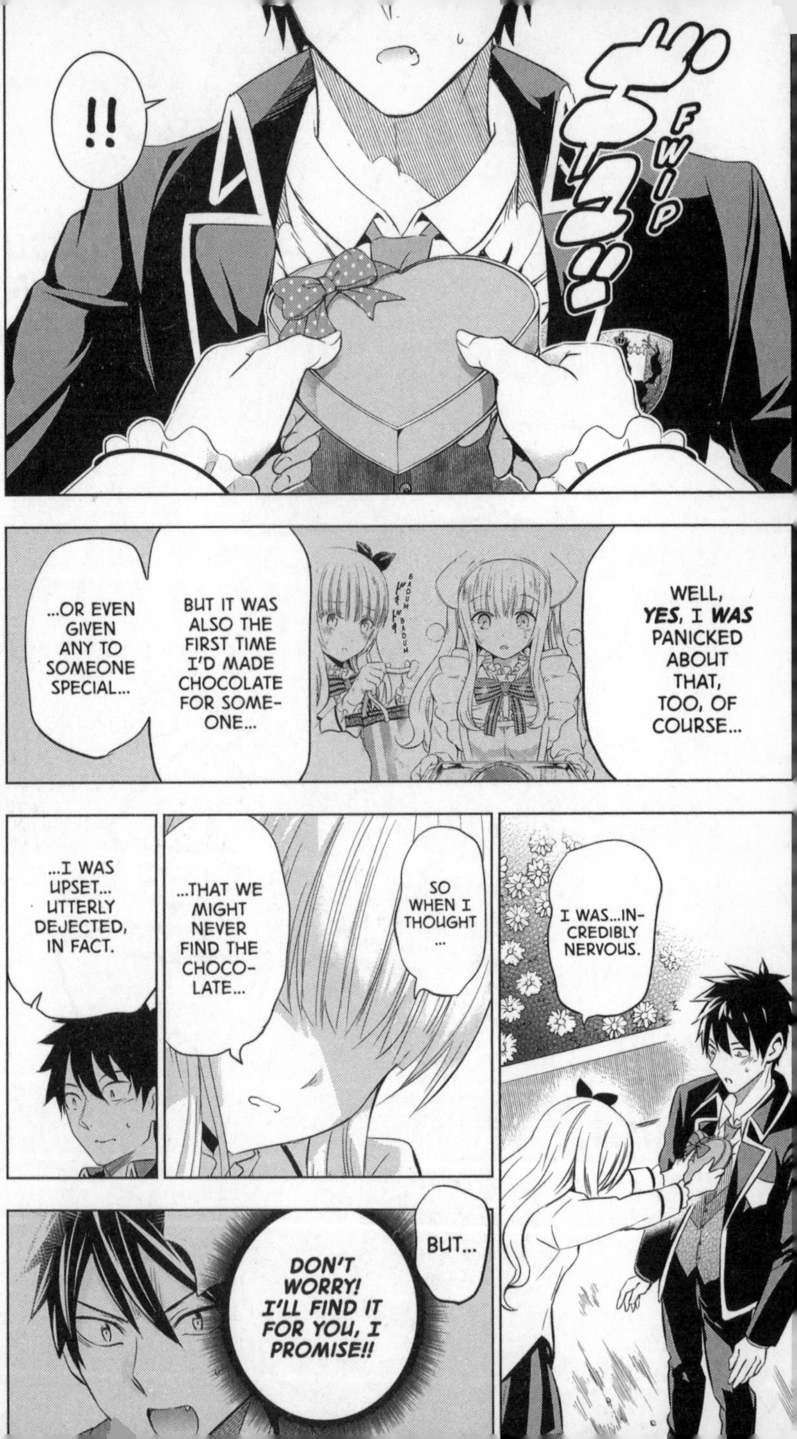
FWIP
!!
WELL, YES, I WAS PANICKED ABOUT THAT, TOO, OF COURSE...
BUT IT WAS ALSO THE FIRST TIME I'D MADE CHOCOLATE FOR SOMEONE...
...OR EVEN GIVEN ANY TO SOMEONE SPECIAL...
I WAS...INCREDIBLY NERVOUS.
SO WHEN I THOUGHT...
...THAT WE MIGHT NEVER FIND THE CHOCOLATE...
...I WAS UPSET... UTTERLY DEJECTED, IN FACT.
BUT...
DON'T WORRY! I'LL FIND IT FOR YOU, I PROMISE!!

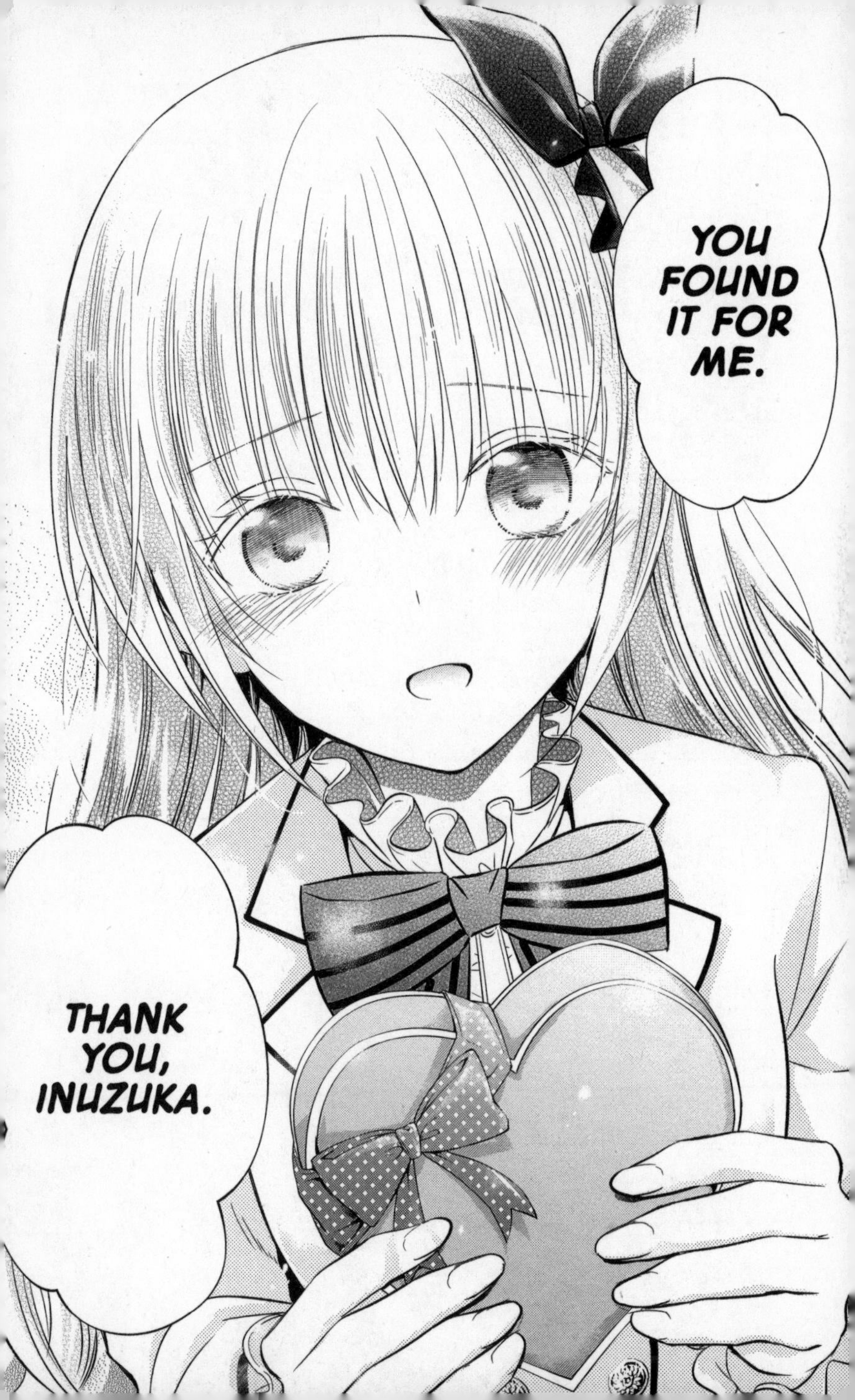
YOU FOUND IT FOR ME.
THANK YOU, INUZUKA.

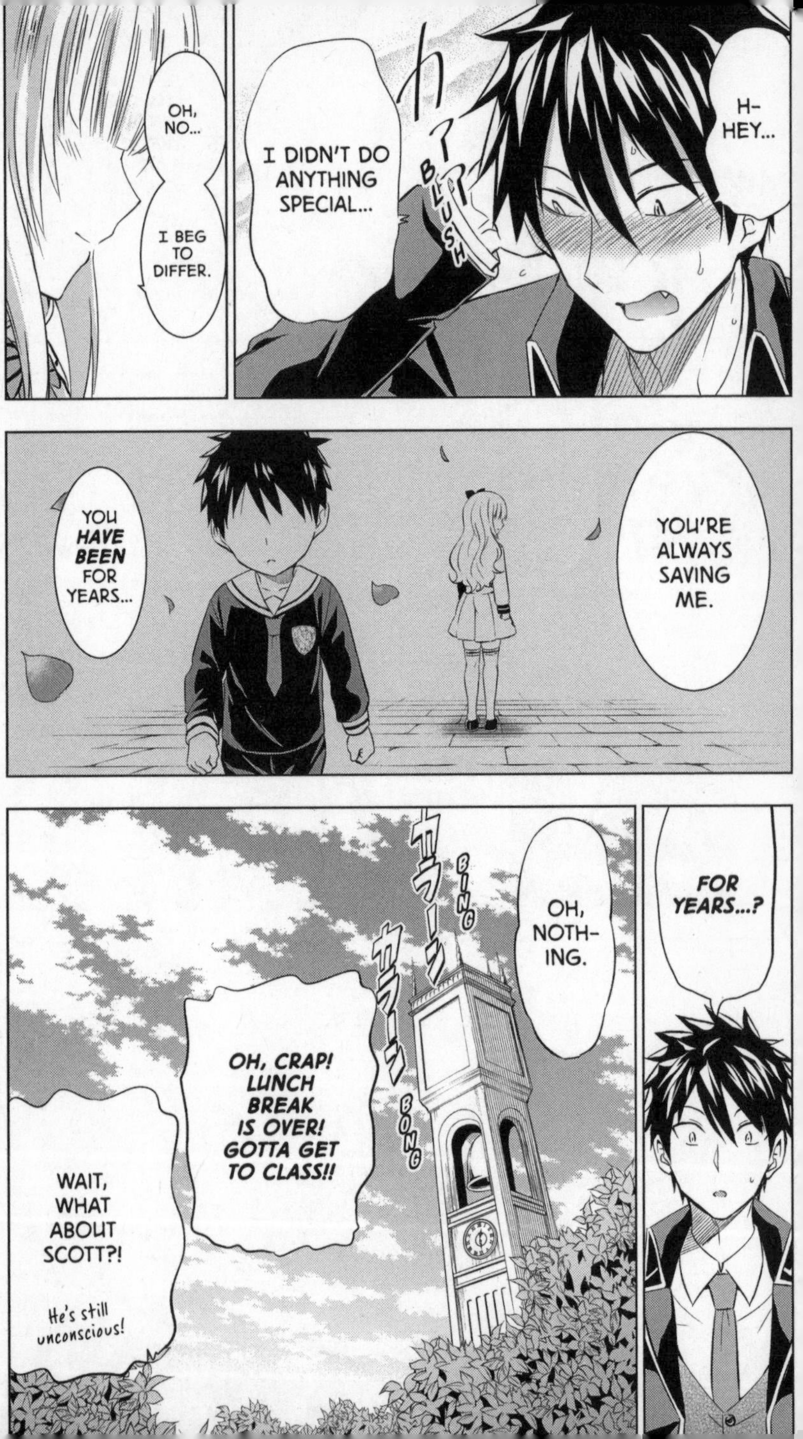
H-HEY...
BLUSH
I DIDN'T DO ANYTHING SPECIAL...
OH, NO...
I BEG TO DIFFER.
YOU'RE ALWAYS SAVING ME.
YOU HAVE BEEN FOR YEARS...
FOR YEARS...?
OH, NOTH-ING.
BING
BONG
OH, CRAP! LUNCH BREAK IS OVER! GOTTA GET TO CLASS!!
WAIT, WHAT ABOUT SCOTT?!
He's still unconscious!

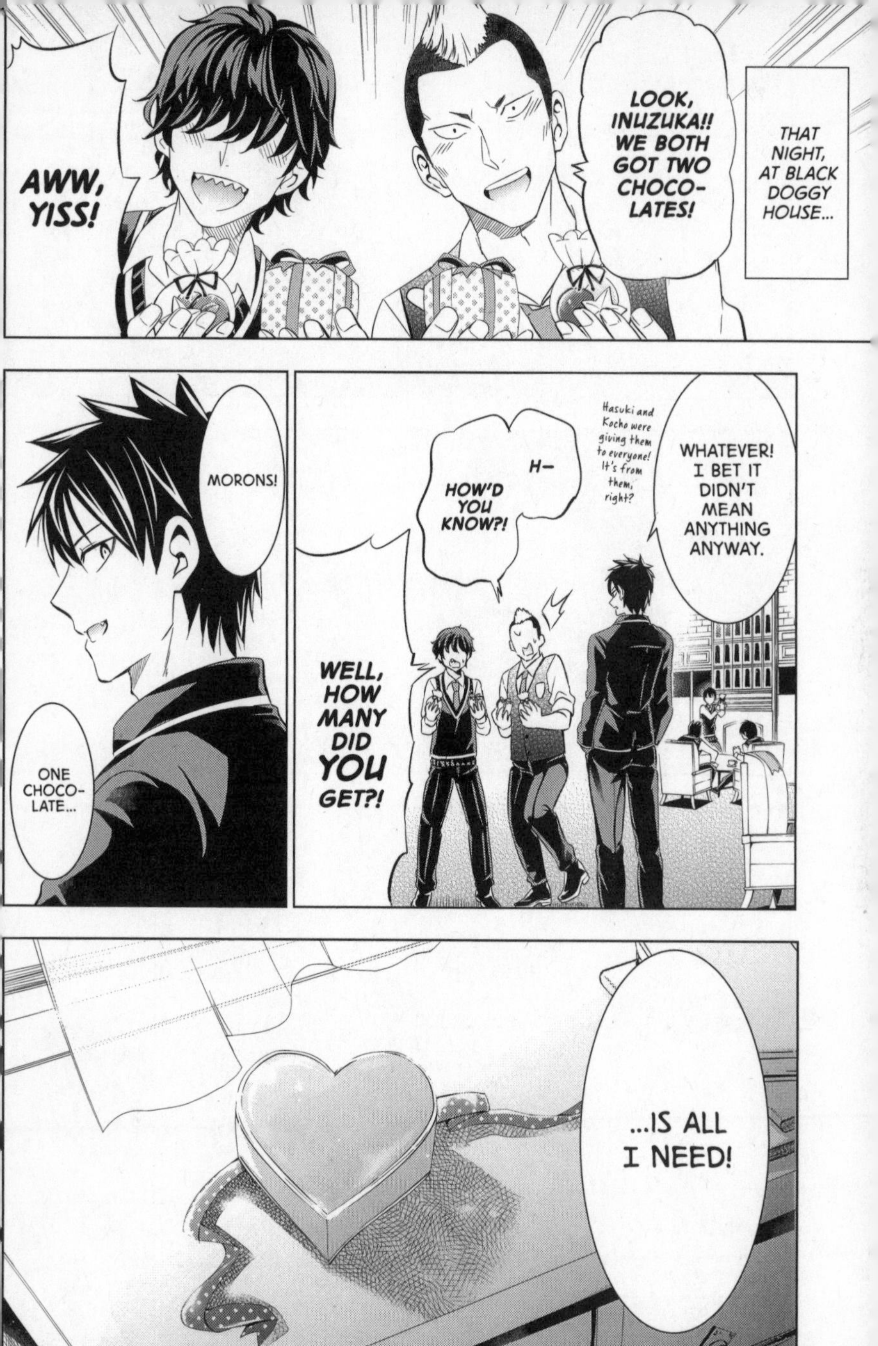
THAT NIGHT, AT BLACK DOGGY HOUSE...
LOOK, INUZUKA!! WE BOTH GOT TWO CHOCO-LATES!
AWW, YISS!
WHATEVER! I BET IT DIDN'T MEAN ANYTHING ANYWAY.
Hasuki and Kocho were giving them to everyone! It's from them, right?
H-
HOW'D YOU KNOW?!
WELL, HOW MANY DID YOU GET?!
MORONS!
ONE CHOCO-LATE...
...IS ALL I NEED!

CONTINUED IN VOLUME 11

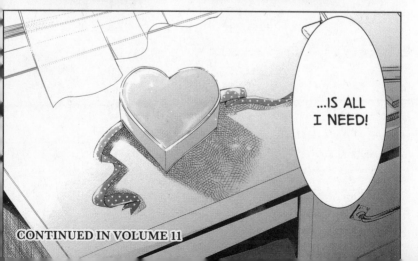

THE MOMENT I KNEW MANGA WAS MY CALLING

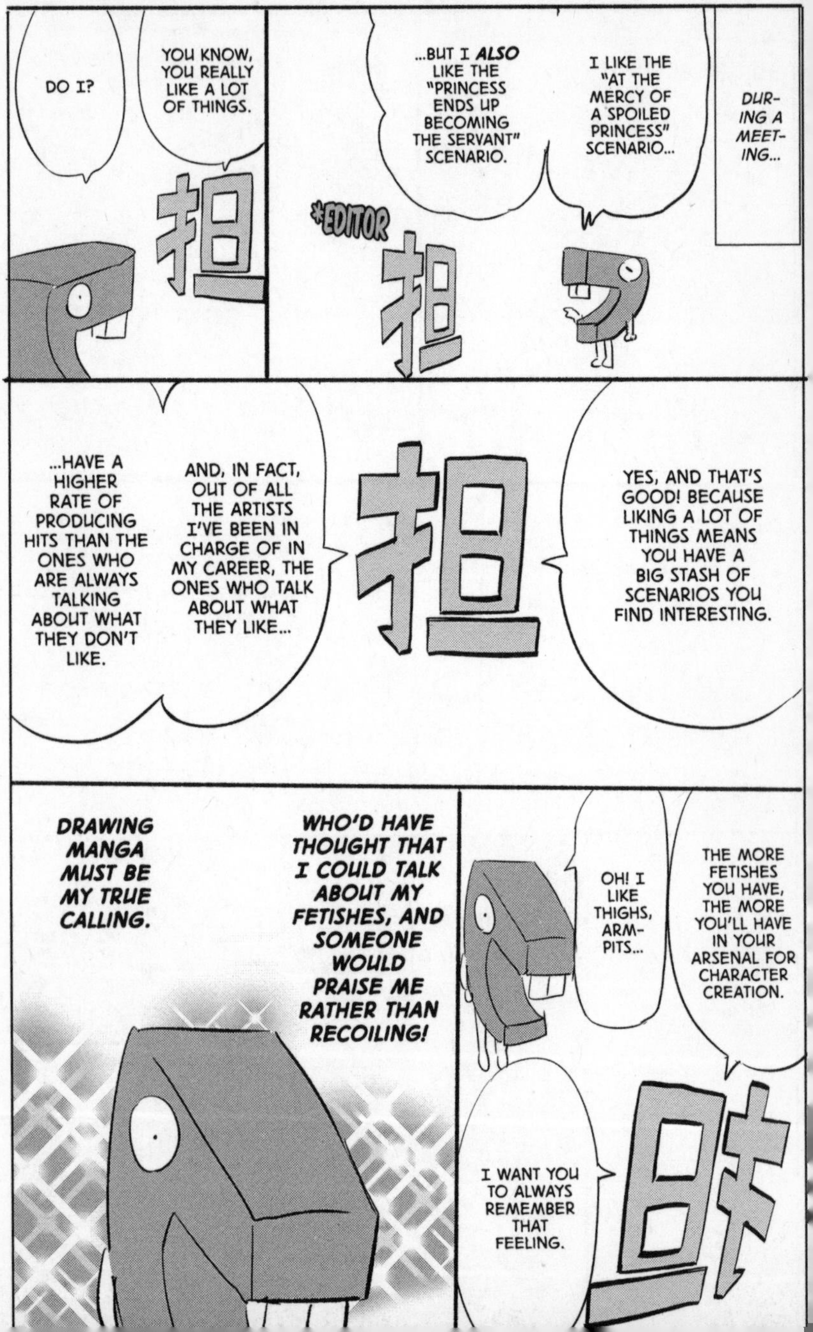

DURING A MEETING...
I LIKE THE "AT THE MERCY OF A SPOILED PRINCESS" SCENARIO...
...BUT I *ALSO* LIKE THE "PRINCESS ENDS UP BECOMING THE SERVANT" SCENARIO.
*EDITOR
YOU KNOW, YOU REALLY LIKE A LOT OF THINGS.
DO I?
YES, AND THAT'S GOOD! BECAUSE LIKING A LOT OF THINGS MEANS YOU HAVE A BIG STASH OF SCENARIOS YOU FIND INTERESTING.
AND, IN FACT, OUT OF ALL THE ARTISTS I'VE BEEN IN CHARGE OF IN MY CAREER, THE ONES WHO TALK ABOUT WHAT THEY LIKE...
...HAVE A HIGHER RATE OF PRODUCING HITS THAN THE ONES WHO ARE ALWAYS TALKING ABOUT WHAT THEY DON'T LIKE.
THE MORE FETISHES YOU HAVE, THE MORE YOU'LL HAVE IN YOUR ARSENAL FOR CHARACTER CREATION.
OH! I LIKE THIGHS, ARMPITS...
I WANT YOU TO ALWAYS REMEMBER THAT FEELING.
WHO'D HAVE THOUGHT THAT I COULD TALK ABOUT MY FETISHES, AND SOMEONE WOULD PRAISE ME RATHER THAN RECOILING!
DRAWING MANGA MUST BE MY TRUE CALLING.

RECORDING STUDIO REPORT

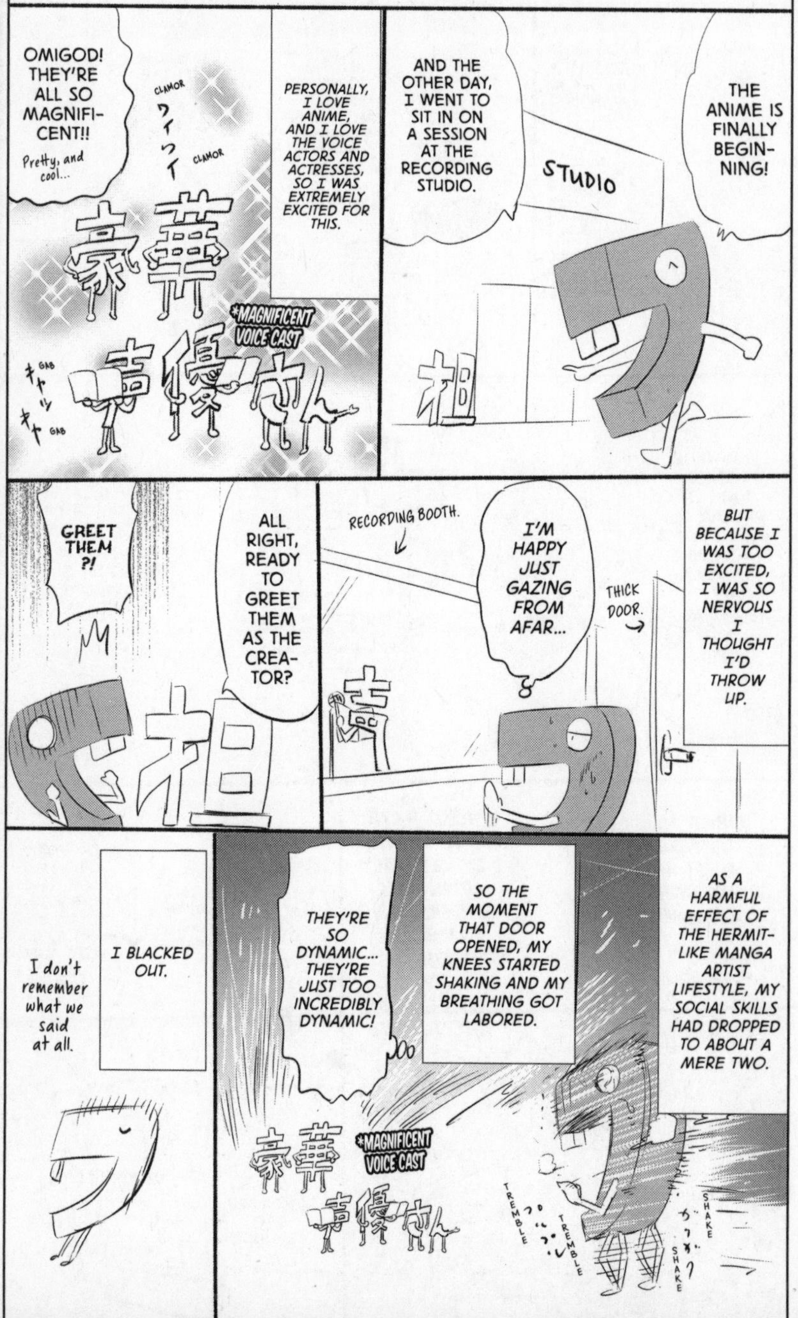
THE ANIME IS FINALLY BEGINNING!
AND THE OTHER DAY, I WENT TO SIT IN ON A SESSION AT THE RECORDING STUDIO.
STUDIO
PERSONALLY, I LOVE ANIME, AND I LOVE THE VOICE ACTORS AND ACTRESSES, SO I WAS EXTREMELY EXCITED FOR THIS.
CLAMOR
CLAMOR
OMIGOD! THEY'RE ALL SO MAGNIFICENT!!
Pretty, and cool...
*MAGNIFICENT VOICE CAST
GAB
GAB
BUT BECAUSE I WAS TOO EXCITED, I WAS SO NERVOUS I THOUGHT I'D THROW UP.
THICK DOOR.
I'M HAPPY JUST GAZING FROM AFAR...
RECORDING BOOTH.
ALL RIGHT, READY TO GREET THEM AS THE CREATOR?
GREET THEM?!
AS A HARMFUL EFFECT OF THE HERMIT-LIKE MANGA ARTIST LIFESTYLE, MY SOCIAL SKILLS HAD DROPPED TO ABOUT A MERE TWO.
SO THE MOMENT THAT DOOR OPENED, MY KNEES STARTED SHAKING AND MY BREATHING GOT LABORED.
THEY'RE SO DYNAMIC... THEY'RE JUST TOO INCREDIBLY DYNAMIC!
*MAGNIFICENT VOICE CAST
SHAKE
SHAKE
TREMBLE
TREMBLE
I BLACKED OUT.
I don't remember what we said at all.

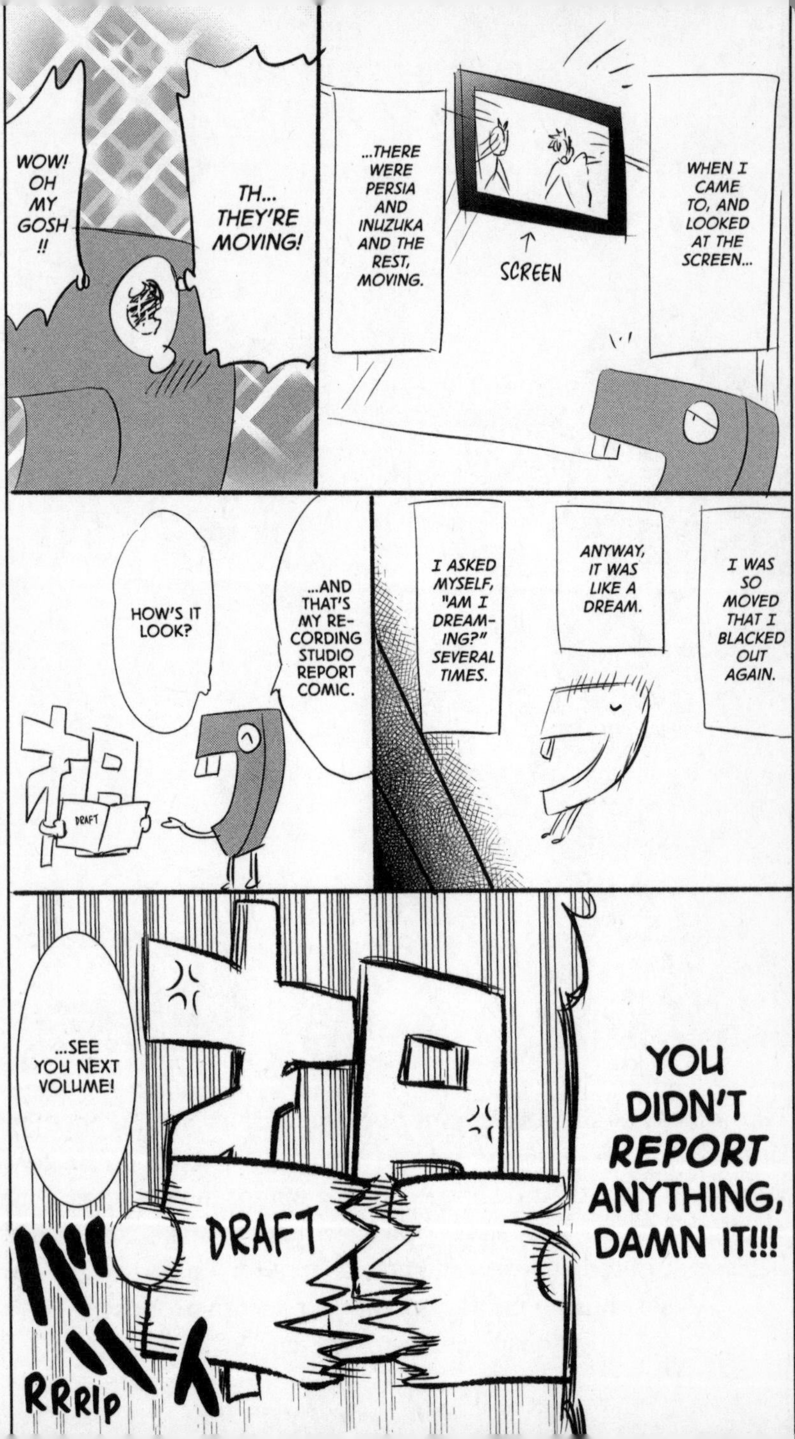
WHEN I CAME TO, AND LOOKED AT THE SCREEN...
SCREEN
...THERE WERE PERSIA AND INUZUKA AND THE REST, MOVING.
TH... THEY'RE MOVING!
WOW! OH MY GOSH!!
I WAS SO MOVED THAT I BLACKED OUT AGAIN.
ANYWAY, IT WAS LIKE A DREAM.
I ASKED MYSELF, "AM I DREAMING?" SEVERAL TIMES.
...AND THAT'S MY RECORDING STUDIO REPORT COMIC.
HOW'S IT LOOK?
DRAFT
YOU DIDN'T *REPORT* ANYTHING, DAMN IT!!!
...SEE YOU NEXT VOLUME!
DRAFT
RRRIP

In love, there are
no save points.

NOW AN ANIME!

ヲタクに恋は難しい

WOTAKOI:
LOVE IS HARD FOR OTAKU
by FUJITA

Narumi has had it rough: Every boyfriend she's had dumped her
once they found out she was an otaku, so she's gone to great
lengths to hide it. At her new job, she bumps into Hirotaka, her
childhood friend and fellow otaku. When Hirotaka almost gets
her secret outed at work, she comes up with a plan to keep him
quiet. But he comes up with a counter-proposal:
Why doesn't she just date him instead?

A picture-perfect shojo series from Yoko Nogiri, creator of the hit *That Wolf-Boy is Mine!*

Mako's always had a passion for photography. When she loses someone dear to her, she clings onto her art as a relic of the close relationship she once had... Luckily, her childhood best friend Kei encourages her to come to his high school and join their prestigious photo club. With nothing to lose, Mako grabs her camera and moves into the dorm where Kei and his classmates live. Soon, a fresh take on life, along with a mysterious new muse, begin to come into focus!

LOVE IN FOCUS

Praise for Yoko Nogiri's *That Wolf-Boy is Mine!*

"Emotional squees...will-they-won't-they plot...[and a] pleasantly quick pace."
—Otaku USA Magazine

"A series that is pure shojo sugar—a cute love story about two nice people looking for their places in the world, and finding them with each other." —Anime News Network

Boarding School Juliet 10 copyright © 2018 Yousuke Kaneda
English translation copyright © 2020 Yousuke Kaneda

Published in the United States by Kodansha Comics, an imprint of Kodansha USA Publishing, LLC, New York.

Publication rights for this English edition arranged through Kodansha Ltd., Tokyo.

First published in Japan in 2018 by Kodansha Ltd., Tokyo as *Kishuku Gakkou no Jurietto*, volume 10.

ISBN 978-1-63236-904-8

Printed in the United States of America.

www.kodanshacomics.com

9 8 7 6 5 4 3 2 1
Translation: Amanda Haley
Lettering: James Dashiell
Editing: Erin Subramanian and Tiff Ferentini
Kodansha Comics edition cover design by Phil Balsman

Publisher: Kiichiro Sug
Managing editor: Maya
Vice president of marketing & publicity: Nano Yam

Director of publishing services: Ben Applegate
Associate director of operations: Stephen Pakula
Publishing services managing editor: Noelle Webster
Assistant production manager: Emi Lotto